Managerial
Psychology

Harold J. Leavitt

Managerial Psychology

An introduction to
individuals, pairs, and groups
in organizations

Fourth Edition

The University of Chicago Press
Chicago and London

Harold J. Leavitt is Walter Kenneth Kilpatrick
Professor of Organizational Behavior and Psychology
in the Graduate School of Business, Stanford University.
He is the coeditor, with Louis R. Pondy, of *Readings
in Managerial Psychology* (second edition, University
of Chicago Press, 1974), a companion piece to
Managerial Psychology. Leavitt has also coedited
Organizations of the Future and is the coauthor of
The Organizational World.

The University of Chicago Press, Chicago 60637
The University of Chicago Press, Ltd., London
© 1958, 1964, 1972, 1978 by The University of Chicago
All rights reserved. Published 1978
Printed in the United States of America
82 81 80 79   9876543

Library of Congress Cataloging in Publication Data

Leavitt, Harold J
  Managerial psychology.

  Bibliography: p.
  Includes index.
  1. Psychology, Industrial.   I.   Title.
HF5548.8.L35   1978   158.7   77–13852
ISBN 0-226-46974-3 (text edition)
ISBN 0-226-46975-1 (trade edition)

Contents

v

Preface to the
fourth edition

The last edition of this book was written during the American "Days of May," the period of student protest, of Vietnam, of black-white confrontation, and of the emerging women's movement. This edition is written in a somewhat different milieu.

Those earlier issues have not gone away, but the sense of urgency has receded. The acute pain has been succeeded by the steadier ache of uncertainty.

Environmental and energy issues are now prominent concerns in all our lives. And while students are back at their desks, a certain residual cynicism about the establishment remains and, presumably, so do the new "we" generation values—more search for the good life, for the sailboat and the long weekend.

For the top executive this seems the era of the uncertain and sticky world; the era of regulation, of litigation, and of cloudy crystal balls.

On the inside, organizations are worrying more about getting the best from these strange young folks they're recruiting, and worrying more about motivating older people in organizations whose growth rates have slowed down. They're concerned, too, with the internal inflexibilities that follow from closer external regulation and control. Innovativeness in products, technology, and organizational design, comes harder in the sticky, vigilantly guarded settings of today.

While I try in this edition of *Managerial Psychology* to respond to these more recent concerns, I also try to stick to the basics. The psychological underpinnings of the first edition continue in this fourth edition. The book is still divided into four parts, moving from the individual, to interpersonal relationships, to groups, to larger organizational issues. The fundamentals within each section remain intact. But part 1 gives more attention to the problems of judging people and situations under conditions of high pressure and limited information. Part 2 has more on power and a lot more on pay and performance appraisal. There is a new chapter on group decision making in part 3, and a new chapter on experiments (here and abroad) with group-based factories. Part 4 has been modified quite radically to emphasize *managing,* treating the managing process as an ongoing, changing effort to find the right problems, solve them, and implement the solutions.

The whole emphasis of this edition is on the active, flexible, changing nature of both people and organizations; and on strategies and heuristics for managing changing people in changing organizations.

I hope I have eliminated the sexism of earlier editions. For my insensitivity to the implications of some of my earlier words, I can only say "mea culpa." I should point out, however, that I use the male pronoun throughout this book (to include all people). I found that the"s/he" form or random alternation of "he" and "she" interferes with the flow of thought. Nor have I added much material on the special problems encountered by women in management. The book is about managing people, with both sexes seen as doing the managing and both as the managed. Whenever it seemed to me that the sex of manager or managed might play a special role, I have tried to point it out.

My gratitude, as in the past, to Kathy Bostick for her quick and savvy working over of the manuscript. Nina Hatvany checked out lots of specific questions for me. And I am grateful, too, to the managers, students, and colleagues who keep me surprised and, I hope, alert.

Mr. Chocolate Mess, kissed by the Northern Princess, has turned into the Prince of America. And now the clear, bright voice of the Red Queen adds its firm inputs; and so do the Poet Laureate's joyous declamations on misery.

Same wife!

1 People one at a time
The units of
management

Introductory note

In these next several chapters the reader will find a presentation of some concepts of human behavior that seem most relevant to managerial problems. Such consideration of people and their behavior seems a prerequisite to any conscious attempt to learn how better to "manage" people. "Conscious" is a key word, because many persons (including many businessmen), are extremely skillful managers even though they go about their activities more or less intuitively. Those of us who are not so gifted need to think out loud about human relations and about ourselves as mechanisms for solving organizational problems.

Although the book as a whole purports to deal with problems of managing, this first section focuses almost entirely on the individual human being. The reasons for this "impractical" digression are several: First, the characteristics of people in general are a good base from which to build up to the characteristics of people in organizations. Second, managers, unlike parents, must work with used, not new, human beings—human beings whom other people have gotten to first. Third, the manager is his own best managing mechanism. An examination of his own makeup should therefore be useful to him.

Part 1 is designed as follows: It starts with some fundamental assumptions about what is "true" of all people everywhere. It moves then to a more detailed examination of the ways people differ from one another and some of the sources of those differences. Next, personality differences and their influence on the ways people see and deal with other things and other people are considered. Two chapters deal with the problem of *pressure*—the effects of frustration and conflict on behavior. Two chapters are concerned with conscious problem solving, the everyday work of the manager. One chapter is devoted to values and attitudes, the points where thought and feeling meet. Finally, one long chapter is given over to the practical problem of assessing people.

The goal of this section is both to simplify and complicate the reader's picture of people—to simplify by systematizing and interrelating some basic ideas (most of which are not new) and to complicate by pointing out the infinite shades of gray and the multitude of interacting variables that can occur in the behaving human organism.

1

People are alike
Some basic ideas

Managers' decisions, like other people's, are usually based on some combination of fact and theory. They are choices made by interpreting things observed in the light of things believed. And in most of their decisions executives are reasonably aware of the particular beliefs they are using in interpreting the facts they observe. They take supply-and-demand ideas into account in making marketing decisions, for example. And they often use high-level technical theory in attacking engineering and production problems.

Managers also use theory in dealing with human problems. But in the human area theorizing seems to be much more implicit or even unconscious. The theories of human behavior that managers hold seem also to be much more diverse than their economic and engineering theories, perhaps because they are much more the private property of individual executives. Here, for instance, are some pairs of theoretical assertions that have been made by business executives. Each of them necessarily reflects some basic assumptions about the nature of man:

People are basically lazy; or, People just want a chance to show what they can do.

Always be careful of an executive who loses his temper; or, Watch out for the executive who never loses his temper.

A good salesman sells himself before his product; or, A good product sells itself.

Men think more clearly than women; or Women size up the true situation better than men.

If you give people a finger they'll take the whole arm; or, Kindness begets kindness.

People need to know exactly what their jobs are; or, People will work best when they can make their own jobs.

Each of these statements (and the list is not at all exhaustive) is either an assumption about the nature of people or a derivation from

5

such an assumption. Each is a flat, unequivocal generalization, much like the statement, "Air is lighter than water."

The fact that many of these generalizations contradict one another suggests that they cannot all be right and therefore raises difficult questions of proof and consistency. This section of the book does not aim to prove that some are true and some are false. What is does aim to do is to provide a set of internally *consistent* generalizations; generalizations that should be *useful* in predicting human behavior, whether they are fundamentally true or not.

All of us seem to make some kind of generalizations about people, and this is important in deciding what is "practical" and what is "only theoretical." Managers have a reputation for practicality and hardheadedness, a reputation fledgling managers may mistakenly equate with entirely concrete and nongeneral thinking. Yet statements like those above are extremely general, extremely theoretical. They may express theory, but they point up the need for theoretical generalizations to serve as a foundation for practicality. Some kind of psychological theory is just as necessary for the manager dealing with human problems as is electrical and mechanical theory for the engineer dealing with machine problems. Without theory the engineer has no way of diagnosing what might be wrong when the engine stops, no way of pre-estimating the effects of a proposed change in design. Without some kind of psychological theory, the manager cannot attach meaning to the red flags of human disturbance; nor can he predict the likely effects of changes in organization or personnel policy.

The particular theoretical position outlined in these early chapters will not be new to most readers. Most of us already accept it but often do not use it. If it is good theory it should lead to useful predictions. Incidentally, if it is good theory it may not necessarily be true theory. No one knows whether some of the things said here are true or false. The reader can decide for himself whether or not they are useful.

Three basic assumptions about people

Suppose we asked this question of many kinds of people: "What are the fundamental, unexceptionable truths of human behavior?" Suppose one asked it of college students, union members, top- and middle-level managers, engineers, architects, teachers, and physicians. The answers would include generalizations like these:

People are products of their environment.
People want security.
All people want is bread and butter.
People are fundamentally lazy.
People are fundamentally selfish.

People only do what they have to do.

People are creatures of habit.

People are products of their heredity.

Some of these answers, like the generalizations we talked about earlier, seem to contradict others, but at another level the contradictions disappear. If one organizes them, one comes out with essentially the same generalizations that many modern psychologists would offer. For three major ideas are implicit in that list:

The first is the idea of *causality*, the idea that human behavior is caused, just as the behavior of physical objects is caused by forces that act on those physical objects. Causality is implicit in the beliefs that environment and heredity affect behavior and that what is outside influences what is inside.

Second, there is the idea of *directedness*, the idea that human behavior is not only caused but is also pointed toward something, that behavior is goal-directed, that people want to go somewhere.

Third, the list includes the concept of *motivation,* that underlying behavior one finds a "push" or a "motive" or a "want" or a "need" or a "drive."

These three ideas can provide the beginning of a system for conceptualizing human behavior. With the help of these ideas, human behavior can be viewed as part of a double play from motive to behavior to goal. And it is also helpful to think of this causal chain as generally forming a closed circuit. Arrival at a goal eliminates the motive, which eliminates the behavior. Thus, for instance, a person's stomach is empty; the emptiness stimulates impulses interpreted as "hunger"; the feeling of hunger stimulates behavior in search of food. He gets food. The food fills his stomach, causing the "feeling hungry" impulse to stop, which in turn stops the behavior in search of food.

This closed-circuit conception includes one major danger. Many "psychological," as distinct from "physical," goals are not finite and specific. One can consume a specific quantity of food and thereby temporarily stop feeling hungry for more. It is doubtful, however, that one can consume a specific quantity of prestige, for instance, and feel sated. Prestige and other "psychological" goals seem to be ephemeral and boundless; enough may never be obtained to inactivate the causes and hence the motive.

These assumptions of causality, motivation, and direction are nevertheless useful assumptions if they are accepted as universal. Causality, motivation, and direction can be thought of as applying equally to all people, of all ages, in all cultures, at all times. When one makes such assumptions they should lead one, upon observing human behavior, always to seek motive and, behind motive, cause.

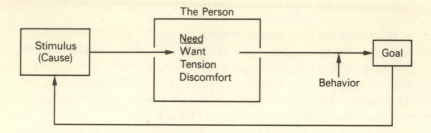

Fig. 1. A basic model of behavior.

A warning is once again in order. These assumptions are relatively modern Western assumptions. Let's not confuse their universal applicability with the belief that that's all there is or ever will be to human nature. There may well exist realms of human thought and behavior that are not encompassed by those three assumptions. And we may—possibly—someday realize that while those assumptions are useful they limit our range of intellectual vision.

But to get back to the assumptions:

There are many different perspectives on them, but the basic assumptions remain intact. For example, one can say that behavior is an attempt to get rid of tension. Tension then equals motivation; and the objective of behavior is to eliminate the necessity for behaving. Words like "motives" or "needs" or "drives" are rough synonyms for each other as well as for words like "tensions" or "discomforts" or "disequilibriums." Behavior is thus seen as an effort to eliminate tensions by seeking goals that neutralize the causes of tensions. Generally, such a view is called a *deficiency* model of motivation.

Such deficiency models are useful in another way. They put the emphasis on the *push* from inside the person rather than on the *pull* from outside. Managers, for instance, often encounter problems with subordinates who "don't know what they want." They feel restless and disturbed but can't seem to say what it is they are after. Most of us behave this way a good deal of the time, feeling the push of tension from inside but not being able to identify the precise goal that would eliminate the tension. We search vaguely, trying one job or another, one boss or another, one idea or another, until—if we are lucky—we hit on something that does the trick. Only then may we be able to tie up that particular feeling or tension with some specific goal, so that next time we can head directly for where we want to go. The baby, after all, doesn't start out crying, "I want a bottle." He starts out saying, "I feel discomfort somewhere inside." He then goes on to try all the different behaviors he can muster until he discovers that the bottle eliminates that particular discomfort. Only then can he identify this goal and narrow down his behavior so that he can get to his goal without exhausting himself.

But no matter how one views these concepts, they suggest that the ultimate condition of mankind can be thought of as an equilibrium condition in which he need not behave. This ultimate will be unattainable so long as one fly after another goes on landing on man's rump to stir up some new need and to force him to go on swishing his tail.

Of course the same landscape can be drawn from a brighter perspective. The tendency not to behave unless one has to can also account for the human capacity to learn. It can account for the baby's ability to become an increasingly efficient food finder. The diffuse kicking, squalling, and rolling give way over a few years to the simpler and more efficient behavior of learning to find and open the cookie jar. If people were not thus naturally stingy in their expenditures of energy, if they did not abhor unnecessary effort, if they were not lazy, then their factories would probably be no more efficient today than they were fifty years ago, if the factories existed at all.

Growth models

Until now we have treated human needs as tensions that arise out of *deficiencies,* out of want or lack. In recent years a strong case has been made for what has been called "growth motivation," a self-generating view of at least some major human needs. It is in the nature of man, this argument runs, to reach out for something more no matter what his state of satisfaction. People do not sit on their duffs even if they are very well fed and very comfortable.

Growth models are thus open-ended in their view of human potential. They see the human beings as continuously developing, moving on from one level of motivation to the next higher one, and so on; and thereby continuously repositioning himself to accomplish ever "higher" ends.

This position is important because it leads one toward a more optimistic posture in approaching the question of motivating people. If one views motivation as arising exclusively out of deficiency, then one begins to think about ways of creating deficiencies for others in order to motivate them. "Let's make him unsatisfied by making him hungry, then he'll work." The growth-motivational view points out that it is when human beings are satisfied in their more basic needs that the "higher" needs are likely to flower. It is when people are freed from the simple deficiencies that they can really begin to work as complete human beings.

Neither growth nor deficiency models allow much room for the idea of "habit," if habit means uncaused or undirected repetitive behavior. If the word "habit" is to fit here, it will have to mean something like "characteristic ways of trying to satisfy certain needs." The disorderly file clerk is not, then, just disorderly because he has disorderly habits. He is disorderly because he has learned to try to satisfy his needs by what we consider disorderly means. Nor is the inmate of the mental hospital just a different kind of human being from those on the outside. He is in there because his best methods for satisfying his needs have landed him there.

So these assumptions (cause, motivation, direction) become theoretical starting points. Perhaps they are worth careful thought. For the reader should consider the implications of these ideas for such concepts as "free will" and "insane behavior." Accepting these assumptions will probably require some revision of the usual meaning of these ideas.

In summary

This chapter has made three interrelated assumptions about human behavior:

1. Behavior is caused.
2. Behavior is motivated.
3. Behavior is goal motivated.

In the process some alternative assumptions have been implicitly discarded. We have discarded the idea that behavior is "random," i.e., that it is going nowhere, for no reason. But we have left room for other ideas, such as the idea of growth motivation, which is not directly generated out of deficiency.

Moreover, the three assumptions are assumed to be interrelated in a circular sequence: from cause to motivation to goal direction. Arrival at the goal inactivates the cause, and hence eliminates the motive, and hence eliminates the goal-directed behavior; although some goals may not be finite.

Many different words can be used to deal with these three ideas. Words like "drive," "tension," "need," and "disequilibrium," for example, are all approximate synonyms for the word "motive." We shall say a little more about growth and deficiency views of motivation in the next chapter.

2 People are different
Motivation and the growth of individuality

While people are alike, they are also different. They are alike in that their behavior is caused, motivated, and goal directed, and their physical equipment is roughly similar. They are different to the extent that they are subject to different kinds of stimulation, that they vary in kinds and degrees of motivation, that they behave in many different ways to achieve many different goals, and that they have different sizes and powers in their physical equipment. The purpose of this chapter is to try to account (only at the broadest level) for the range and kinds of differences that every manager has observed among those around him.

The range of motives

Consider the variety of motives which seem to occur in human behavior. Consider, for example, the class of behavior called "work." What are the motives for work? What are the tensions or discomforts that people try to eliminate through work? Why should people sacrifice so much of the good life to walk into the plant morning after morning, year after year? Clearly, different individuals will give different answers to such questions, and each answer may be perfectly true for each person. Clearly, too, any single individual may come up with a variety of motives to fit his particular case. Direct questioning of a random portion of the American population would certainly include such answers as these:

I work for money and the food, shelter, and goods money buys.
I work for status and recognition.
I work to belong, to be part of a group.
I work to get to the top.
I work because it's only right that people should work.
I work for knowledge and understanding.
I work for security.
I work for the feeling of accomplishment I get from a job well done.

11

This list is not exhaustive. Some of the statements are concrete and specific; others are vague and shadowy. Some seem to overlap one another in meaning. Perhaps the reader will, nevertheless, go along with the generalization that most people work for some variety of reasons like these and that most people would also be willing to do some work for almost any one of the reasons listed, even if the others did not exist. But perhaps before he will go along, the reader may want to add at least one qualification: these motives may be real only for *most people in America this year*. Although some of them may be universal, others may be specific to our culture or to certain sub-groups within our culture. This would be a valid qualification.

The classes of motives

Looking back over the list of motives, one can classify them into at least two major groups. Some arise from needs that are essentially physical and "basic": needs for food, for water, for warmth. One could add others: needs to urinate, to defecate, to sleep, and so on. These are clear-cut, unambiguous needs; they are physiological; they are universal; they are present in infants as well as adults; they are even present in most other classes of animals. They seem unquestionably to be part of the person's original inborn equipment.

The second large class of needs, however, is less easily definable. Needs for achievement, status, and "belongingness" are much more "psychological," more characteristic of human beings, and for the most part not immediately observable in the newborn. They also seem highly individualistic—much more so than the basic physical needs. They seem to be present to an extreme degree in some people and almost nonexistent in others. We do not ordinarily characterize one another as "food seekers," but we do often characterize a person as a "power seeker" or a "prestige seeker." In fact, our judgment of the intensities of psychological needs in other people makes up a large part of our judgment of their personalities. Application blanks for industrial jobs seldom include questions about how much water a person drinks or how many sandwiches one eats for lunch. But they do include questions about his ambitions and his social interests.

It is in these so-called psychological needs that the bulk of organizationally significant individual differences lies; we must try to account for the differential development of these needs in different individuals. This problem could lead us quickly into the question of the importance of heredity and environment, but that would be an unprofitable venture. If the reader prefers to believe that the psychological needs are acquired out of our environment, such a belief will not affect the position taken here. If he prefers to believe that the seeds of psychological needs lie in the genes and that environment only fertilizes and nurtures them, that position is also tenable.

Dependency and the development of personality

The most important issue seems to be this one: Can we, with as few assumptions as possible, account for the development of individually different adult personalities? For the backslapping sales manager and the quiet, methodical comptroller?

A theory, it has been said, is as good as its ratio of predictions to assumptions. To economize on assumptions, we may assume here that only the basic physical needs are inherited and then go on from there. It is then possible to account broadly for the elaborate complex of needs that exists in a twenty-year-old while assuming that all he had to begin with were (1) basic physical needs and (2) a body. In that "body" we must include his sense organs, plus his memory—a mechanism for retaining information picked up by the sense organs—plus a decision-making mechanism, plus a tendency to be stingy in the expenditure of energy. Add to these a muscular system that allows the person to move and act upon his environment. If that is the person's original basic equipment, it is almost enough to account for the accessories he will have added by the time he is ten or twenty or forty.

But he still needs one more characteristic, a characteristic that is not so much a part of the person as of the relationship between the person and the world. This additional characteristic is *dependency*—the dependency of the newborn infant on parents for the satisfaction of his needs; the dependency of the growing child on parents, teachers, and friends; of husband on wife; and of people in industry on their bosses; and vice versa.

If the human infant came into the world with almost complete physical development, like some other animal young, then we might have to devise quite a different theory to account for the adult personality. In fact, if the infant could fend for himself from the start, the adult personality would be noticeably different from what it is.

But any infant who survives to adulthood has necessarily passed through a period in which he was almost entirely dependent upon other people for the satisfaction of his basic physical needs. And this dependency, coupled with the presence of physical needs and a good but incomplete physical plant, plus the capacity to learn, may give us the leverage to account for the development of a great many secondary and tertiary mental needs. To see how this dependency lever might work, consider this entirely hypothetical illustration:

Suppose that you suffer from a magical ailment. The major symptom of the ailment is paralysis—complete paralysis. But though you are paralyzed, your head is perfectly clear and your senses are perfectly keen. You can hear, you can see, you can feel, you can think—but you can't move.

You have a brother who possesses a magical gift. Whenever his hand is on your shoulder you are cured; you can move as well as anyone else. But when he takes his hand away the paralysis immediately returns.

Assume that your brother is a nice guy; he spends a good deal of his time with his hand on your shoulder, and he goes through considerable inconvenience to do this. Through his help you can lead something approximating a normal life. You have not had this disease very long, but by now you have gotten over the shock that it entailed, and you are trying to settle down to the best life you can work out.

This morning you awake, but of course you cannot move. You lie in bed until your brother comes in to put his hand on your shoulder. Whereupon you rise, dress, and wash. You have breakfast, chat, and read the morning paper. You do everything that you may have done before you had the disease.

Over breakfast your brother announces that he forgot to tell you he has a dentist's appointment this morning. He will have to leave the house about ten. He probably will not be back until noon. This is a matter of no great concern to you, since it's just a two-hour absence.

With his hand on your shoulder you arrange a comfortable place in which you can sit while your brother is gone. You set an easy chair by the window, put your feet on an ottoman, and tune in a radio to a program you particularly like. You open the window to let the warm air and sun in and to see what's going on outside. You settle down for the two-hour absence.

Your brother leaves.

For half an hour or so, as you expected, things are fine. You are perfectly comfortable; there's enough activity outdoors to keep you interested; and the radio program is good.

At ten-thirty the program changes to the thing you hate most—country music—but that's of no major concern. A fly manages to get through a hole in the screen and begins to buzz around your nose—but this is just one of those inconveniences you have learned to bear.

By eleven o'clock there's a little itch from a rough place in the chair, but that's bearable, too. The fly is still around. The country music goes on. At eleven-thirty the sky clouds over. The air gets cold and windy. At a quarter to twelve it's raining hard. You're getting wet and cold. If you could shiver, you would. The itches increase. Your bladder begins to get a little too full for comfort.

But you reassure yourself: fifteen minutes more.

At noon you're waiting hopefully for your brother's step, but you don't hear it. He doesn't show at twelve-fifteen. The cold and the wet and the itches and the bladder and the fly and the radio become almost unbearable. By twelve-forty-five you're on the verge of explosion. One o'clock and no brother, but more rain, more discomfort.

At just about one-thirty you hear footfalls. Brother walks in, puts his hand on your shoulder, and says: "I was caught in a traffic jam. I'm sorry I'm late."

Now let the reader seriously ask himself these questions:

1. Just how would you *feel* about your brother at this moment?

2. What do you think you would *do* to your brother at this moment?

Your answers probably fall into one of these major categories: (1) I would feel angry and resentful. (2) I would feel extremely relieved; extremely grateful that he had finally arrived. (3) I would feel mixed up; angry and resentful, on the one hand, and relieved and grateful, on the other.

To the action question, answers range from: (1) I would sock him on the nose to (2) I would throw my arms around him and kiss him.

Each of these answers is appropriate and understandable. Together they represent the necessary conflict of feelings that derive from the complete dependency of one individual on another. The person who says he would feel angry and hostile will probably be ready to admit that those would be predominant but not exclusive feelings. While he feels angry, he may at the same time feel affectionate and grateful. The person who says he will feel grateful and relieved will probably admit that he is also angry and irritated. Some admixture of these almost polar feelings will probably be present in everyone. This is the peculiar phenomenon of *ambivalence,* of the simultaneous existence of opposite feelings in the same place at the same time.

Similarly, at the action level, the individual who says, "I would sock my brother on the nose," might be willing to add, "But I might feel awfully sorry afterward." And the one who says, "I would throw my arms around him," might add that his embrace would include a touch of a bear hug.

Suppose further that this sort of incident happened often, for month after month. Might you then develop an increasing wish for independence from your brother? Might you also seek ways of controlling your brother, of "getting something on him," so that you would not have to count impotently on his good will? And suppose he was a particularly bad brother who didn't care much for you? Wouldn't that intensify your wishes for independence from him or power over him?

Extreme dependency thus serves as a lever for initiating other kinds of needs. To the extent that dependency yields ready satisfaction of existing needs that one cannot satisfy independently—to that extent one's feelings are likely to be positive, friendly, affectionate, protective, grateful, and one is likely to develop strong *social* needs. To the extent that dependency does not satisfy, but rather frustrates—to that extent one is likely to develop feelings of anger and hostility and tò wish more strongly for independence and autonomy, to develop strong *egoistic* needs.

The infant suffers from this kind of magical paralysis. He is entirely dependent on adults for the satisfaction of his inborn physical needs. But because no parent can be entirely satisfying (or entirely frustrating), each child must necessarily develop some mixture of plus and minus feelings, first toward the parents and then, since the parents very often are the world, toward the world.

No parents can entirely satisfy or entirely frustrate an infant for these reasons: Infants who encounter only frustration in their very early attempts to satisfy their needs simply do not survive. Children who don't get fed die. At the other end of the scale, however, no infant can hope for perfect satisfaction. No parent has the prescience to foresee all the infant's wants before they arise or the patience to satisfy every want he does foresee. So no adult in the world grew up through complete frustration in infancy or through complete satisfaction.

The working range is the range between the extremes on the satisfaction-frustration scale. Parents can consciously or inadvertently work predominantly near one end of the scale or the other. And the extent to which the predominance actually is at one end or the other, together with the physiological givens, probably accounts for the *general* pattern of early personality development in any particular child. Teachers, bosses, and other people can perform in the same range later to finish off personality development.

To be more accurate, one can put it this way: Some infants face a world that is mostly non-satisfying, non-predictable, and non-controllable from the beginning. Some infants face a world that is more satisfying, more predictable, and more controllable. Children faced with an unpredictable and uncontrollable world are more likely to grow fearful and hostile early. They are more likely to wish strongly for independence. And they are more likely to be concerned with *egoistic* needs, with mechanisms by which independence may be gained, i.e., with power, ingratiation, acquisition of goods, and so on.

On the other hand, children whose early years are mostly satisfying are more likely to be secure and dependent. They are more likely to develop predominantly *social* needs with only secondary concern (unless they learn it later) about autonomy and independence.

These acquired sets of feelings can now be thought of as two new classes of learned needs. One set is of essentially social needs, for dependency, for affiliation with people (because people satisfy needs), for affection, and the like. The other set is egoistic, i.e., concerned with the self in relation to other people rather than with other people per se. In this class belong the emerging needs for independence, for power (over other people), for prestige (as one kind of power over other people), for knowledge (another path toward independence), and the like.

The extent of parental control

Theoretically, the relative development of one of these sets of needs or the other in a child is partially controllable by an outsider, the parent. Parents can encourage social needs by satisfying physical needs, and they can encourage egoistic needs by frustrating physical needs. In practice, the problem is not quite so simple. For one thing, frustration of physical needs in infancy is likely to be accompanied by two by-products—hostility and fearfulness—as well as by a wish for independence. Moreover, if one were really to frustrate continuously, he would soon have to frustrate not only physical needs but the egoistic needs that begin to emerge from the early frustrations. So now the frustrating parent, having developed in his child a wish for independence, must withhold the right to independence. The next step then is the child who wants independence but cannot successfully get it. Nothing he does for himself is right or successful. Where then? Perhaps a retreat from the world, a kind of internal or fantasy independence. When he grows up a little this behavior may earn him a complicated psychiatric label.

There is another key factor in this picture. When a child, or an adult for that matter, is prevented from getting what he wants, he is apt to become angry and to attack the thing that blocks him. The child strikes out blindly at Mama or Papa, the adolescent uses his fists, the adult often attacks with words. Suppose our hypothetical parent frustrates the child so that he wants to attack the parent. He kicks and he bites and he howls. Does the parent now decide to satisfy or to frustrate this new behavior? Does he let himself be attacked successfully, or does he frustrate the attack by using his superior force to retaliate? If he does the first, what becomes of his dignity? If he does the second, what does he teach the child? Probably he teaches the child that he must suppress or repress his hostility. But the *suppression* of hostility is not the same as the *absence* of hostility. The child who is not allowed to kick still feels like kicking. Extend this behavior over time, day after day, incident after incident, and the pattern becomes one of internalized, unexpressed, "sat upon" hatred and anger, sometimes with a cover of equanimity and calm.

This is not to say that the child is forever what he becomes in, say, his first year of life. On the contrary, the child is always something more than his history. And present needs plus dependency can account for the development of new needs in adults as well as in children. But the outgrowth of very early experiences (experiences in trying to satisfy one's physical needs through a wholly dependent relationship) is a foundation for the broad outlines of later personality. The first years have a good deal to do with determining whether or not the child feels essentially secure or insecure about his place in the world and essentially optimistic or pessimistic about other people.

Dependency in organizations

The things people learn in this first and most important dependency relationship probably also have a good deal to do with the way they face and deal with the less extreme dependency relationships of later life—like the relationship one has with one's superiors in industrial organizations.

In fact, if we want to put this story in managerial terms, we need only to go over the last few pages and change a few labels. We can read "manager" for "parent," and "employee" for "child." And then we go to tone down all the consequences a few notches. The employee, a "used" model of a child, enters a less extreme dependency relationship when he goes to work, and he enters with already existent social and egoistic as well as physical needs. If people in the company are "good brothers," the probability that the employee will learn to feel trustful and affiliative is pretty good—if he is already reasonably trustful of people with power. If people in the company are "bad brothers," his predominant local feelings (superimposed in a complicated way on the general feelings he brought in) are more likely to be hostile and competitive.

It is important to point out here that this view about early dependency may conflict with some widespread beliefs about training both children and employees. For example, this position suggests that strong discipline for the infant will probably lead to hostility and fear and to active power and independence seeking. It suggests further that a history of frustration probably makes later *frustrations* more difficult to take rather than easier. And, in a situation in which great psychological pressure is to be put on a person, holders of this position would place their money on the adult who had *not* gone through an infantile school of hard psychological knocks. They would pick the individual whose parental relationships and preferably his later ones had been comfortable and relatively free from psychological want. (Incidentally, the evidence from studies of successful executives is constant with this view. Successful executives tend to come from harmonious, higher-income homes and to have liked their families and teachers.) For the first year or two, the best way to "spoil" a child would therefore seem to be to deny him what he wants. The best way not to "spoil" him is to help him get everything he wants. And, if one considers the new employee instead of the new baby, the same conclusions might hold. But more of this in later chapters.

The hierarchy of needs

In the first chapter we mentioned briefly the difference between deficiency models of motivation and growth models. The growth view holds that when some motive reaches some level of satiation, then a new set of motives is triggered. That view seems to be particularly appropriate to higher-level motives, the ones that are secondary and tertiary outgrowths of the kind of dependency relationships we just described. So it is worthwhile saying a little more about the growth view here.

One outstanding exponent of growth motivation has laid out the general idea about like this: People start out in infancy driven primarily by their physiological needs. At some later point most of us begin to feel reasonably secure about our ability to get fed, at which point we begin to broaden out into a concern over "safety," a concern about keeping a shelter over our heads, and the wolf from the door. Given some certainty at that level, still another set of generalized motives comes into play, the *social-love-affiliation* motives. Then the *egoistic* motives; until finally, given security about our physical needs, our safety needs, our social needs, and our ego needs, we then go on to needs for *self-actualization*. Self-actualization needs are motives aimed toward fulfilling one's self in one's own way. When a person is "doing what he must do," he is self-actualizing.

Our dependency model offered at least a theory for how such higher levels of motives get generated. The growth-hierarchy model tries to specify the conditions under which they become operational, that is, the conditons under which each set of motives becomes an important driving force in the day-to-day behavior of the individual.

Now suppose that such a hierarchy does operate; suppose we begin to get interested in social relationships after our bellies are filled, and in achievement after our social relationships are secure, and in doing our thing when we have filled all our other needs. What implications does such a hierarchy have for management? One implication is that when management tries to reward or punish, it had better reward or punish the needs that are operational and not those above or below that operational level. If I feel psychologically safe about my physical needs, threats or rewards will have effects different from those produced by the same threats or rewards in someone who is operating primarily at the level of physical safety. Conversely, if my next meal is the problem that is real to me, don't expect me to be diverted with offers of promotion or threats to my status.

It has been suggested, in fact, that the general level of operational needs in a society changes as the society develops and that managers often lag behind that development in their methods of rewarding. They may thus use incentives or threats that would have worked in the less developed America of a hundred years ago, but are as meaningless in our present affluent society as a penny is as a reward to today's teenagers. Our society, in other words, is probably at a stage in which social or egoistic needs are more operational for many of us than physical or safety needs.

Motivation and managing

Now that we've talked a little about how motives develop and about some models of motivation, it's time to raise questions about the relevance of this whole motivational problem to managing. We've already suggested a couple of points of relevance. If we accept the deficiency model, it's an easy jump to think about employee motivation as a problem in creating deficiencies. If we keep 'em hungry, they'll work to eat. That, of course, is not only an ethically questionable route, but a very dangerous one. For if we try to keep our employees short of the basics they need, a new problem arises. Deficiencies may motivate all right, but the behaviors they will generate are not necessarily the ones we are trying to get. If I am hungry, one thing I might do is work harder. But another is to break the windows in the local bakery. Still another is to attack what I believe to be the source of my hunger—you! Motivating by creating deficiencies may start a wide range of actions we may not be able to control.

We said a little, too, about the implications of growth-motivation models for managing. Essentially a reward is only a reward if it matches some unsatisfied motive. We will not get much behavior—good or bad —by offering food to someone whose belly is full. The key managerial implication of the growth models is to point managers toward trying to develop relevant rewards for working which are matched to the contemporary motives of workers. And if, in developed America, most of us are operationally motivated more by social or esteem or self-actualization needs, then we had better start rethinking reward systems built to motivate people worried about their physical and safety needs. Only operational motives generate behavior.

There are at least three other points that now need to be made about the relationship between motivation and managing:

First, power and achievement motives seem to be operational motives for successful managers. This conclusion derives from a great deal of work done over the last couple of decades on three specific motives: the achievement motive, the power motive, and the affiliation motive. Each of the three means about what it sounds like. Achievement motivation is a concern about getting things done, reaching some standard of success. Power motivation is motivation to influence and control behavior of other people; and affiliation motivation is motivation toward positive relationships with other people, toward membership and belonging.

A good deal of evidence has been put forward to show that successful managers tend to be high in achievement motivation and particularly high in power motivation. The kind of power motivation that seems to make for success is not so much *personal* power but a concern about *institutional* power. Successful managers tend to be people who want to influence and control other people in order to get organizational work done, not in order to glorify themselves. But successful managers in business and industry have tended to be fairly low on affiliation motivation. It's possible (perhaps probable) that we are heading into a time when affiliation will become a much more significant requirement for the managing process. But as of now, the data indicate that power and achievement orientations are more closely associated with executive success.

Second, the same researchers who have worked with achievement motivation in managers have made a case for a relationship between levels of achievement motivation in different societies and the rate of economic development in those societies. If two societies are equivalent in every respect except achievement motivation, the argument runs, we should still expect a more rapid economic development in the one with higher achievement needs. The argument is simple: if a nation develops a large number of people who are driven by motives to achieve —to build and develop things—then that resource (achievement-motivated people) will generate economic development. The early New Englanders, for example, faced a physical environment that seemed to offer nothing by way of physical resources save rock and ice. But perhaps because they were achievement-motivated people, they did not lie down and die. They went into the rock and ice business. In the early 1800s, New Englanders literally became ice merchants, shipping ice to tropical nations, promoting the uses of ice for ice cream, iced drinks, and the preservation of food. Those early promoters were achievement-oriented people.

A third point about managing and motivation:

Most of the empirical work on motivation (until very recently) was done with males. But what about achievement behavior in women? Is it any different? Some say yes. The proposal has been put forward (with research data) that American women show a high frequency of "fear of success." Essentially the argument runs that otherwise ambitious women are hesitant about succeeding, lest their success be seen as "unfeminine" and dangerous to their relationships with men. Secondly, there is some reason to believe that women have traditionally been socialized, at least in our society, to try to achieve *vicariously* rather than directly; that is, that women have been taught to get things done, not directly, by acting upon the world, but indirectly via relationships with other people; either by supporting those others or by manipulating them.

Note that there is nothing in either the fear-of-success or the vicarious-achievement arguments to suggest that such behaviors are inherent in the nature of women. What is suggested is that if these behaviors are more characteristic of women than of men, they are probably there because American women have been taught to proceed with caution in competing with men, and to limit their aspirations to the more vicarious, back-up roles and occupations. Women learned (in the past) that they ought to become nurses rather than doctors, secretaries rather than managers, stewardesses rather than pilots.

Suppose, for a moment, that both of these tentative findings turn out to be true—particularly that women are more skillful than men in using vicarious means to get what they want. Should organizations try, as women move into management, to train that vicariousness out of them? To make them more like men?

How about the opposite? Isn't much modern management training for males really aimed at increasing vicarious skills? Don't technical managers, more than bench technologists for example, need to get their achievement kicks more vicariously through their peoples' accomplishments? Don't sales managers have to be vicarious managers, who back up their salespeople instead of competing with them? If so, women may in general represent a partially pretrained managerial resource!

Extrinsic and intrinsic motivation

We haven't yet mentioned another interesting area of recent research in motivation—the differential effects of intrinsic and extrinsic motivation. Intrinsic motivation means what it sounds like, motivation from inside the self; a person doing something because he wants to do it. Extrinsic motivation is generated from the outside. One does something to win a reward that is specifically offered for that behavior.

Imagine, for example, that I am a crossword puzzle addict. I am intrinsically motivated to do crossword puzzles. I do them just because I enjoy doing them. Now suppose it is in your interest to try to get me to do more of them. Suppose that solved crossword puzzles are a product you can sell at a profit. You want more of them because you run the local finished crossword shop. Having "discovered" me (the world's fastest crossword puzzle solver) you grab me and say, "I will pay you for those finished puzzles at the rate of X dollars per puzzle." You are adding a new extrinsic reward on to my already existing intrinsic motivation.

What's your prediction about what will happen? Will the two forms of motivation sum? Will I now be more motivated because I both enjoy the work and I can also earn money by doing it? Some recent evidence —again still under debate—says no; that instead the added extrinsic motivation tends under many conditions, to cancel the old intrinsic motivation. Now that you are paying me to do puzzles, I may begin to find them much less interesting; they are work, not fun. I'm doing it for money, not for kicks. What we have is a little like what Tom Sawyer knew when he got his friends to help him whitewash his fence. If it looks like fun, they'll do it.

So perhaps we had better be careful, in managing, of the implicit assumption that different kinds of motivation can just be piled on one another without danger. Human beings are more complicated than that.

In summary

People are born with physical needs. They later either acquire or blossom out with a host of other social and egoistic needs. These new psychological needs can be thought of as outgrowths of (1) physical needs, (2) the nervous system of the physical body, plus (3) dependency on other people.

The child is dependent on adults. Adults can make that dependency predominantly satisfying or predominantly frustrating. Satisfaction builds security and social needs; frustration builds insecurity, hostility, and egoistic needs.

The dependency conditions of infancy recur in later life in industry and elsewhere. The same infantile learning formula may prevail at the adult level.

But the operational needs of adults may be different. For the needs we respond to tend to form a hierarchy, with physical needs taking precedence *if they are severely threatened*. But if we are physically secure, social, followed by egoistic, followed by self-actualizing, needs become the ones we work to satisfy.

Motivational issues become relevant to management in many different ways. If we accept the deficiency model, we had better make sure that we know how to create deficiencies that will lead to the behavior we want, and not to what we don't want. When we use growth models, we need to worry about the levels of motivation which are operational in our particular people, and we need to design rewards consistent with those levels. In addition, there is some evidence that successful managers score high in both achievement and power motivation; that some societies raise their children to be more achievement motivated than others; and that such high achievement motivation may then contribute to more rapid economic growth. There is also some as yet unclear evidence that women in our society tend to avoid highly visible success and also use more vicarious means for achieving what they want than men do.

Finally, to complicate the issue even more, extrinsic rewards proffered by others may not simply add on to our intrinsic motivation Sometimes extrinsic rewards cancel intrinsic motives.

3 Perception
From the inside
looking out

The two preceding chapters were about the world's influence on the development of the person; in this one the issue is the person's influence on the world. The major questions are these: How and why do people see things differently? How objective can people be? Do people see only what they want to see? Or don't want to see? What part do people's personal views of the world play in the supervisory process?

The perceptual world

Most of us recognize that the world-as-we-see-it is not necessarily the same world as the world-as-it-"really"-is. Our answer depends on what we heard, not on what was really said. The consumer buys what he likes best, not what is best. Whether we feel hot or cold depends on us, not on the thermometer. The same job may look like a good job to one of us and a sloppy job to another.

Fig. 2. Old woman or young woman?

To specify the problem, consider the line drawing in figure 2. This is a picture of a woman. Here are some questions about it: (1) How old is the woman at the time of the picture? (2) Does she have any outstanding physical characteristics? (3) Is she "reasonably attractive" or "downright ugly"?

Show the picture to ten other people. Do they all see the same thing? If some think she looks between twenty and thirty, does anyone think she's over fifty? If some think she's over fifty, does anyone think she's between twenty and thirty? How does one account for the conflicts? Are the differences simply differences in taste? Or in standards of beauty? Or is each person distorting the "real" world in a different way?

This old psychology-textbook picture is intentionally ambiguous. It can be seen either as an ugly old hag with a long and crooked nose and toothless mouth or as a reasonably attractive young woman with head turned away so that one can barely see one eyelash and part of a nose. More importantly, the "truth" will be based on the "facts" as they are seen by the viewer, which may be different from the "facts" seen by another viewer.

Incidentally, if the reader still sees only one of the two figures, he is getting a good feeling of what a "need" is. The tension or discomfort that one feels when he thinks he is missing some things others can see or when he feels he hasn't quite closed a gap in his knowledge—that is a need. And it will probably be difficult to concentrate on reading further until he satisfies that unsatisfied need by finding the second face in the picture.

The influence of our needs on our perceptions

The ambiguous picture is another demonstration of a commonplace observation, i.e., that people see things differently, that the world is what we make it, that everyone wears his own rose-colored glasses. But consider some additional questions: Whence the rose-colored glasses? Are the glasses always rose-colored? That is, does one always see what he wants to see, or does he see what he is afraid he will see, or both?

These questions are important because the primary issue of "human relations" is to consider ways in which individuals can affect the behavior of other individuals. If it is true that people behave on the basis of the perceived world, then changing behavior in a predetermined direction can be made easier by understanding the individual's present perception of the world. For if there is any common human-relations mistake made by organizational superiors in their relations with subordinates, it is the mistake of assuming that the "real" world is all that counts, that everyone works for the same goals, that the facts speak for themselves.

But if people do act on their perceptions, different people perceive things differently. How, then, is the manager, for example, to know what to expect? What determines how particular people will perceive particular things?

The answer has already been given in the preceding chapters. People's perceptions are determined by their needs. Like the mirrors at amusement parks, we distort the world in relation to our own tensions. Children from poorer homes, when asked to draw a quarter, draw a bigger than actual one. Industrial employees, when asked to describe the people they work with, talk more about their bosses (the people more important to their needs) than about their peers or subordinates, and so on.

But the problem is more complicated than that. People may perceive what is important to their needs, but does this mean people see what they want to see, or what they are afraid to see? Both wishes and fears are important to one's needs. The answer seems to be that we perceive both, but according to certain rules. We magnify a compliment from higher up in the organization but we also magnify a word of disapproval. A man may dream of a beautiful woman, but he may also have nightmares. And sometimes we just don't pay attention at all to things that are quite relevant. We forget dentist's appointments; we oversleep when we have examinations coming up; we manage to forget to clean the basement or to call on this particular customer.

Selective perception

What, then, are the rules of selective perception? The best answer we can give is this one: If one reexamines his memories of the past, he may find that his recall of positive, satisfying things is better than his recall of negative, unpleasant things. He may find it easier to wake early to go fishing than to get to a dentist's appointment. He may look forward, in fact, to doing pleasant, satisfying jobs but may evade mildly disturbing and unpleasant jobs. A senior executive once commented to the author that the biggest problem he encounters with young management people is their tendency to avoid the little unpleasant decisions—like disciplining people or digging through boring and repetitive records or writing unpleasant letters. This executive felt that his younger people would be far more effective if they could learn to deal as promptly with these uncomfortable little decisions as they did with the big ones.

But we can see some sense in this selective remembering if we look for it. There are some advantages to a person in being blind to unpleasantness, even if such blindness cuts down his working effectiveness. Ignoring the unpleasant may represent more than "laziness." It may be a sensible defensive device, psychologically speaking. Thus, most people are able to ignore soft background conversation while working. In effect they are psychologically deaf to a potentially distracting part of the real world. And this defense helps them to concentrate on their work. Similarly, most people manage to ignore the threat of the hydrogen bomb and to go on eating and sleeping as though this dangerous part of the real world were not here. It can even be shown experimentally that words with unpleasant connotations tend to be recognized more slowly when exposed for very brief intervals than words with pleasant connotations.

The strange part of this defensive process, however, is that in order *not* to hear the distracting music or *not* to see the unpleasant words one must first hear and see them. One has to see the word, recognize that it is unpleasant, and reject it almost simultaneously, so that one can say, "No. I didn't see what that word was." Hence the label "defense" attached to this phenomenon—defense against the entry of preselected things mildly disturbing to one's equilibrium. So two of our rules of selective perception become: (1) see what promises to help satisfy needs, and (2) ignore mildly disturbing things.

Suppose, though, that while one is successfully ignoring background talk someone back there starts to shout; or, while one is successfully ignoring the H-bomb, an H-bomb falls on London. At those points, when the unpleasantness becomes intense and dangerous, people stop defending and begin attacking. They stop ignoring the irritation and start directing all their attention to it. This reversal seems to happen suddenly, at some specific threshold. The distant irritation increases to a point at which it becomes so real, so imminent, and so threatening that we reverse our course, discard the blindfold, and preoccupy ourselves completely with the thing previously ignored.

This is the third rule: Pay attention to things that are really dangerous. The whole picture now begins to look like this: *People perceive what they think will help satisfy needs; ignore what is disturbing; and again perceive disturbances that persist and increase.*

There is yet a fourth step in this process. What can happen when perceived threats become even more intense and imminent? When the soldier in combat watches his buddies die around him? That one we shall consider later, in the chapter on conflict.

This process may not seem entirely logical to an outside observer, but it is quite reasonable psychologically. For this kind of self-imposed psychological blindness helps the person to maintain his equilibrium while moving toward his objectives. An organism lacking this ability to fend off minor threats might well find itself torn apart in its attempt to deal simultaneously with all of them. Or, at least, an individual unable to ignore unpleasant realities might spend so much of his energy dealing with them that he would make little progress toward his major goals. For once a person has learned to perceive a multitude of threats and dangers in his world he needs a system of defense against them. One should add, however, that some individuals may see relatively few things as dangerous and therefore have little need for defense, while for others the world holds dangers at every turn.

In the preceding chapter we suggested that a person who has encountered a relatively helpful world is likely to perceive more of his environment as potentially helpful. If, however, the world has been mostly frustrating, then more of it, and especially new things in it, will be seen as potentially dangerous. Being dangerous, they must be fended off. But, paradoxically, to be fended off they must first be seen. So to protect himself from more insecurity, the insecure person must first see the things that will provoke insecurity and then manage to deny to himself that he has seen them.

Projections of the perceived world

The basic point of this chapter, the point that the world as it is perceived is the world that is behaviorally important, underlies the development of the now generally familiar projective tests. Originally projectives (which we shall discuss in chapter 9) were designed for the diagnosis of aberrations in personality, but they are also widely used in industry. The same idea also underlies what market researchers call "motivation research" into consumer attitudes, techniques for discovering people's personal views of the "facts" of advertising and product design.

Perception and managing

For managerial purposes, the importance of the perceptual world is clear. If one's concern as a supervisor or counselor or committee member is to try to effect some change in the behavior of other people, and if in turn people's present behavior is determined largely by their perceptions of their environments, then it is critical that one seek to understand their perceptions if one is to understand the circumstances under which their behavior might change.

For example, managers assume almost universally that subordinates want promotions. And yet more than one subordinate has been driven into panic and disappointment because he felt psychologically forced to accept a promotion that no one (sometimes even himself) bothered to find out he did not want.

Often assumptions about the perceptions of others are wrong because they are incomplete. One may assume correctly that employees want more money, but he may fail to understand that more money is acceptable only within a certain framework of independence. This is the paternalism problem.

Sometimes the problem is simple lack of sensitivity for other people. Thus a foreman once complained to the writer about how odd people seemed. He said one of his employees had gotten terribly upset "for no reason at all." The foreman had said, "Hey, boy, go over there and pick that up!" The employee got angry. He had said, "Don't call me 'boy'; I have a name!" The foreman couldn't understand why the employee, a black, should get angry about a "perfectly reasonable" request like that.

In recent years, especially, many of us in the United States have come to realize just how narrow and stereotypical some of our perceptions of other groups have been. And, more importantly, we have come to realize just how much those narrow perceptions have generated both injustice and distress. Certainly what may have seemed to many of us like stubborn demands from blacks, minority groups, and from women has finally penetrated some of our perceptual defenses. We are beginning, one would hope, to see a little better just how much we have been using denigrating stereotypes to deny both dignity and opportunity. Indeed, as some women readers have let me know, earlier editions of this book have been guilty of many distortions. I hope this one has corrected them.

Many parents argue for the importance of heredity over environment because their own children seem to be so different from one another. "Our second child," they will say, "was just a completely different person from the first, though we treated them both *exactly* alike." Parents may quite truthfully feel that they treated two children alike, but it is unwise to assume that the children were therefore treated alike. The first child's world did not include the second child; but the second's did include the first. Indeed, the evidence is now quite good that certain personality variables are related to the birth order of children in families. First-born children tend to be more affiliative and more dependent than later-born, for example, and generally more susceptible to social pressure. Moreover, for the infant whose slate is relatively blank, the minor marks made by parents may be major marks for the child. Thus many parents pass lightly over the differences between feeding an infant now or ten minutes from now. But the child is not likely to pass over the same thing nearly so lightly. The manager is likely to pay little attention to his criticism of a subordinate's work. But for the subordinate it is a week's food for worry.

One more example. Sales managers often complain of the difficulties they encounter in getting salesmen to make "cold" calls. The salesman says he was too busy, or there were better prospects, or he had to catch up on some reports. Is he lazy? Or just defending himself—perhaps unconsciously—against a perceived threat? If it is a defensive process, there are two general ways in which the manager can try to shake the salesman loose. He can teach him to feel comfortable about cold calls, or he can change the mild threat to a major one so that it can no longer safely be ignored. But if he chooses the latter course he had better consider the by-products.

Perceiving oneself

So far we have talked about perceptions of things and other people. But one of the people each of us perceives is himself, as he is, and also as he would like other people to see him. Each of us struts his own act before the world, as it were, in an effort to have other people see us as the kind of person we value.

Quite early in life, we begin to learn what kinds of groups we want to join, what kinds of social classes to aspire to, what kinds of status to achieve. Two of us may have equally intense needs for status and prestige, but if we have grown up in different environments, one of us may seek that status by acting masculine and powerful, or by growing long hair and a beard. Another may seek to fulfill the same needs by costuming herself in high fashions or by bedecking herself in jewels.

Teenagers are often painfully awkward as they strive to perfect their own private acts. They seem to feel it terribly important to appear to be what they doubt they really are. Later they become more skillful, either because their acts are better or because their acts are not very far from what the actors really are.

Note that our acts are functional for us. They are performed by both teenagers and adults for good reasons. An act is a way of filling a role. It is also a way of protecting the vulnerable parts of ourselves from real or fancied attack. But our act is effective in performing its functions only if other people accept it. And other people usually accept acts when the gap between our acting selves and their estimate of our "real" selves is small. Other people tend to be reasonably accurate judges, too. So acting problems arise as the distance between act and reality increases.

It is also true that acts are often uncomfortable for the actor. The boy and the girl may happily abandon their courting dances as soon as the wedding is over. But until each feels secure enough with the other, they must play their self-protecting version of the mating game, no matter how much worry and fret it requires. Similarly the company executive must act decisively, though privately he may yearn for a chance to weep on someone's shoulder.

But though our acts are functional, they contribute to a social world full of distorted signals. You are telling me that you are strong, worldly, and decisive (and you may be—or you may not), and I am just as busily communicating to you that I am the sagacious, understanding, intellectually stimulating character I would like to be (and may actually be—or may not). We have both been practicing our acts for a long time. So we have both developed subtle ways of being convincing, ways that the inept adolescent has not even dreamed of. But we have also developed clever ways of spotting the other guy's act.

Our relationship becomes even further confounded by the fact that we read one another's cover stories through our own need-distorted glasses. We attribute to your behavior the meanings we have learned, which may not be the correct ones. While you stand there trying to radiate strength and decisiveness, I see you as brash and immature. And you, wanting action and recognition, see my efforts at quiet, pipe-smoking wisdom as dullness and lack of imagination. Looked at this way the wonder is not that we find it so difficult to understand one another, but that we are able to understand one another at all.

The first big problem then is the problem of accuracy, of somehow gaining more accurate information about other people—estimating the discrepancy between the actor and the "real" person. The second problem is to estimate how well our act is working. For surely we are in considerable trouble if the self we want to present to the world is presented so badly, so weakly, so transparently that everyone else is discounting it. We are in a bad way if the people around us are saying: "There is someone who is trying to act decisive and sure of himself, while in fact it is as plain as the nose on your face that he is really unsure, indecisive, anxious."

To the best of this writer's knowledge there is only one general mechanism by which such distortions in relationships can be reduced, and that is the mechanism of *feedback*. If somehow we can develop better ways by which we can learn from other people how our act is getting across, then we can either modify it so that it gets across more fully or we can try to reduce the discrepancy between the act and ourselves, so that it is an easier act to play convincingly. The first course leads to a world of intrigue and gamesmanship; the second, to a simpler, less distorted world.

By this reasoning, other people, if we can get them to provide us with appropriate feedback, can do us considerable service in helping us to bring what we wish to be closer to what we are, and to reduce our uncertainty and anxiety in the process.

We shall talk more about feedback in part 2, when we consider problems of influence and persuasion.

The social side of perception

Although we shall consider social issues more in parts 2 and 3, we cannot leave this short piece on perception without reminding the reader that one of the major contributors to the way he perceives the world derives from his group and community memberships. We are "socialized" by our environments, which means that we learn to see the world through the particular distorted lenses of our kinds of people. If we are women, we are taught to see the world as women of our time and culture are supposed to see it. If we got our Ph.D. in physics, we probably not only learned physics, but to perceive science with a capital S, almost as a religion. And if we become members of a fraternity or the marketing department of Company X or of the British Civil Service we are all initiated (for which one can read "socially distorted") to perceive the world as those groups expect us to perceive it and to define our friends and enemies accordingly.

These social pressures on perception are extremely powerful and wide-ranging. They are strong enough to force reasonable people to see short lines as long ones, or nonmoving target objects as moving in the socially approved direction. If we know a little about the "socializing" that has been imposed upon the person, we can often predict with considerable accuracy a wide range of selective perceptions. We can guess what some of his perceptions are likely to be in realms of religion, politics, sex, and a whole host of other dimensions.

So perception is not just a matter of cute little games and ambiguous pictures. Our whole construction of reality, our notions about what is true and, to a great extent, what is important and what is right derive from ways that we have been taught selectively to perceive the world.

In summary

People see things differently. Even "facts" may be seen quite differently by different people. Relevance to one's needs is the most important determinant of one's personal view of the world. Things that seem to be aids to satisfying one's needs are seen quickly. But things that look like obstacles, if they are not critically threatening, may also be seen quickly, only then to be denied so that they appear not to have been seen at all. By denying obstacles, people "protect" themselves temporarily from them. If they really become dangerous, however, people drop the blinders and face the obstacles.

One of the things we perceive is ourselves and other people. To protect and enhance ourselves, we try to manipulate the picture other people have of us by putting up a front that will make them think we are what we want to be. The problem of our act, and getting it across successfully, depends mostly on our ability to pick up audience reactions accurately. And accurate audience reactions are hard to come by because the audience is acting too.

To ignore differences in perception is to ignore a major determinant of behavior. Yet it is easy to assume unwarrantedly that everyone views the world from the same perspective as the viewer. Communication—mutual feedback of our perceptions—is the best corrective measure we have.

The whole process we call "socialization" can be thought of as a perceptual learning process—a way of learning to see the world in the way that our society wants us to see it.

4 Frustration
The roadblock

The hypothetical manager we have been talking about is now struggling continually to reach unattainable goals by a variety of means: first, by behaving in an attempt to satisfy his unsatisfied needs; second, by distorting his perceptions of the real world, i.e., by denying a multitude of minor obstacles in his environment that would push him into greater and greater disequilibrium and by spotlighting things that could be aids to the satisfaction of his needs; and, finally, by periodically stopping on his path toward some goals to deal with obstacles so significant he can no longer ignore them.

Another step is left in the development of this picture. It is the step of actually dealing with these serious obstacles between the person and his goals. The major questions are these: How do people behave under one special kind of pressure—the pressure created by a serious block between the person and what he wants? What kinds of people behave in what ways in the face of such blocks? Why do some people seem to run into more roadblocks than others? Why do some managers blow up so easily? Why don't some people seem to recognize what's good for them?

The obstacle course

Here is a hypothetical case that may illustrate some aspects of the problem.*

Let's go back, if we can, to the days when we were eighteen or so. We have met a girl and taken her out once, and we like her. Now the junior prom is coming up and we decide to invite her. We extend our invitation, and Mary accepts.

This prom is important. It's the big event of the year. It will cost some money, and we don't have much, so we start saving our

---

* This is a male-based example. May I ask women readers to try to think up a counterpart from their perspective?

pennies. We take on extra odd jobs, washing cars, delivering groceries. We manage to borrow a car. We even work it so that a close friend and his date will come with us and share the cost of the gas. We manage to scrounge up enough money so that by prom night we've rented a tux, gassed the car, and bought a corsage. Primped and combed and polished, we drive over to pick up our friend and his date, and from there to Mary's house. We park at the gate and go up the walk with our corsage clutched in our little hot fist.

We've never met Mary's parents. When we ring the doorbell and a man appears, we correctly assume it is Mary's father.

We: "Is Mary home?"

Mary's Dad, gruffly, newspaper in one hand, pipe in the other: "Why no, Mary's gone out for the evening."

End of scene. Two questions for the reader: (1) How would you feel? (2) How would you act?

People's reactions to this situation may be grouped into three major classes:

First, there are those whose predominant reaction is *anger*—at Mary.

Second, many people do not feel nearly so angry as they feel *ashamed* and *disappointed* in themselves.

Third—and very rarely—essentially rational rather than emotional feelings occur, i.e., "I wonder which one of us forgot the right date?"

The actions that may follow these feelings can, of course, be direct expressions of the feelings. The person who feels angry may express himself in action—in door slamming, cussing, or in seeking out Mary for verbal or physical attack. But there is another possibility. He may suppress his feelings and act as though he feels calm. Similarly, the person who feels ashamed and inadequate may act accordingly—with weeping and wailing. On the other hand he may act in many other ways. He may, for example, *act* angry as a face-saving device—though he doesn't feel angry.

The rare third person may feel neither angry nor ashamed. He may simply view the situation as a not-very-important problem to be solved. He thus has an infinite variety of actions open to him—to double check or find another date or go alone or spend his money elsewhere—all without major emotional upset.

Two kinds of aggression and who shows them

The third person is a rarity. Most people would feel like one of the other two. These two have one thing in common: intense emotional feelings of aggression. In one case the aggression is directed toward some outside object—toward Mary or toward her parents or toward women in general. In the other case it is directed toward one's self, one's lack of ability in these realms, one's unattractiveness for women, one's stupidity in getting involved with someone like Mary.

Probably there is some admixture of these feelings in almost everyone, much as in the dependency relationship of infancy. But the sets of feelings that would predominate can be guessed at fairly accurately if we know just a little about the person in the situation.

For example, suppose boy A is the Beau Brummel of the high school. Every girl in town would love to go out with him. He is perfectly self-confident about his ability to handle women. This is his area of major success, though in many other areas he is less sure of himself. Now he gets stood up by Mary.

Contrast him with B, the low man on the high-school totem pole. He has acne. He knows he is not very successful in his social relationships. Girls tease him put pay little serious attention to him. He didn't want to go to the prom in the first place, but you, one of his friends, urged him to. You almost had to force him ("for his own good") to call Mary.

What differences would one expect in the way that these two personalities would handle this situation?

Secure, self-confident A, moving toward an important goal and encountering an entirely unexpected and apparently insurmountable obstacle will probably want to attack the obstacle directly. He will be angry. He will want to fight.

B, who is pessimistic about his abilities but who nevertheless would like very much to be successful, might behave quite differently. When he encounters the sudden, insurmountable obstacle, his anger and hostility will probably be directed toward himself—at this further proof of his own inadequacy, at his stupidity in even venturing into this danger area. He will be just that much harder to entice into boy-girl relations in the future.

Frustration is a feeling

This area begins to look like this: When people meet serious obstacles between themselves and their important goals, they become aggressive. If they are optimistic about their ability to reach their goal, they get aggressive outwardly—they attack the obstacle. If they are pessimistic about their own ability, they get aggressive inwardly—they attack themselves.

Clearly a *series* of frustrations can begin to turn the secure optimist into an insecure pessimist. The Beau Brummel may lose his confidence if, having been stood up once, he bounces back only to find himself stood up again—and again and again and again. A point may be reached in the process at which he can no longer feel certain that the world has gone wrong. At this point he will begin unhappily to worry about himself. Similarly, a series of successes may turn the shy boy into a Beau Brummel.

The rare third person is still worth thinking about. He is the one who feels no emotional upset—no anger at Mary or at himself. He treats the incident the way most of us might treat running out of ink in the middle of a letter—troublesome, but not worth getting into a stew about.

An explanation of the third person requires us to go back to the chapter on perception. Different people perceive the world in different ways. What kind of world can the third person be perceiving that permits him to toss off this obstacle so lightly? His world probably includes, for one thing, a wide range of alternative behaviors to fall back on when he meets a roadblock, so that no single roadblock seems insurmountable. His is a bigger world. It is probably also a world in which most of his other egoistic needs have been successfully satisfied, so that being stood up is not so important.

But what distinguishes an important goal from an unimportant one? The word "important" here means something like personal, or where-the-hair-is-short, or dear-to-one's-self-esteem-or-survival. What is the goal that is blocked for our frustrated subject? He is not upset because he cannot get to the dance. He is upset because his personal egoistic needs for status and self-esteem are challenged. Most of us will agree that being stood up on an important date might have been a major frustration when we were adolescents. But as older adults whose social relationships have jelled, whose range of interests has expanded, we are likely in this situation to be more like the third person. Just the experience of a few years may make the problem look much less important or even emotionally minor. Adult security and self-assurrance usually hang on firmer threads, not so readily ruptured by a single social setback.

Incidentally, we usually save the word "frustration" for incidents that cause emotional reactions. For the third person, and for most "minor" obstacles, we talk about "deprivation."

The explosive manager

Some odd implications evolve out of these generalizations about who reacts to frustration in one way and who reacts in another. The position taken here, in effect, is that the confident, secure person will be less likely to encounter serious (for him) obstacles, but that he will be more likely to attack such obstacles when he does encounter them.

Yet, although it is generally true that organizations prefer secure, solid, optimistic people to shy, withdrawn, insecure people, it is also true that organizations are likely to look askance at executives who have emotional outbursts. Emotional blow-off is seen as unbusinesslike behavior that earns the young executive only black marks on his boss's evaluation sheet. Hence, we are likely to find in industry many cases of internal emotion and the external appearance of calm.

Thus it is possible for the secure optimist to avoid part of this problem—he can *feel* like blowing up but then stifle his corresponding actions so that what the boss sees is a controlled and rational facade. In fact, many executives in industry probably do just that, thereby perhaps contributing to the psychosomatic illnesses industrial executives are said to develop. For chronic failure to express intense emotion and through that expression to utilize the physiological products of emotion can lead to chronic physiological disturbance. Moreover, encountering an obstacle, then wanting to attack it, and then finding the avenue of attack is cut off by the disapproval of organizational superiors—such a series itself constitutes a secondary kind of frustration.

The occasional blow-off, therefore, ought to be viewed as an appropriate reaction by an imperfect but hard-working, highly motivated individual when he encounters, as he must at times, a difficult, unexpected, and apparently insurmountable obstacle.

It may be true that an executive would be an even better executive if he did not get frustrated to begin with; that is, if obstacles that were important for other people seemed minor to him, so that he did not have to worry about controlling his emotional reaction. Most of us would consider it ideal if our model executive could be the rare third person, who would simply shrug his shoulders (both at himself and at the world) and start thinking about where to go from there. An ideal executive might then be one whose tolerance for things frustrating to other people would be so great, whose areas of personal security would be so broad, whose breadth of perception would be so wide, that only very, very few incidents in his lifetime would include insurmountable obstacles (because he would always have ways around them) or really important self-esteem needs (because his self-esteem would be so solid that few things could threaten it). His egoistic needs instead would be needs for accomplishment of organizational goals.

The problem is one of people's expectations about their ability to satisfy their needs; and expectations are, in turn, largely determined by past successes and failures. If through life one has come to expect failure, to feel unsure of his ability to satisfy his personal egoistic needs, then these needs loom larger in his perceptions than they do for others. The martini that is not dry enough stops being just a deprivation, i.e., just a martini that is not dry enough. It becomes instead a sign of disrespect from the bartender—a threat to one's self-esteem.

It follows that people whose self-esteem is easily threatened are less likely to be rational about their efforts to satisfy their needs. It follows, too, that if one can build up people's feelings of self-confidence, so that their expectations are optimistic, they will be able to deal with problems less impulsively and more objectively.

Frustration and standards of success

Perhaps the most important key to whether we encounter frequent frustration or not is our own individual standard of success. Two people may both want to make money, but "to make money" for one may mean $30,000 a year, while for the other "to make money" means $300,000. If two such persons are of about equal ability and have about equal opportunity, and if both actually achieve $50,000 a year, then one will be satisfied and the other frustrated. Both have achieved the same external level of success, but one may perceive himself a failure.

This problem has many facets: It is a question of the relationship between our aspirations and our ability to achieve our aspirations. If the two are close together, frustration is relatively unlikely. If our ability exceeds our level of aspiration—if we are much *better* than we need to be—then society probably suffers because we do not contribute as much as we can. If aspiration and ability are out of line in the other direction —if we want what we do not have the capacity to obtain—then we have a potential source of serious frustration.

It is useful to examine the ways in which people develop their individual ideas of how good is good and how high is high. Many of them seem to develop early in life. Even when quite young, some children seem always to need to win any game they play, while others seem to want only to be "better than average." And occasionally we see still others who apparently can be perfectly happy as low man on the totem pole. Similarly, in industry some people seem consistently ready to accept the level at which they are working or only want to move ahead in small (but perhaps steady) steps. Others feel they are at the bottom unless they are at the top.

An illustration may show how such differences develop: Suppose someone puts a target on a wall and then leaves you alone with a set of darts and the target. Suppose you have never thrown darts before and have shown no particular interest in dart throwing. Do you set yourself a score to shoot for before you throw the darts for the first time? Probably not. But suppose you throw the five darts and score 75 out of a possible 250? Now what do you do? Before you throw the next dart do you set yourself a standard? Is the standard 250? Or is it anything better than 75? For most of us it would be the latter. In situations in which we are perfectly free to set our own standards, we are most likely to keep setting our goals just slightly ahead of our present abilities. Thereby, through learning and training and exercise, we can feel that we are continually moving ahead successfully.

Incidentally, it is probably worth pointing out that people with high achievement motivation characteristically behave in just that way—that is, they set their goals *moderately* high. They set them high enough so that reaching them represents a real but not impossible challenge. They neither set goals which are almost impossible to achieve, nor do they set goals so easy that the achievement wouldn't be any fun.

Let us suppose, however, that instead of being alone in the room with the target and the darts, someone else is present—another person who has been a constant competitor of yours. The other person throws first and hits 100. Now what is your goal? And now how do you feel when you hit only 75?

Once other people enter into the goal-setting process the more or less "natural" tendency to set goals a little ahead of past achievement begins to give way. Goals may then, in fact, be set without any regard to ability. Thus one occasionally encounters a person who *must* become a great industrialist because his parents have hammered that notion into him since childhood. Failing to become a great industrialist constitutes failing to satisfy the people he wants most to satisfy and, hence, means frustration.

Consider the case of a young engineering student who was unhappy at school. He had never wanted to be an engineer; he had always wanted to be a coach. But his father had been an engineer. His father, on his deathbed, had extracted a promise from the student that he would become an engineer, and a good one. So the fellow was stuck first with a goal that had been imposed on him and, second, with abilities and interests that were not likely to allow him to reach that goal. He had no good solution to the problem except to continue through life jumping for the ring he would probably never reach—unless he could somehow change his attitude toward his now unreachable father.

It is commonplace in organizational work situations to feel that one must set high standards for employees to "motivate" them. But may not standards beyond an individual's reach lead him into one of two other behaviors? They may lead him into a hopeless struggle to reach a goal that his abilities will not allow him to reach, and hence into a series of failures, and hence again into panic and insecurity. Or else overly high standards may lead a better-adjusted individual simply to remove himself physically or psychologically from the situation, to refuse to accept the standards that are set for him.

Perhaps one can argue that a person who is in a position to set standards for other people has a responsibility to set those standards neither so low as to provide inadequate opportunity for full expression nor so high as to guarantee feelings of failure. And maybe joint goal setting will help to reach that happy medium.

In summary

Frustration is a "feeling" rather than a "fact." It is a feeling that arises when one encounters certain kinds of blocks on paths to certain kinds of goals. These feelings arise when the block seems insurmountable and when failure to surmount it threatens one's personal well-being—when the goal involves the self.

When people encounter such obstacles, they react with aggression: aggression mostly toward the obstacle when the person is sure of his own ability and aggression mostly toward oneself when the person is pessimistic about his ability, i.e., when he has had a history of failure.

Many obstacle situations are depriving rather than frustrating because the obstacles do not seem insurmountable or the goals are not central to the self. Some people may therefore meet fewer frustrations than others because they have more ways around more obstacles or because they are self-confident enough so that their self-esteem does not have to be proved again by every new problem they encounter.

Moreover, if a person's goals are in line with his abilities, then he may avoid another major source of frustration. If his objectives extend far beyond his abilities, he may consider himself a chronic failure because he cannot see that the carrot is really tied to his own nose.

Other people—parents, peers, managers—have a good deal to do with the development of self-confidence and hence with the ways people deal with obstacles. For self-confidence is tied to success, and success is in large part what other people may decide it is.

5 Psychological conflict
Roadblocks on the inside

Conflict may be thought of as a class of frustration, the class characterized by a pulling in two directions at the same time. The obstacles one meets are not brick walls but drags that pull one back as one goes forward. Conflict situations are frying-pan-and-fire situations, or donkey-between-the-bales-of-hay situations. They are choice situations, decision-making situations. And this class of psychological situations underlies both major emotional upset and irrationality in everyday problem solving. In later chapters we shall consider conflicts among groups. But this chapter is about conflicts on the inside, conflicts within ourselves.

Internal conflicts occur at all levels of personality and in all degrees of importance to the person. Some are minor. Few persons are likely to be psychologically crippled by trying to decide between two movies, though the presence of conflict is often visible in a tendency to vacillate before the choice is made. Nor is the donkey nearly so likely to be paralyzed between the bales of hay as the old story makes out. On the contrary, most of us encounter numberless conflicts in the course of everyday life, conflicts we manage to resolve in short order and without permanent scars.

Some of the same generalizations that apply to frustration also apply to conflict. Some conflict situations involve important central needs that appear to be inescapably opposed. Others involve relatively unimportant needs or offer so many substitute possibilities that we hardly recognize their existence. As with frustration, serious trouble arises from conflicts between intense central needs involving long-term critical goals, where no satisfactory alternatives are visible. Such conflicts can be a real threat to the personality.

In this chapter we consider some extreme illustrations of more serious personality conflicts, in search both of better understanding of the process itself and of the ways in which the organizational environment can irritate or even create such conflicts. Then, after looking at some

43

samples, alternative ways of handling and resolving them will be considered.

An extreme illustration

Here is a nightmarish illustration:

Suppose I build a large cage and put you in it. Suppose you live in it for a long time and get used to it. This is home. Life is dull but not unbearable. You have a good bed and the food is good. But there is a peculiarity about the food. On the table in one corner of the cage is a box. The box has a cover. When you get hungry you lift the cover and inside you find an attractive meal. So whenever you get hungry, you just open the box, take a few things you like, and let the cover close again. You eat and then you go over to your bed and take a nap.

One day something happens. When you get hungry, you go to the box as usual. You reach out to lift the lid, but when your fingers hit it you get a strong electric shock.

You draw back and rub your hand. You think about it for a while. You decide it must have been static electricity and reach out again. This time you get another shock, one that seems more intense than the first. This upsets you somewhat, so you begin to look around to see if there is something wrong. You look for a plug or a wire you can pull out. You look for some rubber gloves. But you can't find anything that will do the job. Of course, you're not very hungry—yet.

An hour later, you are hungrier, so you go over again. You say: "What the devil; so I'll get a little shock, so what?" You touch the cover, but the shock has now grown quite intense. It really hurts. You drop the lid in a hurry. You again sit down on your cot and think for a while. After twelve hours of this, with no food, you begin to get a little frantic. You begin to poke around the place, looking for the answer to the electrified box. You call for help. Nothing seems to work. You start looking seriously for a way out of the cage, something you haven't done since the first few days you were in it. You try to pull the bars apart, to break the lock, to crawl out. Nothing works.

You can smell the food in the box and your hunger begins to get desperate. You decide to risk it. You pull open the lid, get knocked back, but you still manage to reach in and grab a bit before you let the lid drop. You eat your morsel and go back to your cot to think the thing over again.

The situation goes on. As you get hungrier, the shock seems to get stronger. As you approach the box, driven by your hunger, you can almost feel the pain of the shock you'll get when you touch it. You manage to get enough food to stay alive, but instead of adapting to the shock you seem to get more sensitive to it.

What do you do?

The sanity in insanity

The conflict here is an extreme one involving two basic, critical, physical needs: the need for food, and the need for the avoidance of pain. There is no physical escape, and the needs increase in intensity with time.

What, then, would happen?

Probably you would "go crazy." After some days of this, you might huddle in a corner in a dazed and stuporous state. If we opened the cage and took you out, you would probably stay dazed and stuporous for a long time. If we tried to feed you, you probably wouldn't eat. If we tried to wake you, you probably wouldn't wake up. You're gone—even though you're alive and there's no specific physical defect.

If we sent you down to Florida and put you out to bask in the sun, if we held your hand and talked with you and reassured you, and if we used some of the methods that have been developed in psychiatry, we might be able to get back into contact with you. We might tease you into accepting food and into discovering thereby that things have changed and the world is no longer what it had been during those terrible days in the cage. We might, in other words, be able to cure you of the effects of this intense conflict. The cure might be complete, but most probably, no matter how many years passed, you would still get upset when you met up with cages or electric shocks.

Now suppose that we step inside your mind while you're in this stuporous state. What will we be likely to find? You may be off in some fantasy world. You may be the gourmet of gourmets, eating your way through quantities of delicacies while in one fist you hold the only key to the master electric switch. You would be dealing with the conflict by escaping upward into unreality and fantasy. You cannot escape physically; you cannot handle the stresses as they exist; so you escape psychologically, through a neurosis or psychosis.

Such behavior thus becomes, in a sense, reasonable behavior. It fits with the view that the organism defends itself from intolerable attack and seeks to keep itself together. Cutting off one's communication with the real world in favor of a world of fantasy is a desperation measure for meeting intolerable conflict. It is not necessarily a healthy way of meeting it, but to a person at a particular time it may be the best available way.

This illustration is extreme, of course. And it can only work because a cage exists. If we had not enclosed you in the cage, then you would have dealt with the conflict simply by walking away from it and looking for food elsewhere. In fact, one might say that the presence or absence of the cage makes the difference between conflicts that lead to extreme emotional reaction, especially withdrawal reaction, and conflicts that are handled more easily. But the cages one encounters in real life are usually built of social and cultural bars rather than steel ones.

Consider just one more illustration of major conflict before taking up the question of conflict in industrial situations. Consider two spouses, A and B, each married to an impossible partner. Both have been married for a long time, both have children. A has a political job, in the public eye, has no religious values of any significance, is not interested in his children, has no scruples about divorce. B loves his children, is intensely religious, and feels that divorce is sinful. Assume that the partners of A and B continue to make their lives miserable, and suppose further that the intensity of this misery increases continually. Suppose that A and B reach the same point at about the same time. Each decides that the situation is unbearable and runs away.

Which one will be more successful in his attempt to escape? Which one will be able to settle down to life and work in a new community? The answer clearly is that A may be quite successful, and B quite unsuccessful.

The conflict for A is between career and desire to escape. Though much intensified in degree, this choice is not essentially different from the choice one must make in deciding between two TV programs broadcast at the same time. A's choice involves little guilt, little threat to his idealized picture of himself. The stimuli are largely external to his person. All he can lose is his career. But for B, leaving the field is no escape at all. His conflict resides entirely within himself. It involves conscience, self-esteem. No matter how far he may be from the physical location of the conflict tomorrow morning, feelings of guilt and loss of self-respect will be with him, for he has no easy way of cutting out communication within himself.

The troublesome conflicts, then, are those that involve needs "central" or "internal" to the personality. Usually these turn out to be conflicts between needs at different *levels* of the personality—between more or less basically impulsive needs and "conscience" needs.

Conflict in people in organizations

Much supervision is an attempt to control others through the use of conflict. For example, the threat of discipline to prevent some unwanted behavior is an attempt to introduce a conflict into another person's (B's) perceptual world. Where B had only one need, to get what he wanted, now he has a second and conflicting one, to avoid the punishment that getting what he wants now entails.

Such control, through conflict, cannot be classed glibly either as good or as bad. For the most part, such measures do not introduce dangerous conflicts because they do not set up situations that involve feelings of guilt or threaten people's feelings of self-esteem. They are largely external to the personality. But insofar as some people may see rules as a challenge to their basic autonomy, the reaction may be intense.

Other uses of conflict as devices for controlling behavior can get more serious. Suppose, instead of the threat of discipline, we choose to try to develop "positive" feelings of loyalty and duty to the company —suppose we try to build a "company conscience" into our employees as we do into our children. If we succeed, we are setting up *internal* conflicts this time. Now it is not the boss that the employee must worry about, but his own feelings of guilt. People who thus begin to feel honor-bound can get themselves into a tense emotional tizzy. And the probabilities of an irrational emotional blow-off are consequently greater. Paternalism is that kind of problem. One simply showers employees with gifts or benefits and then makes it clear that they are expected to show their gratitude by submission. For those with strong needs for independence, the resulting conflict is essentially internal, and it includes the possibility of violent reaction.

There are many other places in industry where one may find serious long-term emotional conflicts. Many of these center in the same fundamental desires for independence and autonomy, on the one hand, versus one's desires for dependence and support, on the other. The whole pattern of industrial organization encourages this sort of conflict. Subordinates are by definition dependent on their superiors. Subordinates are therefore bound to feel ambivalent to some degree, i.e., to feel uncomfortably bound and yet pleasantly protected.

Sometimes one finds individuals who have managed to strike a balance between their needs for autonomy and for dependency, perhaps by finding a particular job at a particular level that satisfied both needs— like a job as assistant to a powerful superior. Or an executive may find a middle-level spot at which he feels both competent to do the jobs assigned and satisfied with prestige and status. Often, however, higher management, blind to the subordinate's perception of the world, decides to "reward" him by promoting him. Promotion for one who has thus struck a satisfactory compromise between conflicting needs may result only in reinstating the old enervating conflict with greater intensity than ever. Now perhaps our subject begins to feel panicky about his ability to do this bigger job. It frightens him. However, he wants the status and the money it will bring, and he wants to conform to the social necessity of accepting a promotion. ("You'd be crazy to refuse an offer like that!") Shortly following such a promotion, one often sees beginning signs of active conflict: anxiety; "unpredictable" lashing out against subordinates; "inexplicable" refusal to delegate authority; self-isolation from peers and subordinates and, if possible, from superiors; and so on. In fact, many such cases end up in physical illness or alcoholic escapes or some other unacceptable solution. Top management then usually decides it has misjudged the person—he wasn't as good as he looked.

This is not to suggest that fear of promotion should keep people from accepting promotion. Fears can be overcome by success in meeting them. But awareness of the existence of needs that drag against the rewards of promotion can help a promoter to plan the promotional process more wisely.

Sometimes a job demands of a person activities that do not mesh with his conception of what is right or his conception of what is dignified or proper for him as a member of society. Salespeople seem to suffer from this conflict more than some other occupational groups. Sales managers beat the drums and wave the flag to get them to go out to sell Ajax iceboxes to Eskimos. But some Eskimos seem not to need iceboxes; or some other iceboxes look more useful than Ajax; or the salesman feels uneasy and uncomfortable about putting his foot in people's doors when he hasn't been invited.

Some sales managers try to resolve this job vs. moral-social conflict by "proving" to the salesperson the social importance of selling. They point up his responsibility to carry the good life to the ignorant consumer. They try to resolve the conflict by building up the pressure on one side to such an extent that it overrides the other. The difficulties here are two: First comes the problem of the morning after. His enthusiasm drummed up by "inspirational" sales meetings, the salesman goes out and sells—temporarily satisfying his job needs and reducing them to zero. He then finds himself feeling depressed and guilty because the still unsatisfied moral-social needs are now naked and exposed. The second difficulty with this inspirational method is that it requires continual recharging. The sales manager must maintain the initiative by injecting periodic shots of enthusiasm, lest the salesman wake up one morning deciding his product and his job are really no damn good.

Finally, one can mention the role of conflict in consumer decisions. All the recent activity in motivational research centers in a conception of the human personality as a multi-storied structure. The occupants on each floor are at war with the others. Thus some people may deny that they buy a product for its snob value, because their self-respect requires such denial; but they may be able to buy the product for its snob value nevertheless, if the snobbery–self-respect conflict can be rationalized in terms of "good value," or "quality," or "utility."

Conscience

The conflict problem seems to be one of disorder in nature itself. If the development of human personality were entirely orderly, perhaps the need system of an individual would be so designed that there would never be two opposing simultaneous needs. But people do not grow up with any such well-integrated system of needs. On the contrary, they seem from the very beginning to develop more or less opposing needs which frequently demand simultaneous satisfaction. People get hungry and sleepy at the same time; they want to fight and to run at the same time; to love and to hate; to overpower and to submit.

Although the mere presence of opposing needs accounts for the existence of conflicts, it does not account for the intensity or the variety of reactions to conflict. What is required to account for these interpersonal differences is an additional dimension in the picture of the structure of human personality. We need to introduce the concept of conscience, of internal control by the person over his own behavior.

The development of conscience seems to pass through several phases, and you often can actually see them going on in a child. First, the child begins to avoid some things he wants to do because he fears reprisals from his parents or because he wants to please them by showing his self-restraint. When he finds he gets punished for throwing his milk at Mama, he may begin to think twice about throwing it. The next time the same impulse shows up, he may try to do it when Mama's not looking. But as he gets more socialized, as he begins to realize he can't outguess Mama, he begins to internalize and accept as his own the restrictions that originally came from outside. At this point he begins to act, for himself, *like his parents*. He may throw his milk to satisfy the impulse, but then he will slap his own wrist to punish himself for what he has done. The final stage in this process is the child's refusal to throw the milk because *he* now feels it is a wrong act.

This is conscience. It is the difference between the person who is aware of the law but is afraid only of getting caught and the person who himself feels that the law is right and proper and that to break it is morally wrong. So learned conscience needs can be satisfied only by denying the satisfaction of other needs.

The conflicts that cause difficulty are long-term conflicts between increasingly strong action needs and severe conscience needs. Thus, in the military situation, one troublesome conflict may center in the soldier's duty and loyalty needs at the conscience level and his desire to avoid danger at a more basic level. In a husband-wife case, the conflict may be between the conscience notions of morality and propriety and the desires to escape physical and psychological harassment at the hands of the other. In organizations the conflict may be between desires for psychological safety and the conscience wish to be what people expect one to be.

If, in early life, we develop an oversized conscience—if many things come to be seen as sinful or improper or dangerous—then we may encounter many serious conflicts. If one learns early that aggressiveness or sensuality or hostility are wrong and to be feared, and yet, in the course of living, one encounters situations that call for aggression or stir up sensual impulses or engender hostility, then one may be caught up in conflict much more than the next person. And if one's perceptual breadth is too limited to find ways around such problems, then the conflicts will be severe.

On the other hand, if one develops an undersized conscience, if he can lie, or steal, or turn on the showers at Auschwitz* without guilt, then he may suffer very little, although society may suffer a whole lot. Such people are usually labeled "psychopaths." At the extreme they sit in a special psychiatric filing category because they are not exactly sick, except socially. They may make other people sick, but they themselves feel fine.

Unconsciousness

At this point we must add one more concept to the whole picture: the concept of unconsciousness. It has been pointed out that one extreme way to handle conscience-impulse conflicts is to deny the existence of one or both of the needs. Amnesiacs do this. This process of denying from memory something the conscience disapproves is the process called *repression*. It can be viewed as defense mechanism, another way of holding a personality together in the face of otherwise unsolvable problems. If there is no acceptable solution in reality, then the solution must somehow be found in unreality, and repression is a way of denying reality by literally forgetting about it. The conflict then no longer exists. Thus the soldier with combat fatigue is in a completely stuporous state and remembers nothing of what has happened. Except, of course, that he actually does remember. In fact, one might say he remembers too well, since his memories may be so threatening and so dangerous that he must deny them to himself. So unconsciousness is in part the burial

* It's worth noting that most of the concentration camp killers were probably not weak- but strong-conscience people. They had been taught "duty," the duty to obey superiors, perhaps more strongly than the duty not to torture other human beings. They were caught in a conflict. They were in a psychological cage.

ground for dangerous or guilt-provoking needs and experiences. Day dreaming and night dreaming are cues to such unconscious activity. Temporary, voluntary escape into unconsciousness through alcohol or hobbies or movies are other less extreme ways of temporarily holding oneself together by forgetting the conflict. Psychosomatic (psychologically caused but physically manifested) illnesses are often unconscious ways of channeling off some of the tension that deep-seated conflicts may engender.

Handling conflict

Obviously none of these many unconscious or semiconscious methods of handling conflict is particularly satisfactory from the point of view of mental health. Each of them is a last-ditch holding maneuver which itself requires a great deal of energy. So much energy, in fact, may be devoted to repressing what is feared that not much is left for the behavior required to satisfy the multitudes of other more mundane needs that most of us must satisfy in order to survive.

So we are left with this question: How can one *really* resolve emotional conflicts? Conflicts, like other psychological phenomena, are conflicts only because they are perceived as such. They are not part of the real, but of the perceived, world. A conflict exists for a person because to him certain needs seem mutually exclusive. His conflict would be resolved if (1) he could find some new, previously unknown means to satisfy both needs fully, (2) he could change his mind about one of the needs so that he was no longer interested in it, or (3) he could reorganize, in one of a number of other ways, his view of the world so as to set the conflict in a new and less significant perspective.

For example, consider again a husband or wife caught between an impossible spouse and social duty. Several alternative resolutions are *theoretically* available. First, the person may come to feel differently about his or her notions of duty. If he or she decides it is, say, socially, religiously, and morally appropriate to leave the partner, then perhaps he/she can do so without trouble. Or he/she may come to see the partner in a new light, so that instead of being an ogre, the spouse becomes an unhappy human being in need of help. Still again, a person may be able to change his expectations about life, to reorient his standards and philosophy so that the sufferings he endures are not so much sufferings as the-things-one-must-expect-from-life.

This is not to say that one can resolve conflicts simply by asserting, "I feel differently about this." The problem is really to feel differently. The counselor and the psychiatrist offer to help people reorganize their perceptions of problems so that they can perhaps find new solutions.

One way to illustrate the idea of "reorganizing perceptions" is to ask the reader to compare himself today with himself as an adolescent. Consider what a skin rash might have meant in adolescence and what it would mean when he is thirty-five and settled down. The problem is simply not the same problem. As our worlds have grown, as new knowledge and new experience have been added, we have changed our perspectives, reorganized our perceptions.

Sometimes an adult conflict exists only because a person cuts off his channels of information from the world. The combat-fatigue victim, for example, may withdraw completely into himself, apparently seeking to avoid emotional repetition of arduous experiences. Unless he eventually opens his channels, he will never get an opportunity to learn that the world has changed and that he is surrounded by sunlight instead of explosions. Similarly, the process of repressing old conflicts so preoccupies many of us that we cannot observe our changing environments. We do not learn that elaborate defenses are unnecessary because now nothing needs defending. Thus, the poorly educated executive, after a series of perceived failures in coping with technical innovations, may go on avoiding technological change, never realizing that now he is—if he can bring himself to try it—perfectly capable of handling the situations that he is expected to handle. This tendency to narrow one's incoming communication channels in order to avoid psychological dangers is one major social cost of conflict. People avoid much of the world because they fear much of themselves. They "take leave of their senses," literally.

But though many reactions to emotional conflict are psychologically unhealthy and inefficient, they remain psychologically lawful reactions. They, like other behavior, can be thought of as attempts by the organism to bring itself into equilibrium.

Conflicts, beliefs, and decisions
The great balancing act

These processes for dealing with emotional conflict—efforts to reorganize or to reduce incoming communication—have their parallels in the less emotional but equally important processes of making decisions and solving problems. In the next chapter, we will concentrate on the thinking part of people, so at the end of this one it is useful to build a bridge between the emotional side that we have discussed so far and that other, everyday problem-solving side. The processes that we use to deal with conflict provide such a bridge; for conflicts occur not only in human guts but also in human brains. Decisions, the essence of managerial life, are, after all, resolutions of conflicts.

Some of the dilemmas that need explaining are things like the apparent irrationality of many decisions, even hardheaded business decisions; the frequent failure of executives to abandon a course of action even after it seems obviously to be the wrong one; and the tendency to believe in our plans more after we have decided to carry them out than we ever did before.

All of these can be thought of as a part of a great balancing act taking place in the emotions of most of us as well as in our heads. We search for consonance, for consistency, for balance, in business decisions and in the choices of everyday life. When we have invested a large amount in a course of action—like a new line of products—we find it hard to accept reports showing that the products aren't selling. To maintain an internal balance, to reduce psychological dissonance, we may do "irrational" things—like blaming the sales force or investing *more* in promotion and advertising, on the grounds that we haven't given our ideas a fair test.

When the scientist puts a year's work into a problem and his hypotheses don't check out, he is in a state of dissonance, too. He can either give up the hypotheses—to which he has given much of himself —or he can seek a larger grant to develop finer instruments to give his ideas a "really" fair test.

And so on. A well-known study of an offbeat group that predicted the end of the world is a good example. They predicted the end would occur at a special hour on a special date. They disposed of their worldly goods, informed the newspapers, and gathered at an appointed place to await the end. When the hour passed and nothing happened, did they quit and go home? Not at all. Too much imbalance, too much dissonance. Instead they "received" a late message from outer space telling them that this had been a test run to check their readiness and their faith. A new hour was then duly set, and it passed. And now how could the imbalance be handled? It was handled ingeniously. A new message arrived. It announced that because of the faithfulness of this little group the earth would be spared for a few centuries more.

The salesperson moves to another company and begins to sell for competitor B after firmly believing in product A for twenty years. How can he sell B if he thinks A is better? Dissonance again. So he looks into B "more carefully," and he "discovers" that it is a far better product than he had thought. Quality control is much better, etc. Now he can get back in balance.

The lame-duck executive is likely to have the same problem. If he has been obviously shunted aside by the company he has been loyal to and is on the way out, he is in imbalance. How to resolve it? Either by admitting that he is less good than he thought—which is difficult indeed and ought to create greater dissonance—or by beginning to look on the company differently; to mobilize his list of the company's weaknesses and stupidities; to prove that they don't deserve him. That's the more likely course. He makes himself ready to leave by searching more than ever for the negative side of what he is leaving. By so doing, of course, he speeds up the process, irritating his colleagues even further. In their turn, they can assuage their guilt and uncertainty by using his present negative behavior as evidence that they were right in unloading him.

Of course, the company that decides to try a third or fourth test market may be right. So we must be careful here, as elsewhere, about "psychologizing" too easily to explain things our way. The problem is to distinguish "real" logic from the selective logic generated to deal with psychological dissonance.

Thus, feelings and facts get intertwined and almost inseparable (though we often think of them separately) in many of our problems. It is the whole person who makes the decisions, not just the logical part of him.

In summary

The development of personality allows for the coexistence of opposing needs. Conflict situations are those requiring decisions between such coexistent opposing needs.

When conflicts involve critical needs and seem to offer no ways out, reactions may be severe. Fantasy, delusions, and amnesia are such extreme ways out of conflicts.

Conflicts that require extreme solutions usually involve "conscience" needs, centering in morality and social propriety. Extreme solutions often require the person to push one of the needs into unconsciousness and thereby—by forgetting—to deny the conflict.

But such repressive defenses cost energy. Less enervating solutions call for reorganization of perceptions, finding new ways out of apparently dead-end situations.

Serious chronic conflicts may develop in the industrial organization. Conflicts between needs for dependence and for independence are especially prevalent because the industrial environment emphasizes dependency but values independence.

Less deep but equally important conflicts occur in everyday decision-making situations. There emotional and logical mechanisms get mixed into one another. It often then becomes hard to tell how much of our commitment to a course of action is objective and logical and how much of it is an effort to maintain our psychological balance. For human beings seem to want to maintain balance, to avoid dissonance between mutually contradictory beliefs and ideas. Hence, when we make a difficult decision, we tend to build up our support for our solution and to find more and more reasons for feeling we were right in rejecting the alternative.

6 Learning, thinking, problem solving Some reasoning parts of people

A first purpose of this chapter is to counterbalance the general impression of human irrationality and emotionality we have built up thus far. In preceding chapters we emphasized emotional, unconscious, "illogical" aspects of human action. But even a cursory look at people's behavior will show that much of it is quite reasonable. It represents conscious effort to satisfy conscious needs. Students learn to type and to solve arithmetic problems; workingmen search for ways to add to their incomes and their job security; architects try to improve the beauty and functionality of their plans; managers try to choose the most effective ways of budgeting their capital and of designing and marketing their products.

Not long ago, however, a chapter about these matters probably would not have been included in this book. Psychologists and social scientists were so deeply concerned with the emotional life of man that they ignored his conscious thinking life altogether.

This emotional emphasis was partly a reaction against still earlier, entirely rational approaches. Fifty or sixty years ago, for instance, we assumed that workers worked only to earn money and that managers, in turn, sought only to maximize their profits. We built theories of economic behavior and industrial organization around these assumptions. Early industrial engineering grew up as a logical, "scientific" process, treating irrational human quirks like hostility and resistance as outside the realm of science. Later, with the emergence of such odd bedfellows as Freud and the Western Electric studies, attitudes turned in the opposite direction. Foggy conceptions of social and egoistic needs took precedence. Workers sought to satisfy ephemeral needs for "belongingness"; managers were not managing, they were unconsciously competing with childhood images of their fathers.

Only very recently have social scientists from many fields set about to integrate and modify these views; to deal with the undeniable whole man—the manager who may be unconsciously competitive but who

55

also spends a fair share of his time trying to decide what materials to buy and what marketing strategies to follow. This chapter, then, is about those conscious efforts to learn, to think, and to solve problems —issues that most managers work at for many hours each day.

What does it take to learn?

Earlier chapters have already said a good deal about learning. In effect they have said that people learn continuously; they learn their personalities; they learn many of their social and egoistic needs, their attitudes, and their habitual ways of behaving. At the same time they learn to speak, to walk, to read, to build airplanes, and to make managerial decisions. They are learning whenever their behavior at time 2 is modified as a consequence of experience at time 1.

The question now before us is this: What does it take for someone to be able to learn? If we set about to build a "thing" capable of learning, what would we have to build into it? And just how would the thing work?

This thing we are trying to build must demonstrate that it is a learning thing by behaving more effectively—perhaps more quickly and with fewer mistakes—the second or third time it tries to solve a problem than it did the first time. What characteristics do we have to build into it to permit it to pass such a test?

Our thing will really need two kinds of mechanisms in order to learn. It will need some hardware, some gadgets, some devices that will "allow" it to do certain kinds of things. But it will also need some "rules"—it will need a program that will permit it to decide which of the several alternatives to select.

On the hardware side, our thing will first require some *input channels* so that it can have "experiences" to learn from. It will need some means of getting information into itself from outside itself, something like human eyes or ears (some photoelectric cells will do).

Second, it will need some *output devices,* some ways of acting and searching. It will have to be capable of moving through the world or of sending signals out into the world. It will need some equivalents to human muscles or the human voice, like wheels or a typewriter. For how can it modify its behavior if it cannot behave. How can it search for easier paths if it cannot explore?

We are not through yet. If this machine is to improve performance with experience, it needs to remember its experience. It needs a *memory device* for storing up its experiences as well as a way of using this stored-up information when faced with new problems. Lacking such a storehouse, or lacking access to it, each experience will be a first experience.

Besides these external mechanisms it will need several inside gadgets.

It will need some *associative device* to connect inputs with outputs. The device may be a simple one that makes only one choice—to connect or not to connect a given input with a given output. But without such a device the thing won't be able to close the circuit between what comes in and what goes out and hence will be unable to profit behaviorally from its experience.

Besides all this hardware, which allows the thing to receive, process, and put out information, the gadget will need software: a program, a set of rules so that it doesn't just input and output completely at random.

One of these rules ought to be a *stinginess rule.* If the selective device has a choice among outputs, it can be built either to select the most "efficient" of all outputs—the simplest and shortest one—or to select the first output it comes across that will work (which may be easier in the long run) or to use some other specified decision rule.

It will also need a *response rule.* It cannot be allowed to sit still and ignore all inputs. It has to be built so that it is *on* when inputs are coming in and so that it stays on until it gets an answer. It will have to have, in other words, something vaguely like human needs—some motivation to work.

One final requirement: the thing will need some way of getting *inputs about it own outputs.* It has to know whether its own actions were right or wrong. If the archer could not see that he had missed the target, he could never know how to modify his aim. If the manager could never learn about the effects of his past changes in plant layout, he could not know by himself how to improve his layout. But this means that the input mechanisms have to be somehow related to the output mechanisms. If the only input device in our gadget is a photoelectric cell that is sensitive to light, and our only output gadget is a buzzer that signals with sound, then our thing might have a tough time learning. So there has to be some kind of correspondence between the nature of the input and the nature of the output. If it inputs and outputs in the same language, it can learn about itself.

Given all these characteristics, our learning thing begins to look like figure 3.

Notice that the thing is full of closed loops, with the arrows completing full circles. It is also a relatively elaborate system; it is not a cellulose sponge. Notice, too, that it looks a little like the design of a control system that one might find in many engineering situations.

Theoretically, then, if we could build a thing like this, it could learn. If any of these characteristics were missing, it could not learn; nor, theoretically, could people. If we knock out all a person's input senses—his sight, hearing, touch, taste, smell—he can't improve his

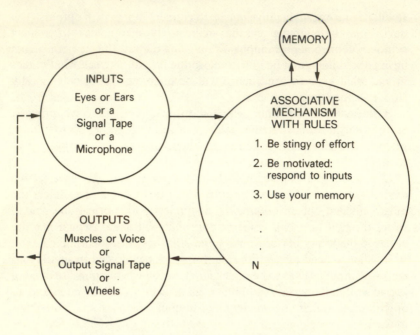

Fig. 3. A learning mechanism.

performance over time because he can't find out how he did the first time. If we knock out his memory, he can't learn because each new try is his first try. If we knock out his outputs—his voice and his muscles— he can't try at all. If he has no brain to make choices, he can't improve because he can't change; he can only repeat his behavior. If we knock out the stinginess principle or his needs, he won't improve because he doesn't give a damn—the hard way is as good for him as the easy way, and no behavior at all is as good as anything else. And if he can't see or feel his own hand—that is, if he can't determine the effects of his own outputs—he has no way of deciding how to change his outputs.

If we put all these requirements together, we come out with an essentially mechanical but nevertheless dynamic view of learning— learning as a process of doing things, finding out and evaluating what has happened, storing the experience, and trying again—using past experience as a jumping-off place. Psychologically speaking, one can say that (1) we act, (2) we perceive the effects of our actions, (3) we reorganize and remember our perceptions, and (4) we act again on the basis of our reorganized perceptions.

Artificial intelligence and machines that learn

Engineers have been able to design machine equivalents for each of these requirements for learning in order to build machines that can learn. Using such machines—computers are the best example—psychologists, mathematicians, and others are able to program them not only to solve problems but to learn to solve similar problems faster after experience. Computers can be programmed to learn to solve problems in symbolic logic or chess or to work out answers to riddles in ways that are surprisingly human. In fact, computers have been programmed to make a variety of rather complex learning decisions. One program, for example, can simulate an investment officer at a bank so that it will make almost the same selection of stocks that he would make, when the two—man and machine—are given the same data to work with.

Sometimes the computer programs behave very differently from human beings, working in a routine mechanical way and checking out every possible choice no matter how patently foolish it is. But other programs are quite human. Such *heuristic* programs (as distinct from *algorithmic* ones) are designed to behave like people. They are built by observing how people solve problems and then programming the computer to do likewise. And heuristically programmed computers therefore make mistakes much like the mistakes made by people when they are learning new games or solving new problems.

Some of us remember, for instance, the way our geometry textbooks used to trap us back in high school, by giving us a series of similar problems and then springing a new one on us. We would generate a rule about how to solve the first lot, and then try to use the rule on the new problem that looked like the old one. After hitting dead ends half a dozen times, we would finally realize that the rule simply didn't apply to this problem, and we would finally go off in a new, perhaps simpler direction.

Heuristically programmed computers behave in much the same way. They do not behave as machines "normally" do. They do not just try everything whether it looks sensible or not, nor do they forever keep banging their heads against walls. Instead they are specifically programmed to behave in a human way. They use strategies or heuristics of the sort that people use—for example, "If the problem is complex, try to reduce it to a simpler form first" or, "If this problem looks like a problem you can remember that you have already solved, first try the method you used to solve that other problem."

While these artificially intelligent programs often simulate human learning and problem-solving methods, they do not at all simulate the human brain. The simulation is not of neurons and synapses; but of information-processing methods.

Several questions about these man-machine comparisons have stirred up considerable emotional heat. It seems clear that by usual definitions of learning, machines really can learn to solve difficult, nonroutine problems. They can do much more than arithmetic. It is not clear that machines are necessarily going to end up smarter or dumber or more important than people, though many observers, including this one, are convinced that many present-day management jobs will ultimately be filled by programmed problem-solving machines—after an intervening period of programmed problem-solving people.

But perhaps the most important issue that needs to be stressed here is not whether or not machines can learn, but the critical importance of the closed loop, of the feedback system in both human and machine learning. *It is only by obtaining accurate information about the effects of our own behavior that we can correct and modify our own behavior.* It is only by knowing what and how we have done that we can learn to do differently.

Feedback—the flow of return information about our own outputs— is important not only in learning to solve intellectual problems; it is also critical in learning to solve social problems. To learn to be skillful in our relationships with other people, we must rely upon the feedback we get from other people about our impact on them. And therein lies the problem we shall be discussing at much greater length in later sections of this book. The problem is this: It is relatively easy to get feedback about the effects of our actions on *things*. We can see whether or not the ball has gone down the fairway or off into the rough. And we can then make efforts to correct our stroke on our next drive. We can put a part into a jigsaw puzzle and see whether or not it fits. We can play a note and hear whether or not it is off pitch. But when we say something to someone else, we do not necessarily or automatically get immediate feedback to tell us whether or not he heard what we intended. For now we are working through the perceptual filters of another person. And his outputs in response to our inputs are subject to great distortion.

While we *know* that the golf ball sank into the water hazard, we do not always know whether or not the bright idea we just gave to our boss sank into his brain.

Teaching machines and behavior modification

It is probably worth pointing out to the reader that teaching machines and other programmed learning techniques are applications of the feedback principle to human learning. The essence of the teaching machine idea is to provide the student with factual and immediate feedback about the effects of his own performance. The student fills in the blank and immediately learns whether or not he was right. But in much regular, nonprogrammed teaching there are long intervals between learning and feedback—between lecture and examination, for example. And in many areas no evaluative feedback is ever forthcoming.

In the last few years another much more far-reaching effort to apply these principles has taken place. It operates under the general label of behavior modification, and, as the name suggests, it is concerned not just with intellectual learning but with changing human behavior in general. But the argument is similar. If people behave and get quick feedback about the effects of their behavior, then their behavior can be modified. And since other people can often define the positive or negative rewards, then we should be able to modify behavior by generating positive feedback for desirable behavior and negative feedback for undesirable behavior. Thus, if a person is afraid of snakes and we want to help him eliminate that fear, we can put him into situations with snakes in which the immediate feedback is positively rewarding, rather than painful and frustrating. By carefully controlling both incremental exposure to such situations and the feedback that emerges therefrom, perhaps we can eliminate the fear.

Of course, the implications of behavior modification go much further than the treatment of fears. The implications extend to child rearing, education, and social development—into the shaping of all human behavior. And the behavior modification movement has theoretical implications, too. For it takes the position that one needs to know relatively little about the internal dynamics of the human being or about what caused the present behavior of an individual. It is essentially a behavioristic point of view, arguing that what needs to be changed is behavior and that what changes behavior is feedback that appropriately reinforces particular behavioral changes. We shall say more about this approach in later chapters on managerial problems of changing human behavior.

Some complicating factors in human learning and problem solving

People's decision rules about what is relevant to a problem are usually broader and more diffuse than those programmable into a machine. Our rules reflect the complexity of memories and needs that exist within us at any one moment. As a result, we are likely to learn more from an experience than we intend to learn. The new management trainee not only learns about the company's finances; he also learns that the financial vice-president likes to push people around. He learns not only about geometry, but about the geometry teacher and attitudes toward geometry. He perceives all these as parts of the problem-to-be-solved because his need satisfactions are tied up with all of them. Learning to solve the geometry problem is only one of several potential satisfactions to be gained by the student. Learning to please the teacher is another; learning that geometry is something to stay near, or to escape from, is another.

Certainly one difficult task of a teacher who sets out to teach geometry (or management, for that matter) is to be sure that it is geometry and not himself that the students see as the major problem-to-be-solved. In fact, one of the major advantages of the movement toward impersonal teaching machines may turn out to lie precisely in this area. By eliminating many activities now done by the human teacher we also eliminate many special and often irrelevant learning problems that the human teacher creates for the student. With the machine almost all the student needs (or is allowed) to learn is the subject matter. In the classroom he needs to learn both subject matter and people in an inextricably interrelated way.

Another complexity stems from people's limited storage capacity. We cannot hold many raw bits of information in our memories unless we classify and categorize them. It is as though we had only a limited number of file folders to work with but could label them any way we chose. If we insist on putting just one piece of information in one folder we soon run out of space. But if we can find useful ways of grouping information, the same set of folders can hold an almost limitless quantity of information. Indeed, "organizing" is one form of categorizing information.

The problem of finding appropriate categories thus becomes a key issue in developing our ability to learn. The manager who insists on separately classifying each bit of information about his operation will soon be overwhelmed by detail, as some managers are. But if he can set up an efficient system of categories, he can handle all he needs to remember.

Unfortunately, categorizing systems, once set up, are difficult to break down. The clerk has difficulty giving up his clerical categories even though he is not in a managerial job. He goes on "thinking like a clerk." As a later chapter on management development will point out, one weakness in up-through-the-ranks and job rotational training is that it demands frequent and difficult recategorization at each step on the ladder. Why, one may ask, teach a person to think like a clerk if we later want him to act like a manager?

A third source of complexity in human learning lies in the fact that mistakes in problem solving are both costly and valuable. We often (being stingy) want to learn only the "right" way of doing things. But learning only what is right means that all the other possibilities are unknown, uncharted, and unstored; and, hence, they cannot be categorized for dealing with similar but not identical problems in the future.

Suppose, for instance, that you are in a hotel in a strange city. You want to drive to plant X. The hotel clerk gives you directions, and you follow and memorize them. What have you learned?

Suppose, instead, that you just got into your car and started out, stopping to ask for help, noticing landmarks, and finally, after many mistakes, getting to X. Then you try again the next day, and the next, until you end up on the same route the clerk would have given you anyhow. Now what have you learned?

By the first method you learned one efficient path through an otherwise unknown jungle. By the second you learned a lot about the jungle and alternative ways of getting through it. You have a list of alternatives against which to apply your decision rules—but at the cost of time and energy.

Now suppose the clerk's route gets dug up for road repairs one day; so you must detour. The advantage of earlier explorations becomes obvious: you have a mental map to work from. You can "feel" your way through the city; the list of mistakes you have stored up will help you solve this new problem.

Insofar, then, as the world of the manager is a world of new problems, one must worry about balancing what the fledgling manager learns by costly experiment and exploration against the high cost of those explorations. If management were a series of repeatable routines, the choice would be easy. But if every problem in management is a new problem, why teach routines?

Problem solving as a multistage process

Learning and problem solving are inseparable processes. When we solve problems we learn about them. But for convenience let's shift our attention now to the problem-solving part of the learning–problem-solving process.

One of the first issues that arises, is this: Just what, after all, constitutes a "solution" to a problem? What is *the* best solution to the problem of college for the children? Or *the* solution to the problem of allocating our capital budget?

We could assume, and often do, that *the* solution exists, and that people should and will look for it; that people will rationally select the very best alternative from an array of all possible alternatives laid out before them.

There are two things wrong with that assumption. The first is that we do not usually have anything like a complete array of alternatives laid out before us. The manager does not know all the machines on the market or all possible marketing strategies, and *it would cost him a great deal to find out*. The second thing wrong is the idea that only the best actually satisfies most people most of the time. In practice,

people often save themselves a great deal of time and effort by searching only until they find something that works well enough to meet their
own private standards of satisfaction. In fact (as the chapter on frustration pointed out), it is precisely when people feel impelled to find the
very best method, when their levels of aspiration are set (usually by
others) far above their abilities, that they are likely to be inefficient
problem solvers, unable to decide and act because every available
decision and action looks less than satisfactory.

Notice that we have been talking about problem solving as a two-
stage process. Usually when we think of solving a problem we are apt
to think only in terms of finding the right answer from among the possibilities. But we have tried to define problem solving here in a little
broader sense, so that it includes not only the selection or decision
process, but also the *search* process that must precede it. For it is very
seldom indeed that the world supplies us with free road maps fully
describing all possible routes, all possible choices. Before we can solve
a problem we must search for paths, routes, ideas, tools. This search
involves the expenditure of time and energy, and often the expenditure
of money or other resources. So part of the problem of deciding which
car to buy is the search problem of deciding which cars to look at and
how much to shop around. In the new car market, at least in big cities,
the search process costs relatively little. Most of the makes are likely to
be lined up in a single street.

But suppose we enter the private used-car market. How many
classified ads shall we respond to? How many newspapers shall we
study? How many individually owned cars do we go out to see before
we decide to buy? How far will we go to see them? Will we ever reach
the point where all the potentially satisfactory used cars are simultaneously known to us, in full detail, so that we can make a choice among
them? This is quite unlikely, because the market is dynamic; while we
are searching for the last car, the first ones have already been sold.
And it is also unlikely because few of us are willing to pay the price
of such a thorough search. Instead we search until we have some idea of
the comparative advantages of different kinds of cars and then on until
we find a satisfactory one. From there on, with any luck at all, our
balancing processes go to work to help us support the decision we have
already made. But we all know perfectly well that there may still have
been a better buy that we never found. So the search process and the
costs associated with it become a large part of the problem-solving
process.

Another large part of the problem-solving process is, of course, the
decision itself. Having gathered as much information as we can afford;
having arrayed as many alternatives as we are willing to, what then?

Then apparently we combine some of our emotional balancing processes with our brains, and either select some standard guaranteed tools for making the choice, or we use heuristics.

Heuristics are rules of thumb, strategies for making complex decisions. Sometimes our heuristics are not very good. Sometimes they aren't bad. We kick the tire on the used car. We start the engine and look at the exhaust to see if it is burning oil. We try to figure out whether or not the car has been repainted. And on the basis of these less than perfect tests (plus our emotional reactions) we make a decision. Some of us have longer check lists than others. Some of us find a mechanic we can trust and bring him along with us to help make the decision.

Man as a "satisficer"

But notice that in most cases, whether selecting a job or a used car, deciding which of several package designs to adopt, or trying to choose among several applicants for a job, we follow what has been called a *satisficing model*. We usually indulge in a limited amount of search, until we reach a *satisfactory* rather than an optimal alternative.

This model of the person as a satisficing problem solver—as an individual using both his head and his guts with a limited degree of rationality and with large elements of strategic guesswork—this is quite a different model from others that have existed in the past. Some earlier conceptions of problem solving laid almost exclusive emphasis on the impulsive and emotional aspects of behavior. That kind of model is still finding lively application in such areas as motivational research in marketing.

But these emotional ideas are not negated by the satisficing model; they are simply placed in a different setting. When one talks about the "cost" of search, one must take into account the *psychological* cost. And the locus of search—the segment of the market in which the buyer searches—may be very much a function of his unconscious (or conscious) need for status and prestige. Some buyers may look only at used Lincolns and Cadillacs; others, only at used sports cars. And their selection of these areas to search is quite likely to be related to their personalities.

The satisficing model is also very different from still a third model that many of us carry around with us. The third is a rational model of problem-solving behavior.

The rational model began as a description of how people *ought* to solve problems rather than how they do solve them. Somewhere along the line this distinction became blurred; researchers and even industrial problem solvers now sometimes treat the rational model as though it were a description of the way people actually behave in problem situations. The rational model, of course, assumes that people will behave rationally—that is, in terms of our two phases of problem solving, that they will first perform a complete and rational search and that they will then select the optimal alternative from among the alternatives evoked by the search.

To borrow an apt analogy, the distinction between the rational and the satisficing models is made clear when one thinks of someone looking for a needle in a haystack. The "rational" person searches all through the haystack collecting all the needles he can find there. He then measures the sharpness of each needle and selects that one needle which is the sharpest. The satisficer searches through the haystack until he finds a needle; then he tries it and if it is sharp enough to sew with he gets on with his sewing; and that's the end of it. If not, he searches some more until he finds one that is satisfactory.

It seems quite clear that most of us do behave more like the second person than the first, whether we ought to or not.

Can some people satisfice better than others?

There is another big issue in the problem-solving process that we have only touched upon, and that is the whole question of the way we *analyze* problems; the way we analyze the search part and the way we analyze alternatives in the decision part. If we are really satisficers, and if we often use heuristic rules for solving problems, then we are rather closely bound by our earlier experiences. Faced with a new problem, we try heuristic rules that we have found to work well on earlier problems that look similar. It is as though most of us carried around a rule saying, "If it worked before, do it again; if it doesn't work, try another." This is a kind of *local* problem-solving process. In the television industry someone tries a program about doctors or cowboys, and if it works, other people pick it up and try it the next year. When the ratings begin to drop off, the producers begin to search for new themes. If we have had pretty good luck using engineering students from a particular college, we are apt to go on recruiting from that school. We keep our ears and eyes open to see whether or not this year's students from that school are doing all right, and only if they aren't do we begin to search in other schools.

But of course it is possible that somewhere in the world there are potential employees who will do this job a good deal better than the ones we are now getting. Or that there are better television themes. But as long as present results are *satisfactory,* our search for new solutions is likely to stay minimal. If there are better solutions, we won't know it until someone else gets them first. Or so it will be *unless we have better analytic tools than the next person*—unless we can use an x-ray on the haystack, or can take finer measurements of sharpness.

Consider this example:

Suppose I have a big box in which I tell you truthfully there are a thousand marbles: 750 black and 250 white ones. I tell you I am going to select 25 marbles, one at a time, and I want you to predict what color the next marble will be.

I am now ready to reach into the box and pull out the first marble. What color do you think it will be? Black or white? Write the answer down before I pull the marble out.

In fact the first marble was *black*.

Now predict the second marble.

In fact the second was *black*.

Now predict the third.

In fact the third was *white*.

Now predict the fourth.

In fact the fourth was *black*.

Now predict the fifth.

In fact the fifth was *black*.

Now predict the sixth.

How did you go about working on this problem?

If you are like most undergraduate students, you begin to develop *local* hypotheses. You notice that there were two blacks followed by a white and then two blacks, so you begin perhaps to generate a hypothesis like this: "There should be more blacks than whites because there are more blacks than whites in the box; and there were two blacks and then a white and then two blacks, so it looks as though there may be a pattern of two blacks and a white. So I will guess that the next one will be white." And you would go on developing new hypotheses as your experience increased. If the next one was in fact white, then you might feel more sure of your theory about two blacks and a white. But if that pattern broke, you would search for a new theory. If five whites came up in a row, you would probably even bet that white was less likely to come up on the sixth, and therefore bet on black.

But a statistician, or someone who had taken a course in these kinds of problems, would not use this approach at all. He would say something like this: Three-quarters of the marbles in the box are black; one-quarter is white. So on any try the probability is 3 out of 4 that a black will come up. I shall, therefore, *always* predict black. And that trained analyst would beat you most of the time, *because he had a better analytic tool than you did.*

The point is that there may be methods in the world for solving problems which are unknown to some of us. And which in fact seem almost contrary to "common sense." Some of us learn some of these tools and apply them quite naturally. Some readers, I am sure, were not for a moment trapped by the marbles problem, because they were armed with a tool that they were not likely to have developed for themselves out of common sense. Someone else developed it, and they were taught it, probably in a classroom in college.

In the history of man, great numbers of tools have been developed and have passed eventually into the realm of common sense. None of us has to figure out any more how to add two and two. Other people have long since worked out rules, and we learned them in the second grade. But in more complex problem areas, where very few tools have existed, new ones are being developed. And especially in management, the competitive advantage may often lie with that manager who is expert with such tools, or who is expert enough to realize that other people are expert with such tools. Managers do not always take easily to the notion that other methods better than their own are being developed. They resist the staff analyst's, or the operations researcher's, complex formulations for solving simple problems. But in many cases (not all cases) their own local methods simply do not work as well.

We shall have much more to say about individual styles of thinking in the next chapter, not only in support of analysts, but in criticism of them as well.

Active and passive learning and problem solving

Learning and problem solving, as we have been looking at them, are *active* rather than *passive* processes. People don't absorb things, they *work* at learning. They search for information, they make decisions, they act upon their decisions, they remember, and they modify their decisions after observing the effects of their actions. People do learn from exposure to experience, but, in this context, experience means doing things to the world as well as letting the world do things to you.

This distinction between active and passive learning is important in management. If we take the passive view, it follows that the trainee should be pumped full of knowledge and experience. So we probably invest heavily in classrooms, lectures, and job-rotation schemes. If we take the active view, we invest in projects, problems, coaching staffs, and the like.

If we take the passive view, we go on to count heavily on the wisdom and experience of superiors—that wisdom and experience to be communicated to the youngsters through advice, written and verbal. We encourage juniors to learn from authoritative seniors. If we take the active view, the wisdom and experience of seniors is relegated to a supportive, behind-the-lines category, available when juniors need it. We encourage juniors to learn first from the problems they are trying to solve, and only secondarily from seniors.

If we take the passive view, we assume that learning should precede action—that we should first learn potentially useful things and *then* try to apply them. If we take the active view, we, in effect, encourage the learner to get himself stymied and then to search for useful ways out.

Moreover, if we generalize a little, the passive view would probably support the sequence of school first and job practice afterward. It would suggest that the business school ought to come before the business job. The active view would support a back-and-forth sequence; one that started with the job, then went *back* to school, and so on—back and forth as, and if, required by the problems encountered on the job.

In defense of schools of business, however, even the most assiduous activist must face up to one dilemma. If we start with active problem solving, how does the problem solver know *where* to search for solutions? How can he know what better tools may be available?

One answer might be that the motivated business problem solver is probably highly accessible to new tools and ideas, because he has competitors and because his level of aspiration doesn't ever quite settle down. But to get to those new tools, he, or their inventors, had better open up channels of communication. This is to say that industry, with its host of opportunities for trying to solve problems, is an ideal active learning ground for management—a better one, in many ways, than any university can hope to be—*if* it can maintain close and solid communication with universities and other tool-developing groups.

Learning and motivation

Active learning occurs, we said earlier, when people are motivated; and people are motivated, we also said earlier, when they are *not* satisfied. So we come up against another curiosity. On the one hand, psychologists, this one included, have been arguing that stability, security, objectivity, and many other fine things emerge when needs are satisfied. But now we discover that effective problem solving, which is what business is all about, emerges when needs are *not* satisfied. What's the escape from that paradox?

One answer is that there need be no escape. If the purpose of business is to get things done at a profit, and if things get done by discontented people, then let's keep people discontented, whether they are stable and secure or not.

But even if we argue that people's stability and security are not the business of the businessman, objectivity is. We would like problems to be solved "reasonably," "rationally," "sensibly," and discontented people may not be objective ones. So we are still in a box.

Another way out can be derived from the distinction made, in the chapter on frustration, between the words "frustration" and "deprivation," or from the earlier idea of growth motivation and the need hierarchy. People can be dissatisfied, it was pointed out, without being frustrated. They can want to solve problems without being in an emotional uproar, if they feel reasonably confident that they can satisfy their lower-level emotional needs. So the trick (if that's a fair word) would be to let people develop their own dissatisfactions about job problems—about making the sale or designing the package—while staying comfortable about more basic needs, about being competent, appreciated salesmen or package designers. Then they can concentrate their energies on the job to be done and do it with some degree of objectivity.

Note that if we learn actively through motivation, experience itself need have little to do with learning. Repeated experience, without appropriate motivation or feedback may teach us almost nothing. Pulling dollar bills out of our pockets for years has not taught most of us much about dollar bills as such. We have learned a good deal about their use, but whose picture is on them? How many signatures? Whose? How many times does the number 1 appear? Where?

Repetition of an act may help people to perform the act more skillfully, not *because* of the repetition but because the repetition gives a chance to try out different methods long enough to find a good one. So let's not assume that frequent exposure to selling situations has *necessarily* taught the veteran to be a better salesperson than the novice. It has only given him the *opportunity* to learn. Whether he took the opportunity, and what he learned—these are quite separate questions.

In summary

People are not perfectly rational, but neither are they incapable of thinking and learning reasonably and consciously. They are endowed with all the equipment they need: input senses, output muscles, memory apparatus, motivation, and a decision or choice mechanism. Only recently have we come even close to equipping machines with like endowments so that they can perform a few intellectual acts as well as competent people can.

On the other hand, people seem to use their endowments with considerable inefficiency. Partly because their equipment is too good, they can and do "learn too much." They learn feelings and attitudes that often interfere with other learning.

People's capacities for learning are in one sense limited; in another, almost unlimited. By devising categories—systems by which they can classify and remember things that are appropriate to the levels of problems they are dealing with—they can store and use huge amounts of information.

If capable people are not lured by the rest of the world into seeking "perfect" solutions for their problems but limit their searches instead to finding satisfactory solutions, they can operate with considerable savings in effort. For to find a *good* product design usually costs far less, in both money and psychic energy, than to find *the best* product design.

But this is not to say that some tools for searching and deciding are not better than others. On the contrary, new analytic tools are being invented every day; and they are likely to be very different from the commonsense methods of today—though our children may use them as we now use addition and subtraction.

It is useful to consider thinking and learning as active processes that begin with motivation. All the activities of searching the world and the memory, of making choices, of trying out new behaviors—all get actively under way when people want something.

7

Thinking and
problem solving II
My style and yours

We said in earlier chapters that people are all alike and yet people are all different. We were referring then to the emotional sides of people—to their needs, their conflicts, their feelings. But people are alike and different in another important dimension, too—in their thinking styles. We all think, but we think differently. Some kids grow up with a "natural" skill at numbers, for instance, but others are "intuitive" or "good with words." Women, some men like to say, tend to think "illogically." Men, some women like to say, are "insensitive." We may say of one person, "He has a logical, orderly mind. He reasons things out"; and of another, "He's tremendously imaginative. He thinks up ideas that would never occur to me."

Such differences in the ways people think and solve problems are both real and important. To some extent these differences may be inborn, and to some extent they are related to general intelligence. But it is also quite clear by now that the whole process of formal and informal education strongly influences the particular "style" of our later thinking, if not its quality. At the extremes, that effect of education isn't hard to see. The engineer's professional education teaches him not only facts but manners of thought, analytic manners of approaching problems. An arts education teaches thinking manners, too, but probably quite different ones; and those manners are likely to carry over into other parts of life. Moreover, such differences in style may lead to interesting and significant organizational problems. For instance, individuals in an organization who think in one "language" may have trouble communicating with individuals who think in other languages. The sales manager complains that he can't understand those whiz kids in systems analysis. The account exec in the advertising agency handles his creative people with kid gloves, because they think in peculiar ways which the rest of us simple folk cannot comprehend.

In this chapter we shall consider some categories of thinking styles, and then talk about the normative question of whether some styles are "better" than others for solving organizational problems. Finally we shall consider some of the implications of these differences for getting coordinated action in big organizations where many people with many different styles have to solve problems together.

Some different kinds of styles

I ask you to throw six dice. They come up like this:

I now tell you that in the set you have just thrown there are three windblown roses and six petals. You ask, "What the hell is a 'windblown rose'?" I reply, "That's the game. Your job is to tell me what a windblown rose is and what petals are. So now throw your dice again and tell me how many roses and how many petals you come up with this time."

So you throw again and this time the dice fall like this:

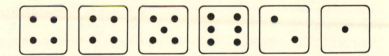

Now how many roses are there? How many petals? The right answer this time is that there are two windblown roses and four petals.

Have you caught on yet? Have you developed a rule? Do you know what a windblown rose and a petal are? If you think you do, or if you think you don't, here are three more samples:

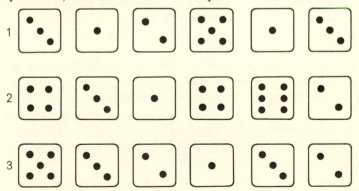

Now have you got it?

Here's the answer, or more properly, here is an answer. The only relevant dice are the odd-numbered ones. Every odd-numbered die has one rose, because the rose is the dot in the middle. The number of petals is the number of dots other than the center one on odd-numbered dice. So the die with the face showing one is a rose with no petals. A three is a rose with two petals; a five is a rose with four petals.

But that's only one way to express the answer or to think about the problem. And indeed it's a very difficult problem to solve if you do think about it that way; that is, if you think about it as a numbers problem. If you don't think of it that way, if you forget about numbers, and if you think about the phrase "windblown rose" and imagine the picture of a rose, the problem is much easier to solve. What does a windblown rose look like? A real windblown rose? It's a rose blown by the wind with just a few petals left on it. Now the face of each die is not a number but a picture, a kind of skeletonized picture. The dot in the center is the center of the rose; the dots around it are petals.

The windblown-roses problem is apt to be solved more quickly by people who think in pictures than by people who think more symbolically. Children do pretty well at it; so do artists; so do women. Accountants and many engineers have a lot of trouble with it.

Let's elaborate on that idea of pictorial (or iconic) thinking versus symbolic thinking.

In recent years developmental psychologists have tried to observe the ways that children go about finding meaning in things. The development of such understanding in children seems to move through three gross stages. Very young children tend to find meaning in things *enactively*. Enactive here means acting upon the thing, touching it, feeling it, handling it. An apple is what it feels like.

Later, around the age of five or so, children begin, by some unclear maturing process, to think in images. They begin to understand things *iconically*. If you ask them now about an apple, they tend to generate an internal mental picture of an apple, an almost one-for-one representation of the real object.

Later still, children go to another stage in their thinking process. Now an apple can be understood *symbolically* by using abstract symbols to think with. It becomes an edible fruit of about such-and-such a size with such-and-such attributes. It is understood with word symbols or perhaps with numbers. Reasonably enough, the rate and extent of symbolic thinking is closely related to education, since most of the symbols we think with are man-made and taught to us by other humans. Thus some children and some societies develop symbolic vocabularies more quickly or over a wider range than others.

This whole developmental idea provides one way of thinking about thinking styles. It may be, for example, that particular kinds of occupations or educations encourage more elaborate and skillful thinking in enactive terms; others in iconic terms; still others in symbolic terms. A mathematician or an accountant couldn't get very far unless he could manipulate abstract symbols pretty darn well. But perhaps a painter or a photographer or (if we allow for sound images) certain musicians might develop high degrees of skill in the iconic realm. And perhaps a ballerina or a good mechanic might develop a large enactive "vocabulary," developing an ability to sense very small differences that the rest of us might miss entirely.

But there seems to be at least one other quite separate dimension to the problem. Not only are some people more skillful than others at manipulating images or tactual sensations or symbols, but some people think much more *analytically* than others, and some think more *imaginatively* than others. The words *analytic* and *imaginative* are rather difficult to pin down in fine detail; but grossly, the reader can quickly sense their flavor. An analytic thinker is one who can take a complex problem apart, break it down into its logically interconnected pieces, and then put it together again. An imaginative thinker is one who might be quick in generating ideas and multiple solutions to problems or who will move through a problem in a "local," trial-and-error way, taking step one and then seeing where he is, and then trying for step two and seeing where he is, and so on. Contrast him with a more analytic type who lays the whole problem-map out in front of him and then finds the best route. Psychologists have tried to measure analytic ability with logic tests and arithmetic reasoning tests. The sloppier concept of imaginativeness has been tested by giving people problems like this: In the next three minutes think up all the uses you can for a brick.

And again, as the reader might guess, certain occupational groups—engineers, technologists, accountants—tend to score higher on analytic than on imaginative tests, while art students and salesmen tend to score higher on imaginative tests. In fact, in one study which compared freshman engineering students with senior engineering students and freshman fine arts students with senior fine arts students, the following results emerged: The senior engineers were much more analytic than their freshman counterparts, but significantly less skillful on imaginative tests. The seniors in fine arts on the other hand, got higher scores on imaginative tests, while they fared worse than their freshman counterparts on analytic tests. The four years of professional education had succeeded, it seemed, in spreading the two groups apart, increasing the engineer's analytic skill, apparently at the expense of his imaginative powers, and increasing the fine arts student's imaginative powers at the expense of his analytic skill.

That finding might be important. If one unexpected outcome of professional education in those two fields is to spread the thinking styles of the two groups apart, another effect may be increased difficulty of communication between the two professions.

This distinction between analytic and imaginative thinking has been noted in different ways for hundreds of years by many observers in many cultures. But in the last decade, some seminal work has been done at the neurophysiological level. We are beginning to find what looks like a parallel separation in the human brain. Experiments with people who have had the two hemispheres of the brain surgically separated are showing similar differences between the capabilities of the left and right hemispheres of the brain. The left hemisphere seems to be verbal, serial, and logical. The right hemisphere (controlling the left half of the body) seems to be the imaginative half. It is "emotional," almost mute verbally, but holistic in that it seems to look at whole things more than at parts.

It is easy to speculate therefore (and speculation is mostly what it is at the moment) that most Western analytic education is left-hemisphere education. We may not yet have exploited the "gutsy," "intuitive," "imaginative" right hemisphere.

Which style is best?

We come now to the normative issue: Is imaginative thinking "better" or "worse" than analytic thinking? Is symbolic thinking "better" or "worse" than iconic or enactive thinking?

Clearly the thrust of most education in the Western world has been toward developing symbolic and analytic skills. We have put much less effort, in our formal educational processes, into developing imaginativeness or iconic skill. What, for example, is your model of a good thinker? Isn't it the technician, skillful with symbolic tools, analytic in process? Or the philosopher? And don't we tend to pooh-pooh those people who are "irrationally" intuitive? Or to believe that it is a little simpleminded and childish for people to think in pictures?

And clearly, too, the progress of man, as we usually define it, has been very heavily dependent on his skillful use of symbolic languages and analytic methods. For it is by those means that knowledge has been passed along and institutionalized, and the complex made simple. If, for example, we said to a senior engineer, "Here's an interesting finding: science and engineering students after four years of education score better on analytic tests than freshmen do," he might well reply that the finding didn't seem interesting at all. For what, after all, was engineering education all about if not to teach analytic methodology? If, on the other hand, we said to him, "But after four years of education, science and engineering students seem to be less capable of solving intuitive-imaginative problems than were freshmen," that might upset him. For most scientists and engineers this author knows are not anti-imagination, they are just pro-analysis. They are pro-analysis for two reasons: first, it has worked; second, the buildup of functional analysis is the foundation from which the next generation of the profession will advance to new knowledge. We need transferable languages and transferable analytic procedures.

If we turn to the artist, on the other hand, we may find that he thinks quite differently about all this. He may be much less interested in transferability or uniformity, and much more interested in uniqueness. The education of the artist reflects that difference. Certainly one key variable in his education is his *individuality,* with the hoped-for consequence that every work he produces will be a unique reflection of himself. Can you imagine an engineer whose training aims for uniqueness, whose professor criticizes the way he has solved a problem because, "That isn't *you*! That isn't unique!"? But such criticism is common for the artist.

Another aspect of the normative problem: The analytic-symbolic approach to the world not only places a positive value on "objective" thinking, but in some ways it places a negative value on "emotional" thinking. Some observers have argued that an important effect of this imbalance in favor of symbolic-analytic thinking is an impoverished emotional development in our society. We have not educated our people to attend to, to understand, and to express feelings and other perceptions which are not easily symbolized or analyzed. By this argument educational emphasis on the symbolic-analytic has yielded a significant unforeseen cost to the humanness of human beings, although some of the deficit is being made up by the recent wave of interest in sensitivity training and encounter groups.

One more normative issue: Just from the point of view of the quality of problem solving itself, is it true that the symbolic-analytic kind of approach is better? In many realms it clearly is. The application of symbolic-analytic style has led to the solution of many complex problems that people unequipped with those tools have simply been unable either to discover or to solve.

But curiously enough, people less competent in analytic-symbolic realms, but more competent in imaginative-iconic styles, sometimes discover solutions which the analysts miss, because the analysts may limit their search to those segments of the world predefined by their languages. We refer our reader back to the windblown roses game, but we can find many other examples of "better" solutions by nonanalysts, even when "better" is defined by analytic criteria. One can legitimately ask whether a world of highly analytic but not very imaginative thinkers will necessarily turn out better, by any standards, than one peopled by more imaginative but less analytic types.

How can people talk to one another
if they think differently?

We need, don't we, both analysis and imagination. We need symbols; we need pictures; and we need to feel. We need many kinds of people with many kinds of education and training and many kinds of thinking propensities. But beyond that, we need some way to bring them together into that beautiful blend that will yield the best of all possible worlds.

But that bringing together is rather difficult. As the languages and thought-modes of specialists move further and further apart, the problem of reuniting the specialists becomes harder. Thus the arts and engineering students we talked about earlier move away from, rather than toward, one another over the four years of college. Male freshman engineers might date fine arts freshman women, but by their senior years the engineers are living in one world and the art students in another. Their differences show in their dress, in where they choose to live, in their haircuts.

One British author has pointed to a variant on this problem on a much larger scale. He has argued that the entire cultures of science and the humanities have grown quite apart in Western societies. Scientists deal with critical problems in ways that are simply not comprehended by less scientific types, and yet it is the less scientific politicians who govern the world that scientists are so rapidly and independently changing.

Certainly within the organization the dangers are real, though on a smaller scale. The notoriously frequent failures of technical people to implement their analytic solutions are a case in point. So too is all the laughing talk by general managers about "long-haired" computer nuts and "weird" operations researchers and "unrealistic" systems analysts. In our view, integrating the many thought-styles of many occupational specialties into some kind of organizational whole is becoming a major problem in modern, differentiated organizations.

Although we can offer no easy solutions, we do know some things that *don't* work. It is not enough, for instance, to "bring people together." The engineers and art students we talked about earlier occupy buildings that are within fifty yards of one another, but the two groups have nevertheless moved apart. A better solution may be to develop a new breed of interpreters, generalists with feet in all camps, who can translate one thought-language into another. In some ways the modern MBA has tended to perform that function. Another suggestion (offered, of course, by an analytic type) is to devise computer programs which will serve as interpreters, converting symbolic data into iconic form or vice versa.

The present fact of the matter, however, is that we don't know very much about how to *un*educate people who have been so educated into one style that they cannot think in others. Perhaps we shall have to learn a good deal more about uneducation in the next decade or two. Meanwhile, encouraging people to speak to one another in mutually foreign languages will not in itself breed understanding.

Thinking styles and the process of working problems through

Later in this book we shall emphasize a tripartite model of problem working. We shall be talking about (1) *problem finding,* (2) *problem solving,* and (3) *solution implementing.* The discussions of human motivation and perception in the earlier chapters were mostly concerned with part 3 of that process, the implementation part, the part that aims at influencing and persuading people to do things. It is in part 2, the problem-solving part of the process, that analytic skills become particularly valuable.

But the third element, problem finding, is not primarily concerned with either influence or analysis. Problem finding occurs at the front end of the whole process. It is about finding the right problems to solve and implement. It is, therefore, about issues of creativity and purpose. The imaginative and iconic components of thinking become important for the manager because they affect this problem-finding question. Questions like: What are the interesting and important problems? How do I look for them? What problems do I really want to work on?

The difference between problem finding and problem solving is something like the difference between the architect and the engineer. The construction engineer tries to figure out how to build a building, given the blueprint, the budget, and some other constraints. What the architect adds is the element of design. Design is imagination. Design is problem finding. For even given a fixed budget, a site, and a function for a new building, an infinite number of different designs can still be created. The "right" design, in this sense, is the product of imagination, of love, of personal standards of beauty, and of a collection of other soft, nonanalytic concepts. These problem-finding skills are probably more related to our imaginative than analytic styles of human thinking.

But more about problem finding in later chapters.

In summary

People differ in their languages and processes of thought just as they differ in other aspects of personalities. Education, particularly professional and vocational education, tends to emphasize particular thought-languages, symbolic languages, iconic (pictorial) languages, and en-active (touch and feel) languages. One can conceive of processes differing, too, along a scale from analytic to imaginative.

It is not perfectly obvious that any particular combination of these languages or processes is "better" than another. But it is obvious that people trained in and connected to one style may find it difficult to communicate with those committed to another. Hence we might expect greater emphasis within organizations, as they build in more and more specialists, on bridging this communication gap by introducing "thought interpreters" or other means of increasing understanding. The issue is not only one of communication, but of the importance of imaginative as well as analytic thinking in organizations. Analysis provides a base for high-quality problem solving. Imaginative thinking may provide a base for high-quality problem finding: helping the person or the organization to identify the new, the beautiful, and the exciting problems.

8

Attitudes, beliefs, and values
Motherhood, Old Glory, and civil rights

1/4/82

People not only develop needs and styles of problem solving, they also develop beliefs and opinions and attitudes and values. Those people believe in God; and these are atheists. Those over there think women's place is in the kitchen, and these are parading for women's rights. Those others believe that if you work hard, you'll get ahead; but these think work is a form of slavery set up by the establishment, and who wants to get ahead in a materialistic society anyway?

This collection of very important "stuff" in people properly belongs neither in the realm of emotionality nor in the realm of cognitive problem solving. This realm of beliefs and values seems rather to constitute some mixture of the reasoning and the nonreasoning parts of people.

Moreover, the mixture appears to be changing in some very important ways. People don't seem to believe what they used to believe. Their thinking processes haven't changed much, nor have their emotional processes; but surely values, beliefs, and opinions are changing fast. Viewing from one side, one can argue that Americans seem to be losing their pride and interest in their work, and that they seem to be changing their traditional standards about sex and morality. Viewing from another side, one might say that people are becoming freer and less hypocritical, and that they are fulfilling themselves!

The purpose of this chapter is to consider attitudes and values from a psychological perspective. We shall put forward several questions: Conceptually, what are attitudes and values? Where do they come from? How do they change? What do changing attitudes and values mean for the managing process?

What are attitudes and values?

Junior has just come home from college on his Christmas vacation. He and Papa are chatting after dinner.

> "What did you take this quarter, son?"
> "Well, let's see. I took a course in Chinese art and a seminar on

81

religions of the East. Then I had a course on the history of revolutions. Oh, and then I had a great course in Welsh mythology."

Pause.

Papa says, "Well, that's nice, son. Did you take any math?"

"Oh, Dad, you know I'm not interested in math."

"Did you take any science?"

"No, Dad, science is for the birds. I'll have to take one science course to graduate, but I think I can get credit for that astrology course I took last year."

Pause.

"Tell me, son, what do you plan to do when you graduate?"

"Well, Dad, I thought the first year after I'm out I might kick around Europe. There's this girl I've gotten friendly with. And she and I decided that we might bum around together for a year or so."

Longer pause.

"And what will you do after that?"

"Well, I'm not sure, Dad, but I've always been interested in leatherworking. I think I might make belts. Or sandals."

Another long pause, then Papa says, "I think you ought to get more math and science and things like that into your program."

"Why?"

"Because those are the things that will be useful to you, that will help you get ahead in the long run."

"But I don't want to get ahead in the long run."

"You'll change your mind about that, son. Wait 'til you have a wife and kids to feed."

"I'm not sure I ever want a wife, and as for kids, there are too many of them in the world already. Why, Dad, do you know how many people there will be in the world by 2000?"

With some emotion: "Oh, you can spout crap like that now, son, but you'll change your mind. You know, I'm not always going to support you."

"So if you don't support me. I'll support myself, Dad. That's not a problem; it's trivial. You have this funny, old-fashioned idea that somehow I'm supposed to go to college and then go to work and get married and live in the suburbs and retire at age sixty-five, and go and live in Florida until I die. That's not my picture of life at all."

And so on.

Papa is trying hard to keep his blood pressure down, to understand, to maintain communication. This kid doesn't seem to want to go to work the way Papa did. He doesn't see college as vocational preparation. He doesn't value math and science as instrumentalities to success; indeed, he doesn't seem to value success itself. He doesn't seem to worry about traveling around Europe with a girl to whom he isn't married. And he doesn't seem to be very much concerned with planning ahead. His attitudes and Papa's are different. His values and Papa's are different. If Junior ever does take a "normal" job (which, incidentally, he probably will), he will probably take it not as an instrumentality to Papa's kind of success, but as a means of getting enough bread so that he can go skin diving. Or so that he can take another trip to Europe.

Attitudes and values, viewed this way, are orientations toward things in the world. Generally, values are considered to be more basic, more fundamental. Attitudes are a little more direct: propensities to look at more or less specific things in particular ways. What's your attitude toward the Catholic church? Toward big business? An attitude is a readiness to respond, an overall framework within which to cast particular beliefs or opinions. Attitudes are usually pretty conscious. People can express them, although in many cases they may choose not to. We tend to call the same kind of things values when they are a little broader, a little more deep-seated, and include more unconscious elements. We usually treat as values people's deeper orientations toward issues like getting ahead, or justice, or virginity, or family.

Two quite contradictory points about people's attitudes and values are particularly worth noting.

On the one hand, there is a kind of patterning that goes on; so that if we know some of a person's attitudes or values, we can make better than chance guesses about many others. If we know an American attitude toward communication, we might make some pretty good guesses about his attitudes toward religion, free enterprise, and so on. There is a certain amount of consistency in people's patterns of attitudes and values.

On the other hand, and contrariwise, patterns of beliefs and attitudes often seem highly illogical. Junior tries to pin Dad by saying, "If you say you're against war, how come you were for winning a victory in Vietnam?" Papa retorts, "If you're a conscientious objector, how can you justify violence on the campus?" Junior adds, "You're against pot, but you smoke and drink." Papa retorts, "You're all for punishing the car manufacturers for ecological problems, but you want a fast sports car!" So we need to worry about a paradox: "consistent" patterns of attitudes and values that are also inconsistent.

Changing attitudes
Again the great cognitive balancing act

Back in the chapter on conflict, we talked about cognitive balance. Much of this paradox can be dealt with by calling once more upon this concept.

The balance idea is simply that human beings try to maintain *internal* emotional consistency and balance among their attitudes, values, and decisions. Hence, any of us is apt to stay stubbornly with a position long after it is seen by others as either rationally wrong or inconsistent with other positions we have held. Our attitudes can be emotionally consistent even while they are rationally inconsistent.

If we return to Papa and Junior, perhaps we can account for their inconsistencies in attitudes and values in the same way. Junior, for example, thinking of himself as a pacifist, refuses to go hunting. Some of his other attitudes and values certainly appear rationally consistent with pacifism. He doesn't believe in capital punishment; he begins to think football is too violent. But then he gets picked up one night for helping to smash windows in the applied physics lab. If we now confront him with the inconsistency between his violent acts and his non-violent ideology, will he acknowledge the conflict? Not likely. The window smashing is a road toward peace, he may argue, because by stopping war research he is stopping violence, and so on. Emotionally, though, his behavior is consistent.

Maybe it is because we often sense just this propensity in ourselves and our organizations that we seek help from uncommitted outsiders. Because they are uncommitted, they can examine some areas about which our involvement has created psychological blind spots. On the other hand, though outsiders may be more objective in their judgments, they may have a tough time communicating these judgments to us. For if the effect of truth, as outside judges report it, is to aggravate the emotional imbalance, we will have a strong inclination to reject it. The consultant who tells us that our decision was wrong is just another dissonant force with which we need to cope. And one easy way to cope is to find reasons for believing that we hired the wrong consultant, unless, of course, this is a very expensive consultant—in which case firing him may create more dissonance than sticking with him.

This balancing mechanism thus provides the individual with a way, sometimes tortuous and unsuccessful, of trying to pull things together psychologically so that he can feel emotionally comfortable; in effect, he tries to do it by modifying the psycho-logic of his position, and then bending the logic to it. It is, after all, the whole person who makes choices, not just the reasoning part of him. So if we want to predict or to change patterns of attitudes and beliefs, we must use our knowledge of the whole person. If we try to predict only by considering logical, rational connections among attitudes, our predictions may be rather poor.

My father, for example, was both an active atheist and an active Republican—and a right-wing Republican, at that. I, and others, used to chide him about the logical inconsistency of being both. Good Republicans, we argued, were God-fearing men. It was the left-wingers who were atheists. But the discrepancy didn't bother him at all. He could argue for hours about how the two positions were perfectly consistent with one another. No one, I am convinced, could have argued him out of his position on *logical* grounds.

The psychological consistency of his pattern emerged because he was an immigrant to the United States. He wanted very much to make it on the American scene—to be a real American. This meant giving up the traditional, old-country ways and really joining up with America. So he went into business and became, naturally enough a Republican businessman. But if he had also remained an orthodox, old-country Jew, how could he have become a real American? Hence, atheism. I don't think the same problem would have arisen if he had been a Scottish Presbyterian. That could have been consistent with business and Republicanism. But traditional European Judaism seemed to him old-fashioned, unprogressive, and irrelevant to this new world of his. For the whole man, his pattern made sense. Viewed by external logic, it was an inconsistent set of positions. But he had no trouble walking the tightrope.

Values

We've used the word *values* as well as the word *attitudes*. Values are the more primitive, basic, all-encompassing of these two concepts. A useful way to think about values is to consider them as a pervasive, underlying set of attitudes, not always conscious. A pervasive belief in individual initiative is a value. So is a belief in the inviolacy of the family. So is a deep faith in science.

Such values may remain only quasi-conscious until something comes along to spotlight them. Since, in a given community, many values are widely shared, we may not even realize we hold them until we enter another community. While I was working with a group in France several years ago, one of my unconscious values was made obvious and apparent. The group had been arguing for a long time, and I had been taking an increasingly strong position in favor of getting everybody together into a cooperative team to solve some problems. One of the Frenchmen turned on me at this point. "Ever since you've been here," he said, "you've been making a pitch about all of us cooperating to solve problems. What makes you so sure that cooperation is such a wonderful thing?" I was stunned by this reaction, because the questioner had pointed out something I hadn't consciously realized: my strong, underlying value about cooperation as a basic way of approaching social problems. I had never questioned, indeed never even thought about it. How many Americans have?

Not only are values apt to be semiconscious, they tend also to take shape early in life and to last long. Not that they can't be changed, but the process is slow. Peer groups, for example, can be extremely influential in modifying one's values. Thus one study shows that, as undergraduates, college women tend gradually to take on the values of the college group. But that part is no surprise. Most of us know that we can take on much of the coloration of our local peer-group culture, especially if we are exposed to it intensively in a cultural island like a women's college. But the values thus picked up by women tend still to be there fifteen or twenty years later when most of them have become suburban, executives' wives. If they had become political liberals during those college years, they were still showing strong liberal leanings twenty years out. Which means, of course, that if we expect those radical college kids to "come to their senses" as soon as they have to earn a living in the real, harsh world, we're probably wrong. There may be modifications, but turnabout is unlikely. Besides, don't we also try to match our jobs and careers to our values? So won't emancipated kids look for career patterns that will support their emancipated life-style?

More on changing attitudes and values

Most of what we shall have to say about changing attitudes and values will be said in the next section of this book, when we discuss influence and persuasion. But one or two ideas are more appropriate here.

Consider the relationships between people's attitudes and their behavior. Note that changed attitudes are not always reflected in changed behavior. We may change (or have changed for us) our attitude toward cigarettes, but we may also go on smoking. However, there is a gross connection, isn't there? We tend to bring our behavior into line with our attitudes over the long pull. That's what advertising is for. To a considerable extent, that's what education is for.

So one way to change behavior is to change attitudes. And the ways we try to change attitudes are legion: peer-group pressures, propaganda, simple reward for expressing the attitudes we want—and introducing dissonance may help, forcing the person to reassess his existing attitudes. If a person who is strongly anti-Semitic falls in love, for example, and then discovers his lover is Jewish, he may begin to reassess his attitudes—or his lover.

But it is also true that one can change the attitude by changing behavior *first*. Not only does behavior gradually line up with attitudes, attitudes line up with behavior!

For example, if I can get you to debate in favor of X, even though you don't like X, you will probably hold a more positive attitude toward X after the debate than before. If I can get you to sing my commercials, you will probably feel more favorable toward the product. If I can get you to throw a rock at the policeman, your attitudes toward the police will become more negative. If I can get you, the union steward, to argue the company's behalf, you will feel more positive toward the company.

Values develop or change more slowly than attitudes, but the principle holds for them, too.

But the most important thing to keep in mind when you are thinking about changing attitudes or values is that change in these dimensions is largely an *emotional* process. Perhaps our biggest mistake in our efforts to change others is implicitly to treat the human being as though he were only a rational, reasoning critter. Indeed, it may be because those of us in the West value rationality and analytic thinking styles so highly, that those values in us influence our approach to trying to change the values of others. We tend to think that we can argue people out of things, that logic will prevail. And we tend to ignore the huge emotional component in the change process. Even as we debate with others, and even as we line up our reasoned arguments, we can usually feel our own emotions building up. I want to convince you that the apartheid policies in South Africa are both morally wrong and will never work. But even as I give you my logical reasons, I can feel my heart beginning to pound, my voice beginning to rise—and you are experiencing the same thing. It soon becomes obvious to both of us that we are getting caught in a hopeless trap; that the spiral of argument will proceed downward, with each of us becoming more emotionally resistant, even while we couch that emotion in phony logic. And yet we seldom are willing to accept the notion that it is precisely at the emotional level that the heart of the issue of attitude change lies. I will not get you to think differently until I get you to feel differently. And notice, too, that we often denigrate those people who try to change attitudes by using emotional means. Because we value reason, we tend to deride salesmen, advertisers, evangelists and other persuaders who make emotional appeals.

Perhaps the central message of this chapter is that though we may wish for a rational world, we are not likely to achieve it by exclusively rational means.

Managing and attitudes

Here are two attitude questions for the manager:

1. Do you want all the people in your organization to share roughly

the same attitudes and values? What are the costs and benefits of having them do so?

2. How are the changing attitudes of the outside world relevant to your organization? How do you find out just what those changing attitudes are?

So far in this chapter we have emphasized how attitudes grow and change in individuals. But their importance to the managing process goes well beyond the individual. Almost all organizations have "cultures." Their members share certain values and attitudes. And most organizations work hard (although not always consciously) to mold a set of common attitudes. Organizations write creeds to be hung on office walls. They tell the world in television ads that "our people" are always kind, loyal, and honest. In one way or another, they also punish people who violate those creeds. They set up expectations about loyalty to the company and its products. They establish dress codes and standards of ethical behavior and proper respect for authority. No organization can avoid some degree of "brainwashing" of its people toward some common set of attitudes. Every organization needs some set of shared attitudes just to hold the organization together. But if our organization tries to impose a set of attitudes that becomes too tight, too different from what's outside of it, then some people will choose to leave the organization, or avoid entering it in the first place. A technical organization, for instance, may gain a reputation for treating nontechnical people as second-class citizens. So young MBAs don't swarm to its recruiters.

But much more important is whether or not we encourage like-mindedness or diversity in our company. In our present, highly volatile environment, the advantage seems clearly on the side of diversity over uniformity—up to a point. Diversity drives toward adaptiveness, but uniformity provides the internal glue of stability. Diversity also drives toward innovativeness. But how individually innovative do we want all those bank tellers to be?

These days, the wise manager must think very carefully about the sort of "culture" he wants to establish in his organization. What kinds of beliefs, values, attitudes, does he want almost all members of the organization to share? And where should he encourage individual variation?

Let's turn for a moment to question 2, the match between the organization's attitudes and those of the world outside. We are back immediately to the notion of *organizational legitimacy*. If our company's values and attitudes appear to deviate a great deal from the standards of the society, we become "illegitimate" and subject to severe punishment—like saloons after prohibition or, perhaps, the FBI after Watergate. Such disparities between an organization's values and those of its environment may be highlighted because the organization overtly acts in disapproved ways; but in recent years they also show up when the organization does *not* act in approved ways.

Sometimes things happen the other way around. I once spent a day with a man whose family had manufactured condoms for three generations. As he spoke, it became increasingly clear that his whole life had been shaped by the fact that his family was in the "rubber" business. His childhood and adolescence were probably peppered with sarcasm and ridicule. It must have been a constant source of embarrassment to him. But I met him at a prestigious conference on population control, a topic which had recently been legitimated by government agencies and large foundations. Perhaps for the first time in his life, his company and its products were now publicly welcomed. He was, in effect, pulled out of the closet and onto center stage as a hero. But it still took him more than two years after that episode to exploit what the new legitimacy of his products meant for the market behavior of his organization.

Those attitudes out there seem to change fast and in unforeseeable ways. It behooves the manager to tune up his external sensors, to make sure he has an effective early warning system. One way to do that is to include diverse people in the organization, people representative of the diverse groups in society. Another way is to develop attitudes and values among employees that encourage them to scan a wide segment of the world, not a narrow segment. Perhaps senior members of any large, modern organization should be reading underground newspapers along with the *Wall Street Journal,* and going to rock concerts as well as the symphony. But more about the organization-environment relationship will come up in the last chapter.

In summary

People not only develop thinking styles and patterns of needs, they also develop patterns of attitudes and values. Attitudes and values have strong components and are usually publicly supported by elaborate rationales. But there are strong emotional factors supporting them, too, so it is not easy to change them by argument or debate.

To change attitudes or values, it is often useful to think of the human being as a "cognitive balancer," who tries to keep his attitudes and values grossly consistent with one another. Hence, we find more or less clear attitude and value patterns in most people. If we know some attitudes, we can usually guess others. If we can change some small attitudes, other changes often follow. But that isn't a perfectly safe bet, because most of us also can do balancing tricks that allow us to feel comfortable with patterns that look inconsistent to outsiders.

The important thing is that people try to reduce internal dissonance, to get things into internal balance. If we look at the internal behavior process, rather than the rational facts, we can often better understand and predict attitudes and also change them more effectively than by logical argument.

While we can often change behavior by first changing attitudes, the reverse is also true: to change a person's attitudes, change his relevant behavior.

Organizations, to some extent, "brainwash" their people, trying to develop common attitudes that simplify managing. But while uniform attitudes provide stability, they tend to make organizations less adaptive and perhaps less innovative. The organization needs some shared culture, but it also needs diversity.

9

The assessment and evaluation of people
One application of personality theory

One famous scholar used to define management as "the process of getting things done through people." Whether or not that's a sufficient
definition, every manager knows that success in managing hangs on
two issues: First, on the manager's own human skills, and second, on
the "quality" of the people in his shop. Finding "good" people is a
critical and continuing problem in any organization.

An associated problem that keeps most managers hopping is the
evaluation problem. How shall we evaluate people's performance after
we get them? Is Mary Smith performing better than Joe Blow? Which
one is the "better" person for the promotion that's coming up? And
both Mary and Joe want feedback; they want to be told how well or
badly the company thinks they are doing. They want to know specifically what they need to do to improve their evaluations next time.

And still another related problem: You've just spent half an hour
talking to Henry Brown (he may be a new customer or a job applicant
or a consultant the company is thinking about using). Your boss then
drops by to ask, "What do you think of Brown?" How do you *say* what
you think of him? How do you say it accurately and succinctly?

That's what this chapter is about: "Assessing," "selecting," "evaluating" human beings. It's about the formal tools, like selection tests,
that have been invented to help out on those problems; and also about
the informal tools, like talking with people to find out what they're
like. It's about judging people, getting a fix on people in a limited
time, in the ongoing real world, without the help of professionals or
elaborate measurement devices.

I've intentionally emphasized a lot of evaluative words in the last
couple of paragraphs to highlight a fundamental moral problem in all
this. For this chapter is about human beings making judgments about
the worth of other human beings, deciding whether one is "better" than
another. That whole process stirs up issues of democracy, Christian
ethics, man's basic acceptance of other human beings, regardless of

what they are. Those are real problems, not yet resolved in modern organizations. We shall talk about them more as they arise in the pages that follow. For the most part, however, we shall have to ask the reader to keep his own attitudes and values at the ready as he goes through this chapter.

The scope of the assessment problem

Both professionals and laymen have frequently failed miserably in forecasting how people will behave in specific jobs. It's a very tough task. If our earlier chapters were right, forecasting the behavior of one individual is much like trying to predict exactly what pattern of cracks will result when a particular thrower throws a particular ball against a particular pane of glass. We can be fairly certain that the glass will crack. But we seldom know enough about the ball, the air currents, the thrower, and the particular pane to be sure about the directions and lengths of the cracks that will result.

Nevertheless, we cannot escape in organizations from the problem of having to assess people for tasks. Every contact with a customer, with a new member of his own organization, with each individual who is relevant to the manager's work, includes some need for assessment—some evaluation of how this person will behave when faced with this kind of suggestion or that kind of job or this other kind of person.

So assessment is not limited to "formal" problems like selecting new employees or rating the performance of old ones, nor is it limited to the assessment of personality. It must necessarily involve assessment of knowledge, experience, education, and many other aspects of the person.

For the formal phases, like personnel selection and performance evaluation, a good deal of research and experience is available. Every executive in industry these days is aware of personality tests, patterned interviews, personnel-rating forms, and the like. Underlying each of these is a large (but not large enough) body of theory and empirical research. Unfortunately no comparable amount of work has been done on the day-to-day problems of assessment to help the executive make increasingly accurate spot judgments about other people. Even so, some useful things are coming to be known. So, when the boss asks, "Well, what did you think of him?" the executive can honestly say something more than, "He's a nice guy" or " I don't like him."

Formal methods of selection and evaluation

One can single out at least three more or less separate formal approaches to the selection and evaluation of personnel for industry.

Looked at right now, the separations among the three are indistinct, for they have been growing together. But historically, each has made its way over a different route.

Pencil-and-paper tests and the empirical method. The first approach, one largely American in origin, can be roughly labeled the "pencil-and-paper-test approach." The great bulk of short intelligence tests, aptitude tests, etc., belong under this heading. So, too, for the most part, do standard interview forms, most merit-rating scales, fitness reports, and the like. Until recently, they were mostly tests of specific skill or abilities, like numerical ability, finger dexterity, and so on.

These are typically American products in the sense that they derive from American behaviorism, with its emphasis on quantification and measurement and on empirical data gathering and with its corresponding de-emphasis on unquantified, introspective, judgmental data. As a consequence, the pencil-and-paper approach has been characterized by efforts to improve the empirical reliability and validity of the procedures more than by efforts to improve the rationale or depth of the material being sought. It is considerably harder to apply to overall personality than to specific aptitudes or abilities.

The pencil-and-paper position is this: The task of selecting people for jobs is a task of predicting in advance how people will behave. Clearly, then, what is required are some measurable advance predictions and some corresponding measurements, taken at some later time, of how people actually performed. If the task is to select a store manager, these are the appropriate procedural steps:

1. We gather—in a standard way—information about people who are possibilities for jobs as store managers. We can do this by setting up standard questions about, for example, education, asking them of job applicants, and coding the answers into several categories. We can do the same with questions about home ownership and applicants' preferences for one kind of occupation or another, and we can measure the time required by applicants to solve certain arithmetic problems, and so on.

2. Ideally, we next lock up the test answers in the nearest safe and allow *all* the applicants to go to work managing stores.

3. Now we wait a predetermined time, perhaps a year.

4. During that year, or before it, we set up some standards about what constitutes success in managing our stores. What is needed is an unequivocal, quantifiable criterion of success. In store management, a theoretically ideal approach would be to permit all test subjects to manage stores in exactly comparable locations, with precisely the same amount of training and precisely the same budgets. One might then use

dollar sales at the end of the year, or number of sales, or percentage increases, or some combination of them all as the criterion of successful behavior.

5. The tester now has available (*a*) the scores of test-subject Jones on the tests he took a year ago, showing his rank on the test in relation to the other applicants, and (*b*) a measurement of his subsequent actual job performance in relation to the other applicants. The next move is statistical: to measure the relationship between predictions and performance, to estimate the reliability of this relationship (i.e., to guess how frequently we could expect the relationship to be about like this in the future), and then to decide if any of the tests are worth keeping.

We may discover that a test of intelligence actually predicted performance somewhat better than chance. The tester would then consider his intelligence test useful for selection. And, logically, it would not matter what direction the test-performance relationship might take. That is, it would not matter if more successful managers were significantly more intelligent, or significantly less intelligent, than the less successful ones. For the method is rigorous here. The problem is not whether the predictions make sense, but whether they predict. If they predict, they are useful; if they do not predict, they are not useful.

The only connection between this kind of rigorous pencil-and-paper approach and any theory of personality lies in the manner in which particular tests are selected and constructed. For the pencil-and-paper approach is itself a method of measurement rather than a theory of human behavior. Any theorist of any persuasion may use it. Some test items may be based on a theory of physiognomy, some on Freudian psychodynamics, some on the color of one's shoes. In actual practice, the current pencil-and-paper personality tests used in business derive largely from a semibehavioristic theory of personality. In the last few years, some tests aimed at more basic "personality styles," especially those that have been around long enough to build up a large data base, have come into wider use.

This pencil-and-paper method has a great many advantages and some practical disadvantages. It has the huge advantage of quantification and empiricism. It also has dollar advantages. Pencil-and-paper tests, once standardized, are easy to manufacture, administer, and score. Professional testers are often needed only in the developmental stages because administration can usually be turned over to trained, but not professional, technicians. Such devices are not very time consuming, so that large numbers of people can be tested, frequently in groups of indefinite size, at reasonable costs.

Perhaps the greatest disadvantage of such procedures is that they are designed for statistical, rather than individual, prediction. That is, they are most useful in making predictions about the behavior of large numbers of people rather than about particular individuals. Thus, a pencil-and-paper tester may be able truthfully to tell management that, if his tests are adopted, "Of every fifty applicants whom my tests pass, you can expect an adequate job performance from forty. Under your present selection methods, you can expect adequate job performance from only twenty-five." The tester could not go on, however, to say whether or not Joe Doaks, subject number 23, who received adequate test scores, would be among the successful forty or the unsuccessful ten. Further, the tester would also have to admit that some rejected applicants would be "false positives"—people who would have been successful but whom the tests nevertheless rejected. He could not predict who those individuals would be.

To put it bluntly, most pencil-and-paper tests can help very little in predicting how a particular person will behave. Too many other things affect those predictions. But if you're running an army, pencil-and-paper tests can often help you get the overall quality up enough to be worth the cost of administering the tests.

This tendency of pencil-and-paper methods to predict en masse rather than individually raises three broad questions. The first is ethical. It is "right" to turn any job applicant away, even if he is only one in a hundred, who would have been perfectly competent if he had been hired? Is it "fair" to the applicant to so depersonalize him that he becomes simply a score among hundreds of scores, his fate inexorably tied to a numerical system? Perhaps this is a valid question, and perhaps it is somehow more fair to tie an applicant's fate to the rose-colored perceptions of a nonquantitative interviewer. It would seem, however, that this ethical issue properly attaches to the whole selection problem itself, not to the issue of selection by tests.

Secondly, most pencil-and-paper tests are, it has been argued, "culture bound." They are tests built by and for WASP males. The deficiency, to the extent that it was real, is being corrected in many cases, though the debate about "standards" vs. racial or sex bias is by no means over. And the future of testing programs hangs on its outcome.

The question that can be asked is about the utility of pencil-and-paper devices at higher organizational levels, where the number of applicants for particular positions may be small. The usual statistical indexes of validity do not apply to very small samples. So if the task is to select VPs rather than typists, the utility of the method is sharply reduced. It is even more sharply reduced when the task is to decide which of two applicants ought to be selected for a particular key post in, let us say, the research and development division of an electronics corporation. At this level so much depends on the correctness of a specific prediction, that the pencil-and-paper method becomes inapplicable.

Projective tests and the clinical method. A second approach to formal selection lays much more emphasis on the dynamics of personality, much less on empirical validity. The approach may be labeled, somewhat unfairly, the projective approach. Projectives are much more "head doctor" techniques than pencil-and-paper tests. They are European in origin, springing theoretically from Freud and technically from the Swiss psychiatrist Rorschach. They build on the internal, perceptual frame of reference talked about in chapter 3, assuming that one can get a valid picture of a person quickly by assessing the way he projects his personality onto some standard, ambiguous parts of the world. All projectives contain these elements of standardization and ambiguity. The "questions" on the Rorschach test are some standardized inkblots that the subject is asked to describe. The tester then interprets the number, quality, and variety of the subject's responses against the tester's theory of personality and against his and others' experience with the responses of other people to the same blots.

Similarly, in the Thematic Apperception Test, the subject is asked to tell stories about a standard series of pictures. The tester records the stories and the subject's behavior. He then interprets the subject's personality in the light of the themes used in his stories.

The end result of a battery of projective tests, then, is not a numerical score comparing subject X with other subjects. It is a verbal report assessing the subject's dominant needs and ambitions, his tolerance of frustrations, his attitudes toward authority, the major conflicts that seem to be operating in his personality, and so on. Given such a report, a manager clearly must decide for himself whether the tester's judgment deserves heavy weighting in the final decision.

One important industrial advantage of projectives is also their scientific weakness. They are essentially individualistic, and they cannot be easily "proved" right or wrong, even by their proponents. Projectives, therefore, push decision making back to where it belongs anyway, into the hands of management. The projective tester says to the manager, in effect, "Here is my expert judgment of John Jones. You have your judgment of him to which you can now add mine. I have tried to add information to your fund of relevant information, but I cannot guarantee that my judgment will be right. You make the decision."

When one considers the history of projective tests, it is reasonable that they should be used in this way. Projectives have their origin in clinical psychology, in the atmosphere of psychiatry and pathology, rather than in education or industry. In the clinic and the hospital, their primary function has been to help the physician seeking to diagnose the meaning of the psychological pains of a new patient. Perhaps, if the physician had known his new patient intimately for five or ten years, he would have no need for the projective tester. But the patient is an individual, and it is his individuality that accounts for his illness; so the physician needs a highly individualized, relatively detailed, and speedy picture of this personality. This is what the projective tester tries to give him.

Unlike the pencil-and-paper tests, personality projectives seldom get to the stage at which they can be scored by anyone, because the interpretation always remains individual. The judgment of the tester is a large factor. When management buys pencil-and-paper tests, it buys a quantitative tool from which most subjective elements of interpretation have been eliminated. Any honest technician counting up the yeses and noes on an interest inventory will come up with the same score as any other honest technician. Not so with honest projective testers. The professional judgment of the test administrator plays a far more important part than the projective tests themselves in determining what comes out. In effect, then, when management buys projective tests, it buys the tester, just as when one buys x-ray, one buys the judgment and experience of the interpreting physician rather than the plate itself.

Projectives are expensive. Although efforts are being made to standardize and simplify them for mass administration, they remain largely one-at-a-time tests. A professional tester may spend eight hours or more testing and interpreting a single subject. Consequently, projectives have entered industry at the levels at which they are most likely to be both useful and worth the money—at the higher executive levels, where pencil-and-paper tests are relatively useless.

Management's only bases for determining whether projectives are worth the investment are, first, its own opinion of the tester it has hired, and second, *its experience over time in relating the actual behavior of applicants with the predictions that testers have made.*

In the face of these difficulties, one wonders how projectives have made their way into supposedly hardheaded business circles at all. One reason may be that projective reports seem to catch the subtle realities of executive behavior better than most pencil-and-paper tests. The reports are complicated and qualified, full of ifs and buts, somewhat like managerial life itself.

Here is a typical excerpt from a projective test report on an applicant for an executive position:

Mr. X is of superior intelligence. Problem situations, even those for which he is momentarily unprepared, do not throw him. He usually does not become emotionally involved when he has to work on a problem but adheres to, as he says, a strict formula which forces him into an intellectual and rational approach. . . . The problem is uppermost and feelings are disregarded. More specifically the feelings of others are disregarded, for when his own personal satisfaction is involved then his approach to problems is somewhat less systematic. For example, he wants others to think that he is a very capable individual and tries hard to maintain this impression because of the satisfaction that this gives him. However, because of this attitude he is apt to become too self-confident, or "cocky," and thus makes errors in very simple situations or problems that he usually would not make under such circumstances. . . .

Mr. X is an overly controlled individual in the sense that feelings play a minor role in the execution of a job. The job is paramount in his mind and he believes that he and others should subjugate themselves to it. Consequently, he is highly critical of the performance of others who work for him—but he demands as much of them as he demands of himself. Furthermore, because the job is so important to him, he does not take sufficient time out to realize the nature of the personalities working with him. He does not accomplish a job by the "human approach" but by insisting that there is a job to be done and all must do it regardless of their personal needs. . . . If he could realize that other people may have the same needs as he and that they, too, may want the satisfactions that he wants and that by giving them these satisfactions they will in no way threaten his position, then he may become more effective on the job than he is now. . . .

Being a competitive individual with a high level of aspiration, Mr. X may be a member of a group with whom he is associated but he will not feel as part of them sharing with them all that he knows, etc. To some extent he feels superior to those with whom he is associated; he feels that he could direct and lead them. But he does not win their confidence, since he is too forward in this regard, and they may resent his attempts to be in the limelight. When working with his subordinates, his status is well defined; but with colleagues, when he has to win the status he desires, he is somewhat uncomfortable. This lack of comfort makes him put forth even more effort to demonstrate his brilliance and ability, which in turn is definitely resented by the group. He is apt to be impatient with those with whom he is working because they do not see things as quickly as he. Although he tries to control himself under such circumstances, his impatience is obvious. Others would work more effectively with him and he would become more successful if he could pay more attention to and accept more of what others have to say.

Managers sometimes react against these qualifications, wishing for more "practical," definitive decisions. Realistically, though, selecting an executive is not a clear problem. It is not usually true that people simply succeed or fail. They succeed or fail "if," or they would have succeeded or failed "but." They might have succeeded if they had worked for another kind of superior, or if management had given them a little looser or a little tighter rein, or if they had been provided with a high-powered assistant, or if the job description had been rewritten so that the new person was given more responsibility in area A and less in area B. For success on a job, especially a decision-making managerial job, is not a function of the person alone but of a person in a situation. Any testing procedure that tends to describe the complications of a personality, rather than to contract and simplify it, provides extra data for relating the person to the environment. If the person is relatively unmodifiable, perhaps the environment is not.

This may be the best place to point out another major dilemma. How much does a person's behavior in a particular situation tell us about that person? If a military recruit cracks up under the pressure of basic training, can we safely say he is a "weakling" or a "neurotic" or an "incompetent"? Might we not as well argue that the recruit's failure indicates that his non-coms were "incompetent" or "insensitive" or "cruel"? But if only one recruit out of fifty cracks up, isn't that proof that that one is the weakest of the recruits? On the other hand, the fact that he failed in military training doesn't mean he isn't a potentially great accountant, does it? Yet, if he gets some kind of questionable discharge, won't the world always remember his military failure and treat it as a sign of general weakness, even when he is being considered for a quite different situation?

The difficulty is that we only see people-in-situations. In the forties and fifties, we probably overemphasized the person part of the equation. In recent years, in our attempts to match person to situation, we have put much more emphasis, properly, on the situation. Projective tests, used well, can be sensible examples of this matching, since such tests ask not, "How good a person is Joe Blow?" but rather "How will Joe Blow probably behave in situations like this or this?" And as informal assessors, without tests, we probably ought all to be doing the same thing, always asking, "How would this person behave in job X or crisis Y?" Notice, too, that questions of the person-in-situation type are much less evaluative than questions like "Is he or she a good person?"

If a projective tester, therefore, can start management worrying about whether to put a new employee to work for systematic department-head Smith or for loose, easygoing department-head Jones, that in itself may be a considerable service to the company.

Sociometric methods. Sociometrically, people are not assessed by tests or by professional testers but by other people around them: peers or subordinates or superiors. The "buddy rating" system used by the military in the Second World War is a typical sociometric device. A platoon of potential officer candidates, for example, trains together for several weeks. Then each member is asked to nominate the three men he thinks would make the best combat officers and the three he thinks would make the worst combat officers. They might be asked, too, to rate their buddies on honesty or intelligence or sense of humor or any of a number of other characteristics. Positive and negative votes received by each man are totaled and a score assigned to that man. The score represents his peers' joint estimate of his aptitude for a particular job.

Sociometric techniques do not require the judge to give a rationale for his judgment. Individuals are simply asked to express their overall feelings about other individuals. The sociometric method thereby short-cuts across an area of great difficulty, since both our language and our communicable knowledge about people are woefully inadequate. More-over, what we do know about personality, however inadequate, suggests that it is not a thing to be torn apart and dealt with as a set of separable elements but is more susceptible to a kind of all-at-once, whole-person evaluation. For, as the first five chapters of this book tried to show, personality—if it can be thought of as an entity at all—is an elaborately dynamic kind of entity. When, sociometrically, one simply asks people to make an overall judgment of one another, one is, in a way, automatically taking both the wholeness of personality and the wisdom of the assessor into account.

The reader will surely smell the impressionistic, intuitive flavor of the paragraph above. As we have indicated elsewhere in this book, it is important not to underestimate the value of our own intuition. "Intuition" in this context means the very rapid processing of large amounts of information against the background of a rich experience with other human beings. There is evidence that broad, holistic judgments of other people can be very good—especially if several observers make the same judgments. It is when we try to specify *why* we make such judgments that the trouble starts. Feelings like "I'd like to work for that guy!" are quite useful, especially if aggregated. But be careful about destroying their value by asking too many questions about *why* we feel we'd like to work for him. Then we often come up with garbage like "Well, he's very honest, honorable, and clever." Total judgments, when decomposed and itemized, often lose their essence.

This coin has another side. When data consist of the general feelings of some people about some other people, the dangers of distortion are many. Such distortions may be partially eliminated by using large numbers of judgments. Although the judgment made by one platoon member may be far off base, the judgments of fifty platoon members are reasonably valid—at least more valid, as World War II experience showed, than many paper-and-pencil tests, rating scales, and even military-school grades.

Sociometric methods have been used in a variety of ways for a variety of purposes. Sometimes one asks several judges to observe and listen to a group of applicants talking to one another. The judges sit on the periphery and observe the applicants. They then decide which one of the applicants would best perform a particular job. A number of variations of this "leaderless group" method are in current use.

Only in the last few years have sociometric methods picked up speed in industrial use, though their validity has been known for decades. A partial explanation for their lagging development may be the indirect organizational implications of their use. Sociometric methods, especially buddy ratings, are something like the voting process. Voting democracy in industry carries many dangers for traditional managerial "prerogatives" and for the whole power balance within an organization. If operators are allowed to select their own foremen, managers will argue, political plots and fixed elections may not be far behind. Selection by popularity, they add, will replace selection by ability, despite the fact that research to date has shown that such ratings are not popularity contests.

The assessment center

Despite these objections, sociometric methods are taking hold, particularly in executive selection. Several major companies have, in the last few years, established assessment centers for their executives, either as separate entities or as parts of management development centers.

These assessment centers typically lean heavily on sociometric measurements of several kinds. Usually they work like this:

Some small numbers of middle- to high-level executives are brought together at a special site for, say, three days. The assessment staff includes one or two professionals—psychologists usually—and several senior line executives who arrive in advance for a short period of training in assessment procedures. This assessment staff then puts the "subject" executives through a series of tests and exercises. The tests may be conventional ones—pencil-and-paper or projectives. The exercises have a sociometric flavor. Groups of the subject executives are given, for example, a group task—a company problem—and asked to discuss it and put forth some recommendations. This discussion is observed by the senior executive staff, often with one senior executive particularly observing just one or two subject executives as they debate and discuss the issue. This process is repeated in several forms, several times, with the seniors building up their observations of each person relative to the others.

Usually peer assessments are added. Subject executives are asked to rate one another on a collection of factors.

At the end of the three days, the whole batch is put together. The staff talks over each man, using observations, peer ratings, test scores, and anything else available, and makes an assessment of his executive potential and, usually, of his development needs.

Sometimes all these data are kept confidential in the center files. Usually they are fed back to each person in a series of interviews; occasionally they are made available to the boss of the person in question.

Technically the process is probably quite effective. It uses a team approach to assessment, exploiting "soft" observational data as well as more hard-nosed test scores. It provides good training in observation and evaluation for the senior executives who work as staff members.

On the other hand, it is clear that such schemes generate ethical problems. May we ask the reader to ponder those broader concerns for himself? For example, is it proper to subject a candidate to three days of assessment, whether he wants it or not? May an executive not want it? Is refusal really possible? What about the findings? Who sees them? What are they used for? How long do they remain in the personnel file?

Day-to-day assessment of people

The people directing an organized human effort must necessarily spend some of their time making judgments about the fitness of certain members for certain tasks. Some judgments can be formalized, but it is at an informal, day-to-day level that most assessment goes on. Top management informally, gradually, imperceptibly, perhaps even unconsciously, decides that Jones looks like presidential timber and that Smith is never likely to go anywhere.

The professional psychologist has surprisingly little to offer the industrial manager in this area. The social scientist has offered industry tests and measurements and forms and systems to help with the massive formal job of screening and selecting and record-keeping. But he has helped comparatively little with the job of improving the manager's personal skill in making judgments about the people he encounters in his business life. Of course the capacity to judge other people is not one that can be easily handed from one person to another. It is a skill requiring effort and practice and also requiring the absence of certain personality blocks. Parental and other early environmental influences probably have more to do with this skill than anything else. A person's capacity to judge probably correlates positively with the extent to which he can view the outside world undistortedly, i.e., it correlates with his own security and self-knowledge. For judging is one kind of problem solving. It can be reduced to three phases: determining what information is necessary to make a judgment; obtaining that information, usually through communication with other persons; evaluating that information into a judgment. Each of these processes is likely to be as good as the judge's own internal information-processing system.

The first, deciding what information is relevant, requires also that we ask: "Relevant for what?" Is he being considered for a specific job? What kind of a job? Working with whom? And so on. If we can get a good psychological picture of the task, we may be able to isolate the kinds of psychological information that would be relevant in a personality.

But even with a clear objective, how shall we go about ordering the information we can hope to get? The scheme that follows is a crude one, but perhaps it will be useful in helping to order the problem. It is made up of three categories: first, the givens in a personality; second, the goals of a personality; and third, the methods by which a personality uses its givens to achieve its goals. Put another way, we can say that the accuracy of our predictions of a person's behavior would increase if we could adequately answer this question: How does this person use what he has to get what he wants? This question asked in conjunction with the question "What are we judging him for?" constitutes a reasonable starting point for the assessment process.

The givens in a personality. By the time we are adults, all of us show some relatively unchanging characteristics. Some of these characteristics are givens in the sense that they were inherited, some in the sense that they were learned early and intensely and aren't given up easily. The general energy level of a person is such a characteristic; so are his skills and knowledge, his educational background, his thinking style; so, too, probably, are his sensitivity to others, the level of concreteness or abstractness with which he thinks; and certainly his physical makeup and appearance. We can find out something about these things directly or indirectly. When we know them and when we know what we are judging for, we begin to have some basis for making comparative judgments.

The goals of a personality. To a considerable extent people are known by their needs. We can communicate something to a third person if we can describe the dominant pattern of needs in a personality. Something imprecise, but nevertheless meaningful, is achieved by saying of another person that he has an uncommon need for orderliness or that he is unusually affiliative or that he has a strong need for power. Long lists of such needs can be set down, and, though they are likely to be poorly and overlappingly defined, communication about the pattern of a particular personality's needs contributes toward defining it, at least temporarily.

A personality's use of its givens to satisfy its needs. One can also seek information about a person's "style," his means of getting what he wants. These characteristic methods of behaving must represent the personality's characteristic ways of trying to achieve what it wants. Certainly, we can expect people to use methods that have worked for them before. At this level one is asking: How does X perceive other people? What is the nature of his social relationships? What are his relevant attitudes toward relevant issues? To what extent does he satisfy his needs through methods that conform to the culture of the organization in which he must work? To what extent does he use methods which do not conform? How does he control his moods and his areas of insecurity? Are his methods consistent or variable?

People vary, for example, in the means they typically use to achieve their goals. Some people tend to be "direct" achievers, taking direct action to get what they want, usually feeling personally responsible for getting things done. Others are more vicarious, more indirect, using relationships with others as their primary route to getting whatever they want; preferring to work through people and taking pleasure in other people's achievements.

But each of these styles may be appropriate in some settings and not in others. Thus a bench technician or an entrepreneur may need to take a direct-achievement orientation; but most supervisory jobs probably need people who get at least some of their kicks vicariously by helping others to accomplish their goals.

It is possible to follow out each of these three categories in some detail: to provide a list of givens, a list of needs, and a list of means for using givens to satisfy needs. But the usefulness of such a process for this book is doubtful. Perhaps what is most useful here is to suggest that a judge order the information that he can obtain about another personality into a few broad categories like these and then compare what he finds with the purpose for which he is judging.

Getting information about a person

A good deal of information about A can be obtained by talking to B or C. A good deal more can be gotten by talking to A. If the assessor has lived closely and intimately with his subject, the process of gathering additional information to make a new judgment is minimal. He probably knows all he needs to know, and his task is to order it against the problem for which the judgment is being made and to try to extricate himself from his prejudices. If one is dealing with a relative stranger, however (and it is in this category that many problems of assessment reside), then gathering information is a major part of the problem. Historical sources provide the assessor with one kind of information. He can use records, biographical information, recommendations from other people, and try to infer future behavior from this second-hand knowledge of past behavior. But he will have to form some large part of his judgment in the here and now by talking with the person being judged. The conversations may consist of one or more formal interviews or several brief informal discussions of business problems, or they may take a social form, a cocktail party or an evening at home. In all cases, the personal evaluation process goes on, even if there is no particular job about which an evaluation needs to be made.

The role of "intuition"

Such personal, face-to-face evaluation always means that information about the other person filters through the screen of the judge's own needs and prejudices. It also means that it filters through the judge's history of learnings. So informal judgments are both dangerous and rich. Indeed, it is probably true that we form very strong impressions of persons (whether we intend to or not) in the first minute or two of our contact with them. Often we form those impressions before any words have been said, deriving our information from clothing, bearing, "body language," and a collection of other inputs that get processed very rapidly through our own nervous systems.

For instance, there is a man who used to work on the same floor as I do, but who moved recently to another floor. I don't know him very well—our relationship is just at a "polite recognition" level. Today I met him outside the men's room. I said something facetious like, "Hey, you're on the wrong floor!" He replied, "I'm getting tired of people saying things like that to me!" And he said it without smiling. I suddenly became aware that that response was typical of almost all the responses I had gotten from him in the past. They always seemed to have (at least from my perspective) a note of negativism, of some hostility.

Question: Is that response of his a useful datum in making an assessment? Answer: Whether it is useful or not, I can't help but use it. I have an impression of him as a somewhat feisty, hostile man. That impression was highly unconscious until today. Now I've brought it up to consciousness. I think I'm better off being consciously aware of my impression of him. At least now, if the occasion arises, I can check it out before acting it out—which I might not have done if I were not conscious yet.

The point is that we often build more or less thorough evaluations of others semiconsciously or intuitively well before any formal interview has occurred. In fact, it has been argued that interviews really consist largely of checking out hypotheses that the interviewer makes about the person in the first minute of contact. If subsequent questions clearly disprove the hypotheses, the interviewer may reject them, but most of us tend to hang on to judgments even when the data don't fit very well.

So the wise judge may not always try to discard his own feelings and prejudices entirely in favor of an "objective system." Discarding such feelings might be desirable if it were possible. But it is doubtful whether it is possible. The alternative for the judge is to recognize the characteristics of his own filters and then to pay attention to what comes through these filters.

For whether one tries to or not, he listens to another person at two levels: at the level of the speaker's words and the information they carry, and at the level of the listener's own feelings about the speaker's words and the feelings these words convey. For example, most people can decide quickly whether or not another person seems to be afraid of them, or angry at them, or comfortable or uncomfortable with them, whether he talks too much for their liking, whether he has what they consider a good sense of humor, etc. And yet, in most formal evaluation situations, we often try consciously to block out and ignore this fundamental source of information, preferring to deal with what we like to think of as "the facts."

This tendency to discard our own semiconscious but nevertheless valuable insights probably derives from our justifiable caution about our own subjectivity and prejudice. Certainly such self-doubt is warranted. Most of us would like to have something more solid to lean on than our own amorphous judgment. We prefer to draw inferences from grades in school, test scores, number of jobs the applicant has held, and any piece of objective, "factual" information we can find. Yet, paradoxically, especially outside the office, only the most insensitive of us would try to estimate another's friendliness by asking whether he has read Dale Carnegie. Instead, data about friendliness are obtained by talking and socializing and then filtering the results through our own conception of what "friendly" means. In effect, we listen with our "third ear." Of course, the third ear is only as good as the person using it is objective about himself. But the same can be said about the first and second ears.

In organizations, "subjective" personal assessment carries great danger, however. "Good" people may become people that today's management likes. And the people today's management likes may well be people like today's management. Subjective, personalized assessment, with little reference to the question of assessment-for-what, may indeed ultimately yield an in-group of "all-alike" people. But since all-alike people may be able to work together better than all-different people, an organization may, under certain conditions, profit from just such prejudice. For example, one can argue that in a period of growth and youth an all-alike team has many advantages. Later in an organization's life the same subjective prejudices may be stifling to the birth of new ideas.

There is another side to this picture. When people are being assessed and know it, they behave in ways they think will evoke the best assessment. If a personnel interviewer asks Mr. X, "How do you get along with people?" his answer might be, "Oh, just fine. I like people. . . ." But if a psychiatrist for whose services Mr. X was paying asked him the same question an hour later, his answer might be different: "Well, Doc, that's just the problem. Some people don't seem to pay any attention to me. . . ."

One method for dealing with that problem is to evaluate in disguised situations. This alternative immediately introduces procedural as well as ethical questions. A second alternative is to make the evaluator an inkblot. Thus the interviewer does not ask, "How do you get on with people?" but instead asks, "What are the kinds of people you like best?" By opening up his questions, by modifying them so that the "right" answers are not at all obvious, the interviewer at least provides a situation in which the subject's answers are his own and not the interviewer's. Even so, people being assessed through interviews will make some guesses about the "right" answers, but, as long as they remain guesses, they represent a valid projection of the personality being interviewed. The major assumption underlying what has come to be called "non-directive" interviewing is just that one. It is the idea that an ambiguous stimulus (an uncommitted interviewer) requires the interviewee to "project" his own attitudes into the interview. An unambiguous interviewer, for whom the "right" answers are obvious, yields only a reflection of himself.

The idea is simple and sensible. The purpose of an interview is to gather information about another person, not about the interviewer. It is appropriate also that the interviewer provide a situation free enough so that the interviewee can talk about himself and be himself. In practice, the application of this principle suggests that an information-gathering interview should be designed like a series of inverted triangles. The interviewer opens each area of information he is seeking with big, broadside queries so that the interviewee can talk at length about his perceptions of the question, raising points in the order that seems significant to him and with the intensity that he thinks is appropriate to them. If the interviewer is still unsatisfied because he wants specific areas of information in more detail, he can then proceed to narrow his questions down to greater and greater specificity. Then he is ready to open up a new area with a new broad and ambiguous question.

These thoughts about day-to-day evaluations of other people are general and incomplete. Ultimately, after all, an evaluation of one person by another is a judgment and nothing more. A good judge needs all the information he can get from all the sources he can find. To an extent, scales, forms, and categories can be helpful. But no "system" provides a means for escaping from one's own lack of sensitivity or understanding in making such judgments. There are no formulas that can rule the judge out of the judging equation.

Assessment and the atmosphere of the organization

Drawing from earlier chapters, we can predict that people in an organization will try to evoke the best assessment they can get. They will (and should) try to stack the cards in their own favor. More than that, however, we can predict that they will have mixed feelings about assessment, both resenting it and seeking it out. We should expect resentment because assessment is a threat to independence and autonomy. But we should also expect people to "want to know where they stand," to want to know whether they are loved and thought well of by those on whom they depend.

From the managerial point of view, then, the problem of assessment is more than a problem of technique. The tests, the interviews, the other ritualistic paraphernalia of assessment, are only a small part of the problem. The bigger parts raise questions like these: Shall we consciously assess our people? Shall we formalize the process? Shall we report back results? All results? Or only "good" ones? Who shall assess? Superiors only? Or peers? Or subordinates? What is to be assessed? Personality or performance? Shall we build a work environment permeated with an atmosphere of assessment?

This book can offer no pat answers to such questions. There are none. What it can and hopefully has done is to run up a danger signal, warning the manager that assessment is a dangerous game. The chapters that follow are devoted, in large part, to considering the implications of issues like assessment for effective team behavior.

In summary

Three general approaches to formal assessment have been described: pencil-and-paper tests, projectives, and sociometric methods. Each has its own advantages and costs. Pencil-and-paper devices are relatively standardized, but their use is largely limited to mass-selection situations. Projectives go deep and are rich in the material they dredge up, but subjective, individualistic, expensive, and poorly validated. Sociometrics are easy and relatively valid but carry serious implications for the power relationships in an organization.

Day-to-day assessing of people is a more difficult problem. It can be helped by a set of categories for thinking about personality, by utilizing modern interviewing techniques, and by increasing one's insight into oneself.

The larger questions of assessment are not "how" questions but questions of "why," "how much," and at what costs.

2 People two at a time
Problems of influence and authority

Introductory note

The focus of this second section shifts from the singular to the plural, from one person to relationships between people and especially to the efforts of one person to influence and change the behavior of others.

The moment we begin to talk about things like persuasion or influence, a major ethical consideration pops up: When is it right and when is it wrong for A to try to change B's behavior? And then come all the questions associated with the use of power: When is it right and when is it wrong to order people to do things? To use blackmail? Coercion? Is it ever right to con people, to "manipulate" them in order to get them to do what you want them to do? What about "brainwashing"? Those are all good and proper questions in a free society.

Notice that these questions are by no means limited to business organizations. They are pervasive in our society, arising continuously in the family, in education, in politics, in international relations, and in every other phase of human interaction.

Indeed, those ethical problems, along with the technical issues of behavior change, are growing more and more complex. Our technically specialized culture has made each of us increasingly dependent on others for need satisfaction. Some years ago, an observer called us (Americans) an "other-directed" people—a people who need others not only for bread and warmth but to justify our existence and to provide us with standards of value. The young executive finds it hard to separate good work from his boss's approval of it. The author cannot feel sure he has written a good book until the critics laud it.

The reader will find a great deal of emphasis in this section on three central ideas relating to influence:

First, the idea of communication, because communication is the prerequisite to any attempt to change human behavior. Present-day understanding of communication has emerged from engineering and the physical sciences much more than from the behavioral sciences.

113

Many of the following pages, therefore, have their origins as much in the technological world as in psychology or sociology.

The second idea is a sharply contrasting and much more psychological one. It is the idea that influence is more an emotional than a rational process. Although we can rationally analyze how people communicate, we would be foolish indeed to think that that is the end of it. Most persuasion and influence is not the result of logic or argument. We are influenced or changed because we have been touched in our guts, not in our heads, and no matter how we pride ourselves on our objectivity and rationality, our fears and our fancies become critical here. To say, however, that we are influenced emotionally more than rationally is not to denigrate us, not to reduce us to primitive beasties. Emotionality is by no means equivalent to stupidity. The emotional, nonintellectual, feeling side of our beings can be wise and sophisticated and truth-seeking, too!

The third idea of this section centers on the concept of the relationship. People communicate with one another. They try to change one another. The central unit is the pair rather than the individual. And the space between the two members is the territory we call the relationship. Relationships are characterized by dependency; and dependent situations are likely, among adults, to be dynamic and ambivalent.

In chapter 2, in the discussion of dependency and the paralyzed brother, one important item was omitted. We treated the case as though only the paralyzed brother were dependent. The big brother was free of dependency. But is that ever really true? Isn't big brother dependent too? Clearly the child is dependent on the parents, but aren't the parents also dependent on the child? The employee is dependent on the boss, but why does the boss put ads in the paper asking literally, for "help"?

What was omitted, then, in the first section was the emphasis on interdependency, the idea of the relationship. We can define relationships as situations in which individuals or groups seek mutually to satisfy needs. In this section, we try to broaden the spotlight to include a bit of the forest of relationships as well as the individual trees.

Anyone who lives in an organization is living in an atmosphere of dependency. He should therefore feel some love and some hate toward the organization. The intensity and direction of feelings should, in turn, vary with the ups and downs of organizational life.

The morals of this tale are simple but important ones. Don't look for psychological equilibrium in organizations (or in marriage or any other relationship, for that matter). Look for variation and change. Don't look for statics; look for dynamics. Don't look for a permanently "happy" organization; look for one that is self-corrective, that doesn't build up unexpressed grudges.

Big brother (the organization) must always be frustrating as well as satisfying. He fools himself if he thinks he can be otherwise. But what he and the paralyzed brother can do is to limit the duration and build-up of frustration by providing mechanisms for expressing and acting upon it. Big brother had better also be satisfying as well as frustrating, because the dependency is mutual.

These issues bring us to the big question of conflict between the individual and the organization. Endless arguments go on about whether or not human beings can live complete, fulfilled lives in the constricting, dependent environment of a large organization. Indeed, a senior executive I know, one who has spent many years in both the public and private sectors, concluded recently that all contemporary organizations are essentially prisons; that the differences between the best and the worst are small at best. In the best ones, the food in the cafeterias is a little better, the cells are perhaps a little larger or decorated a little better, but no organization allows anything approaching full human freedom.

That seems a cynical, embittered view. But suppose we carry it further. Couldn't we say the same thing (and haven't many people said the same thing) about marital relationships? About family life? About small towns? Or about any lasting relationship? That is, isn't it true that any interactions between people always involve some degree of mutual dependency and mutual constraint? And can't it also be argued that to the degree that A is dependent upon B, A is less free?

But that is the negative side of it. How about the positive side? Isn't it fair to argue that life without mutually dependent relationships would be unbelievably barren? That if most organizations and most relationships are prisons, then non-organizational and non-relational life would be like solitary banishment into outer space? All of which is to reiterate the yang-yin theme of oriental thought, and its more flippant equivalent in Western thought: "There ain't no free lunch!" Relationships involve responsibility.

Chapter 10 treats some of the issues of relationships through a consideration of the communication process, the basic mechanism of influence. Chapter 11 hits the influence problem head-on, describing some dimensions of influence and their implications. Then we devote four chapters to four different approaches to influence: The first considers the possibilities and limitations of authority as a tool for influence; the second examines coercive power; the next looks at manipulation as a tool for influence; and the fourth examines motivational and collaborative tools for influence. Chapter 16, like chapter 9, picks some major applied problems of influence, the problems of money incentives and performance evaluation as influence mechanisms, and examines them from psychological and managerial perspectives.

10 Communication Getting information from A to B

People begin, modify, and end relationships by communicating with one another. Communication is their channel of influence, their mechanism of change. In industrial organizations it has become popular recently to communicate about communication—to talk and write about the importance of communication in problem solving. The talk about communication is appropriate because communication is indeed a critical dimension of organization.

Unfortunately, though, much of the talk has been either nonsensical or unusable. For one thing, the word *communication* has been used to mean everything from public speaking to mass merchandising. For another, most of the talk has been hortatory rather than explanatory. Managers are urged to use "two-way" communication, because it is "better" (what does "better" mean?) than one-way communication. The fad has extended to "three-way" communication, again without evidence or precise definition.

The purpose of this chapter is to describe some major dimensions of the communication process, to examine what can be meant by "better" or "worse" communication, and to relate the idea of communication to the ideas of interpersonal influence and behavior change.

Some dimensions of communication

Sometimes there are advantages to asking simpleminded questions. They can help to strip away some of the confusing gingerbread surrounding an idea so that we can see it more objectively.

Suppose we ask, simplemindedly, what are the things that can happen when A talks to B? What is involved in two people's talking to one another?

First, A usually talks to B *about something*. The process has a content. They talk baseball or they talk business or they talk sex. The content is what usually hits us first when we tune in on a conversation. Content of communication, in fact, is what psychologists and businessmen alike are usually thinking about when they think about human relations.

We can see subclasses within content too. We can differentiate categories of content like, for example, *fact* and *feeling*.

Other things, quite independent of what is said, take place when A talks to B. Some conversations take place in the presence of a great deal of *noise;* others are relatively noiseless. In this context "noise" means things that interfere with transmission. We can encounter channel noise like the static on a telephone line that makes it hard for B to hear what A is saying. We can also usefully think of psychological noises, like B's thinking about something else, so that again it is hard for him to hear what A is saying; or like B's being so afraid of A that it is hard for him to hear what A is saying. Language or code noise may make it hard for B to hear: he doesn't understand the words A is using in the way A understands them.

All sorts of noise can occur independently of content. We can find noisy or noiseless communications about any content. We also can usually observe that A, in the presence of noise, is likely to communicate more redundantly—to repeat his message in the hope that B will be able to hear it better the second time or to say the same thing in a different way. Redundancy is one of the most common weapons for combating noise. It is "inefficient" in the sense that repetition is wasteful of time and energy. It is "efficient" in the sense that, so long as noise exists, redundancy helps to push the content through.

Besides the content and noise dimensions of conversation between A and B, a third dimension is the *communication net.* Usually we think of A to B conversation as direct; but many such conversations, especially in organizations, are mediated through other people. One thing an organization chart is supposed to tell us is that A can speak to B only through C or D. As a later chapter will show, the structure of the net a particular organization uses can have a lot to do with the speed and accuracy of members' communications with one another.

One more dimension of the process is worth noting, especially since it has been ridden so hard in managerial literature. It is the *direction* of communication—its one-wayness or two-wayness. Again it is an independent dimension. No matter what A and B may be talking about, no matter how much static may be involved, no matter what the network, A may talk to B this way: A→B; or this way: A⇆B. A can talk and B can only listen, i.e., one-way communication; or A can talk and B can talk back, i.e., two-way communication.

This last aspect of the process, one-wayness versus two-wayness, gets special attention in the remainder of this chapter. Is two-way communication really better? What does "better" mean? Better for what and for whom? When?

One-way versus two-way communication

Essentially our problem is to clarify the differences between these two situations: (1) one person, A, talking to another, B, *without* return talk from B to A; versus (2) conversation from A to B *with* return conversation from B to A. The differences can be clarified best by testing one method against the other. Here is such a test situation:

The pattern of rectangles shown here is an idea you would like to tell some B's about. Suppose you try to communicate it in words to a half-dozen of your friends who are sitting around your living room:

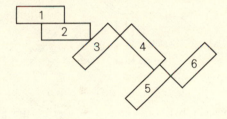

Assume that the rectangles touch each other at "sensible" places—at corners or at midpoints along the line. There are no touch points at any unusual places. All the angles are either 90° or 45° angles; there are no odd ones. This pattern of rectangles is an idea comparable perhaps to a complicated set of instructions you may have to give to a subordinate or to the definition of a policy that you would like to pass along or to the task of explaining statistical quality control to a sales manager. This idea can be communicated to others under (1) one-way or (2) two-way conditions.

If you are the communicator, these are your *one-way* instructions:

1. Turn your back on your audience so that you cannot get visual communication back.

2. Give the audience blank sheets of paper, so that they can listen and draw exactly what you are communicating. Ask them to try to draw as accurate a picture of the pattern of rectangles as possible.

3. Describe the pattern of rectangles to them in words as fast as you can. The audience is not permitted to ask questions, or laugh, or sigh, or in any other way to communicate back to you any information about what it is receiving.

This game is a good parlor game, if you can find some people to try it on. Try it, time it, and then check the accuracy of your communication by determining whether or not your audience has drawn what you have described. If they received what you tried to send, so their pictures match the test picture, then you have communicated. To the extent that their pictures do not match the one in the drawing, you have not communicated.

Two-way communication can be tested for contrast in the same way. The same rules apply, and here is a similar test pattern:

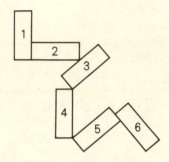

This time the basic job is the same, to describe the pattern verbally so that the people who are listening can draw it. But here are the differences:

1. This time you may face your audience.

2. They are allowed to interrupt and ask you any questions they want to at any time they want to.

Try it this way and time it. The differences between what happened the first time and what happened the second time are the differences between one- and two-way communication. (The order in which the two methods are used matters, but is not critical.)

Under experimental conditions these findings have emerged from this game: (1) One-way communication is considerably faster than two-way communication. (2) Two-way communication is more accurate than one-way, i.e., more people in the audience correctly reproduce the drawing under two-way conditions. (3) The receivers are more sure of themselves and make more correct judgments of how right or wrong they are in the two-way system. (4) The sender finds himself feeling psychologically under attack in the two-way system, because his receivers pick up his mistakes and oversights and let him know about them. The receivers may make snide remarks about the sender's intelligence and skill, and, if the receivers are trying very hard and taking the task seriously, they may actually get angry at the sender, and he at them. (5) The two-way method is relatively noisy and disorderly—with people interrupting the sender and one another, with the slowest person holding up the rest, and so on. The one-way method, on the other hand, appears neat and efficient to an outside observer, but the communication is less accurate.

Such a demonstration points out both the advantages and the costs of one-way and of two-way communication. If speed alone is what is important, then one-way communication has the edge. If appearance is of prime importance, if one wishes to look orderly and businesslike, then the one-way method again is preferable. If one doesn't want one's mistakes to be recognized, then again one-way communication is preferable. Then the sender will not have to hear people implying or saying that he is stupid or that there is an easier way to say what he is trying to say. Of course, such comments may be made about him whether he uses one-way or two-way communication, but under one-way conditions he will not have to listen to what is said, and it will be harder for anyone to prove that mistakes were made by A rather than B. If one wants to protect one's power, so that the sender can blame the receiver instead of taking blame himself, then one-way communication is again preferable. The sender can say: "I told you what to do; you just weren't bright enough to get the word." If he uses two-way communication, the sender will have to accept much of what blame there is, and it will be apparent to all that he deserves some of it; but he will also get his message across.

If one wants to simplify managerial life, so that even a rank amateur can handle it, one-way communication helps. It tightens and structures the situation so that A only has to make decisions about one kind of thing—content of the problem. When he opens up two-way communication, he has to be professional—for now he must make many kinds of decisions at once—content decisions and also decisions about people (Whom shall he recognize? How long should he work to make sure Joe understands while everybody else waits?), about personal strategies (When shall I cut off the discussion? Shall I accept sarcasm or fight it?), and about lots of other things. Like some formations in football, two-way communication is too powerful a device for safe use by people who are amateurs at management. But skillful use by a competent professional can be as beautiful and impressive as the work of a good T-formation quarterback.

Those are the major differences between one- and two-way communication. They are differences that most people are aware of implicitly. If a person gets a chance to ask questions, to double-check what he might have missed, then he can make sure he has gotten exactly what he is expected to get. On the other hand, if he must only sit and listen, he may or may not get the word, and he is likely to feel frustrated and uncertain about what he does get. Moreover, that bit of frustration and uncertainty is likely to grow because he has no way of making sure of things he isn't sure of.

To put it another way, one-way communication is not likely to be communication at all. It is more likely to be talk. One can talk by passing words out into the air. Those words don't become communication until they enter meaningfully into somebody else's head.

Of course, it is simple for a communicator to claim that his responsibility is only to pass a message along, that the receiver's responsibility is to make sure that he understands it. But this is not a very adequate claim. If one really were to argue through the question of who is responsible for the success of communication, one would certainly conclude that communication is largely the communicator's responsibility. For if the communicator's job is to communicate—and if to communicate he must get his message through to the receiver—then his responsibility cannot end until the receiver has received. And he cannot be sure that the receiver has received until he gets confirming feedback from the receiver. On the other hand, the location of responsibility becomes a far less significant issue when one perceives communication as a two-party process to begin with.

A partial definition of communication is now possible. First, to communicate is to shoot information and to hit a target with it. Shooting alone is not communicating. Second, to have more than chance probability of hitting a target requires that the sender get feedback from the target about the accuracy of his shots.

If an artilleryman had to fire over a hill at an invisible target, he would have to fire blind and hope that by luck one of his shells would land on the target. He would spray the area with shells and go away, never being certain whether he had or had not destroyed his objective. But by the simple addition of a spotter standing on the hilltop, the likelihood of accurate shooting can be greatly increased. The spotter can feed back to the gunner information about the effects of the gunner's own shots. "Your last shot was a hundred yards short. The second was fifty yards over." And so on. The advantage is obvious, and it is precisely the advantage of two-way over one-way communication—the communicator can learn the effects of his attempts to communicate and can adjust his behavior accordingly. Like the learning machine we discussed in chapter 6, the decision maker needs inputs as well as outputs to correct his own behavior.

One-way and two-way communication
are really different methods

By this definition two-way communication is not just different from one-way in degree but also in kind. For when one switches from one-way to two-way, a great many changes take place, changes not only in the outcomes but in the inputs. For example, one-way communication usually calls for and gets much more planning than two-way. When you tell a sender in these experiments that he is to send one-way, and you show him the diagram and tell him he can take a few minutes to get ready, it is almost always true that he uses more minutes getting ready to start than he does in the two-way system. The reason is probably obvious. The sender needs to choose carefully the code he will use, even the precise words he will use. But in two-way communication he is apt to start out much more quickly, not worrying too much about a general plan or strategy, because he knows that the feedback will provide him with opportunities to correct himself. The first system is like a phonograph record. Once it starts, it must be played through. Hence it must be planned very carefully. Two-way communication is a different strategy, a kind of "local" strategy, in which the sender starts down one path, goes a little way and then discovers he is on the wrong track, makes a turn, discovers he is off a little again, makes another turn, and so on. He doesn't need to plan so much as he needs to listen, and to be sensitive to the feedback he is getting.

There are important differences associated with these two kinds of approaches. Planfulness, order, systemization: these are associated with one-way communication. The two-way method has much more a trial-and-error, "let's make a stab at it and see what happens," kind of flavor. It is understandable, therefore, that certain kinds of personalities tend to favor one of these or the other because one method or the other is apt to be much more consistent with one's personality.

With our definition of communication, the issue of one- and two-way communication in organizations can be cast somewhat differently than is usual. For now one encounters apparent conflict between the short-run efficiency of two-way communication and the long-run need to maintain power and authority at various levels of the hierarchy. Two-way communication makes for more valid communication, and it appears now that more valid communication results not only in more accurate transmission of facts but also in reorganized perceptions of relationships. Authority, for example, may under ideal conditions of two-way communication cease to serve as a sufficient protection for inadequacy. The dictum that a well-informed citizenry is democracy's protection against autocracy may also be applicable to the well-informed staff or the well-informed employee. And though "democracy" may connote things desirable in government, its connotations for industrial organizations in our society are far from clear.

Barriers in the communication process

In our experiment we set up two-way communication simply by telling our subjects that we wanted them to talk back to the sender, to ask any questions they wanted to, any time they wanted to. Moreover, the experiment was just an experiment anyway, and nothing really rode on it. So there wasn't any reason why people shouldn't talk back—apparently. But, in fact, in almost every case, it turned out that some people in the two-way situation did not get complete and perfect answers. And it was also true that most of these people knew they were wrong —*yet they did not ask questions*. Why not?

When we asked people why not, we got a variety of answers. Some of them didn't ask questions because they were bored; they didn't think much of the experiment anyway. Some of them didn't ask questions because they didn't want to occupy the group's time. Sometimes they were just plain mad at the sender because of the way he was encoding the material. They wouldn't give him the satisfaction of asking him a question. Sometimes they were scared. They had noticed that when Joe Blow asked a question earlier, the sender had given a curt and nasty answer. So they just quit asking questions. Some people said that they had wanted to ask questions, but so many other people were talking all at once that they couldn't get in.

So even in this gamelike little experiment, where nothing much rode on what was going on, where the sender was not the boss—even in such a situation, there were lots of things that kept people from saying what they should have. Lots of barriers to two-way communication remained even after we had tried to set up a situation in which no such barriers would exist.

In the real world, of course, the barriers are likely to be greater and much more numerous. In the real world the boss's statement that his office door is always open has much less meaning, probably, than the experimenter's statement that people should feel free to ask any questions they want to, any time they want to.

There is, then, a moral to this tale. The moral is that if someone wants two-way communication in his organization, he had better plan to work for it. It does not come naturally or by issuing a proclamation. If a sender wants to make sure that two-way communication will in fact occur, he will need to be extremely sensitive to what the people in his group are thinking and feeling. He will have to have his eye open for the person who wants to talk but doesn't dare. He will have to be alert to the extent to which his own behavior is deterring people from asking the questions that need to be asked. He will have to worry about some degree of order or discipline in the group, so that people can get in questions they want to ask. He will even have to worry about the inter-personal relations among the members of the group, for sometimes people do not ask questions of the sender because they are fearful of one of their colleagues. He will have, in other words, to take many new kinds of responsibility.

Communication about novel and routine problems

In chapter 6, when our focus was on individual learning and problem solving, we pointed out that people learn; they use their memories of past problems to solve similar present ones.

Correspondingly, it is obviously true that if the problem in the experiment on two-way communication had been a familiar instead of a novel one, the results might have been quite different. A, for instance, could probably have communicated the English alphabet accurately and rapidly through one-way communication alone. In fact, it has been shown that if we use two-way communication on these rectangle problems again and again with the same group, communication soon becomes one-way anyhow. People stop asking questions. They don't have to. They have learned the code; so A and B understand one another.

From the point of view of speed and accuracy, then, one could make this tentative generalization. Two-way communication improves the accurate communication of previously uncoded or insufficiently coded ideas. But two-way communication contributes considerably less to accuracy after the code has been clarified—after new problems have been programmed and routinized. Coupling this generalization with the notion that new unprogrammed problems tend to occur more frequently in upper organizational echelons, we can also tentatively conclude that two-way communication may be generally more useful for problem solving within the management group than further down the line—except when the problems are people problems, and those are unprogrammed everywhere.

What gets communicated?

One aspect of the content problem deserves mention here, although it will be dealt with more fully later. The problem is that people usually communicate more than information; they communicate feelings as well as facts. Suppose the artillery spotter, instead of simply announcing where the last shell had landed, decided to add a few typically human comments of his own. Suppose the spotter said to the gunner: "Look, you stupid s.o.b., your last shot was three hundred yards over. Where the hell did you learn to shoot?" That kind of communication of unsolicited information will complicate the psychological picture, just as will the communication of inaccurate information, sometimes causing the now frustrated gunner to change his target from the farmhouse to the spotter.

These problems of the content of communication are the subject matter of the next few chapters of this book—the chapters on (communication as a tool for) influencing people's behavior.

In summary

Communication is a primary tool for effecting behavior change. We can isolate at least four independent dimensions of the communication process: content, noise, network characteristics, and direction.

One-way communication has some advantages in speed over two-way. It also has the advantages of protecting the sender from having to recognize his own faults and protecting him from some more complex problems of managing. Two-way communication has the advantages of greater accuracy and greater feelings of certainty for the receiver. But two-way communication involves some psychological risks to the defenses of the sender. Two-way communication also means less *planning* work for the sender as far as the message itself is concerned but opens up a whole new series of managerial problems in maintaining and expanding the two-way system.

11 Influencing behavior Some dimensions of the problem

The purpose of this chapter is to scan panoramically some things that happen when one person, A, sets out to communicate with another person, B, for the specific purpose of changing B's behavior.

The problems under consideration here are largely tactical ones, like these: A sets out to get B to quit smoking; or A sets out to "discipline" B, who has again shown up late for work; or A sets out to stimulate his passive staff into more energetic activity; or to get B to accept his (A's) great idea; or A sets out to get B to like him better or to respect him more. When we watch A's undertaking such tasks, several common aspects become noticeable; some seem to center in A, others in B, and still other in the interactions between the two. Let's begin with a clear code. A is the chang*er*. B is the chang*ee*.

Influence and emotion

Perhaps the most important idea in all this is that when A sets out to influence B, he had better realize that he is undertaking an emotional as much as an intellectual task; that change—individuals, organizations, societies—always involves large components of emotionality. Of course, most of our education has taught us to believe that we influence people through reason, or at least that we ought to. People *should* be persuaded by facts, by evidence, by truth. But any careful observation of reality will show us that reason is, in most cases, only a small component of the process. Most of us accept or reject new ideas or change our behavior more in response to feelings than to facts. We change because we are terrified or flattered or loved or threatened.

The reader who is deeply committed to logic and reason may reluctantly admit that some (other) people are more emotional than reasoning. But that offers all the more reason to work toward a more rational world. It is important, however, even for the most rational reader rationally to consider the positive, even desirable, side of emotionality. Surely there are some times in each of our lives when it is appropriate

127

to behave out of loyalty, out of love for people close to us, out of commitment to a moral cause, even if pure reason might lead us elsewhere.

So when we argue that change and influence are largely emotional processes, we do so neither regretfully nor cynically. Love, commitment, loyalty need not be seen as imperfections and noise in human affairs. They can be perceived, can't they, as what reason is for?

The changer's motivation

In the next few pages let's look at the three key elements in this behavior-change picture—the changer, whom we call A; the changee, whom we call B; and the relationships between them, which we shall call (with considerable originality) "the relationship."

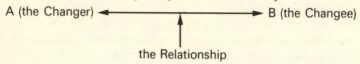

One oddity about people who seek to change others in their readiness to undertake the job without thinking much about their own objectives or their own motives. A friend of mine told me a story recently about his extended efforts to get his daughter to stop sucking her thumb. He had been worried about it for a long time and had seen the family doctor about it. The doctor had examined the child, found no physical damage, and advised the father to forget about the problem.

But when the child got to be about three years old, Papa began to worry about it again. He was worried, he said, about what thumb sucking would do to her teeth and jaws. This time he took her to a psychiatrist, who talked to the child at some length and came up with the same advice the family physician had given: forget about it; it would take care of itself.

Six months later Papa decided on his own to try some of the popular methods for stopping thumb sucking. He put some nasty-tasting stuff on the thumb; he spanked her; and he made her wear mittens. But these methods didn't work either. Now he had come to me.

His objective *seemed* clear enough: it was to stop the child from sucking her thumb. But when pressed, he agreed that there were some secondary objectives that were perhaps not so secondary when he thought about them. He wanted the child to stop sucking her thumb, but he was not willing to pay any price to accomplish it. He was not willing, for instance, to exchange thumb sucking for stuttering or even for nose picking. Moreover, when we talked more generally about what he was trying to accomplish, he finally admitted that what he really wanted was to start making an adult out of his daughter, to start socializing her. He was disturbed because this three-and-a-half-year-old extension of himself was behaving in a way that he considered childish and shameful. He thought that other people disapproved of little girls who sucked their thumbs and that their disapproval reflected on his capacity as a parent. He finally decided, after thinking a good deal about himself, simply to stop the whole attempt.

Such confusion of motives is not at all unusual, even in business. A supervisor, under pressure from his own superiors, starts pushing discipline without thinking much about its effect on production. If an observer raises these issues, the supervisor will argue that his goal is to get more work, purely and simply. But his behavior may suggest that some of the needs involved are personal and emotional, e.g., to get the approval of his boss.

A personnel manager tries to get his staff working hard on a suggestion system. His objective is to build a system that will help the company. But under a microscope one can see other objectives that the personnel manager may not admit very readily. He received a copy of *Business Week* from the president the other day with a note about an article on suggestion systems: "Joe, please let me know what we are doing about programs like this one."

Perhaps the most common form of unclarity about motives for changing others stems from conflicts between immediate and long-term needs. In most industrial situations, no matter how simple and specific the case, a secondary, long-term factor is likely to be lurking in the background. It is the factor of the continuing relationship. Any time a supervisor performs some specific act to get more or better work on a specific job at a specific time, he is acting like the big brother of chapter 2. He is influencing his long-term relationship with his employees. Unlike the big brother's, the supervisor's acts almost always have a large audience. And every specific incident in a supervisor's handling of his people can be thought of as one frame in the long movie which determines his people's general willingness (or unwillingness) to work, their optimism or pessimism, their approval or resentment. The difficulty is that workaday pressures tend to push executives, like parents, toward the short-term problems and toward the satisfaction of short-term personal and egoistic needs, at the expense of long-term objectives.

It isn't always easy to take the long view in the face of short-term pressures. Since every superior in an organization is usually a subordinate to someone else, each is likely to be intensely concerned with the short-term problem of doing what his superiors want him to do. And if the executive feels squeezed by his superiors, he cannot simply ignore his own tensions in order to work for the long-term good. But, perhaps, if he can recognize for himself the several motives that may be relevant to an effort to change someone else's behavior, he can select a course of action that can better accomplish all the ends he wants to accomplish.

So if any generalized rule of thumb exists for the prospective behavior change, it might be this one: Let him examine his own reasons for wanting to effect a particular change before plunging into the effort. Let him examine his own motives. If he does, he may be more likely to effect change successfully because he will be more clear-headed about what he wants to do; or he may alter or give up his efforts altogether if such an examination brings the realization that changing other people would not satisfy the needs he most wants to satisfy.

The changee is in the saddle

No matter how much power a changer may possess, no matter how "superior" he may be, it is the changee who controls the final change decision. It is the employee, even the lowest paid one, who ultimately decides whether to show up for work or not. It is the child who ultimately decides whether to obey or not. It is the changee who changes. A can exert more or less influence on the situation. A can cut capers before B; he can cajole, threaten, or punish; but B (and he may be an irrational and unreasonable B) makes the ultimate decision about whether or not he will change. Moreover, it is not just B but A who feels the tension, whose needs are unsatisfied. So it is A who is at least partially dependent on B.

B, after all, is a whole person; and A's activities in trying to get B to change constitute just one set of forces in the multitude of forces that determine B's behavior. B, in effect, sits behind the solid fortifications of his own history and his own personality, integrating A's activities into all other forces that act upon him and coming up with a new behavioral pattern that may or may not constitute what A wants.

Greater power in A's hands is not necessarily a better weapon for control over B's attitudes or his behavior. B is never completely dependent. So the industrial worker finds numberless ingenious techniques for evading, avoiding, or retaliating against changes imposed by his superior.

Change is uncomfortable

Very often during the process of behavior change changees become disturbed. B, during the course of a significant change in his own behavior (whether the change results from A's actions or not), gets upset and anxious. A, the changer, may mistakenly interpret such action by B as a sign that his change efforts are a failure, that he has gone too far.

In fact, however, some disturbance seems invariably to accompany change. The absence of signs of disturbance may, therefore, be a more negative warning than their presence.

Signs of upset in the process of change are visible in many situations. The child is likely to become upset when switching from diapers to the toilet. The bachelor suffers from sleeplessness and loss of appetite as he wrestles with the idea of marriage. The executive somehow feels anxious and upset, as well as happy, when he learns of his promotion to greater responsibilities.

Moreover, these upsets are likely to lead the changee into aggressive and hostile activity or into moodiness and withdrawal. A is often the nearest target for tensions created by such disturbances; so B is likely to become aggressive and hostile toward A.

The explanation of these upsets takes us back to chapters 4 and 5. We have introduced frustration and conflict into the situation. People change when their present behavior begins to appear inadequate, either because they have been frustrated—something in the world has thrown a block across a previously open path—or because some new path has become visible and looks as if it *might* (conflict) be a better one. In either case a kind of behavior that had in the past been adequate has now become less adequate. If the present path is now inadequate, but no alternatives are immediately available, we have a classic frustration situation—and hence manifestations of aggression are to be expected. If one's present tack does not look as good as it did because another has begun to look better, we have conflict between the safety and security of the old path and the risk of an uncertain new one. Once again we should expect some emotional disturbance, the particular nature of which should be grossly predictable from our knowledge of the individual.

What does A need to know about B?

Different changers in different change situations have different ideas about the importance of "diagnosis," of gathering information about B.

An A who uses force as a prime device to effect change usually does not worry much about diagnosis. The effects of a whip, after all, are fairly predictable even if one doesn't know much about the psyche of the particular person being whipped. But at the other extreme one can find As (and many psychiatrists are among them) devoting a large portion of their effort to finding out a great deal about the changee—about his background, his childhood, and his personality down to the finest detail.

In organizations the whole range of changers are represented, with most exponents of "modern management" favoring the diagnostic side.

One finds, for example, the common supervisory dictum "Get the facts before you act." That seems to mean that diagnosis is a useful predecessor to change.

A great deal can be said here, as elsewhere, in favor of gathering information about a problem before trying to solve it. But three easily overlooked points are worth considering. First, who most needs the information thus gathered, A or B? Second, what kind of information does A (or B) need? Third, how much information is worth chasing after, especially if the chasing process costs time and effort?

Behavior-change problems may be somewhat different from some other problems in this regard. Often it is more important for B to understand the problem than for A to understand it. If the ultimate control for change lies with B, and if it is for B to fit A's efforts into the larger framework of B's own perceptions, then B can best make a reasonable change decision when he, not A, understands what is going on. A may understand B inside out, but he may not be able to communicate that understanding to B or even to plot a very effective course of action. Somewhere along the line B has to line up the facts in a form *he* can understand and utilize. This is the problem with giving advice. A looks over B's situation, thinks (often correctly) that he sees it more clearly than B, and says: "What you ought to do is. . . ." B thereupon feels that his defenses have been violated or that A's advice represents poor understanding; or he takes the advice literally and utilizes it poorly and finally rejects both advice and adviser. Perhaps if A spent less time diagnosing B and more helping B to diagnose himself, the likelihood of successful change would be enhanced.

The second problem involves two kinds of information that are available to both A and B—information about facts and feelings. Facts in the usual sense of observable phenomena are likely to be much less important than feelings in change situations. Fears, doubts, feelings of confidence, inadequacy, ambition—these are much more likely to be significant information for behavior changers than the cold facts of duties or salary bracket. Moreover, these feelings may be hard for A to get at, even if he needs them. This is so partly because our language and our culture make verbal communication of feelings so difficult and partly because feelings often touch on people's psychological defenses.

An A who wants to know how B feels needs to have a sharp third ear. He has to be able to pick up information from such cues as the tone of B's voice, or the raising and lowering of B's eyebrows, or the secondary emotional connotations of B's words. Any A who sets out ot find out why a B is doing what he is doing had best think of the job as something considerably more than a simple fact-finding expedition.

He had better recognize that he will have to listen for some subtle cues and that, because they are likely to be subtle and indirect, they may be easily misinterpreted.

One of the best of many good things to be said for a serious effort by A to understand B's feelings is that those As who undertake such diagnosis often end up changing their own objectives. An A who takes time to find out about an employee before disciplining him may end up changing his attitude toward the employee and hence changing his own behavior instead of B's. The guy isn't a lazy bum after all; he had reasons.

The "how much" question is an important one, too. In chapter 6 we pointed out that if we demand perfect information for a decision, we may never get to the decision. In the kind of human decision making we are talking about here, the same statement holds. To what extent must the manager be the psychiatrist of everyone in his department? To what extent need he know about their sex lives to improve their working efficiency? Most managers implicitly recognize the diminishing-returns aspect of this problem. "Counseling," listening to people's personal problems, is tricky, for one thing—it has a way of changing the focus of a relationship from its value for business problem solving to its value in its own psychological right. More than that, after a while it costs a good deal more than it returns in improved performance. If A needs to know about B, he needs to know the factors immediately relevant to the problem at hand. More might help, it is true, but it often costs far more than it is worth in the total business picture.

The location of responsibility in change situations

In watching As trying to change Bs one may also notice that the responsibility for effecting the change seems to settle in different locations on different occasions. Sometimes A takes all the responsibility, and B none of it. Both A and B tend to see A as the person in charge and B only as an actor. On a road gang, for example, each laborer often seems to be saying to himself: "It is not my responsibility to work, it is the boss's responsibility to make me work. Therefore it is perfectly proper for me to do as little as possible, to do only what the boss can directly manipulate me into doing."

The location of responsibility in A is not limited to labor gangs, and it does not always occur against A's wishes. If anything, many As accept the idea that it is their responsibility to change B and to see that he stays changed. Sales managers sometimes take this view in an extreme form. They properly consider it their job to stimulate salespeople but mistakenly assume that what is their job cannot also be the salesperson's job. Since the effects of such stimulation seem to wear off, they feel it must be periodically reinforced. Hence one finds a great deal of emphasis by many sales managers on incentive gimmicks, on "inspirational" sales meetings, and so on. Very often even managers who talk a lot about "delegation" take such a view and succeed too well. Their people often end up taking the same view, i.e., that it is not their job to sell so much as it is the manager's job to use magic and gadgetry to get them to sell.

Clearly, the responsibility for change does not have to lie solely with the changer. It can be shared by changer and changee or even be taken over altogether by the person being changed. From the changee's viewpoint change is equivalent to learning, and learning, we argued in chapter 6, is an *active* process. If teachers want to motivate their students to learn, one thing they can do is try to get the student to take the responsibility for his own education, to come to want to learn on his own rather than to sit passively while the teacher pumps learning into his head. Many psychiatrists and counselors will even argue that there is no real hope for effecting much "deep" change in clients unless the clients take such responsibility. But in industry, organizational pressures and ideas about authority tend to make As feel that the responsibility is theirs. They thereby encourage Bs to take the easy, non-responsible course of action.

The advantages of shared responsibility are great for both A and B. For one thing, a B who feels that he wants to change is more likely to change effectively and lastingly than a B who feels no such internal tension. Moreover, no A is likely really to understand the subtleties of B's position better than B himself. No matter how successful A's communication with B, there are probably significant things left uncommunicated. So that if A takes sole responsibility, he may find himself trying to solve a problem, working with less information about the problem than is available to B. If, on the other hand, B takes some of the responsibility for changing, he can take some of his own peculiarities into account, and perhaps A and B can find a new behavior that fills the needs of both.

In summary

In this chapter the spotlight has been on a few common aspects of many behavior-change situations. First, we urged the reader to keep in mind that change is a highly emotional process. That expectation should lead the changer to treat logic as a useful but very limited tool for change.

The changer, A, has the serious problem of knowing what he is doing. Often As literally do not know what they are doing or why they are doing it. Their motives may be partially unconscious and unperceived and their objectives equally so. Advance thinking through of one's purposes may lead to a reorientation of objectives or even to the abandonment of a change project.

Changees ultimately control the decision to change or not to change. A can influence that decision but he cannot make it. For the decision that B makes represents the integration of the forces imposed upon him by A along with a whole multitude of forces over which A has no control.

Some As try hard to understand B's reasons for his present behavior before attempting to change that behavior. Others make no such effort but depend instead on observed similarities in all people. There are advantages to some degree of diagnosis of B. But if B ultimately controls the decision to change, then perhaps it is more important that B make the diagnosis of himself than that A make it of him. Moreover, the diagnostic process can be conceived of as a fact-finding or a feeling-finding process. The position is taken here that feelings are as important, if not more important, than facts in behavior-change problems.

Final responsibility for changing can rest with A or B, or it can be shared. Behavior changers, especially when they occupy superior positions, are wont to feel that the responsibility for change must lie exclusively with them. But if B can be made to accept some of the responsibility for changing himself, the resulting change may be more lasting and more generalized.

12 Authority
One model for influence

From the previous chapter's discussion of dimensions of the person-to-person influence process, we turn now to means and tools, to models for influencing behavior. In this chapter and the three that follow, we shall consider such models, examining each against the background of chapter 11.

This chapter and the next are centrally concerned with the role of power in the influence process. This chapter focuses on one form of power, authority; the next chapter on less structured and somewhat more extreme forms of power, pressure and coercion.

Perhaps it's important to start with a few generalizations. First: One way that people have often defined power is simply as influence that has worked. All successful influence attempts are thus considered (after the fact) to have been manifestations of power. If you have succeeded in getting me to do something you wanted me to do, then you have demonstrated power over me.

Another way of looking at power is from the input side, in motivational terms. The person who has strong motivation to influence or control the behavior of other people is said (as we said in part 1) to be *power motivated*.

In addition to the question of the nature of power, there is a large value issue. Power is often thought of pejoratively. We talk about "power plays," "power-hungry people," "power politics," and "power tactics." All of these have implications, if not of evil, at least of inequity or gamesmanship. All of them seem to stand in contrast to virtuous notions like "fair play" and "merit." And yet it is obvious to any executive (or any parent for that matter) that if we weren't pretty sophisticated about power and its uses, we would be dead in the water. If most of us weren't pretty skillful power tacticians, neither the organization nor the family would survive for long. This is not to avoid or deny the huge ethical problems that center around the power question. But it does seem important to recognize from the start of this discussion, that power and influence are parts of our everyday life. While each of us must properly be continuously concerned about using power ethically and justly, to deny its central role in human relationships is nonsensical.

What's "authority" in organizations?

This chapter focuses on one kind of power, authority. There are other kinds, too. Some of us have "expert" power, like physicians. Some have what has been called "referent" power—power that emerges from our relationships with other powerful people. Some of us hold "coercive" and "reward" power—that is, the power to punish and to reward other people through the dispensation of resources we control. This chapter on authority is mostly about what is usually considered to be "legit-imated" power. Authority is a slippery concept to pin down. It is mostly about formal rank and role and position as tools for controlling and influencing the behavior or other persons. But the chapter is also neces-sarily a little bit about the other forms of power too.

Industrial organizational structures are designed with formal au-thority in mind. We build organizations in the shape of pyramids in part because that shape makes the exercise of authority easier. Pyra-mids create differences in rank and status, and the people in higher ranks can use their authority to influence lower ranks. Superiors in industrial organizations almost naturally turn to authority whenever a change problem arises with subordinates. The very idea of *delegat-ing* authority rests on the assumption that authority can help people who have more of it to change the behavior of those who have less of it. In fact, we often even define the "superior" in a relationship as the person with more authority.

Like other tools, authority can be used expertly or blunderingly. And like other tools, it must be used by human beings. Top managers have long since unhappily recognized that the delegation of large quantities of authority to middle and lower echelons is no guarantee of effective supervision. If anything, some executives seem to supervise better with less authority than with more. And contrarily, some super-visors function better with more of it than less. The issue is not only how much authority but how it is used and by whom.

What is authority?

Let's try some definitions of authority, not to be academic but to try to clarify an important but fuzzy concept. Sometimes when we talk of authority, we are thinking about something formal, like *rank*. Authority can be defined by one's military rank, for example. The captain may not know exactly how much authority he has or even what it is, but he knows he has more than the lieutenant and less than the major.

Authority also seems, as we said, to be a form of formal power, again like military rank, that can be formally changed or delegated. "They," the "top brass," somebody up above, can change one's rank and thereby one's authority and thereby one's power.

Sometimes, however, we relate the words *authority* and *power* differently. We talk about someone with an "authoritative" (synonymous with "powerful") personality. Here we mean something like "influential" or "respect-evoking," but we do not mean formally delegable. We mean something the person carries around *inside* himself, like expertise, not something he wears on his shoulders.

Besides this mix-up between formal and personal authority, another confusion results from the word. Sometimes we talk about authority from the perspective of the manager who uses it, sometimes from the perspective of the managed on whom it is used. When we identify with the user, authority looks like a mechanism for coordination and control. When we take the perspective of the subordinate, authority looks more psychological; it is a mechanism by which we are rewarded or punished for our behavior.

Here's where we come out on what authority is all about: Authority is one of many kinds of power. It is formal, delegable, worn-on-the-shoulders power. Authority is power that enters the two-party relationship through the organization. It is an institutional mechanism that aims to define which of two members of a relationship, A or B, will be the superior. Authority is potential extra power, given by a third party (the organization) to some of its members in order to guarantee an *un*equal distribution of power; in order, in other words, to make sure that some people are chiefs and others Indians. Sometimes authority has nothing to do with relationships. For example, the organization may assign to A the power to spend some of its money for supplies. But very often authority does include power over other people, power to restrict or punish, and power to reward. Thus the president announces to the superintendent, in the presence of the supervisors: "You are permitted to decide to fire supervisors or keep them; you are permitted to decide to raise supervisor's pay to this limit or not to raise it." Now the superintendent has some authority—some additional, formal, potential power over and above any other power he may have carried into his relationship with supervisors.

A difficulty arises at this point. An organization (or a powerful person) cannot delegate all the power it possesses, even if it wants to. A C.E.O. (chief executive officer) can delegate only certain kinds of power by calling it authority. The forms of power over the satisfaction or frustration of another persons's needs are legion. In industry, power may take the form of control over income—a form delegable as authority. Or it may take the form of control over the terms of the relationship. That, too, is delegable as authority. It may be power to provide status or prestige. That, too, may be partly delegable.

But other kinds of power are not so readily transferred; for example, the power deriving from an individual's competence and skill or from a member's sensitivity to the needs of another. Sensitivity cannot be delegated. One's name, or one's social standing in a community, or one's whole personality may constitute significant forms of power in a relationship, and they too are nontransferable. In fact, only a fraction of the ways in which one person can control another's needs are readily delegable as authority. The delegable forms include mostly external, nonpersonal kinds of power.

This analysis suggests that a superior who turns immediately and exclusively to his authority is either ignoring many other kinds of power he may possess or else he derives all his power from his authority. In either case his effective range of control over other people will be narrow.

Authority as seen by those who hold it

If we ask a manager if authority is useful to him, he will have some ready and reasonable answers, among them these: Authority is indeed useful because authority is a mechanism for coordination and control in organizations. People have to be gotten to work on time. They have to spend some of their time working, rather than telling stories or visiting the rest room. They have to carry out policy and make appropriate decisions. They have to do all these things if the organization is to move toward its goals in some kind of coordinated fashion.

Certainly if authority is used as a tool for influencing behavior, it is not for influence's sake but for the sake of the organization. Moreover, if it is used most often to restrict and limit individual behavior—and thereby it blocks or frustrates people—that is because organizations are what they are. Industrial organizations are places where people cannot do what they please, where people are required to submit to certain restrictive rules and standards. If people finished projects when they felt like it or said what they felt like saying, no industrial organization could survive.

Given this view—and it is an extremely reasonable one—authority is a tool to restrict behavior (even if restriction frustrates), to create necessary homogeneity by leveling out individual variations. It is an important and efficient tool because it has the advantages of the shotgun over the rifle. We can broadcast restrictions, rules, and limits, and then use our authority to back up the rules when someone steps out of bounds. The mere presence of authority (precisely because it can be used to deter nonconformists) will keep most people within the rules most of the time.

The legal structure seems a fair analogy. Laws, in a sense, constitute a threat of frustration for anyone in the population who steps outside the bounds. We need laws, even though most people obey without threat. However, to carry the legal analogy a little further, even the threat of frustration can become insufficient when a specific law is seen by too many people to be too restrictive. The issue here is much like the issue of frustration versus deprivation (chapter 4). Restriction that only deprives is tolerable, especially if it has accompanying rewards; restriction that frustrates can backfire.

Authority as seen from the underside

We cannot observe authority in action just by observing the boss. Whether A has or has not blocked or frustrated B is determined almost entirely by B's interpretation of A's actions. The perceived world, we said in chapter 3, is the world that determines behavior. Thus the mere presence of the company president in a department may constitute a block for some people in that department. Or an extremely insecure employee, with a distrustful set of attitudes toward superiors, may interpret *any* act by a superior as a threat of frustration, even if the superior is busy patting him on the head. In fact, a superior almost always has to work harder than an equal or a subordinate in order to be seen as a rewarding, nonrestrictive force. The reason again is the dependency of the subordinate on the superior. No matter how nice Papa may be, he is still Papa, and the belt of authority around his middle *could* be used as a whip.

Even though the boss's position carries continual implications of potential frustration, the intensity of such implications depends on the boss's own behavior. Certainly many organizational superiors use their authority in ways that generate a great deal of confidence from their subordinates. Limited and consistent restriction can be seen by most of us as "reasonable," if the atmosphere of a department is generally satisfying of our social and egoistic needs.

Basically, then, most subordinates probably see authority in the same way superiors do, as a tool for restricting and controlling their activities. But though they may see the same thing, they attach different meanings to it. While the boss interprets restriction in organizational terms as control and coordination, the subordinates' interpretation may be far more personal. Authority is a mechanism for satisfying or frustrating their personal needs in a dependent relationship.

The propensity to obey authority

A few years ago, some impressive research was carried out demonstrating just how much many of us have come to accept authority and to obey it almost without question. The experiments were typical psychological ones in which volunteers were paid to serve as subjects. They were asked to help as "teachers" in a teaching experiment designed to test the effects of punishment on learning. They were given an electric shocking device and told to push the shock button every time the "learner" in the next room gave a wrong answer. They were also told to increase the intensity of shock with each wrong answer, if necessary, up to a point on the shock machine scale marked with danger warnings. The "learner" in the next room was actually part of the experimental team. His job was to groan and on occasion scream in pain as the shock got stronger. He would, in late stages of the experiment, beg to be released, and complain that he was suffering from a heart ailment.

The results came as a surprise both to the researchers themselves and to many other presumably sophisticated observers. They had forecast that very few subjects would push the shock buttons all the way. In fact, about 50 percent (and somewhere around that figure seems to hold up for many kinds of subjects) followed orders to the hilt, even while thinking that they were inflicting very severe electric shocks on a screaming middle-aged man with heart disease.

What those experiments suggest is that there is a strong propensity for people to obey even very limited authority. Apparently it is not just because we fear sanctions—like getting fired—that we obey. Most of us seem to obey anybody who wears even the simplist trappings of authority (in this case, a white lab coat), even if it is obvious that no significant sanctions can be imposed on us for refusal to obey. We may fuss and complain, but to an almost frightening extent, we also obey.

Perhaps then, we must be careful, as managers, about assuming that our organizations run because we are such effective users of authority. Rather they run because our people (long before they came to work for us) were taught to be obedient to any authority. We aren't masterfully authoritative. They don't just obey us. They obey anybody!

And if that is true, perhaps we should be more concerned about how *not* to use authority than how to use it. Perhaps we should worry, that is, about getting our subordinates to question our authority, to talk back, to ask why, before they do what we tell them to.

The advantages of authority

From the manager's viewpoint, the advantages of authority, especially restrictively used authority, are huge. We have already cited two of them, the control and coordination advantage; and the easy-because-any-damn-fool-can-use-it advantage. There are many others.

For one thing, one doesn't have to know much about any particular Joe Doaks to be fairly certain that firing him or cutting his pay or demoting him will strike at some important needs and thereby keep him in line. But one might have to know a good deal about the same employee to find out how to make work more fun for him.

A corollary advantage, then, is simplicity. Authority as a restrictive tool does not require much subtlety or much understanding of people's motives. How simple it is to spank a child when he misbehaves, and how difficult and complicated to distract him or to provide substitute satisfactions or to "explain" the situation. Given a hundred children, how much easier it is to keep them in line by punishing a few recalcitrants than to teach them all to feel "responsible."

No matter how "improper," we cannot ignore the fact that exerting authority is often personally gratifying to superiors, and therefore attractive. The exercise of discipline can be reassuring to those who need reassurance about themselves. Moreover, authority fits neatly with a superior's needs, if he has any, to blow off aggression deriving from his own frustration. When the parent spanks the child, not only does he change the child's behavior, he also provides himself with an outlet for tensions built up in him by his own boss, or by his spouse, or by the irritating, troublesome child.

Similarly, authority is sometimes seen, perhaps properly, as a way for a superior to guarantee his superiority. If one's subordinates know that a superior can and will punish readily, they are likely to behave respectfully and submissively, at least in his presence. The reassurance derived from these demonstrations of respect may constitute a great distortion in feedback channels, but it can be helpful to the superior's own uncertain psyche. The superior who takes an essentially supportive approach has no such reassurance. Like the good big brother of chapter 2, he may be complained to and complained against. He may get true feedback, even if it is unpleasant. He may have to tolerate emotionally upset people telling him stupid, even insulting things.

Restrictive authority has another kind of advantage: speed. A do-it-or-else order eliminates the time-consuming dillydallying of feedback.

But speed, as chapter 10 pointed out, may cost accuracy or morale. Where those issues are not critical, speed may be worth its costs.

Restrictive authority, we have said, also has the advantage of imposing orderliness and conformity upon an organization. By a threat to reduce some opportunities for need satisfaction, large numbers of people can be made to conform to fundamental regulations. A manager must make *sure* that his people stay through the required eight hours of the day. Even though the great majority may conform without external threat, the superior has to guarantee minimum conformity by all employees. The job of obtaining willing or self-imposed conformity without threat just looks too big to handle.

Moreover, this restrictive authority is efficient because it can be used on large numbers of people at the same time, even when one doesn't know much about the people.

If those are the pros, here are some cons worth thinking about. First, restriction may have some by-products. When A's activity interferes with B's efforts to satisfy important needs, B may not sit still very long. A often finds he has caught crabs instead of lobsters. He has changed behavior he had not intended to change as well as (or instead of) behavior he did intend to change. The child who is spanked every time he puts his hand into the cookie jar may learn to keep his hand out of the cookie jar, or he may learn to go to the jar only when Mama isn't looking. He may also learn (irrationally) that his parents are out to keep him from getting what he wants. Employees who expect to be censured whenever they are caught loafing may learn to *act* busy (and *when* to act busy) and also that the boss is an enemy. They are thereby provided with a challenging game to play against the boss: who can think up the best ways of loafing without getting caught—a game in which they can feel that justice is on their side, and a game they can usually win.

Restrictions, then, can be effective in changing specific *actions* in the direction A wants (B will *act* busy), but often only to the minimum that B can get away with. It is less likely to change B's attitudes, and when it does it may change them in the wrong direction, in the general direction of distrust and hostility.

Moreover, the circular element described in chapter 2 often enters the scene when restrictive authority is called upon. Restriction includes the possibility of a downward spiraling relationship. A begins by trying to change B through threatening frustration. B changes to the extent that he feels he must, but because he has been frustrated he will feel aggressive and in one way or another he may try to retaliate. A uses more restriction, this time to control the retaliation. Again B is frustrated, and wants even more to retaliate. And so it goes.

It might seem that a serious downward spiral can occur only in relationships between equals. If B is extremely subordinate, he should not have enough power to retaliate effectively. But subordinates do have power in relationships, even though the power may be considerably less than the superior's. As long as B has any power, and as long as the relationship exists, he can retaliate. Sometimes he does it by joining together with other Bs, perhaps to form a union. Sometimes he does it by cutting down or distorting the flow of feedback on which the superior depends so heavily. Often several Bs work together informally. I know, for instance, of a group of middle-management people who succeeded very well in defeating a superior they had come to dislike. Their method was passive resistance. They simply did everything the superior asked them to do—*and no more*. For every problem that arose, each of the three went to him for a decision. They took no initiatives, solved no problems by themselves. The superior was soon forced into the impossible position of trying to do every job in the department by himself.

The tenuousness and the self-defeating weakness of reliance on restrictive authority becomes apparent right here. When his authority has been "undermined" by the "sabotage" of subordinates, the superior who has depended on authority is likely immediately to assume that what he needs is *more authority,* because authority is the only tool he knows how to use. But can the president, in fact, delegate any authority by which the superior can coerce his subordinates into doing more than they are told? More likely the president simply begins to view the superior as the person on whom it is now appropriate to exert his (the president's) restrictive authority.

Such cases are many, and they are understandable. It is a serious error to assume that the *greater* power in a relationship equals the *only* power. As parents we may start out feeling that power lies exclusively in our hands, only to change our minds radically when one of the children runs away from home or gets hurt. It is also a serious error to think that delegable power—authority—is a useful weapon in *all* conflicts.

Still another difficulty with restrictive authority is its relative irreversibility. It is just not so easy to pat a subordinate's head after spanking him as it is to spank him after patting. For human beings have memories, and since restriction tends to reduce feedback loops rather than to build them, a series of restrictive experiences for B may destroy the possibility of further communication between A and B. Once A has lost communication contact, *no* tools of influence are useful.

In fact, the irreversibility methods sometimes creates difficulties even for those who preach a supportive, "human-relations" approach to these problems. A restrictive industrial manager, exposed to human-relations propaganda, will sometimes suddenly see the light and change his methods completely. The scowl turns to a smile; the office door is thrown open; a ration of grog is distributed to all hands. Then comes the rude awakening. Subordinates don't behave right. They don't dance in the aisles. They get drunk on the grog. They "take advantage" of their new freedom. A then decides he was taken in by the longhairs. He reverts to the "right" way, the way he had been using to begin with.

Obviously this kind of sudden reversal from frustration to satisfaction is silly, just as it is silly to leave a candy-starved child alone with five pounds of chocolates. The child is likely to stuff himself. His behavior is then taken as proof that letting children have their own way does not work.

Added together, the pros and cons of restrictive authority lead toward the conclusion that, in general, restrictive methods may be effective in situations that meet some or all of these conditions: (1) the change that A is trying to bring about is a change in specific overt action, rather than in generalized action or attitude; (2) the restrictions are seen by B as depriving rather than frustrating; (3) the balance of power is such that B's power is minimal and A's maximal. One might add a fourth condition: restriction can be effective when speed and/or uniformity are critical.

In a way, industry has learned some of these lessons, mostly the hard way. Authority as a direct and open restrictive weapon is, in fact, used more consciously at lower levels than at higher ones. Lower levels are (or once were) the levels at which B's actions, more than his attitudes, are the targets. They are also the levels at which employees have generally already retaliated against frustration by organizing, so that restrictions, openly imposed, are now depriving more than frustrating. And lower levels were also the levels at which the power difference between A and B used to be greatest, though those conditions, too, obtain less clearly today than they used to.

At higher levels we have tended to be more interested in changing attitudes than actions, and we have perceived that Bs have power, too. So, broadly speaking, we lean less heavily on restrictive authority as we move up the pyramid. A vice-president who shows up a half-hour late is not likely to be "disciplined." We use other, more subtle weapons to shape managerial behavior.

Key ideas in the authoritarian model

Consider now the relationships between this discussion of authority and our discussion in the preceding chapter of the dimensions of the influence problem.

First, what kinds of motives is the user of authority likely to be working from? Toward what objectives? Usually when we label someone "authoritarian," we intend to connote domineering, power-seeking motives. And certainly many of us are motivated by needs for power and dominance when we order our subordinates around. But many of us also use authority for less emotional, more rational reasons. Authority, in any complex social system, is a means to orderliness. We use authority as a mechanism to coordinate complex, multiperson activities, as well as a mechanism of control.

Second, what kinds of assumptions about B's motivations are made in such authoritarian views? One may be the old white-man's-burden assumption: the assumption that other people, like our children or our subordinates, are too dull or naive to understand anything but the direct use of authority or too lazy to work without a push. Another very different assumption that more rarely underlies the use of authority is that B perceives the world as we do, as far as authority is concerned; that he perceives our use of authority as reasonable and *legitimate*. It may not be that B is stupid at all. He may be quite intelligent, intelligent enough, in fact, to recognize the need for legitimate authority in this realm of activity. By the first view, the commanding officer gives the orders because the troops can't or won't make their own decisions. By the second view, the CO gives the orders because the situation demands some single center of control; because the CO's role is legitimate and necessary.

Third, what assumptions do the authoritarian models make about the relations between A and B? First, they assume that the responsibility for change lies with A rather than B. In fact, it is precisely out of authoritarian models that the idea that "authority requires responsibility" has emerged. When I give an instruction, by this view, its outcome is *my* responsibility. Responsibility is the burdensome but legitimate price I must pay for the right to give such orders.

Clearly, then, authoritarian motivation may range from needs for self-aggrandizement or protection of the status quo to needs for efficiency and achievement and orderliness. Notice, however, that these motives do not involve social needs for affiliation or love, nor is there very much emphasis on A's drive for personal success or upward movement. These latter two sets of needs show up much more strongly, as we shall see, in other models.

Notice, too, that the use of authoritarian means is usually quite direct and open. There is no slipperiness or circumlocution about an honest-to-god authoritarian boss. He gives his orders straight, clean, and, perhaps, nasty, too. Moreover, there is an impersonal quality to authoritarian influence. It is rules and contracts that are called upon for justification, rather than personal emotions like affection or hate.

The authoritarian father takes his son to the woodshed—or he believes he does—because the boy has broken known rules, or because the boy "has to learn." He does not consciously take him there out of hate or vindictiveness. Conversely, he does not offer rewards out of love or personal esteem, but rather because B has lived up to the rules, won the race, carried out his "duties."

It is these ideas, then, that prevail in the authoritarian model; the ideas of order, efficiency, system in a world full of people who are at best basically lazy; the idea of legitimate "rights" to use authority; the idea of impersonal, rational "contracts" between employer and employee.

Let us contrast these ideas now with the ones we shall encounter in the next three chapters on other approaches to influence.

In summary

Formal authority is a delegable kind of power. Power to influence behavior may also derive from other sources, largely from the skills, personality, and possessions of the changer.

Restrictive authority is seen by managers as a tool for coordination and control. It has advantages in simplicity and speed and in personal gratification to powerful changers who feel unsure of themselves. It also helps to establish a minimum level of conformity by all subordinates to the superior's standards.

A major difficulty inherent in restrictive authority is the probability of secondary changes along with desired changes in act-behavior. Restriction may constitute frustration and may consequently be followed by aggression toward the changer. Restriction may then incur only a minimal amount of the desired behavior change while also incurring significant increases in hostility and decreases in feedback. Restriction may thereby destroy relationships.

One big reason that authority works as well as it does lies in the subordinate, rather than the superior. Bosses can give most orders successfully not because they are inspiring or persuasive, but because most of us have been taught—from a very early age—to obey *anybody* who wears the trappings of authority.

Authority, as a restrictive mechanism, seems to be most useful in short-term, specific situations, where B's retaliatory power is minimal, where the change sought is change in specific overt action, and where the restrictions are perceived as depriving rather than frustrating.

The authoritarian view of influence is likely to be motivated in part by needs for order, efficiency, and control. It assumes either that B is less competent than A or that A's role legitimizes A's use of authority on B. And it assumes a kind of B who will accept and live by impersonal rules and social contracts.

13 Power tactics, pressure, and coercion A second model for influence

The authority we considered in the last chapter was a largely formal kind of power, organized into a quasi-legal system of roles. Everybody knows that colonels can give orders to majors. Indeed, the extent of that colonel's authority may even be quite clearly specified. But the kind of power we consider in this chapter isn't that bounded, legitimated kind. It's the power that one picks up where one finds it, and uses for his own or his group's end only so long as it works. In this chapter, then, we focus on coercive power—on blackmail, pressure, threat— the power tactic almost all of us despise, and almost all of us use.

Power as reduction

We need not remind the reader that much of the influence practiced in the world takes the form of blackmail, terror, threat. Such coercive power tactics usually depend on the *reduction* (or threat of reduction) of other people's means to need satisfaction, accompanied by a demand for behavior change.

The powerful nation masses its troops at the border of the weak one and says, "Unless you return that territory (which is, of course, historically rightfully ours) we will invade you." The gunman demands, "If you want your life, give me your money."

But notice: "Come to work on time," says the supervisor, "or you'll be fired." That's reductive use of power, too, isn't it? But for a supervisor to threaten to fire a worker is just a legitimate use of authority, isn't it?

So one of the big issues that arises here is that issue of social *legitimacy*. When is such reductive power considered by the relevant group, or by the larger society, or by the world, legitimate or illegitimate? When is such behavior within the rules and when isn't it? And who makes the rules, and how are they changed? That supervisor could have "legitimately" threatened to fire that worker in 1920; but because since then workers have used some illegitimate power tactics of their own, they have been able to change the game rules, so that that supervisor's behavior may not be legitimate today.

We are thus dealing with a great big floating crap game in this chapter, with the changing borderland of social rules and social values. We are dealing with the "social construction of reality." But we are also examining the psychological issue of the reductive uses of power.

Let's consider that psychological issue a little more before returning to the broader social issue.

Notice that the attempt to influence by reduction may not work for several reasons. The supervisor may have misjudged the relevance of his threat. This week B may be developing a new life-style that doesn't call for a job at all. The supervisor may also have misjudged B's vulnerability. Our B may have enough support from his buddies so that he's willing to test the supervisor's ability to carry out his threat. B organizes other Bs, for example, and sometimes discovers that the supervisor may be very scared of having his whole department aligned against him. Now carry the same conception along to areas not quite covered by the rules of the game and we are in the realm of this chapter. "Give me an exclusive interview," demands the columnist of the senator, "or I will publish a story about your weekend with your assistant." "Give up those defense contracts," demand some students of the university president, "or we'll sit in your office." "Convince your people to work at our rates," says the company president to the small-town mayor, "or we will move our plant out of town."

Coercive power and dependency

Notice, too, how closely associated coercive power is to the problem of dependency we discussed in part 1. If B is more dependent on A than A is on B, then A has the potential for exerting coercive power over B.

But we come now to the difficult question: How does one decide which member of a relationship is the more dependent? Most of the time the answer to that question appears more obvious that it really is. It is obvious that the lieutenant has power over the sergeant. Or is it obvious? It is obvious that the teacher has power over his student. The teacher can fail the student or discipline him. But if you have lived around a university during the last decade, you know that the balance of power in the teacher-student relationship has become much less clear. Students fill out faculty rating forms these days, and the dean reads them. Or they write letters to the campus paper or stand outside the classroom singing ribald songs about the teacher. Who's really in charge? Who's influencing whom? The reader surely can go on and cite other examples from his own experience. They may range from the father's discovery that his son is no longer willing to do what he's told (and may be able to back up his unwillingness) to the panic of the young officer when he discovers that his men are just going to stand there deadpan and not do what he has ordered them to do.

There is another kind of dependency which for most of us has been so implicit and so pervasive that we are seldom even conscious of it. It is the dependency involved in our relationship with the aggregate of persons we call society. It is our dependency, in effect, on law and order, our expectation that other people on the street, *all* other people, will obey minimal social rules in their interactions with us. When that dependency is violated, when one of us is mugged or someone smashes a window of our home, we begin to appreciate both the extent of our dependency on societal rules and the fragility of these rules. If we consider the other side of that same coin, we can empathize with what must be the exhilarating discovery of power that comes with a successful breaking of the social rules. How exhilarating it must have been for students to discover the vulnerability of the university, to discover, as it were, their own muscle.

Power and the rules of the game

The important point is that A may appear more powerful than B, but may in fact be more powerful *only so long as both A and B play the game within a particular system of social rules.* Those rules, implicit or explicit, may range from the acceptance of the hierarchy of authority in the organization to mutual respect for private property and to a mutual agreement not to use physical force. One important way to influence other people is by unexpectedly violating the rules of the relationship. Those violations can range from captors torturing prisoners, despite the regulations of the Geneva Convention, to students breaking classroom windows, to the politician making up and broadcasting the big lie about an opposing candidate. Notice that rule breaking is not the property of underdogs alone. It can be done by those at the top of the relationship, by a peer, and by those at the bottom. In the short run it is an infuriating and often terrifying experience for its recipients and a most difficult tactic to defend oneself against.

In the late sixties, for instance, blacks and other groups learned the value of "mau-mauing" and other rule-breaking (not necessarily law-breaking) techniques. Most college administrators, most executives, most government officials expect and can deal with "normal" across-the-table negotiations. But they are likely to be surprised, flustered, and, therefore, in a weaker bargaining position, when they are confronted by a hundred men, women, and children crowding the office, shouting approval of their leader's statements, and booing at everything the other side says.

Notice that such power tactics (or perhaps counterpower power tactics) need not be illegal, though they are often seen by their victims as "illegitimate" or "unfair." And notice that the utility of any particular surprise tactic is probably short-lived. Once the other side learns to expect them, defenses against them can usually be improvised. But the process is dynamic. If my defense is getting a law passed that forbids gatherings of more than five persons on the steps of public buildings, two things are likely: First, the creative invention of new surprise tactics, and second, the "freeing" of the other side to go outside the law into guerrilla or terrorist tactics against which "legitimate" defenses don't work very well.

Some sources of coercive power

If the reader is interested in the techniques of using coercive power, we can refer him to a whole variety of handbooks. They include a tactical manual on guerrilla warfare by Che Guevara, police handbooks, and the military interrogation techniques of the Chinese or, for that matter, the U.S. military. Man's skillfulness in coercive persuasion is as old as man. We've been extraordinarily creative in developing everything from torture racks to isolation cells. Man is expert in the techniques of extortion and blackmail, riot and political pressure.

But this chapter is not intended as a treatise on the tactics of coercion. It is intended rather as a discussion of that power which makes it possible for one person to coerce another.

Most of the sources of power we shall discuss supply "legitimate" power, but they can also be used as sources for coercion. Clearly, one such source is ownership. If I have the Bomb and you don't, I can coerce you. If I have money and you don't, I can coerce you if your needs are susceptible to manipulation by money. That last qualification brings up the issue of relativity again: I can coerce you only if the resources I have are useful in reducing your possibilities for need satisfaction. If your needs are irrelevant to my resources, I have no power over you. If your needs change so that they are no longer relevant to my resources, I no longer have power over you.

Another traditional source of power lies in numbers. Throughout the history of man, from the uprisings of the slaves to the organization of workers and the massing of armies, numbers have been one of the great sources of coercive power, modifying the behavior of kings and college presidents and even, on occasion, of generals. But numbers are not always, let us remember, used in the interest of the good guys. Crowds also lynch.

We must not forget still another extremely large and important power source of a very different and much more direct kind, anonymity. This time we are talking about a source which is seldom legitimate in any society and almost always directly coercive. If you have ever received an anonymous threatening phone call or have had a cross burned on your lawn, you have been exposed to this source. Once again, this kind of rule-breaking, coercive behavior is not necessarily limited to the underdog. On many occasions it is used by those in authority: from leaking anonymous stories to the press to having agents start revolutions. And although such coercive behavior is almost never officially sanctioned by society, it is a form of control that is nevertheless widely used, secretly, by many "legitimate" organizations.

Brainwashing

Since the Korean War, the word *brainwashing* has become well known in American society. It first achieved notoriety during that war as a characterization of the "illegitimate" methods used by the Chinese to convert American prisoners to the Chinese ideology. The phrase has since been used again and again in relation to issues like Patty Hearst's apparent collusion with her captors, or with the Reverend Moon's efforts to convert young Americans to his church.

Brainwashing is a loose concept with many different shades of meaning. Mostly it refers to a form of coercive persuasion that is *not* based primarily in threat. People are not "brainwashed" by being thrown into solitary confinement, or by physical torture. Brainwashing involves the rather subtle exploitation of some now well-known truths about the conditions under which people are likely to change their attitudes and behaviors. We know, for example, that most people are much more vulnerable to influence when their social support systems are removed, when they feel they are all alone. So if we can isolate a person from his traditional group memberships, from the people who reinforced and rewarded his old behavior, he is more susceptible to change. Obviously, with prisoners of war, we have the direct coercive power to remove people from their groups or to control the information they get. We can thus set up conditions that can cause an individual to believe that his buddies or his officers or indeed, his whole society, can no longer be trusted. Thus isolated, the individual becomes more susceptible to influence. Now, in his lonely state, we can urge him, cajole him, almost seduce him into taking small steps in the directions we choose. And small steps are enough. If we can now get him to agree to even a small piece of our ideology, we can go on to reinforce that choice and thereby make the next steps easier. We can, for example, now place that isolated individual into a new group composed of people who will support our subject and reassure him that his moves in our direction are right and proper. His new group not only helps convince him that his new behavior is legitimate, they also promise him full membership if he goes further.

The process of brainwashing is thus essentially no more than the process once referred to by a famous social psychologist as "freezing, unfreezing, and refreezing." It is a process, if one thinks about it, that we use widely in universities when we take a student from his home and put him on a college campus, isolating him from his previous group memberships and providing him with new paths, new routes that are locally reinforced. Companies, armies, fraternities do much the same things.

Where do we draw the line between legitimate freezing, unfreezing, and refreezing and illegitimate "brainwashing"? Is it "brainwashing" when parents try to "educate" their children into high moral standards? What if the moral standards favor sexual promiscuity or stealing or bombing institutions?

Business organizations and rule-breaking power

Here is an assertion we are ready to defend, but not to the death: American business organizations are now among the most civilized institutions in American society. *Civilized* in that assertion means using power within societal rules.

That assertion is more defensible when we talk about behavior inside the organization rather than outside. Even within the organization there are still plenty of examples of the use of questionable power tactics by one group against another, very much in the tradition of power politics. Certainly there are conflicts within the executive suite. But outside-the-rules coercive behavior has become very rare indeed within the organization itself. Executives don't strive for power in the same nefarious ways that dukes and princes used to. They don't often assassinate one another or kidnap one another's children or cheat on their employees' paychecks.

But they are by no means clean either, particularly in their relationships outside the organization. Private businesses have been known to bribe government officials. And certainly private organizations, particularly in the financial, marketing and political sectors, have been extremely creative in using tactics just barely within the rules in order to get what they wanted.

Of course, it wasn't very long ago that the tactics of coercion were very widely used by American business, internally and externally. Private businesses hired armies to beat down union organizers. They engaged in physical combat with other business for territorial rights, as in the days of railroad construction. They have used (and continue to use) espionage mechanisms.

But they are cleaner than any other institutions in our society, cleaner than businesses in many other countries, and probably a good deal cleaner than they used to be.

But if so, why? Because they are run by beautiful people? Perhaps because they've made it, because they have achieved legitimate power. They have created enough of the rules so that they don't need to break them very often. They have become the establishment. Sometimes, of course, they make dumb as well as unethical decisions that backfire, as when one large auto company a few years ago tried to get something on one of its then minor critics. All it succeeded in doing was in making him a major critic while losing a great deal of its own credibility.

By this line of analysis, we should expect the greatest use of outside-the-rules power, either by groups on the outside looking in, or by groups on the inside when they feel their kinds of rules are seriously threatened. It follows, doesn't it, that if we are in a period of social upheaval, we should expect more coercive pressures from weak groups trying to make their way to legitimate power, like unions a generation ago and militant black groups now, and more coercive pressures also from powerful groups which feel their power is threatened, like some males and some business organizations.

One can argue that achieving legitimacy makes coercive tactics less necessary. "Legitimate" organizations can make many of their own rules, so whatever they do becomes socially legitimate.

But it's not quite that easy. Society gets its fingers into the pie too. Legitimacy is not a fixed and permanent state. Nor is it entirely under the control of currently "legitimate" institutions. Organizations and behaviors considered legitimate by society change over time. Certainly businesses are one set of institutions for which the societal definition of legitimacy has changed quite frequently, despite efforts to maintain the status quo. In the last few years, more and more of what had previously been considered unquestionably legitimate in business practice has come under fire. Societal controls over business behavior are increasing, from what you can put on the label to how much you can keep secret from your employees.

If the general perspective of this chapter is correct, we should therefore expect more efforts by businesses to confirm their own legitimacy and, at the same time, a greater effort to subvert the increasingly constraining rules being imposed upon them. We are in a time when "strategies of legitimating" are becoming more critical in the lives of American organizations.

In summary

This chapter is about coercive power tactics as mechanisms of influence. Such tactics, ranging from torture to the torch, have been around for a long time. A major protection against them has been the evolution of social rules and humanitarian values. Those rules and those values, of course, depend heavily on forever-changing social consensus. Coercive tactics are periodically used, however, by deviant members or by legitimate organized authority to keep deviants in line. They are also widely and understandably used by deviants, who justify them as the only feasible means to the ends that they desperately seek. No society in history has ever developed foolproof protection against the use of such coercive tactics by other societies, by recalcitrant members of their own society, or by their own institutions under threat. Our society is no exception. Business organizations have perhaps come as close to moving beyond the need for such extreme coercive tactics as any institution in society. One might have suggested a decade ago that universities had come even closer. It is now not clear that they have. It behooves the business manager, even now, to look to his organization's defenses against such tactics and even more to the capacity of his organization to deal with them or with changing societal pressures without resorting to the same tactics.

Moreover, it is important to realize that the line between "coercive" and "normal" persuasion sometimes becomes very fine. The "brainwashing" that most of us deplore is in principle not very different from the "education" that most of us positively value.

So this is a red-alert chapter. Its message: Watch out! Coercive power is not dead. The rules of the societal game can crumble more easily than most of us had thought.

14

Manipulation
A slippery model
for influence

If we were to ask a military officer how he gets his subordinates to do things, he would talk about issuing orders and commands. That's authority. If we were to ask a loan shark how he makes sure his clients repay him, he would probably just point to the large, dour man standing in the shadows. That's coercion. But if we ask a salesman how he gets people to buy things, or a politician how he gets people to vote for him, we are apt to get different answers, but answers that have some common elements. We would expect to hear answers like these: "You've got to make them think it's their idea." "You've got to make them like you." "You've got to sell yourself." "You've got to be sincere." "You have to pay attention to their interests and the things that are really important to them." That's manipulation.

Just how are these answers different—as they obviously are—from the kinds of authoritarian ideas we talked about in chapter 12 and the coercive tactics of chapter 13?

One of the biggest differences, of course, is in the fact that the quotations we just listed pay a great deal of rather sophisticated attention to human emotions and human needs. They recognize that human beings are their objects of influence, and that human beings are complex systems with needs for affection, for dependency, for support, for approval and recognition, and all the rest. In this respect they contrast sharply with the authoritarian model, which assumed a kind of rational, hardheaded person who obeys rules and understands abstract justice. And they contrast with most coercive models which concentrate heavily on only a few human attributes, notably fear and greed.

But those quotations have another distinct flavor too. They have a quality of surreptitiousness, of slipperiness, at least in their implications. "You've got to make them think it's their idea," implies, of course, that the idea is really yours, not theirs.

We notice a third quality, too. These are the kinds of ideas that any of us might spout in talking about dealing with peers or superiors; but we would be less likely to pay much attention to them when dealing with our subordinates.

They differ from the authoritarian ideas in another way too. The person using an authoritarian model is likely to be fairly open and direct. When your boss tells you to do something right now there's nothing very secret about his motives or objectives. Even blackmailers and stickup men are usually quite clear in communicating their purposes! But when the used-car salesman, or the politician sidles up to you, then you begin to suspect some unannounced motives, some hidden purposes.

This point probably gets at the heart of the manipulative problem. It is the reason that so many of us want to reject it and retaliate against it. For this kind of attitude, the I-will-make-you-think-it's-your-idea attitude, is seen by most of us as an effort to degrade us, to play us for suckers. If A succeeds, then B never realizes he was manipulated and A wins. But if A fails and if B realizes suddenly that he is being manipulated, then B is apt to retaliate rather violently.

The growth of the manipulative models

The manipulative models have been with us for a long, long time. They show up in the writings of Machiavelli and even earlier. Since 1930 or so modern versions have become especially popular in sales training, an understandable phenomenon. For the salesman enters into a relationship of his own initiation with customers who are usually at least as powerful as he is. Authority isn't a very useful tool for him. On the other hand, the salesman has a rather clear and precise objective, which varies little from day to day or customer to customer. He doesn't want his customers to buy an automobile, he wants them to buy a Ford, and to buy it from him. So the salesman's problem is very clear. It is to get that person to do what A wants him to do, but to do it without authority and without coercion.

Out of this specific problem—the problem of trying to get someone else to do precisely what I want him to do, without using authority or other direct power—there has emerged a series of sophisticated manipulative models for influence. These models all share six key ideas, although they vary considerably from one to another in other respects. The six ideas are these:

1. A's motives should not be made fully known to B. A wants to sell magazine subscriptions, but he starts out to convince B that A is really not selling anything at all, just offering free samples. The gigolo really wants a white Mercedes, but the motives he communicates are love and nurturance.

2. Second, the manipulative models usually use the relationship between A and B as a tool for influence. Most of the manipulative approaches are essentially two-step processes: step 1 is to develop the relationship with B so that B comes to value it; step 2 is to use the now-valuable relationship itself as a bargaining weapon in bringing about change. The magazine salesman tries to develop in his customer feelings of sympathy and support because he is working his way through night school; and having thus touched nurturant needs in the householder, he offers his magazines as a means for that householder to show his support. The politician offers favors, little services to the people of his ward, and then asks of them only the little personal favor of their votes. The paternalistic manager takes a deep personal interest in his people, buys them gifts at Christmas and in other ways develops personal feelings between himself and his employees; and then, consciously or unconsciously, he uses that relationship, with its implications of loyalty and friendship, to get what he wants.

Just for contrast, it is worth pointing out that the complete authoritarian we described in chapter 12 does not move in the same direction at all. The personal relationship is set aside for him. The complete authoritarian focuses on the rules; the manipulator sells himself.

This manipulation of the A-B relationship can be thought of as an effort to create the kind of dissonance we talked about in part 1. First we make another person feel love and loyalty toward us, and then we demand of him that he change the beliefs he now holds dear. Thus we set up an imbalance. For B to love us and keep his contrary beliefs places him in a dissonant state. So he must choose between his beliefs or his feelings toward us. If we're clever, he changes his beliefs. But if we fail, it is understandable that the failure can be explosive, with the possibility of B shifting from extreme love to extreme hate.

3. A third and related characteristic of the manipulative models is the exploitation of dependency between A and B. While the authoritarian exploits dependency, too, he does so directly and always downward in the hierarchy, demanding that subordinates perform or get fired, that children obey or get punished. But the complete manipulator exploits dependency differently. He exploits it in both directions in the power hierarchy, using psychological power rather than legalistic authority. The manipulative executive, for example, may make his way upward in his organization by forming a close relationship with some higher-level executive and by trying to make that dependency reciprocal. He searches for a sponsor, someone with whom he can develop a parent-child kind of relationship. If he can be successfully dependent on some superior, then the superior will be reciprocally dependent on him. It is not surprising that we ascribe to women, in Western society,

a greater ability than men to manipulate dependency skillfully, for women have typically had to work from subordinate, or, at best, peer roles.

The manipulative executive is likely to exploit dependencies downward, too. He will not count on his impersonal role as the boss, but rather on personal dependency on himself as an individual. He may seek personal, intimate relationships with his people, and then use these deep personal attachments as a base for effecting change.

If he is really a consistent manipulator, he will try to have his superior and/or his subordinates develop very strong attachments to himself, but he will always hold back on the reciprocal end of the deal. A good manipulator never exposes himself completely. Some of his personal motives are always undisclosed. He must never become so entangled either with subordinates or superiors that he cannot abandon them if he needs to.

4. A fourth characteristic of the manipulative approaches is that they are apt to be extremely sensitive about the emotions of people. The good manipulator exploits people's needs for approval, support, recognition, dependency, participation. Aware of the potency of these needs in his two-step process, he makes great efforts to sell himself by satisfying other people's needs for recognition and attention. This awareness of widespread emotional starvation in our society is of course precisely what the over-the-line manipulators—the con men—exploit so successfully. But within the law, it can be these same kinds of needs that a manipulative spouse can exploit in his or her partner, currying favor, flattering, providing satisfactions that may be hard to come by elsewhere in the world. The manipulative partner thus increases the value of the relationship and the extent to which he or she may use it as a bargaining weapon. But the manipulator is also fulfilling the other partner's emotional needs.

5. A fifth related general characteristic of these models, a characteristic that is really just an extension of the two-step process, is incrementalism. The manipulator does not move precipitously, nor directly, nor completely. He influences in bits and pieces. Unlike the coercive holdup man, the con man moves slowly, establishing a relationship with his prey, letting him win a few hands of poker, and only gradually moving him along to where he wants him. If he is a good con man, he even "cools out the mark" after he has taken him; he takes steps to make the widow feel good after she has been bilked of her funds, so that she will not go to the police or retaliate against him.

6. Finally, it is worth pointing out that manipulative models not only exploit the relationship between A and B, but also *the relationships between B and other people.* There is a step beyond the process of

developing a relationship between you and me so that I can later press you to do what I want you to do. That next step is the use of group pressures, pressures by other people, Cs and Ds. The early primitive stages of the human-relations movement represented such a transfer from the exploitation of the A-B relationship to the exploitation by A of the relationship between B and others.

Much of the early talk about group participation, and many of the early experiments on group decisions, represented such an extension of the manipulative models. A still wanted to get people to do what he wanted them to do. And A still kept some of his motives to himself. But now, using group discussion as a tool, A did not work hard to develop the relationship between himself and the group. Rather he tried to develop cohesiveness and rapport *within the group*. Then when the group began to move in a particular direction, the individual member was pressed by the group to conform to the group's wishes. This device was not new, of course, even several decades ago. Any good rabble-rousing politician knows how easy it is to keep someone from saying "no" in a public meeting after 90 percent of the crowd has already shouted "yes."

So group participation as a tool for influencing behavior had its problems, too, especially in its earlier forms. One got workers to accept a methods change (a *predetermined* methods change) by holding group discussions and by getting group commitments to a decision to change. But in our next chapter we will consider some more recent developments on the participative side: collaborative methods for trying to effect change that make large use of groups, but which try to escape from some of the ethical and technical difficulties of manipulation. As we shall see, this fourth model differs quite distinctly from the authoritarian, the coercive, and the manipulative models.

When is it "helping"? When is it "manipulation"?

The line between manipulation and helping people often gets foggy. Psychiatrists score high on manipulation scales, while surgeons score low. But is your local psychiatrist or nondirective counselor or sensitivity group leader trying to manipulate you, or is he trying to help you? In fact, he probably comes a lot closer to manipulating you than does, say, your top sergeant in the army. Almost all of the "helping professions"—teachers, counselors, therapists, clergy, physicians, and nurses—must worry a good deal about the extent to which their efforts to change other people are manipulative. One criterion question, of course, is whether or not the changer's motives are exposed and open. But is it sensible for the physician to tell you exactly what he is doing and why? Might it not be his honest judgment that it is better to with-hold some information until he can build trust with smiles and small talk? Isn't it often wiser for a counselor to let the client begin to see the truth for himself, rather than blurting it out?

The point is that manipulation, as we have tried to describe it, is not always selfish or immoral. Manipulation is a method. One of the critical considerations involved in the choice of any method is the user's own values.

In summary

The manipulative models for effecting change have grown up mostly in settings where the use of authority was impossible, settings in which A is a peer or subordinate of B. The several manipulative models share some basic ideas: Manipulative As withhold some of their motivation from public exposure. Manipulative As tend to develop close relation-ships with B, often dependent relationships, and then to use those rela-tionships as a tool. The manipulative models tend to take two steps in the influence process, the relationship step and then the influence step. Manipulative As are sensitive to human needs and emotions, and they tend to work in bits and pieces, by indirection rather than by direction.

For most of us, manipulation is a word loaded with deplorable con-notations. But in lots of situations, the method is useful and, by most standards, moral.

15 Collaborative models Influence without authority or coercion

Authority is an impersonal, almost nonhuman tool. Coercive power seems a cruel, often hostile tool. Manipulation is a questionable and demeaning one. What then are other alternatives?

Some readers may already have discerned and perhaps been disappointed by the absence of rules of thumb in this section. The absence will continue, not willfully, but because the nature of the influence process obviates magical little rules. The means of influencing behavior do not reside in one person. They reside in the *relationship*. If Bs stood still, As could indeed devise rules for influencing Bs. But Bs move, respond, retaliate, change. So if we are to come up with any rules at all, they must be rules governing the behavior of the A-B relationship, not just the behavior of one of the elements.

It is true that we could play probabilities. We could say to our salesperson: "This is your spiel. Run it off like a phonograph record. Seventy-five percent of your clients will throw you out. Twenty-five percent might be influenced." But if a manager takes that view about influencing his subordinates, or his peers, or his superiors, he is in for trouble.

Without expecting rules for answers, then, we can ask: What are alternatives to the use of authority, coercion, or manipulation?

The AA model

Consider Alcoholics Anonymous. That organization effects deep and difficult influence with considerable success. Their objective is to cause drinkers to stop drinking. What are the methods by which such a goal can be achieved?

Many people have tried many methods on alcoholics. Wives have threatened to leave their drinking husbands. Churches have warned drinkers of everlasting punishment for their sins. Alcoholics have been isolated from alcohol and forced into "cold turkey" withdrawals. These are essentially restrictive methods, using power to punish. They are concerned with symptoms rather than causes. They aim at changing overt behavior rather than the more fundamental need or attitude. Some of them work some of the time. Often they don't work.

AA approaches the problem quite differently. Essentially, their procedure is the following:

They make the availability of their services (and their motives) known to the alcoholic (and he may choose not to avail himself of them).

If he chooses to attend a meeting, he listens to testimonials from ex-alcoholics (and he may be impressed by none of them—in which case he is again free to leave).

If he decides they know what they are talking about, he asks for help (but he doesn't have to).

He is given one or more "buddies"—once alcoholics like himself. The buddies make themselves available (if he chooses to call on them) to talk over his problem or just to hold his hand.

If he decides to try to quit drinking, it is not easy. So he calls on his faith in God, if he has any, and on his buddies. They provide help with support, with hand holding, with a supply of knowledge of the future— i.e., "Sure it's tough, but if you hold on a while longer, you begin to feel different, and then it gets easier, *and we know*." They also provide the knowledge that real changes requires a really new way of looking at the world.

When AA is successful, the alcoholic stops drinking. Often he then helps others to stop drinking as one way of handling the new void in himself.

One finds no threat, no command, no surreptitiousness in the process. The alcoholic stops drinking; he is not stopped. He is helped to change himself. He is helped by being shown alternative means, substitute behaviors, new sources of faith—by anything that will fit his needs. This is a predominantly augmentative, supportive process in which responsibility never leaves the changee.

Is management different from AA?

The manager will point out several differences between the problems faced by Alcoholics Anonymous and the ones he faces. First, AA can afford to wait for people to recognize their own problems and to seek help. The manager often cannot. He must bring about change even when people don't come to him seeking to be changed. Second, AA can let each person solve his own problem in his own way at his own pace. The business organization requires conformity to certain standard behaviors and to pressures of time. Finally, the manager will complain of the risk in this method, the lack of control over the changee. In AA's approach any alcoholic can just walk out the door any time he feels like it without changing at all. In business we have to be sure that people will do what needs doing; we cannot allow them to decide whether they would like to or not.

The alert reader will add still another objection: Where is the diagnosis, the understanding of causes so heavily emphasized in the preceding chapters of this book? In this AA situation effective behavior change seems to occur without any attempt to look into the source of alcoholism, into the frustrations and the conflicts that probably led to it.

These are partially valid objections, both to AA's method and to the whole-hog applications of the AA model to managerial problems. But before considering the modifications that need to be made to fit organizational requirements, it might be useful to consider the similarities between the AA method and those used by some other behavior changers.

Similarities between AA and other approaches

The AA pattern, in its broadest outline, is a pattern that has independently taken hold—for good or evil—in a great many segments of modern American life. It shares with the manipulative models a strong sensitivity to human needs, but there most of the similarity stops. It showed up in chapter 6, with the emphasis on learning as an active, responsible process in the learner. It shows up in educational thinking, in the position that a student's education is an active function of the student as well as of the teacher. The teacher's role is to provide help and knowledge as the student requires it and as he can integrate it. The teacher's job is not to make the student a passive sponge to soak in a pool of pedagogical wisdom, but to help him to help himself.

Child-rearing practices have gone the same way. Today's pediatricians talk to mothers about "demand" schedules, easy toilet training, affection and support. Rigid discipline, even great emphasis on personal cleanliness, have gone by the boards.

Counseling and psychiatry have moved rapidly in the same direction, with "nondirective" therapy and most other present-day forms of psychotherapy, including most of the rapidly growing behavior modification models.

Some may argue that these methods are precisely what is wrong with present-day America. They make us weak and soft and heaven knows what else. Perhaps they do. But if any manager feels that those methods will be our ruination, he had better look over his shoulder at his own plant. Related ideas have probably crept in disguise into his own operations. His first-line supervisors are probably practicing sev-

eral versions of "human-relations" techniques all over the place—
especially on him. His market-research people are going motivational.
They are using nondirective depth interviews and projective tests in
dealing with consumers. Ditto his employment interviewers. His industrial-relations people are probably trying to apply essentially the same
ideas to conflict resolution in their relationship with the union. And his
advertising people certainly are not using whips on the customers. Even
the C.E.O. himself is probably saying things like: "To learn to swim,
jump into the water," or "Experience is the best teacher," or "You can
lead a horse, etc." All these are just other ways of saying that we must
at least help to change ourselves; others cannot do it all for us.

The AA model and the managing process
Getting people to see a problem

We said earlier that three major obstacles block the use of the AA
approach in industrial problems. Let's examine these difficulties one at
a time to see whether or not they really are difficulties and, if they are,
to see what modifications are needed.

Here is a simple, but perhaps typical industrial behavior-change
problem:

> A new manager of a staff department grows increasingly con-
> cerned about the "weakness" of many people in his group. They
> seem stolid and unchanging, unimaginative and uncreative. They
> go on doing things as they have always been done, though it is
> obvious to the manager that many methods and procedures could
> be simplified, many new services could be rendered to line people.
> How can he make them less resistant to new ideas? How can he
> get them to take a new outlook toward their jobs? How can he get
> the lead out of their pants?

Alcoholics Anonymous, for the most part, simply waits for the
alcoholic to become unhappy with his alcoholism. Only then do they
undertake to change him. Similarly, psychiatrists wait beyond their
office doors for the patient to feel bad enough to visit a doctor. But
the social inefficiencies of such a process are obvious. Many people
may be psychologically sick for a long time before the sickness becomes
painful or crippling enough to make them look for help. And it doesn't
make much sense in education for a teacher just to wait for children
to want to learn arithmetic or in business for an executive just to wait
for his secretary to want to become a better speller.

And yet, although the manager cannot wait for people to see a
problem, theoretically his people will not change very significantly
unless they do see a problem, until they feel the tensions of relevant,

unsatisfied needs. So the manager's first task becomes: How do I make these people feel dissatisfied with their present behavior?

A variety of methods exists. Just waiting is one, and we should not discount it too quickly. Certainly many a young person in industry will notice by himself that a new superior is different from an old one and, apparently out of the clear blue sky, will come voluntarily in search of help, say, in learning how to write better reports. He may already have felt uncomfortably inadequate as he compared other people's writings to his own. Now he has his first opportunity to try to do something about it. The manager who had been wondering how to get this subordinate to improve his reports is now in a superb influence position. So, just waiting for B to encounter problems, to recognize his inadequacies, and to screw up enough courage to ask for help should not be thrown out altogether. Moreover, the very act of *not* acting, of waiting, especially by a new superior, may be seen by subordinates as a sign of tolerance and hence of accessibility.

But there are other possibilities besides waiting. One is to throw the subordinate into situations which will make some inadequacy obvious to him. The superior takes an active part here, but an impersonal part. The subordinate begins to see a problem because of the trouble he gets into with other people; the superior has simply caused these encounters to occur. Thus, a manager may cause one of his people to recognize problems by increasing his responsibility, by sending him out on difficult assignments, by exposing him to meetings with people who make no bones about their attitudes toward his staff. Such behavior by managers is unusual, for managers are wont to reduce the responsibilities of "ineffective" people much more frequently than they are to increase them, thereby reducing risk but also reducing the opportunity for learning.

Again, a superior can get a subordinate to recognize a problem simply through his assertion that a problem exists. Thus, a staff group which has been perfectly happy about the way things are going can be made to recognize a problem if the manager simply announces that the group's work is not quite up to standard. The teacher can do the same for a student by giving him a low grade on an exam. The difficulty here is obvious. Although the manager will probably succeed in getting the group to recognize a problem, he will also succeed (though he may not have attempted it) in having the group blame him for it. The group may decide that its work doesn't need to be changed but that the boss does. And sometimes they can do it. But a little anger or disturbance is to be expected and is usually temporary. To get people to see a problem by threatening, directly or by innuendo, that if they don't change they will endanger their bread and butter is, of course, straight restriction and carries with it all the dangers inherent in reactions to frustration. The danger is especially great when the source of the threat is the same individual who later wants to "improve" B's behavior.

This is the point at which a third party often becomes useful. Parents are often abashed at how easily a new teacher can accomplish what they themselves have been unable to accomplish. Some of the credit given the teacher, or the family doctor, or Uncle Joe, does not belong to them as individuals so much as it does to their roles in the relationship. Anomalous as it may seem, a position of lesser power may often be a better position from which to effect a behavior change than a position of greater power. Our manager may try to start a change with a threat, but then he may have to turn over the rest of the job to the personnel department. The third party can often do much more to effect change from there on out than the manager himself can do. In a sense the manager's action has made personnel's job easy. For now personnel, like AA, receives a knock on the door from a B who has already decided he needs help.

There is something paradoxical in this line of reasoning. This chapter is about methods for effecting change without authority. And yet it seems that one cannot effect change unless some restriction has been going on, so that B feels unsatisfied.

But that is only half the picture. It is true that people are likely to start wanting help after they find out that their present behavior isn't as good as they think it is. But there is a second possibility, too. People can want to change because they learn to want more or better or higher goals. We may start looking for a new car when the old one stops performing. We may also start looking because Detroit has put out some shiny new ones. The manager can add new information to his staff's picture of the world. He can open new promotional avenues, new opportunities for learning, for socializing, for satisfying all sorts of needs that can often stir even the most stolid of old-timers into activity.

This is the problem of raising levels of aspiration. It is a difficult problem. It requires the changer always to keep such opportunities for growth and development open—always new ones, always better ones. For as long as B can foresee new, better, and achievable means to the satisfaction of his needs, he will be ready to change his behavior in the direction of those better means.

The alert reader will notice that many of these techniques for getting B to see a problem are not very easily distinguished from some of the techniques labeled "manipulative" in the last chapter. A's motives aren't always fully disclosed, for example. And many of the suggestions call for indirection if not surreptitiousness. In this respect, as in the case of sensitivity to human needs, it is just plain true that manipulative models parallel part of the collaborative approaches. The differences between the two become clearer when one moves on to the way A uses his relationship with B, and in the locus of control over what will happen.

All this is to say that people don't change unless they get uncomfortable. One may use AA's method of standing by until the world makes the person uncomfortable; or one may do it by trying to raise levels of aspiration so that B himself finds his present behavior inadequate and awkward; or one may get a third party to use his power to make B uncomfortable. Some one of these methods or a combination of them is a theoretical requirement for getting B to think seriously about changing his behavior.

Diagnosis: Why is B doing what he is doing?

The second objection raised to the Alcoholics Anonymous method is that AA seems to ignore the causes of B's alcoholism. A good deal of emphasis earlier in this book was placed on the importance of understanding the reasons for B's present behavior, either the factual or the emotional reasons. Now a model shows up in which relatively little emphasis is given to such diagnosis.

The problem really is this one: Who must make the diagnosis? In many cases, it is more important for B to understand the causes of his own behavior than for A to understand those causes. In the AA model the buddy provides the alcoholic with an opportunity to communicate any facts or feelings that may be relevant. If they are communicated aloud, it is true that the buddy may come to understand them, but, much more important, the alcoholic may also come to understand them. And if one already has someone who wants to change, then it is far more important that he understand what he is gaining or losing from his present behavior than that someone else understand it.

This is not to say that A needs no understanding. It is only to say that A's understanding of B's problem is often not nearly so important as B's own understanding of it.

Let us return here to the problem of the new manager of an ineffective department. His job is to revivify the department—without changing personnel. How much does he have to know about why his people are unimaginative, unenthusiastic, unproductive?

He has to know more about *how* they feel than *why* they feel that way. He does not need a case history on every person so much as he needs enough understanding of feelings to estimate the meanings his actions will evoke. He has to know whether his people have just been waiting for a break and are all ready to grab it or whether they have settled firmly into a path of safe stolidity. He has to know something about their dominant needs and dominant fears. He has to know these things primarily in order to know how to communicate his conception of their inadequacies to them. For to suggest great new responsibilities to people who are fearful even of their small old ones may not get them to recognize a need for change but only to deny it more completely. *What's behind these feelings is usually better left as B's own business.* The present feelings, more than their causes and origins, are the most important working materials of the industrial behavior changer.

Who controls the change situation?

The third objection to the AA method is that AA seems to have so little control over the alcoholics' behavior. At any step along the way B is free to reject the whole process and to leave the situation without changing. In organizational situations, allowing B such opportunities would seem an extremely risky process. But those risks are worth thinking about.

Consider again the new department staff manager. First, as manager, he can always veto what his people decide to do. He can give his subordinates opportunities to change themselves, and, finding that they fail to change in accordance with his wishes, he can still resort to his authority. So the only risk added by giving B more leeway is the possible loss of time if the method fails.

On the other hand, if the kinds of behavior changes sought were only changes in overt behavior, then there might be a good case for tight control. If all the manager wanted was his people's putting their shovels into the ground and lifting them up full of dirt at specified intervals, and if the manager could afford to stand over them to make sure they carried out the ritual, then obviously he could actually exercise pretty close control. But in practice the kinds of changes the manager usually seeks are changes in brain as well as muscle behavior. He wants his people *to make decisions differently* than they did before, and he knows perfectly well that many of the decisions will have to be made in the manager's absence. Though he can watch to see that a worker uses his shovel right, he often cannot watch to see whether he is using his brain right. Since that is the case, is it actually riskier to let subordinates decide they want to change and then to make decisions that fit their changed perceptions of the world? Or is it riskier to force them to change, so that when they face a new decision they face it with a mixed feeling of wanting to do it and of resentment against having to do it?

The answer seems clear. The manager's control, in the sense of his ability to foresee his subordinates' behavior, is far greater if he has given them an opportunity to accept or reject change (and knows where they stand) than if he has required change without obtaining "honest" feedback.

Even self-imposed change is uncomfortable

AA does not have an easy time changing people. And people do not even have an easy time changing themselves. Since any behavior change usually represents giving up some previously adequate behavior in favor of some new and untested behavior, any behavior change will be accompanied by some degree of tension and anxiety. So it is with the switch from one job to another—butterflies in the stomach on the day or two preceding the first day on the new job.

Although he uses a permissive, augmentative approach in trying to effect a change in his subordinates, our manager must still expect B to show this kind of tension and anxiety. The changer probably cannot prevent anxiety in B, but he can help to alleviate it by encouraging and supporting B's efforts to change.

A generalized pattern of collaborative influence

So the AA method has some limitations and some difficulties for industrial use. But perhaps by making some modifications we can set up a general set of conditions for effecting behavior change in continuing relationships:

1. *B perceives a problem.* AA waits for people to perceive a problem. In industry one must often take action to get them to recognize that a problem exists and that consequently a change is necessary. We suggested several possibilities, all the way from simply telling B that his present behavior is inadequate to manipulating the world so that he runs into inadequacies in his own behavior. But the changer must always beware lest the problem B perceives is the changer himself.

2. *B takes responsibility for considering alternative ways of behaving (and if possible seeks A's help in discovering additional alternatives).* When B has decided he has a problem calling for change, it is for him to consider the possibilities for change and for A to provide help.

3. *A and B mutually communicate the implications for both A and B of one new method of behavior versus others.* Since A is the person who is seeking the change, and since the change that B selects is

important to A, A must have an opportunity to feed back to B the implications of one alternative or another. Thus possibly B may decide to change, but to a behavior that is *still* unacceptable to A. This unacceptability is one real factor in B's deciding whether or not the alternative is feasible.

4. *B selects an alternative which A can accept.* The responsibility for deciding what B shall do and how he shall do it still remains with B. Especially if A is a superior, B's selection will have to be acceptable to A, although *acceptable* may not be the same as *ideal.* This is a little like collective bargaining but even more like a discussion between husband and wife about where they shall take their vacation. If a location can be found that is entirely acceptable to both, all to the good. If the location is only a satisfactory compromise to each, that is still pretty good. If no compromise is possible, then A, if he is in a position of authority, can always revert to the simple use of the veto.

5. *B tries to change. A supports.* It is at this point that A's role shifts from that of provider of information to helper and supporter and reassurer. For it is here that tension and anxiety may show up in B. After taking a few baby steps in the new method, he may decide that this new behavior is hopeless or ridiculous. A can help by providing knowledge of the future, reassuring, making B feel that he is progressing (if he is actually progressing). It is here, too, that A can expect to come under overt or covert attack. It is A after all who has "forced" B to try this new, awkward, and inefficient way of behaving. The great mistake that A can make is to insist he is not to blame and to argue the facts of the case. What B needs is help, not argument.

6. *B finds the new method successful and integrates it as part of his behavior, or, finds the new method unsuccessful and abandons it.* After being nursed along in his attempt to behave differently, B's skill may increase and he himself may find the new method serving his purposes better than the old. B can then be said to have changed. But if B finds that the new is not so good as the old, he may revert to the earlier method, if that is still possible, or he may move to a third method. If the latter is his choice then the whole process begins again.

These six steps constitute a crude and incomplete set of conditions for collaborative behavior change in continuing relationships. It is a difficult set of conditions to bring about. But the important question is whether it is more difficult and more time consuming than the beguilingly simple use of authority or the strategic planfulness of manipulation. If the time and energy that must be devoted to the unforeseen by-products of other methods are added to the total, the restrictive and manipulative processes may be even more difficult than the collaborative one. Moreover, one of the most important advantages of collaborative methods is that they tend to become easier with time. For Bs who have "been changed" by this method are likely to develop feelings of confidence in A that make future changes in the relationship easier. Such feelings of confidence may even allow A to use authoritarian methods effectively because they are no longer seen as frustrating.

In later chapters we shall try to show how these approaches have generalized to groups and large organizations.

In summary

Alcoholics Anonymous seems to do a good job of changing people without much call upon authority and without the guile of manipulation. Its method appears to be uncontrolled and uncertain, but with modifications it may be much more applicable to organizational problems than one might guess.

The basic assumption underlying the AA approach is that people must take most of the responsibility for changing themselves, and changers therefore must be helpers rather than coercers or manipulators. A superior's authority thus becomes a supply of means by which to help subordinates satisfy their needs through work rather than a supply of ammunition with which to threaten, reduce, or seduce them. The process becomes much more of a shared, collaborative activity, and less of one in which one person simply acts to influence another.

16 Influencing through pay and performance appraisal
Toil and trouble

In almost every organization, some people are paid more than others and some people are promoted more quickly than others. Most managers figure that most people want more pay and more rapid promotion; so most managers try to use pay and promotion as tools for influence. They try to get people to work harder or faster or more effectively or longer by holding out the promise of more pay or a better job. Most managers also feel that if they pay some people more or promote some people faster, they must have a way to evaluate people's job performance. They need a way of deciding who are the "better" people and who are the "worse" ones.

This chapter is about pay and performance evaluation and the ways that they are used and misused as tools for influencing human behavior. The first part of the chapter is about both of them, because very often they are clearly tied together, with higher performance evaluation justifying more pay.

The subtitle of this chapter, "Toil and Trouble," says a good deal about the problems generated in organizations by these twin time bombs. They are messy, difficult, double-edged tools that as often as not yield unintended negative changes along with the intended positive ones. They often generate frustration, anger, sabotage, gamesmanship, and cutthroat competition. But organizations can't seem to get along without them. So let's look at them and try to figure out some ways of using them to produce more positive results.

This chapter is divided into three major parts. The first considers some general problems that underlie both pay and performance appraisal. In the two sections that follow, we look in more detail at some specific issues important to each one.

Some underlying ideas about both pay and performance evaluation

Consider the following generalizations about pay:

173

1. Managers pay people in exchange for good work.
2. Managers pay people as a reward for good work.
3. Managers pay people to motivate them to work harder.

And then consider these generalizations about performance appraisal:

1. Managers appraise people's performance in order to identify the better workers.
2. Managers appraise performance so that they can reward better performance.
3. Managers appraise performance in order to motivate people to do better work.

All those are statements on the managerial side. Now consider these from the employee's side, about pay:

1. Employees want and expect to be paid in exchange for their work.
2. Employees want to be rewarded if they do better work.
3. Employees are indeed motivated by the promise of more pay.

And on the employee side, here are some statements about performance appraisal:

1. Employees want to know where they stand.
2. Employees want recognition for extra effort.
3. Employees want feedback about specifically what they need to do to improve their work and to get more pay.

Within limits, it seems reasonable to say that all of those statements are approximately true, and that should make the whole situation look beautiful. We have a nice match between what managers want to get by paying and by evaluating performance, and, on the other side, what employees want to do to get more pay and more positive evaluations. What can be wrong with such a happy marriage? Plenty! In just about every organization, pay and performance appraisal are thorns in the relationships between manager and employee, in relationships among employees, and in relationships among managers.

Here are just a few of the employee-to-manager complaints that are familiar to every manager: "How come he got a 7 percent raise and I only got 5 percent?" "How come the industrial engineers want to lower the piece rate now that we've finally become good enough at this job to make some real money?" How come, now that I've done exactly what you told me at last year's appraisal, I still get a lousy appraisal this year?"

Or in relationships among employees (often unexpressed): "You want to make the presentation so you'll look good. Why can't I make it?" "You're always sucking up to the people upstairs!" "If I share my idea with you, you'll get the credit I should get." "You got a fatter raise than I did, but I really did most of the work." "But I deserve more. I've been here longer and I've got five kids!"

Or among managers: "How come, when you rate the people in your department, they all get top grades? They can't all be cherubim!" "Just because the estimating department did a lousy job, do we all have to lose our bonuses?" "You just gave that bum a good performance appraisal so that you could get him out of your group and into mine!" "You hired that fresh MBA brat and paid him more than we get, even though we've been here five years!"

It isn't hard to transfer these sorts of problems from the work situation to, let's say, the school situation. For most students, grades are the equivalent of both pay and performance evaluation. And for both teacher and student, grading has been a perpetual source of toil and trouble. For the student, there are questions of justice: "The exam was not a fair one!" "I got just one point less than he did, but I get a B-minus and he gets a B. Yet I always came to class and he almost never did!" "The grades on these papers aren't fair. They were just your subjective judgment." "But I really know the stuff. Just because I do badly on those dumb multiple-choice exams doesn't mean anything." "Why do you have to grade on a curve? If we all did well, we should all get good grades!" "Why did you give us all just about the same grade? Some of us worked much harder, and I learned much more than others, but we weren't rewarded for it."

Whenever we try to evaluate people's performance differentially and to reward appropriately, we always end up with some bills to pay. That doesn't mean we shouldn't do it.

Two relevant underlying propositions about the nature of human beings are these:

The more rapid and accurate the feedback people receive about the results of their past actions, the more quickly they learn. Performance evaluation tries to give people feedback so they can learn where they went wrong and where they went right in order to go righter next time. "Right" of course, is defined here in terms of the organization's interests.

Second proposition: People (or any other animals) will tend to repeat behaviors that have been rewarded. Hence, if we can pay people for doing the "right" things, they will do more of the right things.

There is a third behavioral subproposition that belongs here: The closer (in time) the reward to the activity one intends to reward, the higher the probability of repetition of that activity.

Those are sensible generalizations that support differential reward and appraisal systems. But there are also, in our society, some widely shared human values that become central here. One of them is the democratic belief in equal justice for all. Another one is the belief that harder work deserves greater reward, a belief engendered by the Protestant work ethic. But we also believe in teamwork, in trusting and cooperating with one another. And here, of course, is where the trouble starts—where the behavioral propositions meet the social values. Who has really worked harder? What's just and what's unjust? When should the individual cooperate? When should he compete?

Our individualistic values and our empirical knowledge drive toward differential pay systems and differential performance appraisals. On the other hand, we hold, whether we like the word or not, collectivist values. We believe in teamwork, in cooperation, in mutual trust and mutual support. And everywhere in our society the tension between those two sets of beliefs generates trouble as well as productivity.

So the message here is: *Do not expect to solve pay and performance-evaluation problems in your organization!* In any future that this author can foresee, those issues will continue to boil and bubble. And we will need constantly to be adjudicating, modifying, correcting to try to minimize the costs and maximize the advantages of any system we choose to use.

Alternative ways to pay

Given all these problems, it is not surprising that many different systems for paying people have been devised, defended, and criticized. Here are three of the most prominent efforts.

Tying pay to performance: Incentive schemes

For a long, long time incentive systems for paying people have looked a lot simpler than they have turned out to be. Their history goes back to cottage-industry days, to take-home work in textiles and other industries. The underlying notion is beguilingly straightforward: We pay you for what you produce. For every unit of work that you perform, you get a unit of pay. If you don't produce, you don't get paid. If you produce more, you get paid more.

On the shop floor of many factories today, individual incentive programs frequently take a mixed form. An employee typically receives a basic hourly rate, with incentive bonuses for units produced above some standard. Similar systems can be found in selling groups with incentive commissions paid for sales produced.

Versions of this system show up (over longer time spans) in the executive suite, where bonuses for outstanding performance are sometimes paid at year's end.

It is beyond the competence of this author to assess the overall costs and benefits of such efforts. Certainly many of them have been historically associated with "exploitation" of workers, and with sweat-shops. There are those who feel that they are by their nature socially or psychologically dysfunctional.

One of the major drawbacks to incentive schemes is their tendency to generate organizational game playing, by both managers and employees. The history of individual incentives on factory floors, for example, is fraught with accusations from workers that managers change rates as soon as people turn out to be skillful enough to achieve the existing rate. And on the managerial side, the argument has been that workers often purposely and secretly hold their work pace down or surreptitiously develop tools for beating the system. So instead of generating trust and cooperation between management and worker, they tend to generate enmity.

And understandably, too, individual incentives drive people to do what they are being paid for, and *not* to do what they are not being paid for. So problems arise around issues like maintenance of equipment, helping out others in emergencies. The same sort of game playing shows up among salespeople and in other groups where individual incentives are frequently used. Salespeople may secretely intrude on one another's territories to increase their own sales, or overload customers to make short-term sales records look good, sometimes at the cost of long-term customer relations. Or consider the perpetual problem of the plant manager in a decentralized organization: If, over the short pull, he can turn in an outstanding performance at his plant, he may be promoted to a larger plant or to headquarters. There are all kinds of ways to make that short-term performance look good, at the expense of long-term results. He can reduce short-term costs by letting equipment deteriorate. He can let labor relations go to hell if he knows he will be transferred before the strike vote is taken. He can play games with inventories of finished goods and raw materials.

Just to emphasize some of the difficulties that may arise with individual incentives, consider the following example:

Eight employees work at removing casings from skinless frank-furters. The frankfurters are molded in cellophane-like casings which must be peeled off after chilling. The employees stand alongside a conveyer, pick up the frankfurters, hook a fingernail under an edge of the casing and strip it off. This is the kind of straightforward, repetitive job that is almost ideally suited to an individual incentive rate. So the industrial engineers work out a standard, succeed in getting union and employee approval, and put the incentive rate into effect.

The rate works well for a while until one of the group hits upon the idea of taping a small razor blade to his finger. The "other people" factor shows up at this point. This creative technological improvement is immediately adopted by all the other employees (who are not, for good reason, as "resistant to change" in this case as they are purported to be in many others), and productivity per worker increases several hundred percent. Now the take-home pay of the group is far out of line with the pay of other employees doing comparable or even more skillful tasks in other departments. Management's motives now need reexamination. If management changes the rate, the union will accuse it of reverting to rate-cutting practices and of reneging on its contract to pay for productivity. And so on.

Psychologically speaking, the example shows how the logic of individual incentive pay is wrong as well as right. It is right in the sense that it usually ties meaningful rewards to the kind of effort that the rewarder wants. It is wrong in what it omits: other people, other worker needs, and managerial needs and in its failure to take interdependence into account. The assumption is that the total job of a company can be broken down into individual subparts, each subpart just the right size for one individual in the organization. The work of the organization will be accomplished best (this argument runs) when each person does his job as effectively as he can.

Many psychologists like to point out the fallacy in such reasoning. The whole is not the sum of its parts, they argue, but something much more, because the parts are interdependent. A tune is more than the notes that make it up; the bicycle remains a bicycle even after every one of its original pieces has been replaced. Contrarily, all the parts are not a bicycle, not until they are put together in one particular way. If every person looks at his own small task alone, ignoring its relationship to other tasks, the greatest total productivity will not be attained.

It is easy to show the same phenomenon in experimental situations, just as long as intercommunication and interaction are required. For example, suppose we give each of five individuals several pieces of a puzzle. No one has enough pieces to complete his own puzzle, but among the five there are enough pieces to complete five puzzles.

Suppose we set up an individual incentive system. We say to each: "You will be paid in accordance with the speed with which you can put together your puzzle. The one who makes his puzzle first gets first prize, the one who makes his last gets the booby prize." Under these conditions, with each individual concerned about his own immediate productivity but necessarily caught in the trap of having to give up some of his pieces in order to get others he needs, the total productivity of the group in X minutes is usually less than five completed puzzles.

Change the incentive system now so that each person is given an equal share of the prize money, the prize money being determined by the total number of puzzles the group can complete in X minutes. Five completed puzzles are the likely result.

But it is only when there is such interdependency, such a need to trade off pieces with other people, that this disadvantage of the individual incentive system shows up so clearly. For if we give to each person all the pieces needed to complete his own puzzle, it may well be that he will complete it fastest under conditions of individual motivation. If management can indeed faultlessly divide and plan the parts of an operation so that each part is actually independent of any other part, then management can truthfully say, "All that we want this worker to do is to produce as many of these pieces as he can produce."

Such conditions are rare in the industrial world. We still find them occasionally in home work situations, and they are sometimes approximated at lower levels of industrial organizations. But only approximated, because most managements, when they reflect on it, want people to do more than their job. They do not really want the individual employee to go on blindly punching out blanks when his machine needs lubrication; they do want him to take a few seconds off to show the new employee at the next machine how to cut down his enormous scrappage; they do want him to report a fire when he sees one.

In the puzzle experiments just mentioned, an interesting thing may happen. Subjects often refuse to accept the individual incentive rules of the game. Many of them simply don't serve their own "best interest"; they insist on trading pieces they know will produce puzzles for two other people, even if they can't complete their own. Moreover, they begin to look sheepish and unhappy if they sit with a completed puzzle before them, being stared at balefully by the others they are blocking.

As one goes up the scale in an organization to higher levels of responsibility, these points become far more obvious. At higher levels we seldom say, "Do this—and don't do anything else." For at higher and more technical levels more and more decision making must be left to the individual. He must define for himself more of what a good day's work is.

Although we cannot very well rank people's wants, we can be fairly safe in assuming that money is not all they want all the time. Even as early as 1927 the Western Electric researchers were pointing out that the introduction of individual money incentives could create psychological conflicts by forcing people to choose between money and the important social standards of their own group: between cooperation and competition; or between the need for approval of one's group at work and the approval of one's spouse when he or she sees the paycheck.

Like most conflicts, these too may be solved by unexpected means. One compromise for a person caught in such a conflict is to work out some way to beat the system and yet maintain or even improve his relationships with others. The development of a new jig hidden from management can satisfy both needs. Aggression is another way of working off the tension evoked by such conflicts. And who is the ideal target?

Moreover, the control of individual incentive rewards is perceived by employees to lie almost exclusively in the hands of an unpredictable and not always beloved managerial big brother. One should therefore expect to find ingenious and powerful forms of resistance. Incentive plans then may become pawns in games of strategy, with management seeking always to plug potential loopholes in the system while employees, in ways that can be unbelievably creative, drill new holes in "impossible" places. As a consequence, many industrial engineers find themselves caught up in a frustrating, never-ending, and unpopular holding-action strategy. If the socially determined production ceiling has become a commonplace in plants with individual incentives, so has the unhappy, slightly embittered industrial engineer.

In two ways, then, the simple maxim "A good day's pay for a good day's work" becomes hard to implement. First, we have to specify, as managers, whether we want a good day's work from *every* individual, or a good day's work from *all* the individuals. The two are not the same. Second, even if we want a good day's work from every individual, money isn't always enough to get it, especially if the means we provide for getting money conflict with other available means to social and egoistic satisfactions.

If this picture of the individual incentive seems unattractive, the reader should keep the alternatives in mind. In many, many situations, when the alternative is a flat rate, the individual incentive can and does yield significant improvements, both in productivity and morale. When employee confidence in management's integrity is high and when the "atmosphere" of an organization is cooperative and friendly, the addition of an individual incentive may do much good and little harm.

Group or unit-wide incentives

Another method of paying that has been gaining in popularity involves shifting the incentive from the individual to the group, or even to the whole organization. We've been doing something like that for a long time in the way we pay off members of winning and losing teams in the World Series.

Consider, for example, a small company of, say, three hundred employees, which chooses, instead of individual incentives, one of the many varieties of multiple plans. Assume it chooses the Scanlon plan, which is itself an extreme within the profit-sharing group. In a sense such a plan does not properly belong in a chapter on money incentives, for though it begins with money incentives and though money incentives derive from it, it can be better thought of as a plan for the psychological reorganization of a company.

The elements of the plan are these: (1) A monthly bonus for everyone in the plant based on an index of the overall productivity of the plant—an index that is a satisfactory measure of improvement in the organization's efficiency. (2) The introduction of production committees. If every worker's take-home pay is tied not to his individual productivity but to the productive efficiency of the company as a whole, then the production committee becomes the mechanism for tying everyone's efforts to the goal of productivity.

Notice that this plan includes the same assumptions made in individual plans. But profit-sharing plans also add two others: interdependency and social and egoistic needs.

These two additions are surprisingly important. The underlying proposition of individual incentives reads something like this: Individuals will work harder if they are individually rewarded with money for harder individual work. The profit-sharing modification is of this order: Organizations will work harder if they are organizationally rewarded for harder organizational work.

The two propositions do not even contradict one another. The second is an extension of the first. We do not have to prove one right and the other wrong; we have only to decide whether we are dealing with *independent* or *interdependent* individuals and with simply motivated or multiply motivated ones.

The second proposition assumes that individuals in industrial organizations are both socially and economically interdependent. It therefore defines an individual's job differently than the first. His job is no longer to punch his press as productively as possible; it is to punch his press in a social environment, to think about ways of improving the operation of his press and the company, to help whenever helping other people in the plant will contribute to the overall efficiency of the organization, and finally, when faced with unusual decisions, to try to make those decisions which will contribute to total efficiency.

One result of such a plan is an increase in feelings of responsibility for the total operation on the part of all members of the organization. For now it is harder to make management the scapegoat for all problems. If production, and therefore the bonus share, drops, there is no tight rate to blame it on. If some people work too slowly or stupidly, it costs everyone something. What should everyone, not just management, do about it?

This increase in employees' "ownership attitude," however, is not an unmixed blessing. Even though most managers insist they want their people to develop one, an ownership attitude in each employee means that each employee may take a serious interest in things management considers its private property. It may mean, for example, that the machine operator now expresses interest in the sales manager's decisions. He may question such decisions. He may want an accounting for the sales department's failure to bring in a large order. At this level secondary and tertiary changes in atmosphere and organizational structure are likely to occur. Notions about secrecy, about prerogatives of one group or another, are likely to be battered down.

If profit-sharing plans succeed in developing what they set out to develop, a strongly active desire on the part of everyone in the plant to improve the plant, what then? Where individual incentives so often sharpen the line between management and employees, these profit-sharing plans tend to obviate it. They tend to push the whole organization in the direction of oneness, in which everything is everybody's business. The new control problem may not be how to get people to work on time but how to keep them from henpecking management.

When a management is struggling for productivity, when employees appear obstinate, inconsiderate, and entirely insensitive to management's needs, the development of an ownership attitude in employees may seem wonderfully utopian. But the reality creates difficulties. The senior officers of more than one small company that has adopted such plans have spent some sleepless nights and gone on even blander diets precisely when they have achieved what they sought—a working force intensely and creatively motivated to help the organization to succeed. Management feels the pressure when it has to face up to the reality of long-sought honest feedback. They find that they are hearing not only the happy news of dollar savings but the unhappy public exposure of past managerial inadequacy. For as every phase of production is examined in the bright light of joint committees, almost any management team is bound to discover case after case in which its decisions were not quite so good as they had seemed to be. Yet the fact remains that the multiple incentive system has paid handsome dollar dividends to management and worker alike. Its cost is that management and everyone else must operate in a glass house.

The words "multiple incentives" were used advisedly in the subheading of this section. Although the money incentive is central to the development of such plans, they also encompass changes in the whole organizational structure. Incentives in the form of greater opportunities for independence and for greater participation in planning and decision making are other outgrowths of these groupwide systems. In these ways, they represent an almost total rebuilding of the relationships among members of an organization.

Several of these plans have been used in many companies, with variable success. Psychologically they make sense in that they open channels of communication and create a situation in which at least one goal, the goal of greater productive efficiency, is spread more widely through all levels of the organization. They move people toward an ownership attitude by the simple expedient of providing a kind of ownership.

But they are no panaceas. Sometimes, even an ownership attitude cannot outproduce technically superior people or equipment. They create new, difficult psychological and organizational problems while solving others. They lead us into the pervasive problems of working groups. It is one thing to find a group of people with common goals. It is another to find them working together efficiently toward those goals.

Straight salaries

At higher organizational levels, among white-collar workers and executives, the use of straight salaries has been around for a long time. In recent years some companies have instituted a pay policy whereby everyone, from the bottom to the top, is paid on salary, rather than by hourly or incentive rates. The underlying hypotheses are that people, given the right working conditions, are positively motivated by a variety of things other than money; that money is a "hygiene factor" which has to be there in pretty good supply, but that it should not be used to try to make people work harder or better; that it is for rewards other than money that people will work harder—out of intrinsic interest in the work, or in order to grow and learn, or to move ahead. It is to escape both the negative impacts of incentive schemes and the social-caste implications of hourly rates for lower levels that some companies have turned to straight salaries for all employees.

A large challenge is created by removing pay (at least to some degree) from the manager's motivational tool kit. Now the manager must set up an organization which motivates and challenges through means other than money. He must still treat money seriously, just as he must treat lunch hours and holidays seriously; but if he wants his people to work harder, he must find other methods. He must make the work itself more interesting, or he must set up a climate in which hard work is the standard. Those may be more difficult things to do than to set up incentive schemes, but they may also be much more consistent with human nature.

Some "solutions" to the performance appraisal problem

On the performance appraisal side, a large number of methods have been used to try to achieve many different purposes. Some of them are primarily for managerial use, so that the organization can get an early fix on its young "comers." Some of them are designed chiefly to help identify training and educational needs. Some of them, like some pay plans, have a motivational intent: to stimulate people to work harder.

Almost every major company these days uses some kind of formal individual performance appraisal. Most of them ask an individual's boss to evaluate that individual at standard intervals on a standard form. The forms range from long checklists, designed to help assess the individual's cooperativeness, loyalty, intelligence, and a whole collection of other "traits," to some that require the boss to specify particular incidents which he thinks characterize the best and/or the worst behavior of the employee.

Some of them are never seen by the employee. Others, particularly those which are tied closely to the concept of management by objectives, tend to be more participative. In those cases, the manager and the employee usually sit down together to talk not only about the past but also about future performance objectives.

Some performance appraisal systems operate entirely independently of the pay system; some of them are tied directly to pay. Some evaluate the individual against his own performance; others compare members of the organization to one another. Those forms grade, as it were, on a distribution curve, requiring the manager to rank employee X relative to all his other employees; to say, in effect, "If I could only promote one of my people, it would be this one; and this is the person I would fire if I had to fire one." Some performance appraisals are done by only one supervisor; some require multiple assessments.

Almost all appraisal systems work downward, with superiors appraising subordinates. A very small number also include upward appraisal of superiors by subordinates, or appraisal by peers. The reader may recall in our chapter on assessment that we emphasized the value of gut impressions in assessing people, and the value of aggregate as against single appraisals. In that chapter we also pointed out that peer evaluations were often more valid than evaluations by superiors. But peer evaluations and evaluations by subordinates both raise "political" specters, and are seldom used in business organizations despite their apparent validity. Multiple ratings are also surprisingly scarce.

Another curiosity: In this author's experience, appraisal systems are almost never fully implemented in the way that is intended; particularly when one requirement is that the superior must discuss the evaluation with his subordinate. If one asks subordinates in organizations about the last time they had their regularly scheduled performance appraisal interview (even in companies with elaborately formal systems), it is surprising how often the subordinate denies that any such interview has *ever* taken place.

One reason, of course, is that such confrontations between superiors and subordinates are often terribly uncomfortable. They are at least as uncomfortable for the superior as for the subordinate. So many superiors manage to put them off or to convince themselves that that little ten-minute talk that took place in the corridor last Wednesday was in fact the performance evaluation interview for this year.

This may strike the reader as a rather negative picture. I think it is. I know of no organization that is delighted with its performance appraisal system.

So what's the plus side? What are the things that seem to help? Let's try these:

1. Get more than one opinion on any individual. Take the time to discuss the opinions held by several people of that individual. Talking it over among people who know the individual is a very valuable tool for assessing performance. Of course, talk is costly in terms of time and energy. But poor evaluations can be costly too.

2. Try to build some form of peer evaluation into the system. There is a lot of evidence that peers make more valid judgments about how a person will behave than superiors do.

3. Develop methods that tie performance appraisal to growth and learning objectives, so that we are not simply evaluating people as good or bad, but are rather trying to point out problem areas and paths to their solution.

In summary

One of the ways most organizations try to influence their members to do more or better work is through the manipulation of pay and through performance appraisal systems. Both of these typically generate large amounts of trouble in organizations along with some of the positive impact they are intended to produce.

Individual money incentive systems are most appropriate where workers can operate independently of one another and where their jobs can, in fact, be designed so as to permit independent operation. Difficulties begin to arise when individual incentives are applied to interdependent people on interdependent jobs. Then productive work by each person on his special job (even if it could be attained) may not add up to productive accomplishment for the whole organization.

Company-wide multiple incentive plans are psychologically different from individual plans. Individual plans tend to isolate the individual and his work from the organization and its work. Company-wide plans tend to focus everyone on a common organizational goal rather than his own individual one. This common concern for the organizational goal makes for basic changes in worker-management relationships, for increases in the range of satisfactions available to people in an organization, and for new and difficult problems of interaction.

As influence mechanisms, individual incentives are more likely to effect overt actions than basic attitudes. Multiple incentives, closer to the AA model, may have deep and wide effects.

Wages and salaries are not just money. They are also indicators of progress, worth, and status. And they are equity measures, too, telling us whether our treatment relative to others and to our own performance is right and proper.

To eliminate both the stresses of incentive schemes and social-class distinctions, some companies are moving to straight salaries for all employees, using factors other than pay for motivational purposes.

Performance appraisal methods are many and varied. They show a spotty record as tools for influencing behavior. Multiple judgments, peer evaluations, and learning-oriented methods all have something positive to offer in this otherwise uneasy area of managerial practice.

3

**People in threes
to twenties
Efficiency and
influence in groups**

Introductory note

The third part of this book is about groups, about those committees and task forces and meetings that occupy so large a chunk of the manager's work time. We not only spend time working in groups, we also spend time complaining about them. They are slow, we claim; they make stupid compromises; they are inefficient; they are places for people to put on power shows; they are the abominations of managerial life. And having vented a whole string of such feelings after a long day of meetings, many of us then proceed to do a really curious thing: we march right back into another set of meetings the next day. We curse meetings, yet we go right on having them. Which suggests that either we are very stupid, or that somehow groups, committees, meetings are in fact useful tools for performing some of our managerial functions. I prefer to think that groups are important tools. So the general thrust of part 3 is to try to make the reader worry not about whether groups are good or bad, but about the conditions under which groups are good or bad; and to consider how groups affect people, how meetings can be improved, and how groups can be used for managing organizations.

Groups are critically important intermediaries between large organizations and individual people who compose them. One of the really misleading things about most organization charts is that they picture the organization as an orderly collection of individuals. Each box on the chart represents a job for one person, so that if we add up all those jobs, we would appear to have "the organization." That, of course, is not at all a true picture. It ignores the ever-present small groups that intervene between individual and organization. Whether the organization likes it or not, people form groups. Both the informal groups they form and the more formal groups the organization forms play very important roles in shaping the organization's behavior.

The group, formal or informal, affects the behavior of both individuals and large organizations in at least these ways:

189

1. Groups discipline, mold, and change the behavior of individuals. Both common sense and research results show that the groups individuals belong to are powerful determiners of behavior, attitudes, and values. Whether it be gangs or university departments, groups influence their members. Chapter 19 is specifically concerned with the ways that groups press, form, shape, and control their individual members.

2. Groups are also important decision-making mechanisms in modern organizations. Despite the protest that camels are horses designed by a committee, despite the fact that some organizations have forbidden committees (which is like trying to forbid sex), a great many decisions in organizations are made in groups. Two of the chapters in the next section are concerned with decision making in groups; one with the conditions that make for good or bad group decisions; the other with ways of improving group processes in general.

3. Looking toward the whole organization, instead of toward the individual, groups turn out to be important in another way; as major contributors to organizational decisions. The many groups within an organization bargain, negotiate and compete as well as cooperate with one another. Those active intergroup relationships are large factors in the corporate decision-making process. Chapter 20 is about conflict and cooperation among groups within the organization; about the group politics of organizations.

4. Chapter 21 deals with communication networks in groups. Group networks can tell us a good deal about the advantages and disadvantages of different small group structures and also about alternative ways of structuring larger organizations.

5. Groups are important in managerial development and organizational design. Groups influence the morale, the well-being, the learning, and the development of people in organizations, from assemblyline worker to executive. Chapter 22 is about ways of using groups for developing managers, and chapter 23 is about using groups to improve the quality of working life.

17

Group decisions
Monsters or miracles?

There is a useful set of survival simulation exercises that some readers may have encountered.* Sometimes the simulation is about a group lost on the surface of the moon; sometimes the group has crash-landed in the desert or in the arctic. The exercise always requires six or seven people, isolated and in danger of death, to make decisions as a group. If they're lost in the desert, they must decide whether it is more important to keep a few quarts of water than to keep a loaded gun or a compass, and so on. They must rank order the values of several such items. The exercise is usually set up so that each member first gets a chance to make the decisions alone. Then the group sits down for forty-five minutes or so to talk the situation over and to make a group decision about those same items.

Those are useful exercises for two reasons: First, people learn a good deal about their own and others' behavior in a tightly constrained task situation. But they're also useful because they demonstrate, in most cases, that the group's decision is a good deal better (when compared to a survival expert's ranking) than the average of the individual decisions. Moreover, in many cases the group's decision turns out to be better than *any* individual member's decision. In those cases, the group is "synergistic," yielding a net improvement over the performance of anybody in it. Sometimes, however, the group decision is worse than the average decision of the members.

Why and when are group decisions better or worse?

Group discussion in the survival experiments is a little like some kinds of military intelligence work. If six of us get together and collect all our bits and pieces of information about the desert, the total information available is likely to be a lot more than any one of us had before. More information obviously often helps us make better decisions.

* Some excellent ones were developed by J. C. Lafferty and P. M. Eady and published by ELM, Plymouth, Michigan.

But another reason those group decisions are usually pretty good is probably equally important. When groups talk things over, the logical strengths and weaknesses of certain opinions become clearer to all concerned. Wheat is separated from chaff. It isn't only information that people share; it's also a critical evaluation of the arguments that contribute to the quality of a group decision. Notice that this critical faculty of groups is not guaranteed to work. Some groups are scared and don't dare question member's beliefs. Some are "snowed" by self-styled experts or authority figures. So the critical faculty is something groups often need to train themselves to use well.

A third reason that these survival simulations so often show group decisions to be better than individual ones has to do with the survival setting. In these survival exercises, the groups always exist in isolation, all by themselves. The group is not part of a larger group. The members have only one overweening purpose, to survive. No one in those groups, for instance, wants the group to die. But in most real organizational situations, the members of a given group are much less "pure." They are usually members of other groups. They are not just motivated to do what is good for the group they are presently with. They may have other purposes. They may represent other groups. The person from the marketing department may not just be interested in the best decision possible for the organization. He's also interested in getting a good piece of the action for his marketing group. Or he may want to use the group meeting as a step toward getting himself promoted. In the real world, that is to say, group decision occurs not in a vacuum, but in a world of other motives, other commitments, other loyalties. That's when groups often do create camels when they're trying to build a horse.

Nevertheless, these survival cases point up the fact that groups, when the conditions are right, can make better decisions than could be reached by averaging the decisions made by their individual members. Moreover, there is evidence that groups that have been trained in working together improve their decisions more than groups that have never had training. So group decisions can be good, and they can be made better if the group members are willing to do a little work toward making them better. Those facts are inescapable, regardless of the complications that take place in larger organizational settings.

Groups and commitment

The reader will note that we have jumped head on into the issue of decision quality. But, of course, groups are not called together solely to try for better-quality decisions. They are often called together for another very important reason: to gain commitment to a decision. The "I-love-my-own-baby" proposition holds true over a wide range of situations. If we participate in a group decision, we are likely to be more committed to that decision than if the decision has been made by somebody else. That "fact" is very important in organizational life. It underlies the whole movement toward "participative management." It seems to hold true over a large number of cultures. It is important for the implementation of decisions. Most decisions, after all, no matter how good their quality, are not worth very much if they aren't implemented. One of the most powerful implementational tools we have is the commitment that derives from participation in decision making.

On leadership and group decision making
Contingency models

We have said so far that groups are often useful for decision making because (1) they can bring more information to a situation, (2) they can analyze information critically, and (3) they can generate commitment by their members.

But there are situations in which a manager (1) already has all the information he needs, (2) is perfectly capable of processing it himself (or with the help of his computer), and (3) does not require the commitment of others for implementation purposes. So he might not need to involve a group at all. If we take such a contingent view of different types of decision-making situations, we then identify a whole variety of group-relevant or group-irrelevant decisions. For some, group decisions may look sensible, while some decisions can probably be made faster and better by the manager alone.

In the last few years, much interesting work has aimed at documenting this contingent view of leadership behavior, trying to specify the conditions under which a leader might use one decision method or another. To give the reader a feeling for one of the more useful ones consider the following little case:

> You are supervising the work of twelve engineers. Their formal training and work experience is very similar, permitting you to use them interchangably on projects. During the last few months the backlog of new projects assigned to your unit has decreased, causing you and your engineers to worry about possible lay-offs unless business picks up.
>
> Yesterday, your manager informed you that a request had been received from an overseas affiliate for four engineers to go abroad

on extended loan for a period of six to eight months. For a number of reasons, he argued, and you agreed, that this request should be met from your group.

All of your engineers are capable of handling this assignment and, from the standpoint of present and future projects, there is no particular reason why any one should be retained over any other. The problem is somewhat complicated by the fact that the overseas assignment is in what is generally regarded in the company as a highly undesirable location.*

If you were the manager in this situation, how would you go about making the decision? Remember the question is how you would go about making the decision, not what is the right decision. Will you sit at your desk and make the decision yourself? Will you call each of the engineers in and talk to them, then make the decision yourself? Will you call a meeting and listen to people, and then make the decision yourself? Or will you set up a group decision meeting, in which you would participate, aimed at reaching consensus? If you give this case to a number of managers, you will find a lot of disagreement about the appropriate way to approach the decision.

The model we referred to earlier tries to make sense out of problems like those in the following way:

According to the model, there are two important issues: (1) decision quality and (2) human commitment. To make a good-quality decision, we need the best available information. To get successful implementation, we need people's willing commitment to carry out the decision.

The model then reasons: If only the quality of decision counts, and commitment is unimportant, the leader should gather the information needed and make an individual decision. And that would be the end of it. But if commitment (or the development of people) is also important (or if commitment only is important) then the decision-making process must be more participative.

So if the reader will now review the case, he can ask himself questions like these:

Is the quality of the decision important? The answer seems to be that it is not. Almost any decision will do perfectly well, as long as the engineers go along with it.

Is the commitment of the employees important? The answer has to be yes. The job will not be done very well if the people who work

* Borrowed, with permission, from Professor Victor Vroom of Yale University. See Vroom, V. and Yetton, P. *Leadership and Decision Making*. University of Pittsburgh Press, 1973. © 1973, University of Pittsburgh Press.

on it do so under protest, and if everybody feels it was "unfair." In this case, then, the contingency model recommends a group decision-making process aimed primarily at building commitment and not very much concerned with decision quality.

But, of course, one can find a whole collection of other cases in which quality is critical and commitment unimportant. And in some of those cases one might find that meeting with subordinates can contribute nothing to the quality of the decision. In those cases, the model's recommended solution is that the manager make the decision by himself.

Notice that that kind of contingency model does not put much emphasis on the information-processing part of decision-making activity. It pretty much assumes that if the manager has all the information he needs, he can also make a good-quality decision. Some students of small groups argue that that is an oversight. But the idea that decision making involves both information and human commitment is a good, basic idea which the reader might want to keep in mind the next time he is trying to decide whether or not to call a meeting.

Brainstorming and group creativity

We have not yet mentioned still another function of groups in organizations: creativity. Sometimes we bring people together not so much to make decisions, as to generate ideas or offer alternatives or provide counsel. Sometimes groups "brainstorm." Whether "brainstorming" really works is a subject of some debate. Some studies suggest that the same group of individuals working independently in separate rooms would turn up as many or more creative ideas in the same amount of time as they would brainstorming in a room together. Whatever definition of creativity we use, that elusive concept is largely the property of individuals, not groups. Nevertheless, most of us would probably agree that our own creative ideas are often sparked by interactions with others.

And therein lies the notion behind brainstorming. Get people together in a loose, nonevaluative setting simply to think out loud about anything that might be even remotely relevant to the problem at hand. The process is both useful and fun when "divergence" is more important than "convergence"—when we need new possibilities, new alternatives, rather than solutions. And, as we shall argue in the last section of this book, one of the great weak points in present styles of managing may lie at the root of the whole process, around the question of finding and choosing the right problems. A good deal can be said in favor of occasional opportunities for members of an organization to hang loose, to spin off ideas, dreams, and fancies no matter how screwball they may seem. Sometimes, for the sake of the organization, it is useful to quit working and do a little playing.

In summary

This chapter has tried to encourage the skeptical reader to adopt more positive attitudes toward group decision making. But this chapter has by no means been an all-out pitch for group decision making. It has tried to describe the conditions under which group decisions are better than alternative forms of decision making, as well as the conditions under which they are worse. But groups are important for more than decision making. They can also generate commitment and loyalty from their members. And these two factors, quality and commitment, are perhaps the key pragmatic questions to consider when evaluating the usefulness of groups. There remain, of course, other questions, of style, of morality, of human development, that the reader may also want to think about as he approaches the question of how "groupily" he wants to manage his shop.

We have not said very much in this chapter about how to improve the working machinery of groups. In comparable situations where group decision making seems appropriate, some groups will still make better decisions than others, usually because they are more skillful users of the machinery of group process. The next chapter looks at those problems of group process in more detail.

18 Group process
What really went on in that meeting?

If we simultaneously put two groups to work on the same task, we will probably find that one does a better job that the other. Perhaps one group has "better" people than the other. Or perhaps one group's members work together more effectively than the other's. Maybe one group's people compete with each other or put each other down or don't buckle down to work. This chapter is about the working conditions that increase or decrease the effectiveness of task groups.

Let's begin with a now familiar distinction. In earlier chapters we often distinguished between factual and emotional communication, between facts and feelings. We argued that effective influence in most cases requires communication about feelings as well as about facts. When we switch our thinking from individuals to larger units like groups, a very similar two-part distinction turns out to be useful. This time the distinction is between *group task* and *group process*. "Task" is equivalent to "facts." Most groups in organizations exist to perform some specific tasks: to set next month's production schedules or to set vacation policy. But all groups, no matter what their tasks, also go through a process to complete their task. The members have to communicate with one another, put together information, process it, make decisions, and so on. The ways in which group members go about their task we shall call group process. *Task* is about where you want to go in your car. *Process* is about how the car itself operates—whether the oil pressure is up and the spark plugs are firing and whether the whole vehicle is well maintained.

It's task issues we usually talk about when we're in the group. Process usually gets talked about to our buddies at the bar after the group meeting. Task is about whether or not we ought to hire twelve more technicians. Process is about that s.o.b. department manager who never agrees with anything the rest of us want to do.

We are all process experts

Almost all of us are quite expert on many matters of group process, but, curiously, we seldom use what we know to improve the operation of groups. We are expert in the sense that we can go home after a meeting and describe the group's psychology and social structure in considerable detail over dinner, and we know which particular behaviors were dysfunctional to the group. We detect quite easily the undercover fight going on between Joe and Henry; or we know when Joe said one thing when he really meant another; and we know that the boss appeared to want the group members' opinions, but that he had really made up his mind before the meeting started. All those are process observations that most of us are highly sensitive to, but usually we either simply lock them up in the backs of our heads or we talk about them over coffee after the event. Yet these are, of course, highly relevant, valuable bits of information that could potentially help to improve performance. Certainly if a basketball coach saw a couple of his players tripping each other up, he would consider that very much part of his business. And yet many of us sit in groups and watch our colleagues tripping each other up, and just shut up about it.

Why don't we talk out loud about process issues? The reasons tend to be social, don't they? "It would be embarrassing," we might say, "to call attention to someone talking too much," or "People just don't go around saying out loud that Mary and Sam are always on opposite sides of the fence no matter what the issue is. It just isn't done!" But isn't it? It's often done in the family, and with increasing frequency, it is being done in organizations.

Dealing with emotional "noise"

What the issue amounts to is this: People have feelings at group meetings. Many of the group's members observe those feelings. If such feelings seem to contribute "noise" that gets in the way of the task (or, conversely, seems to be relevant to the task) one sensible thing to do is to talk about those feelings.

To clarify this picture, consider two almost extreme approaches to the way one might handle the emotional side of groups. One common procedure is simply to set up rules to disallow the direct expression of such feelings. The rules may be formal parliamentary ones or informal ones. The chairperson says, "We will stick to the facts in this meeting. We will keep personalities out of this. We will cut off people who talk too long or too much." His purpose is to eliminate the expression of feelings, and his weapon is his authority to enforce organizational rules. This seems a sensible, businesslike approach to the problem, but it needs more consideration.

Another not so businesslike method for handling process is to take the position that feelings should not be kept out of meetings but let in and identified. Here the chair says, "If you want to blow off, blow off. If you want to boast, boast. If you want to deal in personalities, deal in personalities. But when anyone does any of these things, let him or anyone else point it out so that everyone will know what he's doing." This second method also deserves serious consideration.

People's emotional behavior in groups, like all other behavior, is goal related. People boast because they feel that boasting will get them something they want—recognition, or power, or status. People lick boots for reasons, too; perhaps they think boot-licking will make someone they need like them a little better. When several people join to try to solve a problem through committee action, there may be one central problem that is common to everyone on the committee, but there are also individually perceived problems that each member brings in with him. People, we said in part 1, perceive the world in relation to their operant needs. If other members of a group are in a position to help or hurt a particular member, that member is likely to be alert to their power. The emotional "noise" in a group may therefore be made up, to a large extent, of efforts of individuals to satisfy their personal needs in the presence of the group. Thus, this kind of "noisiness" can only be considered wasteful or irrelevant when the group problem is defined as the only real problem. Such a definition is simply unrealistic. This second level of individual problems exists, and attempts to solve them—although irrelevant to the group's problem—constitute, so far as individual members are concerned, a perfectly relevant use of the communication system.

We may object to persons using a group for their own ends, or we may object to the methods that some individuals use to solve their personal problems—methods like name calling or yessing. We may feel that the methods people sometimes use are not effective methods even for accomplishing what those individuals want to accomplish. Nevertheless, those methods are attempts by individuals to solve problems, and to rule them out by authority may be to rule out the individuals as well as the noise. For if these "irrelevant" needs are so important to a person that he tries to use the group as a sounding board for them, then to deny him that opportunity can only do one of two things: it can make him lose interest in the group and the group's problem, or it can make him disguise his communications so that they sound relevant to the common problem.

Authority or parliamentary procedure or social pressures may drive individual motives underground, but such methods do not necessarily eliminate them. Instead of open argument and open emotion, one now gets calm, seemingly rational discussions, but discussions which somehow manage indirectly to discredit opponents or to defend positions beyond any point of reasonable utility.

Everyone who has served on a committee has seen this kind of velvet-glove activity many times. Sometimes it takes the "it's an excellent idea but . . ." form, or, "Well, of course we *could* go about it your way but. . . ." Such tacks are much harder to handle, much less likely to contribute to honest unanimity (or honest disagreement), than an open haggle.

It is quite impossible to exclude individual noise from group discussion by force or by parliamentary procedure. If these devices eliminate emotional noise they eliminate it as ear plugs do—at the cost of much relevant information. Problems may appear to be solved in such restrictive situations when the "solution" is actually a hodgepodge of compromise and half-truth. As in the feedback example in chapter 10, if we want the information, we may have to bear the emotion.

Hence, the other choice: let the communication channels carry whatever pepole want to communicate. Let everything in, but tag the different classes of information, so that everyone knows what's what. Seek out the causes of and get rid of the causes. When people don't need to make noise, they will stop and get down to the problem at hand.

Such a policy need not be as chaotic as it sounds. Perhaps it is more orderly to convert chaos to system than to cover it with system. The question is not anarchy versus order so much as the orderly handling of anarchistic factors in a group. Getting groups to say what they feel is not easy however, especially if time is limited. But patience and some respect for people's ultimate willingness to accept responsibility can help a good deal. Postmortems and bull sessions devoted to what was right or wrong about the last meeting are useful techniques for this purpose if the group meets periodically.

I remember one group of six men working on a research project full time. The project called for the six to break up into pairs and travel to some field locations for a few days. The group spent hours trying to decide who would go where with whom. Afterward, in a bull-session review of the day's progress, someone pointed out that it was silly to have thrashed around so long over this trivial point. This stimulus finally brought a previously hidden issue out in the open. Everyone liked Joe, and everyone wanted to be the one to travel with Joe. But nobody would admit it; so they had used all sorts of "rational" arguments all day about why one pairing arrangement or another wouldn't work. Of course this recognition came several hours too late, but it helped to prevent occurrence of similar stalemates later. Postmortems like this become easier with time. In fact they can often be worked in as part of the meeting itself, so that people are always watching for and pointing up underlying feelings contemporaneously with their discussions of content problems.

Groups that operate with fairly free expression and recognition of feelings follow a somewhat different pattern from more carefully controlled groups. They start slowly, characteristically with considerable hodgepodge and disturbance and little measurable progress. But they can accelerate fast once the air is cleared. Controlled groups, on the other hand, show steadier, step-by-step progress that seems more orderly from the outside.

Barriers to communication in groups

It may be profitable to examine the same problem from the other side. Instead of asking, "What causes noise?" one can ask, "What blocks the communication of relevant information?" This is the same process question we asked in chapter 10. What blocks feedback?

Looking at the problem from this perspective can be useful; for, while it is true that too much is often said in groups, too much may also be left unsaid. The subordinate says, "Yes, I understand your instructions," but later it turns out that he did not understand. The salesman does not think it important to tell the sales manager about the change in the customer's attitude. The production worker does not report that his machine is acting oddly because he forgot to lubricate it. The patient says, "You're the doctor; you tell *me* where it hurts." These kinds of relevant information left uncommunicated are the opposite of noise. The atmosphere of a group may be too quiet—too quiet in the sense that problems do not get all available information brought to bear upon them.

Sometimes the barriers that limit communication are simple mechanical ones. Thus, when the communication system is a one-way loudspeaker, the simple absence of channels in one direction makes it mechanically impossible for the receiver to send relevant information back to the sender. Letter writing is another process that includes at least a partial mechanical barrier. People can write letters in two directions, but the process necessarily involves a time lag that constitutes a partial barrier to the communication of information that may be useful only if it arrives quickly.

Such mechanical barriers, however, are probably the least important barriers to communication in human groups. The most significant barriers are the more ephemeral psychological ones like these examples:

First, there is a *status barrier* between superior and subordinate that limits communication in either direction because of fear of disapproval, on the one hand, or loss of prestige on the other:

"If I ask that question these people will think I don't know enough to be boss, so I'll act like I know the answer already."

"If I admit this to the boss, he'll be wild. He'll think I've lost my touch."

Then there is the *interpersonal-hostility barrier*. This is the one that goes:

"I won't give that guy the satisfaction of admitting he's got a good idea. And I certainly won't let him in on my idea."

And there is the *parliamentary-methods barrier*. It sometimes takes this form:

"I can't speak until I'm recognized by the chair; and if the chair never recognizes me, my information will never come out. If the chair does recognize me later, I'll still say what should be said now—even if it's irrelevant later."

We need not elaborate on the way parliamentary procedures, which were intended to promote and simplify communication, have been used in social and political affairs selectively to prevent and complicate communication.

These kinds of barriers are troublemakers in human groups. They cannot be dammed up or set aside at will. They do not even have the saving grace of remaining stable and fixed. Instead they move and change with moods and feelings of group members, so that now one set is in operation and now another.

The answers to such barriers may be the same as the answer to too much emotional noise. They could be circumvented if they themselves were communicated. If two people, for example, can reach the point where they can tell one another what they think of one another, they may be able to work out an understanding that will allow them to communicate successfully. But ordinarily they do not communicate these feelings—they do not especially in the industrial culture. Instead, they say, "Stick to the facts! Don't get emotional! Let's be businesslike!" This cultural attitude is probably the biggest communication barrier of all because it prevents the communication of interpersonal feelings, and uncommunicated interpersonal feelings, in turn, complicate and sometimes prevent the communication of facts.

Group process and group objectives

If a committee of executives starts out to decide whether or not to institute selection tests for salespeople, their objective seems, at first, perfectly unambiguous. Then someone discovers that one member has quite a different conception of selection tests from other members of the group. Ten minutes later someone raises these quesitons: "Is our objective to decide on selection tests only? Or are we really here to revise all our selection procedures? Are interviews and application blanks tests, or are they outside our scope?"

Ten minutes later still, someone wants to know: "What does the boss really have in mind when he asks us to look into this? How much money is he willing to spend? Is he willing for us to do a major research job? Or does he want us to buy a packaged product even though it may not be very good?"

And still later someone with an irate note in his voice asks: "What are we trying to decide anyhow? Is it whether or not tests are a good idea? Or is it what tests to buy?"

And so on at intervals throughout the meeting. What seemed precise and unambiguous turns out to be diffuse and shadowy.

Defining objectives becomes more or less difficult with the nature of the problem the group faces. But almost every time we find a decision-making committee in action, we also find periodic difficulties with the definition of objectives.

Besides these overt questions, a series of covert problems is often present. A major one is the problem of subgroup objectives versus group objectives. Thus, in collective bargaining everyone may overtly agree that the objective is to work out a best solution to common problems. But everyone also knows that other major objectives are in operation and that they are in conflict. The union wants to get the best deal it can get, even at the expense of management. And management wants the best deal it can get, even at the expense of the union.

Similarly, in a meeting in which several departments are represented, we often find unverbalized objectives lying just below the surface. The sales department wants to make sure that it doesn't lose any of its control over pricing. The production people do not want the sales to be in a better position to dictate production schedules after the meeting than they were before. And so on.

A third level of problems also exists. This is the level of the individual operating as an individual. "How does the boss really feel about this issue? What decisions will please him most? Is my objective really to take the direction that I think is best, or the decision that will most please the boss?" Or, similarly, "Where does this particular proposal fit into the larger political picture? Who will get hurt if we take one direction or another? Who will be helped?"

Clearly the "right" way to cope with these problems will vary with the motives of the coper. Sometimes an individual or subgroup can profit most by blocking the definition of objectives. One can hardly find a better way to keep a meeting from going anywhere than to raise a new specific issue every time the committee gets close to clarifying its purposes. On the other hand, one can equally well befuddle a meeting by overemphasizing objectives—especially if a member chooses so to broaden and complicate them as to take the meeting altogether out of the range of possible accomplishment. The problem is that objectives create difficulties for groups so long as they are differently understood by different people in the group and so long as some of them are not out on the table. Once everyone in the group has a reasonably good feel for the limits of the problem and for the variety of objectives present, something can usually be done about them.

Helping to clarify objectives, perhaps by restating someone else's statement, can help a group to get started and can also put the restater, the clarifier, in a position of strength in the group. Similarly, conscious efforts to talk about covert objectives, if one suspects their presence, can help a committee to function more efficiently; although the person who does this job takes more risks with covert than with overt issues. If one member suggests, for example, that someone else's personal needs are predominating, guards will be quickly thrown up, and the discussion may thereby be led into fruitless defensive argument. So a group member or chairperson who feels that someone in the meeting has ulterior motives had better word and time his suggestion carefully. If he himself is the person with ulterior motives, he may do himself and his cause some good by expressing them—if his cause will be helped by an efficient meeting.

The point is that groups are not likely to go anywhere unless they know where they are going. Even a single human being may have trouble defining his own objectives, and the problem gets much more complicated in a group. Whether it is advantageous for a group member to clarify objectives in the group or to confuse them, to express his own personal objectives or to hide them, these are questions each member of a group must weigh for himself.

From the perspective of the whole group instead of any individual member, the problems to be solved are these: (1) to have every person in the group know where the group is going; (2) to have every person in the group either want to go where the group is going or say where he wants to get off; (3) if there are people who want to get off early, either to change objectives so these people can go along or to let them off and start over; and (4) to take another look every once in a while to see whether objectives need to be changed or modified.

Several actions can help a group in these directions. If people try to communicate about objectives, both personal and official, then at least the problem is out on the table where it can be seen and dealt with.

Objectives are likely to be communicated readily if they are not jammed down people's throats by chairmen, if they are treated as a normal part of the agenda, and if the general atmosphere of the meeting encourages this kind of feedback. If, in other words, they operate more like Alcoholics Anonymous and less like the old-time iron-pants boss.

A census of ideas about the group's objectives taken early in a meeting can also help get these issues out on the table quickly. Often, in meetings, the first idea raised becomes the take-off point for discussion, thereby eliminating expression of some other possibilities. Since the first highway may not be the best one, it can be useful to map out several alternatives before starting the trip.

"Personality" problems in groups

Another class of obstacles that seems to block effective small-group process centers is the personalities of the participants. Such people problems include factors carried into the group by the members, like the leader's personality, his dominance or submissiveness, the intensity of his desire to be liked, and so on. They also include problems of individual members' talkativeness, shyness, argumentativeness, and defensiveness.

There are problems of communication, too, stemming from differences in rank, age, sex, expertness, and prestige in the organization. And certain problems may arise within the group—somebody's idea is ignored, somebody else's is laughed at, somebody else says absolutely nothing and just smiles, thereby frightening some of his colleagues and encouraging others. Finally, this general personality category includes problems of group mood: elation, depression, and regression into dirty stories or golf or anything except the subject at hand.

No way of avoiding such problems has yet been found, but there are ways of dealing with them. From the group point of view, they are problems only if relevant ideas and information are omitted or distorted as a consequence of them. Often, of course, such problems do affect both the kind and degree of communication. The quiet person who sits and smokes his pipe may seriously affect the rate and even the nature of the ideas that are contributed. For out of the corner of his eye each member may be watching him for some sign of approval or disapproval. Depending primarily on any member's own feelings of security or insecurity, this point or that may be modified, withheld, or overemphasized because of the quiet one.

Or a shy person A offers a suggestion which is ignored. He offers it again and it is again ignored. Like the adolescent in the chapter on frustration, one can see A gradually withdraw, thereafter to come out of his shell only infrequently and only in order to jab at someone else's ideas.

What, then, can be done, not so much to prevent such problems as to deal with them? Again the answer seems to lie in the communication process. For if a group can communicate about its people problems, the problems may be resolved. But they are unlikely to be resolved so long as they remain hidden and uncommunicated. This again is the problem of dealing with noise. These issues can be opened for group discussion, or they can be denied entry. If a group chooses to deny them, if it chooses to cut off argument, to require that emotionalism be kept out of the meeting and that dirty stories be excluded, then the group is ignoring data relevant to its own operation. And data about itself are as important to the solution of a group's problem as they are to the solution of any individual's problem.

Discussion of such personnel issues need not mean that the group has to examine the remote causes of people's feelings. Just as in the case of A trying to influence B, the original causes of B's feelings are often irrelevant, but the feelings themselves need airing. Thus, when some members of a group leave the field by going off into jokes or gossip or pipe dreams, it is not absolutely necessary to find out why they are doing it. It may be necessary, however, to recognize that such digressions are not accidental. They represent attempts to satisfy needs, to get rid of tension. It may therefore be wise to permit time to be "wasted" in the release of such tensions, instead of forcing the needs to find outlet through the medium of "rational" discussion. Recognition and acceptance of people's feelings and encouragement of an atmosphere of permissiveness seem to be sensible directions for a problem-solving group to take.

A group that operates this way may seem strange sometimes. It does not progress steadily, but in bursts, with periods of highly concentrated work interspersed with periods of digression or argument or laughter. If a superior should happen to walk in on such a group meeting, the chances are about even that he would be impressed or disturbed by what he found.

As it is for problems of objective, the census is a handy device for getting personnel problems out on the table. It is useful for a group to stop once in a while just so that people can say how they feel—how they feel about the group's progress, how they feel about the methods the group is using, how they feel in general. Periodic stops to examine feelings need not be formally instituted; in fact, they occur quite naturally if we let them.

A third method for coping with personnel problems is, surprisingly, to de-emphasize pre-meeting preparation. It seems, at first, to make sense to urge group members to think about the committee agenda in advance and to come "prepared." But preplanning can also be a source of serious personnel difficulties. For "preparation" may mean that each person works out his individual position before the meeting and then comes into the group to try to sell his position to the rest. If that is what preparation means, every member of the group now has a position to defend. If his position is rejected he may feel he has suffered a personal, egoistic defeat.

Group leaders especially are given to overpreparation. They often feel that the responsibility for success rests solely with them. Consequently, a new chairperson is likely to go home and think out alternative answers to the problem before the meeting and to select the answer that seems best to him. He then comes into the meeting with the wrong expectations about the right answers. Whereupon a whole host of reactive personnel problems arises.

"Preparation" can have other more useful meanings, too. A leader can plan a group meeting without creating much difficulty for himself or his group. It is one thing, for example, to come armed with all the information one can muster to feed into the hopper, and quite another to come armed with conclusions. Moreover, to be prepared with a general procedural plan for conducting a meeting is different from coming with a specific step-by-step outline. Group members are likely to accept information or a general plan but to resist the imposition of conclusions or tight, inflexible procedures. Moreover, if a problem is big enough to call for a meeting, a chairperson who has the answer in advance is often incorrectly prejudging the complexity of the issue.

This whole personnel question involves one of the issues talked about in the section on influence—the location of responsibility. Groups are likely to function with a minimum of personnel difficulty when the responsibility for action and procedure lies with all the members rather than with any particular individual. The responsibility then remaining for the chair or the leader is to help provide and police a communication system that will evoke all the information the group needs to make its decisions.

Problems of navigation

Groups get lost in the problems they try to solve. Often they have difficulty locating their position after they have decided where they want to go and have started out to get there. The problems here include timing, meeting deadlines, laying out sequences. They are programming problems. They can be called problems for two reasons: First, they represent sources of inefficiency in a group. Once a group has decided on a destination, it can get itself so involved in going there that it gets lost. It doesn't notice the wrong turn or the circularity of its movements. Second, navigation is a problem because of the relationship between people's self-orientation and people's feelings. Group members feel uncertain and anxious if they don't know where they are. They may feel they are making no progress when in fact they are. Or they may feel that they are drifting purposelessly. These feelings are often direct consequences of poor navigation.

Skillful navigation is something of an art. A leader (or any member of a group) who begins to feel that his group is getting lost has several ways of trying to do something about it. He can just wait and hope the group will find itself. He can ask the members to stop and go somewhere else. Or he can ask them to stop and try to find out where they are going. If they then decide they like where they are going, they can pick up where they left off; if they don't like it, they can change.

This third alternative is a sensible one for several reasons. Failure to do anything includes the possibility that people who begin to feel lost may also begin to withdraw from the scene. Simply vetoing the present course is bound to create some kind of debilitating emotional reaction, either further withdrawal or aggression. But just asking for a pause to reconsider is likely to yield few side effects and may actually enhance the group's progress.

Any navigational act, however, especially if it comes from a leader, involves some risks. For navigational interruptions constitute restrictions on the group, and restrictions may make the restricter unpopular. But periods of unpopularity, after all, are the fate of a group leader. He must choose between the long-term gain that will come from overall efficiency and the short-term popularity he can invite by abdicating his leadership and ignoring uncomfortable problems like deadlines.

What this navigational problem amounts to, then, is that somebody —the leader or anyone else—has to keep his eye on the group as well as on the problems the group is trying to solve and has to report back what he finds.

Decision-making problems

Another source of difficulty in groups arises at those points at which a decision seems appropriate. Discussion of a point has been more or less completed, and the time to come to some conclusion has arrived. Sometimes groups block impossibly at these points. They seem unable to recognize them or unable to make any decisions if they do recognize them. And sometimes the decisions that do get made do not seem to be meaningful. People don't pay much attention to them, or they don't act upon them once they leave the meeting.

The problem is to get decisions made when they are ready to be made and to get them made in a way that will lead to follow-up action by the people in the group after they leave the group.

Group leaders may approach this problem in one of two extreme ways. Sometimes a leader will push hard for decisions, allowing a specified period for discussion and then asking immediately for a vote. At the other end of the scale is the leader who never gets to decision-making points, either because he doesn't recognize those points or because the discussion of an issue just never seems to be fully completed. Like the individual problem solvers in chapter 6, in other words, groups may fail to search for alternatives long enough or may demand an optimum solution well beyond their realistic level of achievement.

Many managers favor the limited discussion and vote method of the parliamentary variety. They recognize that the best is too hard to get; so they are satisfied with a brief search. The primary weakness of that method is this: although the decision finally reached may be a satisfactory solution to the problem, it may be a decision in appearance more than reality. When a decision is forced quickly and when the method of deciding is by vote, what is left for the minority except psychologically to reject the decision? If they were "rational" human beings, of course, they would accept the majority wish and carry out their part in it. But most of us, even though we may try consciously to accept a decision with which we disagree, have trouble getting very enthusiastic about it. In a sense the minority is challenged to prove that the majority decision is wrong. Such a challenge is easy to meet when the time comes for individual action, simply by acting in ways that "prove" the decision cannot be made to work.

Moreover, if decisions come too early, before people feel that they have contributed what they have to contribute, before they have organized and clarified the issues for themselves, then the decisions reached may indeed by superficial and unsatisfactory. They are therefore likely to be forgotten quickly or passed over lightly once the meeting is over. Vague feelings of hostility and resistance may also follow, feelings that may lead consciously or unconsciously to sabotage or denial of the decision.

A good deal of research evidence shows that decisions are carried into action most effectively when they are group-consensus decisions, when all members of a group can somehow settle by their own efforts on a choice with which they all agree. On the other hand, decisions imposed from the outside or decisions imposed on a minority by a majority or decisions imposed by the leader are not likely to be lasting or effective, for the same reasons that restrictive authority is a poor tool for effecting important changes in attitude.

Consensus decisions are not easy to achieve. People in groups have an unhappy tendency to disagree with one another, either overtly or covertly. And yet, if the group's problems require that every member carry out of the group a desire to act positively on the group's decision, then it is imperative that everyone accept, both consciously and unconsciously, the decisions reached in the group.

Often, it is true, we must fall short of ideal decision-making procedures. Deadlines and other immediate pressures force us to make majority or individual-leader decisions. But this will occur less often when we have built an atmosphere that makes consensus easier. Open two-way communication, clarification of people's feelings, freedom to object—these contribute to the ease with which consensus can be approached. Sometimes even the most efficient group will run into a decision for which consensus seems impossible to achieve. Someone just cannot or will not agree with the position being taken. Here again, however, even if total agreement cannot be reached on the problem, agreement can often be reached about the need for some kind of decision. Then, at least, the minority has expressed its position, has announced that it is not ready to change that position, has had a chance to express its own feelings about its position, and has agreed that some decision short of unanimity is necessary.

Techniques for improving group process

Over the last twenty years, many methods have been developed for trying to train group members to improve group performance. Sensitivity training is one such important effort. In effect, what people are asked to do in a sensitivity training group is to pay attention to process rather than task. They are groups set up without "extrinsic" tasks in order to caricature and highlight process. It is probably fair to say that most people who participate in sensitivity training come away feeling they have a better grasp of the importance of underlying feelings and emotions in groups. They may also feel that they have a little more skill in expressing how they feel—and in getting others to do so.

While sensitivity training has concentrated on teaching individuals to be generally more sensitive to group and interpersonal processes, other related techniques like team-building programs, now widely used in large organizations, have evolved to train groups rather than individuals. In team building, real teams—groups of people whose work is interconnected—are the units. The method is also process centered; group members are encouraged to talk about their feelings and attitudes in order ultimately to improve task performance.

While these formal mechanisms are often useful, much of their essence can be achieved informally, without elaborate programs. For example, if a particular work group meets frequently, one way to try to improve group performance is to save a few minutes at the end of every meeting for "process analysis," to switch the discussion from task to process and to allow a little review of the group process during the preceding meeting. The question for discussion can be simple: What was good and what was bad (in our own opinions) about today's meeting? Let's identify the problems and then think up ways to solve them. Initially the discussion may be "sanitary." People will suggest the meetings be scheduled in the afternoon instead of the morning, or on Wednesdays instead of Fridays. Or, couldn't we serve coffee? But if the atmosphere stays open, after a few such sessions some more important issues will surface. Issues like: Can we propose agenda items, instead of having you always make up the agenda? Or can we ask Joe to stop bringing outsiders in, because that makes it more difficult for us to speak freely? It's not magic. It's not psychiatry. It's just a fairly commonsense way of letting people improve their own meetings.

In summary

Group process is about how groups work, rather than what they work on. It is, among other things, about people problems, styles of decision making, and methods of leadership. Here are some conclusions about process.

The "emotional noise" made by people in groups may represent attempts by members to satisfy personal needs. If that noise is forbidden expression, it may go underground but continue to distort the group's operation.

Conversely, there may be too little noise in a group; that is, available relevant information may not be forthcoming because of barriers in the communication system. Some of these barriers may be mechanical, but many of them are psychological, like barriers created by status differences or interpersonal jealousies.

In either case, too much emotional noise or too little, the preferred course would seem to be to promote rather than limit communication, that is, to accept and deal with information about personal feelings and personal needs as well as with information about pertinent facts.

Problems involving objectives are one major category of process problems. Objectives often seem clearer than they are. These problems can be dealt with by building discussion of objectives into the agenda, by taking an early census of members' conceptions of the questions to be worked out, and by periodically reexamining objectives.

Personality problems are a major process issue. These include problems of moods, individual needs, and the like. Again, open, permissive communication seems indicated to encourage consideration of these secondary but relevant questions.

Navigational problems also plague groups. Groups can get so involved in content matters that they may lose direction. Periodic stops, to shift from content to process, can alleviate these difficulties.

Decision making raises additional problems in groups. Consensus is an ideal goal if action and initiative outside the group are sought.

Sensitivity training and its relatives make up a diverse package of techniques aimed at helping group members understand process issues better and increasing openness and validity of communication in groups.

19

Group pressure on
the individual
Conformity and deviation

The preceding chapters in this section have been pretty businesslike.
They were concerned with issues like effective performance and high-
quality decision making in groups. But groups are human things, too.
They influence people. Sometimes they scare people or punish them
or make them feel great. They shape and socialize people. They generate standards, values, beliefs for which their members may make great
personal sacrifice. They can exert extraordinary power. They can
"educate" or, if there's any difference, "brainwash" people.

This chapter is about how groups press people, and how people press
groups.

Group pressure on the individual

Here is a problem:

You are a member of a committee. It doesn't matter what sort
of committee; you may be trying to select new products, or
working out a strategy for upcoming negotiations with the union, or
allocating space in the new laboratory, or surreptitiously plotting
an attack on the enemy. It is a committee made up mostly of
people at about your level, chaired by a person who is intelligent
and reasonable and rather well liked by all of you. He has circulated
an agenda in advance of your next meeting, and you have thought
a good deal about it and arrived at a position on the very first item—
a position you feel rather strongly about.

You arrive at the meeting room on time, but a few of the
eight members have not yet shown up, so you and others make
small talk until things get under way. The late arrivals show up,
a few pleasantries are exchanged, and the chairman gets things
started. Gradually one member after another begins to express his
views about the first item on the agenda. By the time you get into

the act, it has become pretty clear that most members seem to
agree on one position—a position very different from yours. Most
people seem to be nodding their heads and saying, "Yes, method X
certainly looks like the best way to go."

Then you come in rather strongly for method Y. Nobody seems
very upset. Everybody listens. Some people ask you questions
and make comments that are partially supportive and partially in
disagreement. And the discussion goes on.

After a while the chairman says, "Well, we've been at this for
awhile; let's see where we stand." And he tries to summarize
the two positions that have been taken, position X and your
position Y. It's all done informally, but one after another, each
in his own style, the members go along with X rather than Y.
As one after another of the members goes this way, you begin to
feel some discomfort. People seem to be turning toward you, psychologically if not physically; and the chairman casts an inquiring
look your way. This is a committee that likes to operate informally,
and you approve of this informality. You know that the chairman
doesn't want to have to put this issue up to a formal vote and
say, "We have decided seven to one in favor of X over Y." On
the other hand, in your opinion, Y is right and X is wrong.

So the pressure begins to build and the spotlight begins to focus
on you. The chairman says, "Well look, ladies and gentlemen,
we've got a little time. Why don't we talk a little longer." And
turning to you, he says, "Why don't you give us a rundown on the
reasons for your position?" So you do. You lay it out in a way that
sounds (to you) forceful and reasonable and correct.

The rest of the committee, which is now focusing rather intently
on you, asks questions. It's as though you are on center stage.
Everybody is turning toward you and talking to you. They are
not shouting at you; they are not angry at you; they are simply asking
you "rationally" to justify your position.

This goes on for a while and then people begin to get a little
fidgety. Finally, one of the members turns to you and says, "Perhaps
our differences aren't as big as they look. Perhaps it's all really
just a matter of words. Sometimes differences that are
really small begin to blow up to look like something bigger than
they are." And the chairman adds, "Well, it is getting rather
late and in the interests of getting this job done, I think we have
to arrive at some kind of conclusion." Then somebody laughs,
turns to you, and says, "Why don't you just come along for the
ride, and then we can all go out and have a cup of coffee?"

You are no dope. You can really feel the pressure now. You

know that what these people are really saying is, "You are one of us. We want to get going. Don't hold us up any longer."

But you're a tough and rugged individualist. You're a person of principle. Position Y is right, by golly, and you say so again rather forcefully. There is a long silence. Then one of the members says something forceful in reply: "Oh for Chrissakes! You've been riding that horse for about three-quarters of an hour now, and you haven't come up with a single new reason. It isn't like you to be so stubborn" As though this first opening is a signal, others join the attack. People go at you from all sides. They point out that you've been wrong before when you've held out in situations like this. They attack your loyalty to the group. After all you know this group likes to operate by consensus, and that it is important to all the rest that you all agree. They hit you with everything they've got. Even the chairman seems to be joining in.

But still you hold out. You just can't bring yourself to accept position X when it is so patently clear to you that Y is the only reasonable answer. So there you sit feeling that this is a little like being interrogated by the Gestapo. Your mouth is dry and you seem to be all alone inside your own thin skin. But you've been raised right! You also think of principle and honor. And so you grit your teeth and fight back. And the clock ticks along.

What comes next?

Pretty far down inside you, you know damn well what comes next. The floodlights will be turned off; but not to give you relief. Finally (and rather suddenly), one of the members turns to the chairman and says, "We've been at this for almost an hour and a half. We have other business at hand. I think we should adopt position X, and then go on to the next item." And other people turn their chairs, facing one another and the chairman; but no longer facing you. They summarize the arguments for position X and someone says, "Okay, we've decided to do X; now let's move on."

You've been quiet for the last few minutes because people haven't been talking to you. You have listened to the summary of the reasons for accepting position X, and since one of them is clearly absurd, you open your mouth to say something about it. A couple of people in the group turn and look at you as you talk, but they don't say anything in return. The others don't even look, and the chairman finally says, "Let's get on to the next problem on the agenda." And the group goes ahead.

You know what's happened. You have been psychologically sealed off. As far as the group is concerned, you are no longer there. When you speak, no one hears you. Your influence is now zero. You have reached the last stage in the process by which groups deal with deviating, nonconforming members. You have been amputated.

In one version or another, this story is probably familiar to almost every adult. It is not limited to committees of executives in industry. We encountered the same pressures when we were kids, in the family, in streetcorner gangs, and in school groups. We met it again as teenagers, when we were pressed to conform to group standards of dress and deportment—standards we often tried to resist. And we will continue to encounter it.

The stages of group pressure

But the fact that we have encountered it often doesn't reduce the pain and the pressure. In fact, our experience has taught us so well that we can usually foresee early in the process what we will be in for if we buck the group. We know they are likely to start out being reasonable, discussing the pros and cons of the issue. But even at that stage, it is implicitly clear that the deviant, not the group, is expected to change.

We can sense what will come next, too. We know the seductive pat-on-the-back routine. We know that some members of the group will be friendly and smile and joke with us. They will, in effect, tell us how much they love us and remind us of how valuable the group is to us. They will chuck us under the chin and make up to us in order to pacify us.

And we also know what is likely to happen if we don't come across.

Groups, like children, tire of playing games rather quickly. They will decide that they have wasted enough time on that tactic. Then the silken glove will come off to expose the iron fist. If reason won't work, and seduction won't work, then the group moves to stage 3, attack. Now they try to beat us into submission. They pull out all stops; the gloves are off.

But even that isn't the last stage in the process of exerting pressure on the deviating individual. The last stage is amputation. It's as though the members of the group were saying, "Let's reason with him; if that doesn't work, let's try to tease him by emotional seduction; and if even that doesn't work, let's beat him over the head until he has to give up. Failing that, we'll excommunicate him; we'll amputate him from the group; we'll disown him."

This last and final stage is for most of us a very serious and frightening possibility; the more frightening, the more we value the group.

The threat of isolation, physical or psychological, is a very grave threat indeed. We don't want to be abandoned by our families, nor by our friends, nor by our business associates.

Perhaps it is because we can foresee this ultimate stage that even mild and early pressures can cause us to change positions or beliefs or attitudes. Most of us don't get all the way through meetings like the one we described at the beginning of this chapter. We give in a good deal earlier in the game. We "work things out" when we are still at the reasoning level or at the emotional seduction level. For the paradox in this process is that the greater the pressure the group exerts on the deviant through these steps, the more difficult it is for the deviant to give in. The stage at which we can give in most easily (and still save face) is the first stage; the reasonable, rational stage. If we say "yes" in response to the chucking under the chin and the emotional seduction, we are apt to feel a little sheepish, but that isn't terribly embarrassing. To give in under a beating is a lot more painful, and a lot weaker and more shameful. And to give in after we have been amputated is darn near impossible because nobody is there to accept our surrender.

Is the group being cruel and capricious?

So far we have been viewing the group's pressures on the deviant from the deviant's perspective. For most of us the individual who holds out is the hero, whether he wins or loses. For we value individuality and nonconformity in our society, or at least we say we do. We identify with the underdog, with the deer attacked by wolves. But consider this same problem from the other perspective, the group's. We may ask: Why are these people doing this? Why are they reasoning, seducing, attacking, amputating? Is it just a malicious, devilish kind of behavior to satisfy some sadistic needs of the group members? Not usually. If we think of the times we ourselves have been members of the majority, we can begin to see the other side of the pitcure.

Here is a group that is trying to get a job done. To get the job done well depends in large part on getting wholehearted agreement and co-operation from all members of the group. But there is a clock, and there are other constraints imposed by the world.

We go about the problem in good spirit, trying to cooperate, trying to understand, trying to work out a solution that we can all accept and to do it in a reasonable time. And we come very close to an answer. Everybody seems to be in perfect agreement except for that one character there.

Then what shall we do? As reasonable people, we do not steam-roller a person because he thinks differently from us. We listen to him and we ask him to listen to us. So we go through that ritual. We reason with him. But that doesn't work; he just doesn't seem to be able to see it our way. The clock is ticking away.

What next? Why then we try to appeal to him on emotional grounds, on grounds of loyalty or decency. We almost beg him to agree. This is a difficult thing for us to do, but we want to get the job done and we don't want to hurt him. We appeal to him to join up, to go along, to maintain a solid front. But he stubbornly refuses.

Now what? So now we hit him. Now we really are mad at him, so we let him have it. Maybe if we all jump up and down on him, he will have sense enough to come around. And the clock ticks on. But the stupid, stubborn s.o.b. still holds out.

What then? Well, then we must take a step that is as painful for us as it is for him. We must dismember our group. We must amputate one of our own members, leaving us less than whole, less than intact, but at least capable of coming to a conclusion. With this recalcitrant, stubborn, impossible member, this group cannot remain a group. To preserve it, we have no choice but to cut him out.

Viewed this way, the deviant individual is not such a hero. Much of the world's complex work is done by groups. When a group exerts pressure on an individual, it may thus not constitute an arbitrary imposition of power, but rather a set of increasingly desperate efforts to try to hold the group together in order to get the work done.

Does the deviant do anybody any good?

Besides the argument that it is good and wholesome and healthy for individuals to be independent thinkers—an argument that is not always as sensible as it sounds—is there any other good argument for encouraging individuals to take deviant positions if they believe in them, and for encouraging groups not to clobber people who deviate?

The answer, of course, is that there is at least one very good practical reason, in addition to all the moral reasons. It is the fact that deviants stimulate groups to think about what they are doing. Deviants, whether they are themselves creative or not, generate both creativity and thoroughness in groups.

The process is simple enough and understandable enough. When like-minded people get together to talk over an issue, they are likely to come to agreement pretty quickly and then to pat one another on the back and go out and drink beer. When the same people get together in the presence of someone with quite different ideas, they are forced to reexamine their own beliefs, to go over them in detail, to consider sides and aspects of the problem which they never had to consider before. They must do this in order to argue effectively with the deviant, in order to attack him, in order to reason with him. As a consequence, they end up knowing more about their own problem than they would have if the deviant hadn't been there. It costs the group time and sweat. But what they earn is greater understanding, broader search, more knowledge of their own subject matter.

Can the deviant ever win?

We now come to the next question in this logical sequence: Suppose the deviant is right? Does he have a chance? Or will his presence simply cause the group that is already wrong to believe more strongly but more sophisticatedly in its wrong position?

The answer to this one is rather complicated. There is rather good research evidence that people can and will distinguish better answers from worse ones. And a deviant who comes up with a clearly better answer, even in the face of a large group that has agreed upon another answer, has a very good chance of getting his answer accepted. Such is the case at least for problems with a clear logical structure. If I can demonstrate to you a clearly easier way to add a column of figures than the way all of you are now adding them, it will not be too hard for me to swing you over to my method. So the deviant who comes up with a new solution—one that other people had not even thought of, but clearly a good solution—is likely to have little trouble getting it through.

Unfortunately, many problems, probably *most* problems, tackled by groups aren't quite of that nature. They are fuzzily outlined judgmental problems, in which ordering the quality of solutions is not so easy. The "normal" problems are problems like selecting or promoting personnel, or allocating funds among several departments, or deciding on a sales program. On those kinds of issues the deviant doesn't have much of a chance in most groups.

And here we encounter another paradox. The one with the different ideas, the deviant, is apt to have a better chance of getting his ideas accepted by a group that isn't very solid, isn't very cohesive, hasn't worked together very much, than by a group that is solid, whose members do know and like one another. So the executive may find himself faced with what looks like a strange dilemma. On the one hand he wants solidity, loyalty, high morale in his group. On the other hand, he may want the creativity he can get from the deviant. And yet it is precisely the high-morale, cohesive group that will go after the deviant hard and fast; that will clobber him even more quickly than the new group or the unsure group.

But the paradox may be more apparent than real. In a way all we are saying is that the people with different ideas may be able to pull a snow job on a bunch of people who feel shy and uncertain with one another. He has a chance of influencing them, of getting his ideas through, more readily than he could in a solid group. But he is likely to get his ideas through, not because a pick-up group will examine and consider those ideas more rationally or more seriously than a solid group; but rather because they are constrained, uncertain, unwilling to open themselves up for fear of attack by others. So the aggressive deviant, the one who talks loud and fast, may be able to get to them.

On the other hand, when faced with a solid, self-assured group, the snow job is almost impossible. The deviant will have to prove his case and prove it rather thoroughly. But, of course, the probability of his being able to prove it to a group that is solid and self-assured is not very great. For they are not likely to break ranks unless the logic of the case is so clear, so rational, so obviously better than their own solution, that only a fool could reject it.

What kind of deviant can survive?

Interestingly enough, even powerful deviants don't seem to have much chance against a strong and solid group. As all of us know, a member of the group who is already peripheral and uninfluential—the new, young member of a streetcorner gang, for example—is in a poor position to try to push a new idea through. But we are apt to think that if a person is strong and central in the group—the leader of the streetcorner gang—then he should be almost omnipotent, capable of getting the group to accept even extremely different ideas. The fact of the matter seems to be, however, that even strong members of groups, people with authority or with personal influence and power, have a very tough time pushing a group very far from its own standards. Even the kingpin has to move slowly, by bits and pieces, to get the gang to stop stealing apples and start playing basketball. If he doesn't move slowly, he will get the same treatment as any other deviant and eventually find himself amputated.

The same seems to be true in industry. Even the powerful boss will meet a good deal of trouble in pushing a very different idea through a solid group of subordinates. If he is a real Machiavellian manipulator, he will work first on individuals when he is trying to bring about a radical change, rather than on the face-to-face group.

The lonely executive

It may seem a shockingly soft thing to say, but one can interpret most of the research and commonsense analysis of conformity as essentially a problem in loneliness. Group pressures can be exerted on individuals —lone individuals—much more effectively than they can be exerted on pairs or subgroups. It is when the deviant finds himself alone, without a twig of support, without even another deviant (even one who deviates in quite different directions), that the pressures of the group are apt to become overpowering. It may be this fear of isolation, of singleness, that permits a group to press the individual to conform, even if that individual has authority or other kinds of power. Even the president seems to want and need some sources of support, some assurance of psychological backing from his people. He needs not to be all alone. In fact, much of the effect of group pressure can be washed out by the simple expedient of having just one other member of the group back up the deviant.

Thus again we encounter a paradox. For now we are saying that it is loneliness that will force a person to conform to the group. Which implies that he will feel less pressure to conform (and therefore feel more independent) if he is in the group—a full member of it—and thus not at all lonely. So how now are we to answer the earlier question: Does the group force the individual to fit into its mold, thereby reducing his individuality, thereby brainwashing him? Or is it only when he is a psychologically secure member of the group that he can express his individuality without feeling pressure and restraint?

There is an answer. People need psychological support, an environment free from the fear of loneliness. But if that support is bought at the price of constricting conformity, the individual loses his individuality no matter which way he goes. So the critical issue becomes the nature of the group. On what dimensions of behavior does it demand conformity? Does it demand, as the price of support, that he dress as they dress, that he believe as they believe? Or does it set more open standards, requiring conformity in fewer dimensions and perhaps less critical ones? Does it only require, perhaps, that everyone conform to certain time demands and certain demands of procedure, while consciously avoiding requirements of conformity in opinion or belief? Indeed, can a group set a positive standard of nonconformity?

Since the individual needs the group, the group can exploit the individual, forcing him to bend to its demands. But individuals make groups, and it is possible to make groups that exert tolerable pressures on procedure but do not constrain beliefs and ideas.

In later chapters we shall return to this issue of group pressure on individual behavior. It becomes important, for example, in the design of management-development programs and in contemporary "experiments" with self-managing systems in manufacturing and other organizations.

In summary

Groups put pressure on members who deviate. Usually the pressure moves through several stages, from rational argument through emotional seduction to attack and finally to amputation of the deviant member. But the process is not usually capricious or sadistic. From the group's side, they exert pressure in an effort to survive intact and to get the job done.

Group pressures work mostly when the deviant feels all alone. Given any kind of minimal support, he can hold out much more effectively. And though a powerful deviant has a better chance than a weak one, no deviant can try to push a solid group very far very fast and expect to get away with it.

Clearly, deviants make groups think, even when they don't change the group's mind. But we need to temper two prevalent notions about deviation: The first is the notion that nonconformity is somehow always better than conformity. We must remember that much of the world's work can only be done by conforming to agreed-upon standards. The second is the notion that groups kill individuality by exerting pressures to conform. We need to remember that most of us feel freer to be ourselves in groups where our position and membership are secure, than in settings in which we feel alone and unsupported.

20

Conflict and competition among groups My team can beat your team

Let's suppose that I am the manager of a large manufacturing and consumer marketing operation. I am democratic and progressive, though perhaps not very bright. I also want to get the best possible ideas out of my people. It is clear that we will need a new design for one of our key products to start the next season. So I ask the heads of each of three groups to submit proposals for the redesign. I ask each group head to get together with his people and develop what they think would be an optimal design.

But I don't want to get into the position of having to select the one design I think is best, especially since I am not a very competent designer myself. Moreover, I want to open up discussion and communication. So I inform them that after all three designs are in, I would like to have each group circulate its design to the members of the other two groups. Then when each group has had a chance to look over all three, I would like representatives of the three groups to meet together to decide which of the three designs is, in their joint opinion, the best one for the company to develop.

Thus, by keeping everyone informed of everything, by giving all groups a chance to look over three alternative designs. I figure that I should be able to get (1) the best of the three designs and (2) understanding and agreement among all three groups. Do you think this plan will work?

The experimental evidence says it won't work at all. This scheme of having several groups each work out a problem and then resolve differences among themselves is almost doomed to failure. And most of us know it, but we don't really believe it won't work even when we're right in the middle of it. Perhaps the best way to describe what does happen is to quote an insurance company executive who joined in an experimental version of the same kind of problem:

> We were divided at random into four teams. The instructor then asked us to draft a statement of policy for our Company in answer

to a certain hypothetical situation. Each group, working separately, was to draft its version. It took each group about two hours to hammer out its statement. Each group elected a representative to meet with one another to select one of the four statements. I was elected to represent my group. The members of my group, though naturally proud of their effort (they had reviewed the other three drafts in the interim), were confident that reaching agreement with the others would be easy.

The four representatives sat at a card table in the center of the room; behind each man, breathing down his neck, sat the group he represented. It soon developed that the over-all objectives of the four groups were quite close; it merely remained to choose one of the drafts. At the end of an hour we were further apart than ever. I asked my group for permission to vote for one of the other drafts. My request was indignantly turned down. Feelings had begun to run high. Logic had been tried; gamesmanship had been tried.

Notes were passed forward by each group to its representative. These notes were not helpful at all; they merely urged us to "get" the other man on some point or other. All had failed—the results were shattering.

Four judges, previously elected by their groups, were now called in. They had not participated in drafting the policy statements at all. During the time we had been working out our policy statement, they had drawn up criteria for evaluating the four drafts. The drafts were then submitted to them anonymously. In just one half hour and in a separate room in calm deliberation they had reached a unanimous decision. The experiment was over.

Most of the things that happened were highly predictable. They were predictable mostly because of the role of emotional and psychological elements, which we tend willingly to overlook when we concentrate on getting a task done. The uniform and predictable happenings include these:

1. As each group begins to develop its own solution it becomes more internally cohesive and solid. Morale within groups tends to go up, as their design takes shape. And when they have finally produced something together, they are apt to feel quite high on themselves. Sometimes, of course, a deviant or two pops up; so the happy solidity is a little cracked and shaky.

2. When each group sees the comparable work of the other groups, the initial reaction is apt to be a slight letdown, followed by a quick

recovery and continued increase in group morale. Usually, after the group members have seen the others' solutions someone will say, "I didn't feel very sure of our design until I saw these others. But if these are the only things these other groups have to offer it's pretty clear that ours is the only one worth a damn." Of course that means that the deviants have a face-saving means of reentering their groups.

3. In each group this same solidifying, balancing process goes on; so that by the time the representatives come together each in effect is convinced that the design he is offering is the best of all the designs—"honestly" the best; and, moreover, he has now, he feels, been charged by his group to convince the other two that his design is the one they should all buy.

4. Initially, the representatives, when they meet together, are likely to behave like the majority dealing with the deviant in the preceding chapter. Each provides reasons to support his own group's design over the designs of the other two. But especially if this is a public meeting, this rational discussion soon turns into a duel. The representatives start to cut one another to pieces. They try to top one another in their cleverness and wit. The goal of finding a single best design soon fades out in favor of that of trying to be a hero to his own group. And if the representative cannot appear a hero, at least he must not be a traitor. He must not give in. So the representatives almost never become a functioning group. They become gladiators, battling for the approval of their constituents, trying not to be publicly destroyed by the others.

5. The representatives then usually start gaming each other. They try to form coalitions, two or three against one; but they all know that these coalitions are opportunistic. They cannot count on their allies should they see some kind of opportunity for advancing their own causes. Sometimes, the representatives will thus come to some kind of a half-baked decision. Two of them will outvote a third, or one representative will be weak enough (or his group split open enough) so that he gives in. But most of the time they deadlock and finally give up in favor of an outside decision.

6. Suppose that at this point we argue that the difficulty is obvious; it is the social pressure of the groups on their members that is really preventing a decision. Somehow if we could get to the private opinions of the individual members—if we could get to the people—they, in their wisdom, would recognize and admit to the design that is really the best one.

So now we take a secret ballot among all members of all groups. They have now had a chance to see all three designs, to study them, to discuss them, to debate about them, and they all have some expertise about design.

That doesn't work either. In almost every case the group members vote nearly 100 percent in favor of the design submitted by their own group. Even privately, one's own group's design looks best. Occasionally there will be a break in the pattern. One or two members of the team may admit that another design looks better. Usually these are peripheral or deviant members of their teams who were troublesome from the beginning.

7. So if the groups can't decide, and if the individual members can't decide, we can now throw the decision to authority—to the boss. Or if we wanted to, we could throw it to a board of arbitrators who would sit down impartially, and independently look at all reports, perhaps without knowing which report was written by which group. In most cases, the boss or the arbitrators then have no trouble at all. They come to agreement quickly and quite easily.

8. Now we have a decision. We have taken it to the top and the top has decided. And isn't this the way we should have done it in the first place? Perhaps so, but what does this "decision" mean? The design submitted by group X has now been chosen, group Y's is the alternate; and group Z's is considered completely inadequate. Now what happens? In experimental runs of this sort, what happens is quite uniform. The winning group is elated. It feels good and thinks highly of the board of arbitrators that has chosen its design. The losing group feels hostile, frustrated, depressed. Privately, and sometimes publicly, they will insist that the arbitrators really didn't know what they were doing, and that any really imaginative expert in the field would recognize the superiority of their (the losing) design. So the fact of the decision from above does not completely solve the problem. It certainly has not solved it in the sense of developing commitment by all groups.

9. We can follow this experimental design a step further, and put the groups to work again on some new problem. Then we encounter some interesting new results. The group that has just won is apt to be self-satisfied and comfortable and "frozen." Though its organization and social structure may be less than perfect, nobody dares to change it. The people who were powerful in the development of the first design remain powerful on the next problem, whether they are qualified or not, because even though some members may want some changes, no one dares disturb the winning combination.

The third team, the losing one, may be in serious internal trouble. They may feel their representative has let them down. Individuals who took minority or deviant positions now come back in with I-told-you-so comments that engender further interpersonal bickering and stress. Usually such groups will recover from this internecine warfare; but sometimes they will collapse entirely. If winning groups freeze, the losing team melts. It so readily abandons its original organization that it has a great deal of trouble finding anything to hold it together.

The second team is a lot better off. They have lost but they have not been decimated. They are apt to be analytic and thoughtful in the reexamination of what happened in the first round. They are unfrozen in a sense, but they have not completely melted. Other things being equal they are a good team on which to place a bet for the future.

So psychologists have been conducting experiments of this kind that demonstrate issues that seem obvious and simple; that people develop great loyalty to what they produce themselves, and to one another when they produce something together; that this in-group loyalty may be so overwhelming as to make it effectively impossible (at least within the structure set up in these experiments) for the groups to come to agreement with other groups.

Some morals

Let's turn now to the morals of this tale. In some ways these are negative experiments. They demonstrate how agreement cannot be reached, rather than how it can. They also show how easy it is to start a fight, even among grown-up and reasonable people. They reiterate the old truism that it is easy to build a solid group by providing them with an outside enemy. They tell us—as we all know—that representatives of groups are often much more concerned (and understandably so) about the groups at their backs than the problem before them.

But they also offer some much larger, if tentative, morals. As we begin to realize the almost incredible ease with which conflict between groups can be created, two worrisome, related thoughts arise.

First, one begins to feel wonder at the very existence of large societies. The pressure toward fragmentation is so great and fragmentation itself so easy, that the survival of large groups such as tribes, nations, or even companies looks very impressive indeed. One wonders why we haven't broken up into little bits faster and faster.

Second, if social dikes are really as easily rupturable as it appears, perhaps it is time for more of us to get our fingers into them to try to hold things together.

A third generalization that is perhaps worth noting: Although most of us are properly proud of our uniqueness and individuality, we are to a great extent driven by the structures in which we find ourselves. Psychologists would be hard put to predict the behavior of any single individual in the experiment we described earlier. But it's easy to predict the behavior of the groups. Once we have set up the structure, the overall human outcomes appear almost to be guaranteed. Autonomous and free though we may appear, we live in social structures, and our collective behavior is very much an outcome of those structural characteristics. If we had been raised in the USSR, we would not only speak Russian, we would think Russian, we would perceive Russian, we would fight Russian.

The positive side

How about the positive side? If we want representatives to pay attention to the problem at hand we need either to reduce the pressure from their groups, or to make the representatives a sufficiently cohesive group so that membership in the *representative group* is something meaningful and important in its own right. By doing the latter we will put the squeeze on the representative, making his life miserable by requiring him to owe loyalty to two groups, even though those two groups are in partial conflict. But we will also increase the probability that he will indeed represent both points of view to both groups and thus increase the level of objectivity of the whole show.

There may be several other things we can do to increase the probability of an acceptable solution. We can search for "superordinate" goals; for objectives so large and important to every member that differences go by the board. These may be negatively induced goals—like Pearl Harbor—bringing subgroups together by threatening all of them; or better still—but harder—they may be positively induced, like the coalescence of all groups in a depressed community to lift the community out of the doldrums.

There is a third possibility—the method of education. Perhaps if people are more aware of the traps around them they can avoid them more successfully.

Another note should be sounded here. Organizations can almost be said to have *styles* of conflict management. In some, for example, direct conflict is avoided at almost any cost. The culture demands that people be polite in meetings, that underlying differences not be discussed openly. In other organizations conflict tends to be confronted more directly. People express disagreement and argue for positions. It is easy for most of us to prefer the first to the second. It looks civilized, courteous, and comfortable. But it may be wise at this point to take a better look at the second. For when the world is changing fast, it may behoove organizations to face internal conflicts openly, indeed to welcome argument and debate, as the catalyst for its own change.

Some varieties of conflict and accompanying tactics

We haven't said much yet about the several different kinds of conflict that can occur in organizations. In our example the conflict was among peer groups of about equal size, status, and power. But that isn't the way things always line up. Sometimes a small group finds itself up against a much larger group or coalition of groups. Sometimes power differences arise—workers versus management, for example. And sometimes a small and also subordinate group takes on a larger group with more power and authority, like a dissident subgroup in the larger church, or a small group of student radicals in a large, conservative university.

There are several, quite different means that groups can use to resolve conflicts.

The first is war—coercive power, as we called it earlier. If you're the big powerful group, you clobber the little group. You kill them, jail them, excommunicate them, banish them. You hoist their heads on poles.

If you're the little group in a power war, you must count on other forms of power: hit-and-run guerrilla tactics, blackmail; and of course, you seek alliances to increase your power. You curry public opinion. You try to prevail on other big groups to back you up.

Obviously these kinds of tactics are still with us, largely unchanged from the days of the caveman. But we have added a few new, hopefully somewhat more moderate and civilized tactics to the conflict scene, haven't we? Indeed, isn't the measure of civilization the degree to which conflicts, even between more and less powerful groups, can be solved by less coercive means? We have set up governments, organizations, and legal systems, all of which are intended to move the issue of conflict resolution away from raw power and toward—toward what? Toward reason? Perhaps it's still too early to expect much of that.

How about toward *negotiation* and *trading* situations? Nothing to be terribly proud of, perhaps, but nothing to denigrate too readily, either. From the bread-and-butter bargains made by congressmen who vote for one another's favorite bills, to the informal (and illegal) coalitions among business competitors to fix prices or agree upon territories, to union-management bargaining, society rides on negotiations, trades, compromises, and accommodations to conflicts. Most of them are legal; many aren't. Most don't truly resolve conflicts; they just keep them within bounds. But surely that's better than war.

Sometimes we inch a step beyond that, especially in the relations of large and powerful groups to small rebellious ones in their midst.

Traditionally the resolution of these conflicts was simple: big steps on little. But sometimes because the big groups are unsure of themselves, or sometimes because the big ones are very sure of themselves, they have moved from direct coercive power toward *absorption* as a method for ending conflict with little groups.

All absorption means in this context is that large group A tries to deal with dissident little group B by behaving like a big pillow. University administration A, for example, says to its protesting students B, "O.K. We'll do some of the things you ask. But you must take a large part of the responsibility for doing them. You want to participate; we'll let you participate, part way. We'll put three students on the fifteen-man search committee for a new president," etc.

The big organization bends, backs off, but in bits and pieces. The little one gets some of what it wants, but at a price—the price of partial cooperation, of partial reentry into membership in the parent organization.

This process may at first seem indistinguishable from slaughter, at least to the dedicated and rebellious, small group, for its effect may well be the ultimate demise of that group. Certainly it can be viewed as emasculation, for protesting groups, founded on protest, cannot easily survive if they get most of what they want. But sometimes, depending on motives and intent, the process can represent a considerable degree of civilized effort by the large group to acknowledge the need for change and to bring it about at a price. For the large group pays a price in the absorption process, too. It remains the establishment, but it is a changed establishment, changed by the pressures from the small group.

Does it happen in business organizations?

The reader may well point out that the kind of experiment we described at the beginning of this chapter seems more typical of governments or political groups than industrial organizations. No intelligent manager, they might argue, would ever set up a situation like the one described. He wouldn't put three groups to work doing the same thing, and even if he did he wouldn't let them decide among themselves which of the outcomes was best.

Let's grant that one. But even holding problems of union-management relations aside, aren't there other parallels in most large organizations? Can't we think of large organizations, at least in part, as sets of groups in power relationships with one another? The problem may not be a new product design. It may be the location and size of a new warehouse. And the groups may not be three parallel design groups, but a regional sales force that wants something very different from what a staff analysis group thinks would be optimal. Or the issue may be the allocation of slices of the capital budget. And the members of the capital budgeting committee may be, partially at least, representatives of one subgroup or another. Or sales groups vie for the same classes of accounts; or maintenance people want control of a process the technical people claim is theirs. And so on and on. These are less pure cases of identification of members of organizations with subgroups and special subgroup interests, but their essence is the same.

Some recent approaches to managing intergroup conflict

Traditionally, organizations have tried to handle conflict, we said, by coercive measures or through negotiation and compromise or by "absorption" of protesting groups. Of course, they have also called in higher authority. If there is a fight between the kids, Papa makes the decision. But since two warring groups know that both will look bad if they take their dispute upstairs, conflicts are often "handled" by going underground. Nobody admits there's a war. The kids pinch each other when Papa isn't looking, but behave like little sweethearts in public.

The dangers of such phony resolutions are very great in organizations. Conflicts between groups nefariously eat away at the organization's health.

Are there alternatives? One that has been experimented with widely in recent years is the technique of *confrontation*. It derives from some of the beliefs about the nature of human groups that we discussed earlier. When groups are in conflict, the argument goes, the conflict will necessarily involve feelings as well as facts, process as well as content. Although the groups may argue only about the facts of their positions, they also (as indicated early in this chapter) tend to develop stereotypes and prejudices about one another. We see ourselves more and more as the good guys, and they become more and more the bad guys. They are selfish, power-mad, wicked. We are just trying to do a job. This process of positively valuing one's own group and increasingly denigrating the other derives, as the reader will see, from the tendency of group members to support one another and to overvalue their own position in the presence of outsiders.

Even if this emotional separation accompanies conflicts that may have been started over factual issues, it will have to be dealt with. Hence the notion of confrontation. Let's bring the groups together, usually with a third-party process manager, and let's have them talk, not about the factual issues, but about feelings and attitudes. If we can get those stereotypes and distortions of feeling straightened out, perhaps we can go back to the factual differences and work on them, this time with a problem-solving attitude rather than a game-playing or warlike one.

In summary

It is very easy to set up situations in which groups compete with one another. In such settings the solidity and morale of members within groups is apt to climb steadily as the competition progresses. But the feeling between groups is apt to degenerate into bickering and hostility. In such situations the naive use of meetings of representatives may simply aggravate the problem. What starts out as an honest effort to reach a resolution can quickly become a public display of each representative's capacity to outtalk and outwit the others.

Members of groups identify so closely with their own product, and representatives identify so closely with their own groups, that the likelihood of resolution decreases as the morale of each group develops, rather than the other way around. On the other hand, outsiders, when not identified with the group, find it easy to reach agreement and to rate some group products as better than others. But if these outsiders then try to impose their choice upon the groups (even though the groups have invited it), the result is less than ideal. The group whose product is selected, of course, accepts the outsiders' decision. But the other groups will feel recalcitrant and generally dissatisfied. Nevertheless, while denying the validity of a decision that has gone against them, the losing group is apt to lose its cohesiveness and to degenerate into internal warfare and bickering. The winning group, on the other hand, may sit on its hands, satisfied with itself and fearful of changing anything about its structure, lest it break up the winning combination.

This chapter offers no clear solutions to problems of intergroup struggle and competition. It suggests, however, that greater understanding of the extent to which one's behavior is dictated by group factors may contribute to more objectivity. It suggests that if we can tie representatives together so that they, too, develop loyalties to one another, they may operate more effectively, though suffering more personal stress. Finally, if we can somehow develop stronger identification with the total organization's goals, then, perhaps, the best of all possible worlds will result. We shall consider that problem in a little more detail in the next chapter, which is on management development.

Some tentative generalizations to broader problems of social and organizational conflict were included in this chapter, to try to show some varieties of conflict that can occur, the strategies that can be tried to cope with them, and their relevance to social and organizational survival and progress.

Presently, experiments in resolving conflicts by confrontation methods are under way in many different settings. In labor-management conflicts, management conflicts, and others, these efforts are meeting with some success. Their aim is to help conflicting groups to share their attitudes and feelings about one another, as a precursor to working on more factual differences.

21 Communication networks in groups Designs for getting the word around

Like the relationship between two people, the relationships among members of a group are limited by the kinds of communication that occur. In chapter 10, we pointed out that communication has several dimensions, only one of which is the content of what is said.

The same holds for groups. Group members can talk about all sorts of ideas, but they can also use one-way or two-way communication no matter what they talk about. They can, moreover, carry on more or less noisy and redundant conversations. And, the reader will recall, group members can communicate over different *networks*.

A network, for our purposes, is a structure, a system of connections among people who are members of a group. Sometimes in larger organizations we have formal networks, "official" communication structures. In smaller groups the networks that evolve tend to be more informal, often unknowingly generated mostly by the person leading the group. Some group leaders tend to encourage open-to-everyone networks, and some set up structures in which each member speaks only to the leader. The type of network within which a group works is important, both to the effectiveness with which a group performs its task, and to the morale, attitudes, and even creativity of its members.

Most of this chapter is going to summarize some research done on communication networks in small groups. These experiments may strike the reader as a little abstract at first, but try to stay with them because the underlying ideas have important implications for the way we design organizations and the way we manage small groups.

What we mean by communication nets

Communication nets are a *structural* aspect of a group. They tell us how the group is hung together. Consider, for instance, the difference between a boss who sets himself up to communicate with his staff like this:

234

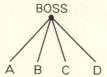

and one who prefers to divide his four staff people into two seniors and two juniors:

The lines here represent lines of communication. These diagrams are structural. They tell us nothing about the people involved—just something about the "system." What differences might such different setups make in the boss's flow of information? In his flexibility? In the originality of the ideas he gets?

Consider also the effects on subordinates of being in one communicational position or another—like B in the two charts. In one case he can talk to his superior directly, in the other he must go through channels?

For example, suppose that for a group of five persons all channels are two-way channels. Then this question still remains: What system of channels will be the most effective system for these five people? Will such a group solve problems best when everyone has an open two-way channel to everyone else? Like this:

Or is *this* system better?

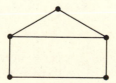

Or this one?

And which of those nets is the most fun to work in?

Even though each of these networks provides enough communication channels to permit intercommunication, the arrangements and numbers of channels differ, and so, therefore, may the effectiveness of the group as a problem-solving body. Moreover, some of these networks fit better with the usual company organization chart than others; some would look very strange indeed on an organization chart.

In practical terms the question now is this one: How does the communication network affect both the efficiency of a group's performance and the morale of the group's members?

Testing communication networks

The best way to answer such questions may be temporarily to strip away the complications found in real life. Then one can set up small experimental committees and put them to work in one or another of these networks. By providing each experimental group with some standard tasks and then measuring performance, one can get some ideas about the relative efficiency of one of these networks versus another. In the past two decades such experimental work has been carried on, and the results have been both consistent and interesting.

The reader might like to try to decide for himself, on a commonsense basis, just what results one should get with one of these networks or another. So, for illustrative purposes, consider these two networks of five people each:

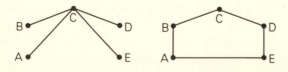

Such groups might be analogous to groups of field staff people, each located in a different branch or district but all reporting eventually to the same boss at headquarters. Let's say communication is by telephone. In both networks, A, E, B, and D are district people, and C is someone back at the central office.

In an experimental setup, one can give each group the same problem, a problem which requires some information from each person before it can be solved. Usually it is some sort of puzzle, in many ways analogous to a pricing problem in a rapidly changing supply-and-demand situation.

Which of these two groups will solve this kind of problem faster? Which group will have the higher morale? Will there be a leader in no. 1? In no. 2? Which particular positions in group no. 1 or no. 2 will be high morale positions? Which will be low morale positions?

Here are the answers that have come out of experiments like these: Network no. 1 will be the faster of the two.

On the whole, the morale of group no. 2 will be higher than that of group no. 1. People will be more enthusiastic in group no. 2.

Only one person in group no. 1 is likely to get a big bang out of the job, and that man is C. The others, A, B, D, and E will probably feel bored and left out of the center of things.

Person C in no. 1 will probably be the leader of that group. Everyone in the group will be likely to turn to him. In no. 2 the leader (the one who gets the answer first and sends it out to the others) can be almost anybody. In fact, there may be a different leader each time the group runs through a problem, or else no identifiable leader at all.

Another finding in these researches is most intriguing in its implications for industry. Two groups are put to work in the circle (no. 2) and star (no. 1) patterns. Their task is as follows: Each person is given five solid-colored marbles of which one color is common to all persons in the group. The group must find the one color that all 5 members have in common. They then write notes to one another over the available channels, saying things like this: "I have red, green, yellow, blue, and brown." Eventually they discover that all have red marbles. After playing this game several times, the groups in both networks become proficient and fast. At this point, the marbles are changed. Instead of simple solid colors, they are given mottled marbles, of odd shades, difficult to describe. Now two people looking at identical marbles may describe them quite differently. One may use the term "greenish yellow," the other may call it "aqua." "Noise," in other words, has entered the system in the form of a semantic problem.

The interesting finding is the difference between these two networks in their ability to adapt to and meet this change. The circle handles it nicely, so that after ten runs or so it is back to high efficiency. The star can't seem to cope with it, still making a large number of errors after many trials. This result certainly suggests that the structure of an organization influences its adaptability as well as its other forms of efficiency.

Communication structure, then, does affect a group's efficiency, at least in this kind of situation. But much depends on the definition one gives to the word "efficiency." Some communication networks allow for faster operation than others, but the advantage of speed may be gained at the cost of accuracy and/or morale. People are happier in some networks than they are in others, and some networks therefore are more likely to keep going longer without blowing up, but these networks may be slower or less accurate than some others. This conflict between "morale" and "efficiency" may indeed turn out to be a generalized conflict in industrial organizations. Some networks make fewer errors than others. Some are more flexible than others. All these words may have something to do with what we mean by "efficiency."

Why different networks cause people to behave differently

If we look at these results in the light of parts 1 and 2, they are not hard to understand. Why is network no. 1 faster than network no. 2? For one thing, no. 1 is like a one-way communication system. Although people can talk back individually to the central person, they cannot talk to one another. No. 1 imposes an orderliness on the group that wipes out extra messages. In no. 2 no such clear organization is imposed. People can send messages to two people; they can get around more and thereby spend more time.

But in sending more messages, members of no. 2 also are taking advantage of more checkpoints of the kind provided by two-way communication. Thus, they can locate and correct more of their errors.

They also have in no. 2 more chance to participate and take responsibility. They are less dependent on one person since they can check with one other person. So they are more satisfied and happy, just as people were in the two-way communication example in chapter 10.

On the other hand, the central person in network no. 1 is quite happy—and for the same reasons. He has responsibility, he has several sources of information and several checkpoints. He is independent and powerful.

In these ways, then, the mere mechanical fact of *structure* can act upon individuals by making them more or less dependent, more or less certain of where they stand, and more or less responsible. The same fact of structure can also act upon the total operational efficiency of the group, causing it to work faster or slower, more or less accurately, and more or less adaptably.

Once again, though, it is worth pointing out, as we did in chapter 10, that structure seems to affect people's feelings in one direction and their speed and accuracy in the other. No one has yet found a structure that maximizes speed and accuracy and, at the same time, morale and flexibility.

Networks in industrial groups

One may argue that these laboratory findings, though interesting, are not particularly relevant to the problems actually encountered in industry. In most face-to-face industrial groups only one communication network seems possible, and that is a fully connected network in which everyone can communicate directly with everyone else.

But the argument that this is the only actual network, even in committees, does not hold water. A clear, albeit informal, notion about who can talk to whom exists in most groups. In fact, in face-to-face meetings, although the *official* network is a fully connected one, the *actual* network may be some other one altogether. Communication networks are much like organization charts: there is likely to be a formal, officially charted organization, and there is likely also to be an informal, uncharted organization that nevertheless plays a significant role in the functioning of the company.

In a committee meeting, for example, a chairperson can usually manipulate the communication setup so that in practice each person talks to the chair and not directly to other people. And even if the chair tries to be "democratic," the same result may occur unintentionally because of differences in rank or power among members of the committee. Privates don't interrupt generals whenever they feel like it, no matter what the official communication network.

In continuing work groups, the possibilities for changing communication nets are better than in meetings. Almost any network is possible if the group in question is the continuing membership of a particular department.

However, the members of a great many industrial groups seldom meet face to face. Where there is physical separation, one would expect the structure of the communication net to have far more direct effects.

"Good" and "bad" networks

What, then, are the characteristics of the "best" communication networks? That question demands another: Best for what? If the question is what is "best" for small meetings and conferences, where everyone's ideas are worth something and where the same people will probably get together again next week, then the answer seems clear. The best networks are likely to be the ones with at least these two related characteristics:

First, more equalitarian networks are probably preferable to more hierarchical networks. That is, networks like the circle, where everyone has access to about the same number of channels, are preferable to networks like the star, where one person has many neighbors and the rest none.

Second, those networks that provide everyone with at least two direct communication channels are probably better than those that give some people only one channel to the rest of the group.

Several different networks meet these criteria. And there are real differences even among these. But as a group, networks that meet these standards seem—in experimental situations—to yield higher morale, greater willingness to work, and a series of other advantages over networks that do not meet them.

But if by "efficient" we mean fast in getting started and fast in its operations, our conclusions about the best network must be quite different. Then differentiated, nonequalitarian networks like the star look better. For they impose a clear-cut organization on the group, defining each person's job and leaving little leeway for wandering away from that job. As a consequence, those groups get started faster and work faster once they have started.

Similarly, the experimental findings would lead to other predictions. For instance, consider a superior, A, who puts himself in the position shown here:

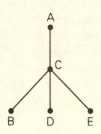

Any superior who does this may be leaving himself in serious danger. And his subordinate C, may find himself in a very powerful spot. For the subordinate has more and faster access to internal organizational information than his boss or anyone else, and by being a little selective in what he transmits (purposely or by oversight), he can end up controlling the organization. Sometimes one sees this situation with the president's private secretary. By being in a position to screen all incoming and many outgoing messages, he can become a formidable personage.

Preferential access to information, after all, is a major source of power in any organization. In experiments in the star network, anyone in the central position, C, is likely to become the functioning boss. His personal characteristics do not matter much. He learns more, faster, than anyone else. In real life, his communicational power may be balanced by someone else's authoritative power. Curiously, one will often find groups so organized that the position of greater authority is not the key communicational position, even where power maximization in the hands of authority is the objective sought.

These ideas are related to some ideas about feedback talked about in chapter 10. Information is transmitted more broadly and apparently more accurately, and people are happier about sending and receiving it, when the people involved have some degree of control over what is happening, that is when they have some feedback, or when they have checkpoints to help them increase their certainty about what they are getting, or when they have opportunities to contribute to what is going on. Free feedback clearly helps in this direction, and now one can add that "equalitarian," "multichannel" communication networks seem also to help toward the same end.

A word of warning may be appropriate here. It may seem to follow from what has been said that the very best network is the fully communicating one, wherein everyone can talk directly with everyone else. Although this is probably true for certain types of problems in relatively small groups, it may not be true as groups grow larger. Purely practical considerations, like how much one person can send or receive at one time, might require limitations in the number of channels to be used in larger meetings, or even in small meetings for special kinds of problems.

Another warning: The research on communication has not dealt much with "real" situations. Problems of authority and responsibility that exist in industrial organizations clearly complicate real-life situations. So we must necessarily be cautious about jumping off into generalizations from such experimental research.

Unfortunately we do not know much about the networks that will or will not work for large organizations. Some of our little ones "look" centralized, some decentralized. But we can't put a thousand people in a laboratory, or at least we haven't yet.

Although it is probably true that many of the results would hold up if we could test them on large groups, many of them would not. We would run into the problem of oversupply of information if we expanded the star network to even twenty-five people with only one central person in position C. We would probably need some intermediate people to absorb irrelevant information and organize the remainder for C. Similarly, if we had a hundred people in a fully connected network, we would probably get chaotic results, at least until a good many channels had been voluntarily closed off. And we cannot even draw some networks for larger groups. Some, like this one,

are unique to a particular number of people. How does one draw that same net for ten people?

Self-defense and the design of networks

If these notions hold, one may ask why work groups are not more often of equalitarian, multichannel design in industrial organizations. One good reason is that these designs conflict, as do many aspects of small-group operation, with the pyramidal, highly individualized structure of most industrial organizations. Another good reason is that speed and control are often more critical than morale or even creativity.

There is also a not-so-good reason that may be worth special mention. Two-way communication in equalitarian networks often seems dangerous and threatening to some people in the group. For instance, people in higher positions in an organization may prefer hierarchical communication networks like the star pattern because it helps to maximize their power in the group (assuming that a superior will put himself in a position like C's). Patterns like this one serve the same purpose as one-way communication. They keep a boss off the psychological hook. His weaknesses are hidden better in a position like C's in the center of the star than in any position in the circle. He can screen information from others. He can blame errors on others, and maybe he can get away with it. The other people in such a group may have no way of checking on the real source of either an error or a bright idea. Often people argue for the star pattern over the circle on grounds of speed or businesslike efficiency when an underlying reason for the preference is the protection for someone's self-esteem. The same reasoning may hold for subordinates. It is easier for them, too, to hide in a hierarchical network.

But, of course, despite these issues, open nets are becoming more frequent on the shop floors of many organizations in many societies. Their advantages in the modern world now often appear to outweigh their costs.

In summary

The simple structure of the communication network in a group, independent of the persons in the group, seems to set limits on the group's performance.

Groups whose problems require the collation of information from all members work faster when one position is highly centralized and the others relatively peripheral. But the morale, the self-correctiveness, and perhaps the creativity of such groups may be better when the communication network is more equalitarian and when each member has more than one source of information.

Highly centralized groups may often be used for their consistency with general organizational designs, their speed, and their controllability; but they are used as psychological defense devices to protect superiors' "weaknesses" from being exposed to subordinates, and vice versa.

22

Developing managers
Applied ideas about
influence, learning,
and groups

Let's turn now to ways we might use some of the ideas about groups discussed in the preceding chapters on a practical problem, the development of managers (*if* managers can be developed at all!)

A problem for the reader:

You are the VP for human resources of a large, multi-product company. You are lucky because your C.E.O. is intensely aware of the need for training at all levels. Top management also thinks well of you.

You are called to a meeting in the president's office one day, where you find the president, the executive vice-presidents, and some of the senior line officers of the company.

The president says: "Joe, as a consequence of your arguments we've decided to go all out on intensive management development. We've spotted a dozen younger people around the company, every one of whom looks like at least vice-presidential timber. Right now they're in third- or fourth-level jobs, as assistant department heads or department heads in some of the smaller departments. They're lightweights now, and we want to make heavies out of them. And we have to speed up the process. We're going to need several top-level people in a year or two. We're willing to stand the salaries of these people up to six months, even if they don't do any productive work. You can have them. Do anything you have to do to make topflight managers out of them. You can keep them here or take them out into the country somewhere. You can hire consultants and experts; you can send them off to a university if you think that's best. Just turn them into competent managers who can take over our top spots."

This is the assignment—you've been given a carte blanche. Now what would you do?

A problem like this can be broken down into a couple of major questions. These seem to be the questions a human resources director would, sooner or later, have to answer.

1. What is a "topflight" manager anyway?

2. What are some of the good and bad ways of trying to teach people to be topflight managers?

What's a topflight manager?

This first question is a terribly difficult one. If we can answer that one, we can set the goals of our development program. But how does one find an answer to such a question?

Some people used to think one answer lay in finding the common personality characteristics of successful business leaders. They were looking for the ideal managerial personality. But as the concept of leadership became more sophisticated, most people abandoned that idea, having found as many different personal characteristics as they did leaders. Besides, our engineering methods for changing personalities are pretty poor; so even if we wanted to build people who are just like already-successful managers, we probably couldn't do it very well.

Another direction to search for answers is through job analysis, rather than analysis of managers themselves. Once we have located and defined the significant aspects of managers' jobs, we can go on to imbue our acolytes with the knowledge and skills that are appropriate for those jobs. This strategy leads us toward a formal analysis of the duties and responsibilities of job X, the skills and knowledge needed to perform those duties. The process becomes deductive; we determine the job requirements, and deduce from those the requirements we'd want the person filling the job to meet.

A third approach is a much more pragmatic one, a managerial work approach. It says: Let's follow managers around and see what they do. Maybe that will tell us what their jobs are really like and give us a fix on the kinds of skills they need to do those jobs. One big danger in going that way is that we may end up training managers of the future to behave like managers of the present. And it's likely, of course, that the world of the future will require different skills.

So again it's not surprising that some people have looked for another way of trying to decide what a polished, finished, developed manager should be like. The fourth strategy is a future problems approach, based on the notion that anything we do now to develop young managers is not likely to pay off until ten or twenty years from now. So maybe we should try to forecast what managerial work will look like in ten to twenty years and then train people for that target. The real weakness in this approach is that most of us are lousy forecasters. It's fun to forecast, and most of us are happily seduced by other people's projections about the future. But most of the time those projections turn out to be wrong, or at least to generate unforeseen second- and third-order consequences that turn out to be more important than what was forecast.

That leaves at least one other approach. A continuous learning strategy, a plan to train flexible people, people who are capable of dealing with whatever comes along. The trained manager is thus seen as a self-adjusting, continuously learning person. This view leads, not to teaching specific skills, but to teaching people to recognize when they need to learn new skills.

In recent years the search for the one and only managerial personality has slowed down. So has formal job analysis. So has the future-problems model. What seems to be emerging more and more is a two-pronged combination of the managerial work and continuous learning strategies. These two blend nicely because careful observation of managerial work points to flexibility and continous change as key characteristics of the work itself, and, consequently, characteristics required of the people who will perform it.

As we go on in this chapter to consider several programs for management development, these different perspectives will surface again. For instance, if you think the most important thing to teach prospective managers is to behave like present managers, some form of apprenticeship program begins to look good. If you think future managers will have to deal with some specific futures, then you will have to teach them about those futures in, perhaps, a much more academic program. If you're trying to turn them into flexible learners, then you may want to set up a wide range of different (and perhaps surprising) tasks, along with frequent opportunities to assess and analyze their performances on those tasks.

What's different about being a manager?

Despite what we have just said, we still have to worry a little right here and now about the critical and unique aspects of "managing," about how managing differs from a lot of other activities in the world.

Many people have put forward many different models of the "essential" nature of the managing process. We have one too. We shall be describing it in more detail in the last section. The key ideas are these:

1. Managing always includes some influencing and implementing activities. Somehow managers always have to get other people to do things. Which means that managing always includes a lot of power problems. Which is also to say that managers have to know a lot about dealing with human beings.

2. Managing also always includes a lot of problem solving. Some of the problems managers have to solve are not very different from the nice, neat problems that all of us had to solve at the end of each chapter in our math books in school. Those are the easy ones for managers, the nice, clear problems that the boss occasionally assigns. All we have to do, as managers, is put our minds and our educations to work on analyzing the problem and coming up with the solution.

But most managerial problem solving is much messier than final-exam problem solving. For one thing, managerial problems have to be solved under far from ideal conditions. Managers not only have to work against tight deadlines, but must also work on a dozen problems at the same time—like taking exams in five subjects all in one three-hour period. And that's one thing that is likely to get worse in the future. The hectic, overloaded setting in which the manager works will not improve. There will be tight deadlines. There will be limited, imperfect information. There will be high levels of uncertainty and high levels or risk in managerial problem solving. Most problems will not even have a nicely satisfying outcome, like getting an A on the exam. The manager may have to make a decision today and perhaps never know for sure whether his decision was a good one or a bad one. Sometimes, of course, he will know very quickly about the outcomes of his decisions, but often he will be blamed for outcomes that his decisions did not cause, or praised for outcomes that had nothing to do with his decisions.

3. The manager has to be a problem finder. Most managers might guffaw at that one. They might well argue that finding problems is the least of their problems. There are plenty of problems sitting on the desk every morning. And yet every manager also knows that he dare not spend all his time putting out the fires springing up around him. He also needs to take an active rather than an entirely reactive stance. He has to decide which problems are really the important ones to solve and which ones aren't. He has to create problems, to set goals, to decide where he wants to go, even though he may have lots of trouble getting there and he may have to make painful compromises and many detours along the way. This problem-finding element in managing, this element of purposiveness, makes managing an effort to move the world instead of just being moved by it. It will probably continue to be critical for managers in the future. It also happens to be an element that we don't know very much about.

4. There is still, of course, another central issue that differentiates managing from most of the rest of living. Managing occurs within an organizational setting. Unlike most other people, the manager operates from a power position within a pyramidal structure. He is blessed (or perhaps cursed) with the authority we discussed earlier. Those below

him in the pyramid usually see themselves as being more dependent on him than he is on them. And whether he likes the power position or not, he is in it, and many forces in his environment operate to keep him in it. But though he appears to have great and independent power, the actual balance of power in the industrial world seems to have shifted rapidly downward, making the manager's position somewhat awkward. The paralyzed brother has recovered the use of some of his muscles. Where once he knew every operation in his business better than anyone else, the manager cannot now come close to such sagacity. Where he once may have needed help only in the information-gathering and executing phases of his operation, he now often needs it even in the analyzing phase. He operates in a position that is peculiarly dependent while seeming to be independent.

From that position he must somehow perform his functions through his influence on other people. For his task is not a one-shot task but must be performed in a way that will permit him always to return for more. Nor is the typical manager the top manager; he is dependent not only on subordinates but also on his peers and superiors. He expects, and is expected, to act as an extension of his superior's ego. He is expected to think creatively and originally but also to act as his boss would act in a similar situation.

All these factors flow from the hierarchy, and they all complicate the managing process.

If this characterization of managing is approximately correct, then management-development programs ought to be devoted to helping people to learn how to influence people and implement change through people, how to solve complex, ill-defined problems under tight deadlines and high risks, and how to find purpose and fulfillment while working in a battering, hierarchical environment.

Notice that so far we have put our emphasis on developing managers who can manage. We have said nothing about developing managers who can live full and happy lives while managing. Indeed, if we succeed in developing a manager who does everything we have just described, he will surely confront a hectic, overloaded, and not necessarily fulfilling life. It won't be an empty life, certainly, but how can we help make it something better than a harried one? Anyone who takes on the job of "developing" managers must, we propose, be concerned with the souls as well as the skills of his students.

Then how shall we do it?

If we're approximately on target with our notions about what managing is all about, the next question becomes how to teach people to do it well. And here modesty is in order. It is not clear that anybody really knows how to do it. But as we move from the conceptual to the engineering phase of the manager-developing process, at least these kinds of ideas seem to emerge:

1. Most manager development ought to take place inside, not outside, the managerial world. It could usefully be an interactive, back-and-forth process between outside educational programs and inside active experience. We talked in earlier chapters about alternation between content and process in groups. We now suggest a similar interactive alternation between "studying" managing and doing it. That argument runs counter to the notion that sending people to management-education programs at universities is management development. It is also opposed to one-shot programs which take place for a week or a month at a resort and are then finished. It supports a long-term view of managing as a continuing learning process, and learning as a continuing managing process.

Incidentally, one of the reasons that we so often use one- or two-week off-site programs and so seldom design continuous development programs is that we use the university as our model of what education should be. But universities do not run two-year MBA programs because they have found that two contiguous years is just right to educate a manager for life. They do it because they are pretty much forced to do it, because they are physically and geographically set up so that students must come to the campus and stay there. A few colleges have tried, with some success, programs that alternate between education and work, but such programs have not become commonplace even in management education.

It is not so much the validity of the continuous-learning model that has limited the diffusion; it is the logistical difficulties of implementation. But if our task is to develop managers within one organization, those logistical difficulties become much less troublesome.

2. Let's try to teach methods and attitudes more than knowledge. This is not to say that knowledge is irrelevant in managing, but much knowledge about managing is transient. Consequently, we ought to be developing in our managers a set of attitudes that makes them want to maintain, update, and thirst after new knowledge. We ought to teach an aspiring manager to develop an experimental turn of mind; an attitude that makes him innovative about the managing process itself; a "scientific" curiosity about the management process, a learning attitude that sends him searching for new ideas and methods that might be applicable to managing; and an open attitude that encourages him to seek counsel from diverse sources. Some of these attitudes are probably teachable; some are beyond our reach by any presently known educational methods. But, fundamentally, we should be trying

to inculcate a continuous learning posture more than a specific body of truths.

Probably the best known way to approach that target is by requiring student managers to take on vague assignments requiring lots of exploration and interaction with others, accompanied by critical discussion and review.

3. A good deal of emphasis in management development needs to be given to the manager's self, his ego. At least three important issues seem to arise here. First, we might try to help the manager to value himself as a problem-working instrument. If managing involves problem finding, it must also require reasonable self-confidence, tenacity, belief that one's own ideas are worth something. We need to try to help managers become at least somewhat "inner-directed."

Second, we probably need to try to teach managers to take their own needs seriously; to look always at themselves as well as at their external tasks; to be consciously concerned with questions of what they believe in, what they feel is ethical, what they themselves want to accomplish. This is not a matter of self-indulgence; it is an awareness that one is himself a significant part of managing.

Thirdly, and perhaps most importantly, we have to teach managers to value and use their "gut feelings." For despite our advanced state of knowledge, despite our sophisticated models and methods, a large chunk of managing still has to be done with "feel," "judgment," "intuition." These often unconscious inner feelings are important and valuable tools, especially since so much of managing must be done in real time, on the fly, with no time available to use other, more elaborate tools. So we should be teaching our managers how to read small signals and how to listen to (rather than ignore) their own feelings; and we should do this not to the exclusion of reason, but as the companion of reason.

Some alternative techniques

With this sort of framework in mind, the developer can begin to select some combination of methods and techniques to use as his training tools. Most training directors would doubtless, at this point, begin to consider the available alternatives currently in use in industry. They include job-rotation plans, classroom-education plans, apprenticeship plans, and various problem-solving plans. They can be found in varying degrees and combinations because they are not entirely independent of one another. Some are techniques that can be used within others; some are primarily administrative devices that leave training itself largely to other people. Consequently, it is not proper to try to label any of these mechanisms as better or worse than any others. Any of them can be carried through naïvely and poorly, or well and with wisdom.

Probably the most widespread formal method of management development, even today, is job rotation. An executive-in-training is systematically (or unsystematically) rotated through many jobs at many levels of the organization. In some plans he simply observes the jobs; in others he may work actively in them for a period of several months or a year.

Underlying these plans is the belief that a variety of job experiences provides the trainee with an opportunity to learn "all about the business" and is therefore good preparation for managership. The advantage to a manager of knowing his own business is obvious. It is questionable, however, whether independent experience in each of several jobs provides a candidate with knowledge of the relationships among the jobs, a kind of knowledge probably more useful to a manager than knowledge of any specific operation. Moreover, rotation plans may—although they do not necessarily—suffer from a kind of passivity and aimlessness resulting from the absence of a clear-cut central goal. Thus, for example, when one works in a department for three months, one, may learn quite different things from what he would learn either as a regular employee or as a manager who had to look into the department to solve some specific managerial problem. The rotated trainee is in danger of learning superficially, like a tourist in a foreign land. Organizations that use rotation systems often become aware of this difficulty. Then they either lengthen the rotation schedule or set up special assignments which require trainees in rotation to be more concerned with the managerial aspects of the job than with its operational aspects.

It is sometimes claimed that a simple rotation plan is a good way of separating the leaders from the followers. Those trainees who are poor tourists, who learn only the minimum, can be differentiated readily from those who take initiative and find things to learn, even if those things have not been defined for them. It may well be true that a rotation plan is a useful selection method. The people who take initiative, who think up problems on their own, may stand out quickly. But that is selection, not training.

If there is a great strength in rotation schemes, it is an ambiguous one we have not yet mentioned—rotation can multiply and fragment the manager's loyalties so that he is part of all groups, not just one. While split loyalties will increase the probability of ulcers, they also increase the likelihood of intergroup cooperation.

Classroom training, including lectures and discussions, is, like rotation, both useful and incomplete. As the rotation system emphasizes experience, most classroom training emphasizes the provision of knowledge. Both knowledge and experience are relevant to the development of management. Both add to the trainee's breadth of perception of the world. But like rotation, classroom courses are likely to be psychologically sealed off from the solution of managerial problems. For in the classroom, learning is tied largely to the trainee's desire to be successful in the class. Only later, when he is faced with managerial problems in which classroom knowledge would have helped, is he likely to be fully aware of how many really useful things he could have learned if he had known then what he knows now. Three months of reading and lectures are likely to train inefficiently unless they accompany rather than precede the need tensions that come from having to solve a management problem. It is paradoxical that industry, which in the eyes of many educators presents an ideal training ground, should be turning to the classroom as an educational device while educators themselves are complaining that the classroom is an inadequate educational mechanism.

One kind of formal management education that has become particularly popular in recent years is the university executive program. These programs are typically conducted for large groups of executives gathered from many different cultures. The programs vary in length from a couple of weeks to a couple of months. Although they are often used as a sort of reward for the good executive, or as a way of showing that the organization thinks well of him, they also do seem to have an important broadening effect, an especially valuable contribution for senior managers who have grown up within the narrow confines of one organization. Such programs also socialize people into a feeling that they are members of a profession called "management."

These are not at all trivial matters for people in senior management positions. They are the ones who especially need a broad understanding of the nature of the larger world around them, as well as an understanding of the implications of alternative financial, control, and accounting practices. They are the ones, too, who need the sense of being professionals, of maintaining high standards of ethics and of skill. They need also to perceive both the uniqueness and the universality of the problems they face. University programs also provide a pause, a breather in the hectic life of the manager. There is evidence from many different fields that such pauses yield useful fallout for the individual himself and for his contributions to his managerial world. It does appear to be true that getting away for a while recharges our batteries.

Again it is worth pointing out that the adequacy of the university classroom must be judged not only against the content and method of classroom teaching but also against the motivation of the student. If a manager-in-training goes to a classroom in search of help with a problem he has already defined for himself, then the classroom, like the AA meeting, can be extremely helpful. But if the student is the passive party in the classroom relationship while the teachers pump him full of knowledge, it is likely to be an inefficient method. For learning cannot be exclusive of the needs of the learner. And what is learned best is what is relevant to the current needs of the learner, not what may be relevant to his future needs.

Such off-the-job, one-shot executive programs are far from perfect. They show a sharp wash-out effect after people leave them and return to the workaday world. They are not very good means for developing specific managerial skills. So they are best seen as useful modules to be combined with others over the course of a career.

Apprenticeship systems, often combined with rotational systems, are another base for developing managers. Sometimes trainees are attached for extended periods to a particular executive, to serve as his assistant, to live in his office, and, insofar as possible, to do his work. Such systems may provide good opportunities for the trainee to practice working on managerial problems. They may also provide the motivation for acting like an executive. But the quality of the coaching is variable. Political and personality factors limit their usefulness, for the variety of executive problems the trainee is given is left largely up to the executive to whom he is attached. If the executive is either uninterested in the apprentice or feels threatened by him, that particular apprenticeship will provide few learning opportunities.

Still another effort to provide motivation and opportunities for practice in a group setting is the junior management "board." A group of lower-level people is elected or appointed to a kind of second board of directors which meets periodically to consider any business problems it chooses to consider, to gather information about those problems, to analyze them, to come to decisions, and to make recommendations to the senior board. While holding their lower-level jobs, young people thus get an opportunity both to tax their own brains on executive problems and to work at the peer level with a group of other "part-time" managers. This approach has the advantage of giving younger people an opportunity to view the world as a manager, to be faced with and wade through problems of impending change, and to create changes of their own.

Task-group–based development programs

In recent years a whole series of different forms of task-group development models have been evolving. They deserve special consideration. In the past, some of them were concerned primarily with groups and very little with tasks. In the fifties and sixties there were a number of experiments based on sensitivity training carried out within particular companies. Most evolved over time into more task-oriented directions and became centrally concerned with what is now called "team building." A few remained primarily "humanistic," concerned almost exclusively with personal and interpersonal sensitivity. Some are quite clearly delineated in space and time. Others are much less separable from the ongoing work of the organization. Here, to provide the reader with a picture of how such a program might work, is a brief description of one recent program of the latter sort.

Company A is a rapidly growing organization staffed largely by technical and professional people. The organization is loosely and flexibly structured. Indeed, until recently it was very hard to get answers to questions like "Whom do you report to?" With growth, the pressure to "get organizated" also grew. So the president increased the number of vice presidents and organized them, together with key administrative and planning people, into what he called a management committee. Almost all members hold Ph.D.s in one of the hard sciences or engineering. The functions of the management committee, though not clearly delineated, were to design company policy and to make sure that policy was communicated and implemented.

A consultant had been brought in to help the company become a little more organized. He proposed that some management development ought to accompany the formation of the management committee.

With the president's agreement, the following plan was devised: The management committee members would meet together for two days just prior to their next scheduled meeting. During those two days, a two-person faculty designated by the consultant (but checked out by the company) would conduct a management-development "workshop."

The faculty designed the workshop. After interviewing a number of members of the organization, the faculty members felt they were dealing with strongly "cognitive types." These were people who were used to using their heads, and using them critically. Second, many of the important problems of the company centered around coordination among divisions. Third, beginning rumblings of discontent could be heard among newer (but not brand new) members of the organization. So the faculty decided that its initial training inputs should focus *cognitively,* on people and coordination issues.

The faculty also felt that management development should blend as much as possible into the ongoing work of the organization. The line between them should be a blurry one. So management development should take place continually, and formal educational inputs and real-world practice should be close. Since groups are such powerful mechanisms for mutual learning and problem solving, the programs should be strongly group-based.

The program that evolved for the first two-day workshop consisted of a series of lectures, cases, and simulation exercises selected for their relevance to this group. These were duly presented at an off-site, two-day meeting.

These formal inputs were alternated with "relevancy sessions." One faculty member would offer an exercise, lecture, or case discussion, followed by a break into small groups to consider implications for the company and then a general discussion. The process was then repeated with a new input by faculty. Sometimes the relevancy sessions pinpointed some company problems that needed action, sometimes not.

As the workshop progressed, several clear issues surfaced, some requiring further study before implementation action. Task forces were set up by the group to deal with some of these problems, and some were put on the agenda for regular management committee meetings.

The group decided that a one-day session following the regular meeting should focus on a few selected issues. Over the next several months, this process continued, though not in a regular or formal fashion. Several short input sessions took place, along with several reporting-back sessions and several self-study activities.

The president and some committee members felt that something similar would be useful at other levels of the organization. Some similar two-day management-development workshops were therefore designed and carried out.

As this process went on, a new problem emerged. The second-level people felt that, while they were beginning to communicate with one another better, and while the management committee members felt that their own interpersonal communication and coordination was improving rapidly, the communication *between* levels continued to be weak. The typical complaint voiced by second-level managers went like this: "The vice-presidents may be able to talk to each other, but they sure as hell don't know how to talk to us! We never know what's going on around here." The consultant and staff then organized some vertical sessions within major divisions of the company.

And these activities go on. They are partially self-generating and highly contingent on what preceded. Some intradivisional activities are spinning off from them; task forces and partial reorganizations are taking place. The faculty's role is rapidly being phased out. They may be useful again at some later time.

Notice that the line between such "management-development programs" and "reorganization" is not at all clear. And rightly so. The
starting point is, in this case, some management-education activity.
Because they are intentionally tied in to the ongoing problems of
work, such programs—when they work—spill over into many other
areas of the organization's life. In the case described here, this loose,
spreading style may be particularly relevant because of the organization's commitment to remaining relatively loose. The organization
does not seek a tight, hierarchical structure. It wants to be people-
based. But as it grows larger, it will be forced to become more structured, though this will surely involve some sacrificing of the present
do-your-own-thing style. Nevertheless if we can increase the quality of
interactions among members of the organization, we can at least
counterbalance some of the need for formal structural controls.

But are such programs appropriate only for loose, fluid, and rapidly
growing organizations? Not necessarily. Here is another example:

Company B has about 17,000 members. It is also a high technology
organization, also staffed by bright, cognitive, technical types. It is
much older and more stable than the company in the first example. It
has about nine levels in its hierarchy, and everyone knows exactly to
whom he reports and how he is evaluated.

Top management in organization B also felt that in its rapidly
changing environment, more managerial skill was needed among its
technical managers, and a somewhat more entrepreneurial attitude
might be needed too, as competition stiffened. The consulting faculty
and management group concluded that this program, too, should carry
a strongly cognitive flavor, that it should be extended over at least a
six-month period, and that it should be concerned very heavily with
people management. But this program was to be organized around a
tight schedule, consonant with the much more schedule-oriented
organization. It was to consist of a three-day "kick-off session" for
groups of thirty middle-level people, with a series of five one-day "reinforcement" sessions, one per month, in which visiting experts would
present a day's worth of input on specifically relevant issues, like
performance appraisal methods. And it would close with a two-day
"wrap-up" session.

The reader will notice that although so far we have met the criterion
of continuity in this program, we have not yet managed to get much
interaction with the workaday world. That was done in two ways:
The first group and all succeeding groups were charged with using
the program as a base for experimentation with any ideas they found
potentially relevant to the management of their own departments. They
were by no means required to take a sympathetic view of the ideas

being presented, but they were asked to act, to try out, to experiment with their managerial behavior. The reinforcement sessions were practice oriented, and the wrap-up session consisted in part of a show-and-tell activity in which the participants talked a little bit about what they had tried to use, what had failed and what had worked.

This program was repeated with a large number of middle-management groups and later with a smaller number of higher-management groups. In this program, measurements were taken by the company that indicated modest but positive changes in the behavior of participants in their interaction with one another and in their concern with their own management skills. Thus far, all groups have continued to meet periodically (some over the course of several years). Many spin-off activities have developed: subsidiary workshops within subunits; meetings between subunit managers to try to resolve difficulties; the introduction of specialized consultants on special projects; and the development of a small in-house staff resource group.

The reader will have to decide for himself whether or not such programs are valuable. They certainly do not cover the educational spectrum. They are certainly not substitutes for course work in accounting or finance. They certainly do not guarantee that all participants will come out polished, topflight managers. But they do seem to contribute something to the development of the individual and to the smoother running and greater flexibility of the organization.

In summary

Anyone concerned with developing managers must deal with three key questions: How do people learn? How can a trainer train? And what is a manager?

Learning is defined here as a process of reorganizing perceptions so that new patterns of relationships are formed. Training, therefore, necessitates providing trainees with problems that require perceptual reorganization for their solutions and providing these problems in a situation in which relevant knowledge and experience are also available—including knowledge and experience about groups.

The "ideal" manager can be defined in many ways. The emphasis here has been on those phases of the manager's job involving the gathering and analyzing of information, decision making, and action, with a recognition of the unprogrammed nature of his problems, his continuous dependence on other people, and the pressures imposed upon him by his position in a hierarchy.

23

Groups on the shop floor
Toward the end of the
assembly line?

In the last few years, a good deal of attention has been given to the reorganization of the Volvo automobile works in Sweden, along with some other Scandinavian manufacturing plants. Similar experiments in the United States have received less publicity. One common factor of all these efforts is a central focus on the autonomous work group. Another common ideological factor is a concern for "humanizing" work.

This chapter looks at and tries to evaluate some of the forces that are driving many modern managers toward intensive experimentation with the use of groups and other behavioral tools. But the major purpose of this chapter is to show the reader how the forty-year history of research on small groups has led toward this potentially important application to the design of organizations.

The growth of interest in group methods

In the late sixties, many of us remember, we in the United States became very much concerned with "the decline of the American work ethic." The then-new Lordstown plant of the General Motors Corporation emerged as a focal case. A serious strike at that plant was interpreted by observers as a sign of significant new attitudes among new, younger workers. Modern young workers were frustrated, it was said, by the restrictiveness of traditional assembly-line jobs, by the very short-cycle, repetitive work patterns, patterns that had characterized many American factories since the turn of the century. There was much talk about making jobs in the modern factory more enriching. Particularly in northern Europe, social and political opinion was pushing hard for improvement in the "quality of working life," and these societal demands were backed up with legislation requiring more worker participation in company decisions. In Sweden, for example, interest in improving work life cut across many sectors: trade unions, government, and management itself. A strong tradition of research in "industrial democracy" provided a technical base for experimental application of these beliefs.

World attention in the sixties and seventies was also focused on Japanese managerial practices. The surging Japanese economy had changed the image of Japanese management from copycats to cats worth copying. We began to set Japanese productivity and efficiency on a pedestal; and we began, therefore, to take more interest in the group-oriented methods of the Japanese enterprise.

Here in the United States, of course, the student demonstrations and black riots of the sixties and the women's rights movement, all contributed to a rapidly growing concern about "humanism" at work. The young seemed to be opting out of traditional business careers. Life-styles were said to be changing. The images of large companies were taking a beating. They were being seen, it appeared, less and less as heroic developers of the American dream, and more and more as wicked exploiters of the environment, of the consumer, and of the worker. And one more thing: Costs were going up!

Add to this combination of outside events the changing profile of American managers themselves: More MBAs; a more "professional" orientation; twenty or thirty years of familiarity with notions like McGregor's theory Y, and sensitivity training, and other moves toward intelligent "people management." Managers didn't have to love such ideas. Many hated them. But they knew about them. These ideas had become part of their world.

Put all these forces together, and it should come as no surprise that the quality of working life now enters the American scene as an important concern.

The technical background: Social science and research on groups

A very large body of research on small groups had been done in the United States by the 1960s. We had "discovered" that groups could be self-disciplining and self-policing; that (under specifiable conditions) they could make good-quality decisions; that they could provide opportunities for enrichment and education to their members; that they could help to reduce feelings of anomie and disaffection so common in assembly-line operations; that they could provide "neighborhoods," little communities that might greatly enrich life on the job; and that they could build commitment to work.

So these ideas were there; but ideas need supporting technologies before they move the world very far. And the technologies were building. We had experimented, with mixed results, with sensitivity training, then with "team building" and "O.D." (organizational development) techniques, and with many other methods of group building, both in and out of industry. In the fifties some of these techniques had been used, with considerable local success, with hourly workers. Many had been tried out with managers. And their ideology was "right" in that it matched the growing concern for "humanism" at work.

These two sets of forces, (1) the growing disaffection with existing factory forms, plus (2) the growing awareness of the possibilities inherent in the small group, have led to a lively set of factory floor experiments and reorganizations both in the United States and abroad.

Since many of these experiments were taking place in manufacturing firms—auto factories, food plants, aluminum production—technical and engineering problems were also central. Soon we began to see some coupling of engineers with social psychologists in experimental efforts to design new factories around the concept of the autonomous small group. As the reader might guess, the dollar costs of the change-over from a traditional assembly line to a group-based plant are not trivial. Setting up a shop in which groups can carry out significant complete subassemblies takes some doing. Equipment must often be redesigned and plant layouts radically changed. Even the product itself must sometimes be modified to permit efficient manufacture in these group-based factories.

What's a group-based factory?

Imagine yourself going to work in an automobile plant in Detroit. You were hired for a low-skill, assembly-line job, given some brief training, and put to work. Your job is very carefully structured and involves a small number of highly specific acts. The job is so designed that you are expected to do the whole thing once in less than a minute. Then a new part comes along the line, and you work on that for a minute, and then a new part, and so on. You get to know the people around you during lunch or coffee breaks, but it takes time. You get reasonably well paid, and there is a whole system of job categories that will yield higher pay if you are upgraded after a period of time. On your job the physical environment isn't bad. It's noisy and perhaps a little dirty, but it's cool. And your union is strong.

Draw your own conclusion about how you might feel about working day in and day out in a setting like that. How long would you do it? What would you feel about your "career"? About the place of your work in your total life? In fact, a lot of people don't mind such jobs; but a lot of people do mind them. There is some evidence that younger people dislike such work more than older people do.

Now switch over to a new group-based auto plant. This time you get a job as a member of a ten-person group that is responsible for assembling exhaust systems for a particular car. You start on a simple job, but you are expected to help other members of the group when they need it and to participate in a briefing session each day when you take over from the previous shift. In those sessions you find out where things stand, how far behind or ahead your group is from a goal set for it. You also are expected gradually to learn some of the other jobs performed by other members of your group. Some members are even getting extra pay to teach you their jobs. There is very little supervision from above. The group pretty much takes care of itself. If somone from management has a complaint, the complaint is usually addressed to the group. The questions might be "How come you guys blew it on this problem?" Or, "We're going to need twenty more units a day starting April 1st. What will we need to get production up that high? Do we need more people?" The questions are for the whole group.

In the eyes of many people these days, that second work style looks a lot better than the first. There is more autonomy, more individual responsibility, more variety, more teamwork, more possibilities. There's also likely to be more debate and argument, more "politics," more "personality" problems.

But it's still a pretty limited world. After you've worked in a group like that for a year or two, you might feel you've learned everything there is to learn, and you might lose interest. Moreover, you might encounter personality conflicts. Perhaps the group doesn't accept you or you don't like the group, and that could make work very unpleasant indeed. But such problems, it can be argued, are appropriate adult problems for adult human beings. The group-based factory seems a step toward more self-control, more autonomy, more involvement in some sort of productive effort, and perhaps a lot more feeling that one is a member of a human community.

But if we back up and look at all this from a managerial point of view, the problems are enormous. Converting from one of the older to one of these newer forms is both costly and risky. It is not surprising then, that in the United States most experiments with group-based organizations take place in new plants, in new settings which don't require remodeling the old. Starting the physical plant from scratch makes it a good deal easier to design a factory that is technically consistent with the group form; and starting from scratch with new employees means that people don't have to be "unfrozen" from their old behaviors.

Not surprisingly, too, a long time will have to pass before the final results of such trials come in. Although the group form seems, on the face of it, to be more "human," it will take a while to find out if it is also more cost-efficient. Some American automobile people, for example, are highly critical of Volvo on the grounds that its changes will sharply drive up production costs. And apparently these critics have been at least partially right. But the Volvo response seems to be about as follows: "It may be true that some costs are involved in the implementation of a new kind of operation. There are technical failures, social problems, and materials problems. But over time," Volvo argues, "we will have an advantage over the older firms because their system is gradually cracking up. They will have to make changes at some time in the future. By that time we will have ironed out the bugs and be on our way. Besides, our way is socially right."

Notice that this whole issue is a very good example of what managing an organization is all about. It is about risk, about analysis, about human values, all bubbling up in a highly uncertain environment. And notice, too, that the results will never be unequivocally clear. If Volvo loses market share (or gains it) we can blame the results on a dozen other factors—inflation rates, import restrictions, and so on. If G.M. later moves in the same direction as Volvo, they can argue that they are acting with healthy caution and conservatism, with the advantage of having let others make the first mistakes. And meanwhile, they can tool up by doing some good quiet staff work so they will be ready to make changes when they want to.

Another large problem we have not yet mentioned: the attitudes of trade unions toward group-based production methods. Scandinavian unions for a long time have pushed actively for more worker participation in the decision-making process. But American unions have traditionally shied away from that demand. They have been perfectly willing, for the most part, to let management make managerial decisions. They have chosen to fight the battle for wages and working conditions. They don't want to run the plant. They just want their people to make money and work under satisfactory conditions. American trade union attitudes seem now to be slowly changing in this regard, just as do the attitudes of managers; but the process, if it is really happening, is gradual and uneven.

It is even difficult to estimate how much movement toward group-based production there is. Is it truly a major industrial movement, or a trivial one? One reason for uncertainty is that many companies experimenting in this area take a proprietary view of their activities. They avoid publicity, going about these changes rather quietly. They have several causes for caution. They would not be happy if some of the experiments failed and negative publicity ensued. And some feel that these costly changes represent large potential competitive advantages. They are not about to let their competitors reap the benefits without having paid the bills.

Where do we go from here?

At this point in history, it is difficult to make anything like an objective evaluation about whether group-based plants are turning out to be better or worse than traditional plants. Certainly it is difficult to do so strictly on the criteria of cost and efficiency. But though cost and efficiency considerations are probably critical factors in the ultimate outcomes, we must remember that much of the drive for group-based redesign emanates from human values and expectations. A lot of the effort also represents an attempt to adapt to the changing world, to maintain the "legitimacy" of the organization as a member of society. It seems a fair guess that this general direction of social change will continue, that more and more people will be pressing, through their governments and all other means, for more "humanization" of the production process. In turn, the short-cycle, highly specialized assembly line will be viewed more and more negatively, more and more as a relic of the past, not unlike the sweatshop or child labor.

Nevertheless, the group solution may not prove to be the best one, especially if it turns out to be costly or to generate other unforeseen problems. Another horse in the race for change, for instance, is automation, which may "solve" the human problems of the production line by removing humans altogether.

In summary

Societal pressures have been moving toward improving the quality of work life. American observations of Japanese managerial successes and Scandinavian experiments with new, more "human" production methods have also spurred action in this area. These forces, coupled with several decades of research on small groups, have led in the last few years to a resurgence of interest in group-based "sociotechnical" alternatives to the assembly line.

These experiments are fairly widespread, particularly in new plants with new employees. The results are not yet in, but it seems clear that more such experiments will be tried and retried. What ever the form these efforts finally take, they will surely result in major modifications of traditional, highly specialized assembly-line methods.

4　People in hundreds and thousands Problems of organizational design

Introductory note

This last part of our book is about managing—managing large numbers of people in organizations. In this last section, we try to describe the nature of large organizations—their structures, their systems of control, their goal-setting procedures. But those descriptive efforts are not at the core of our concern. They are there to provide a background against which to think about the managing process; about the art and science of working problems through in those complex organizational settings.

We have already looked at how issues like achievement motivation affect organizations. We have looked at several approaches to influencing individuals and small groups. We have also seen the extent to which the situation within which people work shapes, controls, and limits their behavior. In this section we try to put all those issues together, and we add a few more. The focus, we repeat, is on *managing*.

Chapter 24 looks at managing as a special case of problem working. All of us work our way through problems all the time. But managers try to do it in those complex structures called organizations, and they often have to do it with problems that extend well beyond the boundaries of those organizations. So we try to lay out a simplifying model for thinking about the phases of problem working in organizations.

The rest of this section is about what managers try to manage. Chapter 25 is about the organizational handles that managers can grab onto to try to steer and influence and change their organizations. Chapter 26 takes an historical look at how our ideas about managing people have evolved over the last seventy years. Chapter 27 considers organizational goals and objectives and looks into the ways organizations find and set goals. Then, in chapter 28, we look at the people part of the large system, at the problems of implementing decisions and effecting changes through the long, human chains that compose those organizations. We follow that with a look at structure and technology and the ways that managers can change structure and control systems. And

267

in chapter 30 we step outside the organization and look at problems of managing the relationships between the organization and that great big world out there.

So though part 4 contains a little about organization theory, it is mostly about the managing process in large organizations. Managing, after all, is an active process of trying to identify the important issues and trying to do something about them. Managing means trying to find the right things to get done, and getting them done through people, in complicated settings. That's what this concluding section is all about.

24

Managing
Working problems
through, through people

This chapter tries to pull a lot of different issues together. So far we have talked a good deal about people and groups, but we haven't said very much about where the action is, about the rather frenetic, ongoing process of managing within large organizations. So this first chapter of our section on large organizations is about what managers do and the special problems of *doing* in complex organizations. But we also try to organize things a bit by laying out a three-part model of the managing process.

What do managers do?

What is managerial work actually like? What is it that managers are supposed to do? People who have spent a long time following managers around, observing and recording their behavior (much as animal behaviorists observe apes), answer that question like this:

First, managers do an enormous amount of work. They are on the go at a fast pace for long hours.

Second, managers do most of their managing on the fly. They often decide and act, that is, without knowing much about what they are doing because they are under time pressures and psychological pressures of other kinds. It is not (as far as we know) that managers can't or won't think. It's just that mostly they don't have much time to. They work under pressure with limited, often impressionistic data, and a lot of uncertainty about many relevant facts.

Managers not only do lots of work on the fly, they do it from formally delineated roles in elaborate organizational structures. (If you think tribes of apes have elaborate dominance and status systems, look at managers.) They are not free agents. They have to coordinate their activities with lots of other people, and they have to influence lots of other people upwards, downwards, and sideways. They are always driving in very heavy human traffic.

269

But what is it exactly that managers *do?* If we were to ask a number of managers that question, they would probably give us answers like these: "I solve problems." "I make decisions." "I put out fires." "I persuade people to do things I want them to do." "I develop young people to replace me." "I do a lot of checking to make sure that the things that are supposed to get done actually do get done." "I deal with emergencies—everything from someone not showing up for work on a critical day to coping with a flood that has destroyed half the inventory we were scheduled to ship this week." And some managers might add: "I think up ideas." "I invent or create new plans, programs, products."

Notice that in one important sense managers don't do very much. They don't mow lawns or drive bulldozers or tighten screws. They do mostly "soft" things, head things, no hand things. People have tried in many ways to abstract from this melange of managerial activities some orderly statement of the fundamental functions of managers. For instance, managers, it is said, plan, organize, execute, and monitor. We shall use a slightly different set of categories.

Managing as problem working

We suggest that the reader think of managing as a problem-working process. In that respect, managing is no different from many other activities that all of us engage in. It's no different from what scientists do, or housekeepers, or artists. The big difference is in the setting, the deadline-pressured, achievement-oriented, crowded organizational setting in which managing takes place. But what does it mean to say that the manager or anyone else is a problem worker? That he works problems through from beginning to end?

One can think of problem working as a four-phase activity. The first phase (which may sound trivial but is actually quite critical) is problem finding. That's the process of choosing the problems worth working on. There's also a problem-solving phase, the often difficult process of finding a good solution to a complicated problem. Third, there is an implementation phase, getting something done, making it happen, getting it from the blueprint to the brick and mortar. And fourth there is the monitoring phase, the checking-out phase, comparing the results with the intent.

Those four phases probably characterize large segments of our lives whether we are managers or not. But one key difference is that most managerial problem working is done while running fast. Managing is not a process that allows much time for contemplation or for analyzing all possible alternatives. In managing, of course, the third phase, implementation, is absolutely critical, too. In some professions, finding the problem may be just about enough. In others, finding the answer brings the glory. In managing, doing something about the answer is essential.

For the next few pages we shall elaborate on this four-phase model, but not in the order just presented. We won't talk much yet about problem finding. We'll begin by considering what problem solving can mean in the managing process and then go on to talk about implementation and a little bit about monitoring. Then we'll back up and take a look at problem-finding processes and how they fit into the larger problem-working scheme.

The problem-solving part of managing

Consider what you were taught in school about problem solving. What were some of the rules of thumb? One was probably something like "Get the facts," or "Gather the relevant information." Then how about something like "Consider the possible alternatives" or "Figure out the possibilities." Then something like "Choose the best solution." The emphasis was probably on logic and orderliness, on searching for causal connections among things, on creating order from chaos.

Probably, too, in most of your college courses that required you to solve problems, you were given the problems as homework or in exams. Your job was to solve them, to produce the correct answers. Aptitude and intelligence tests also gave you problems that you had to solve. Sometimes giving the answer was not enough. You also had to show that you understood the proper method for solving the problem. In some courses, if you solved the problem intuitively or by using your own little tricks, you lost points. So problem solving was treated as something that doesn't begin until the problem is laid out for us.

In much formal education, our problem-solving practice was convergent—that is, we were set up to search for *the* answer, not for *an* answer. And in many parts of our education, the problem-solving process stopped when we had found the solution. The answer was the end of it.

Good reasons exist for using such an approach during the educational process. We were taught "proper" methods because other people in human history had figured out those methods. They were being transferred to us so each of us would not have to repeat the history of our species. We stopped when we got to the best solution because that's what that course was intending to teach us, to find and use methods that the teachers knew would efficiently bring us to the best solution.

But managing in the field is a little different from solving problems in a geometry class in the seventh grade. It is different in several important ways. As we said earlier, problems are not always given to us; we have to find our own. And second, the solution is not usually enough; we have to do something about it. But perhaps even more importantly, the situation is usually much less "pure" than it was in that exam in math class. First, we don't usually have all the information we need to apply a reasonable, known method to get the solution to the problem. All the facts are not there. Second, we often have to solve the problem in "irrational" real time, that is, against deadlines that weren't set by teachers who knew that twenty minutes was "about right" for that problem. And third, the right answer often doesn't make obvious sense—it doesn't possess the helpful attribute of coming out even, like the math test problems usually did.

Each of us has learned enormously useful methods of problem solving based on what was taught to us in school. We have learned, particularly, the power and value of analytic methods developed over centuries of philosophy, mathematics, the hard sciences, and the social sciences. Most of what we of the Western world call progress has emanated from our mastery of methods for solving problems systematically and analytically. And much of what we do successfully in managing organizations, we do because we can apply those analytic skills.

But there is much that those analytic skills cannot do for the managing process. And efforts to apply them religiously to that process often result in negative consequences. If the young technician, now promoted to a managerial role, still maintains the same problem-solving standards that he used at the bench, he may turn into a rather poor manager. He may want to work the problem through "thoroughly." He wants to get *all* the facts. He may accept only optimal solutions. He wants clear definitions of his problem. But managing involves working with ill-defined problems, against unrealistic deadlines, with highly uncertain information.

It's worth reiterating that much of our formal education has been aimed at the problem-solving phase of the total problem-working process. It has taught us how to decompose problems, how to order chaos, how to try to get to the heart of the issue and come up with *the* solution. Most education, after all, is analytically oriented. We were taught reading, writing, and arithmetic—all essentially analytic skills using symbolic languages. But what most formal education has not taught us about problem solving is how to solve problems on the fly; how to accept risky solutions; how to use our guts; how to find good heuristics.

Consider, for example, the issue of assessing people. All managers have to do it. They talk to someone for half an hour and have to decide whether or not to hire him or whether or not to trust his sales pitch. Or they go to a meeting and have to assess very quickly what they will be up against in trying to sell a plan. And we know a lot, formally, about things like assessment of people. We have developed tests and measuring instruments that can often be very helpful to managers for selecting or promoting or evaluating their people. But those kinds of analytic instruments are essentially useless when the manager is confronted with a twenty-minute meeting with a client or a tough negotiating session. He can't put his client through a test battery. He can't—much of the time—have his staff check out the people he will encounter. So he must use the subtle, uncertain cues that are available at that moment. And our education, at least our formal education, has done very little to help us do that kind of on-the-spot, uncertain problem solving.

The best advice this book can offer to its readers in those matters is the same advice offered in the chapter on assessment. Get in tune with your gut feelings and with nonanalytic signals. Develop your skills in these areas, along with your analytic skills, because these skills are critical to effective management.

The implementation part of the problem-working process: Types A and B

Another phase of the whole managing process is best summed up in the word *implementation*. Managers need to get good answers, but they also need to do something about them. They need to make things happen. Managers like to think of themselves as action types, as people who get things done. Implementation is the part of the problem-working process that involves getting things out of the laboratory and onto the market, taking the consultant's report and really reorganizing the company around it, turning out the product, opening up the new market, getting the new plant into production. Implementation also means getting the customer to buy it, getting your subordinates to do it, getting the other guy to use it. Implementation involves influencing, persuading, bullying, selling, building, achieving, and all the other action-oriented words that make up such a large chunk of managing.

Theoretically, implementation can stand independently of problem solving. Somebody else can solve the problem and we can implement it. Somebody else can make the policy and we can carry it out. But in practice, problem solving and implementation become very closely tied together. Any fairly large-scale implementation program, for example, usually includes a series of problem-solving acts which serve as "subroutines" within the larger implementation act itself. If our job is to implement the acceptance of product X in a new market, we will encounter several small problems that will have to be solved along the way. We shall have to decide which medium to advertise in, or whether to advertise at all; and what outlets we shall use; and how to price the product. So implementing generates problems that need to be solved in order to go on implementing.

Implementation is also tied up with problem solving in another, more important way. If we are implementing a decision, that must mean, of course, that the decision has already been made. Or so it would at first appear. Certainly if we take a quick look at the connection between implementation and problem solving, we would say, "Surely one problem-solves first, and then one implements. It's a one-two punch. Make the decision, then implement it. That kind of one-two view is what most of us have learned to be a reasonable way to approach things. For the moment, let's call implementation that *follows* problem solving Type-A implementation.

Type-A implementation not only serially follows decision making, it has another important characteristic. In Type-A implementation, the implementers are usually different people than the problem solvers. Thus, for example, a research division comes up with a solution for a technical problem, and then the engineers or line managers implement the solution. Or the engineers design a pump, and then the manufacturing people build it. And if that pump happens to be a saleable product, there may be a second phase of implementation, in which the marketing people now sell the pump which the manufacturing people have built. But the essentials of Type-A implementation are, first, the serial notion of solving it, then doing it; and second, the separation of the problem solvers from the implementers.

Now consider another view of implementation, Type B. It's a view that has grown up largely out of psychology and is based largely on ideas about the nature of people rather than the nature of reason. Most of the ideas of participative management and of organizational development implicitly carry this Type-B view. Type B emphasizes the interaction between problem solving and implementation. The B view argues that successful implementation requires involvement by implementers in the problem-solving part of the act. Which means that the B view wants to combine problem solvers and implementers and that it also wants the two processes to take place at just about the same time. The rationale is simple: People support what they help to create. If you must implement what I have decided, you will not implement it with love and commitment. But if you must implement what you have helped to decide, then the decision is your baby, and you will both love it and work at it. The B view thus also appears to fly in the face of the rational model of knowing what you want to do before you do it. The reasons are essentially the same. If problem solving is done first, and implementing afterwards, then not only will the implementers be less committed, but the solution itself may be less good because the implementational pitfalls may not have been fully considered.

The difference between these A and B views are deeper and more important than they may look. Type A puts its major emphasis on the quality of the decision, and its secondary emphasis on getting the thing done. Type B puts its greatest emphasis on the implementability of the solution, and is much less concerned about the elegance of the solution itself. Type A is logical; Type B is much more emotional. And the classic argument between the two views has been running for a long time. If you are an A type, you argue. "The important thing is to get the right answer. There's no use implementing the wrong decision. Therefore, concentrate on problem solving before you concentrate on implementing." The B types argue back," "There's no use having a good decision if you can't implement it. Therefore, although you may come up with a less-good answer, the bottom line is implementation, not decision making."

For most of us, these issues seldom reach the debate stage. We go about problem solving and implementing much more implicitly, using the standards and beliefs we have grown up with. Those of us raised in science and technology and/or in large organizations learn mostly the A view. Technology teaches us to value A because we are probably rewarded more for high-quality solutions than for high-quality implementation, and also because logic is valued next to godliness.

If our education emphasized more humanistic issues, or if the problems we have had to confront were mostly small, face-to-face problems, then we may have learned B views. In that world of smaller personal relationships, affective, often irrational issues play a very large part. So in this writer's experience, salesmen, teachers, counselors, and politicians tend to take a Type-B view, to be more concerned with issues of change, commitment, and persuasion than with plans, decisions, or structures.

Where do implementation types A and B work best?

It seems moderately clear, too, if one looks over a whole variety of implementation problems, that Type-A styles have worked best in large, hierarchical institutions, like big companies and governments and the military. In those kinds of organizations, it almost becomes nonsensical to try to combine problem solving and implementing at every level. There staff experts, planners, analysts, and researchers are easily, perhaps necessarily, separable from the line doers and sellers and expediters. In large organizations strategy can be pretty well separated from tactics.

What would one then expect to find as the important tools of Type-A implementation? They are, sensibly enough, primarily the tools of power and authority, and to some extent the socialization tools. For if we already have decided what needs to be done, we then need power and authority to get other people to do it. We need to control rewards and punishments. We need to be able to monitor behavior so that we know that what we want is being done. We need to socialize our people to be loyal and to perceive our authority as legitimate.

Conversely, the great successes of Type-B implementation can be found in the smaller units discussed in the first part of this book, in one-on-one relationships and in small groups and small organizations. It is in counseling, in selling, in managing small, face-to-face teams and project groups that B has generally worked pretty well, and A has often fallen flat. And it makes sense that things should work out that way. In small units, personal commitment is critical; the individual with his own individual motives and attitudes is critical.

And the tools that have evolved around Type B are, understandably, mostly socioemotional tools. They are the tools like the small group discussion, team building, and non-directive methods.

As Type A implementation moves downward, into the smaller settings within larger units, it begins to run into flack and difficulty. Though the general may find it easy and comfortable to use Type-A tools in running his corps, the second lieutenant may find that they will not quite do, even with the well-trained platoon. And certainly the foreman will head into trouble in getting good work from his people if his methods are exclusively Type A.

And, conversely again, Type-B tools begin to run into difficulty as they move upstairs in the large organization. We have been less successful in running armies participatively than in running individual classrooms that way. For in the larger units, sequencing and coordination requirements loom very large.

But it is the manager of the moderate-sized unit, the plant or the small company, who finds himself right in the middle of the battleground. It is there that Type-A traditions are challenged by Type-B experiments. And it is during the growth from small to large that managers suffer the transitional conflict between the informal, but disorganized humanism of the small company and the pressing demands for structure and formalization that growth seems to require.

Problem finding

While productive debates arise between Type A and Type B true believers, at the interface between problem solving and implementation, neither of these camps has paid much attention to the problem-finding phase of the larger problem-working process. By problem finding, we mean the processes by which one creates and selects problems, the front-end issues. Problem finding is not about getting answers, nor about getting results. It is about getting questions. It is about how people find what they want and, therefore, necessarily, about some very soft stuff, like dreams and loves and crazy ideas.

Consider, for example, a new house. For the building contractor, the first order of business is mostly implementational, getting that house built cheaply and quickly. He worries about scheduling subcontractors and buying material and making it happen according to plan. For a heating engineer, problem solving is the central issue. He has to plan an efficient and safe system given a design for house size X and shape Y.

But now consider the architect. One part of him is probably just like the engineer, solving the problems of closet space and stairways and bathrooms and kitchen appliances. But another part of him, the part most of us hire him for, is neither the engineering problem solver nor the implementer-builder. It is the designer, the artist, the creator of unique houses. This design part of his work—the problem-finding part —is divergent, not convergent. There is no single best answer to the design question. An infinite number of designs are possible, even given budget and site constraints. What the architect adds to the problem-working process is a design, a creation. If the architect has mostly an implementational style, he will worry mostly about bringing the house in on time and within budget. If he is a problem-solving type, he will be mostly concerned about building a rational house that will stand for a thousand years. But if he is a good architect, he must also be a problem finder, a designer. He must create that house of all possible houses (is it sensible to think of "all possible houses"?) that will be interesting and beautiful. Notice the subjective, the artistic quality of such words. This is dream stuff, the stuff of imagination. Problem finding is thus partially about the ways one generates (inside oneself) the beautiful and the beloved. And it is that component, the active input, that differentiates innovative architecture from the routine and dull, albeit functional building. That creative input, that problem-finding component, has been much neglected in management education and perhaps in most other areas of formal education as well.

Problem finding is a critical element in the managing process, for though it may be soft, it is also active. It is through finding the right problems that managing really becomes a way of moving and shaking the world. It is here that managing can make futures.

What kinds of managers tend to be good problem finders? Probably not the managers we have trained in modern schools of management. There we have been training young people to be demon problem solvers and implementers. But the classic entrepreneur was a problem finder. He knew what he wanted. He didn't behave like a problem solver, trying to figure out what the future would be like, and then trying to meet it. He tried to make the future he wanted.

Where else should one look for good problem finders? Problem finding involves values, creativity. We do not have very good analytic rulebooks for such issues. Many of them involve internal rather than external search. They involve understanding one's self, knowing how to find answers to questions like "What do *I* want?" "What do *I* believe is right?" "What would *I* really like to be when I grow up?" What kinds of people worry about questions like that? Probably artists, maybe parents, maybe theorists in the hard sciences.

Perhaps because we do not have good, known methods for dealing with problem-finding questions, we often try to deal with them by using the methods we do know. So a student may try to choose a career by trying to figure out which professions will be in demand a decade hence. Or the organization planner tries to figure what posture the company should take by collecting five-year forecasts of economic and demographic trends. That is to say that we often finesse, even for ourselves, the question of "What do I want?" by trying to become what we think the world will demand of us.

There are probably two things wrong with that kind of response, both for the individual and for the organization. First, even our best problem-solving efforts to forecast the future are pretty weak. It has been said that "the future is not." It isn't history backwards, lying out there waiting to be dug up. It is being made as we go along. So forecasting is a very tricky business. Second, if we spend our time trying to adapt to projected future demands, how will we ever innovate? How will we make our futures better than our pasts?

Since we have pushed the reader to attend to the problem-finding process in managing, we ought to say something about how one can learn to be a better problem finder. Unfortunately, we don't know much. At the moment we must mostly speculate. Would a course in creative art be useful for managers? Is it useful to interact with more kinds of people to stimulate new ideas? Can we learn from students of the inner self—from the meditators, the gurus, both Eastern and Western? Should we take more long walks along the beach? What are the conditions under which you get your most creative or most important ideas?

The interfaces among problem finding, problem solving, and implementation

Let's consider a bit more some of the difficulties that arise at the point where problem solving meets implementation. If we do our problem solving first, we said earlier, we can expect trouble in generating commitment from the implementers. On the other hand, if we bring implementers in on the problem solving, things will get messy. Too many people may get into the act and the quality of the solution may deteriorate. A comparison of Japanese and American managing styles may offer some help with that dilemma. The traditional American model is to do the problem solving first, and then quickly to go on to face the implementation issues. Understandably, we Americans run into lots of problems in implementation. Some people don't like the decision, some sabotage it, some don't understand it, some claim it can never work. So we chew up a lot of time on the implementation side.

The Japanese seem to spend a much larger proportion of their time getting everybody in the organization into the problem-solving phase. By American standards, the Japanese talk things over forever before they make a decision. But the Japanese seem to make up that "lost" time at the other end, the implementation end. By the time the Japanese decision is finally made, everybody seems both to understand and support it.

But the problem solving–implementation interface is an easy one, relative to the interfaces between problem finding and the other two. Someone once called architecture "the impossible profession." Perhaps one reason is that the architect must combine some very different cognitive styles. He must be, at the same time, both a divergent problem finder and a convergent problem solver. He must design a beautiful house, but the plumbing has to work, too. Many clients of architects have found them "difficult" or "unreasonable" or "impractical." What those descriptions probably point to is the difficult transition from dreams to budgets. For that dream may not match the client's or builder's requirements and may not come in within budget. The architect cannot easily work from the constraints backward. He works from his imagination forward. Not so the heating engineer or electrician.

The same stress is apt to arise for problem finders in the organizational world. There is nothing about the problem-finding process that guarantees reason, compromise, economic realism. Problem finders—people who know what they want—are likely to look inflexible and even stubborn. And when problem-finding types are in positions of low power in organizations, they are apt to be put into little isolated cells or in other ways treated as interesting and occasionally useful oddballs.

Difficulties occur at the problem finding implementation interface, too. At the extreme, Type B implementers sometimes substitute participation for purpose. They are apt to decide what ought to be done by taking attitude surveys. They tend to believe that leadership is entirely a service function for those who are led, not a process of influencing others to believe as the leader does. The dilemma at the problem finding vs. Type-B interface is this: How do I do what *I* want when my job is to help the group do what *they* want. One unsatisfactory way out is to take a chameleonlike posture: I will want whatever the group wants.

There are positive sides to all this, too. Implementing can operate in the service of problem finding, for example. One way to find what we want is to look at what we've done. Playing, trying out a variety of actions, is certainly one method many of us use to get a clearer understanding of our likes and dislikes. It is an outgoing rather than an ingoing method, but not entirely a foolish one. Since most of us can't see very far ahead, we often encounter new ideas as we go along, and some of these may turn out to be very attractive. Implementation, that is to say, provides new problem-finding alternatives.

At the societal level, the conflicts between problem finding and other phases of problem working are themselves a source of innovation. For a society salted with lots of problem-finding types starts a lot of divergent fires. Some of those fires turn out infeasible and die out. They don't make it when confronted with the hard realities of problem solving and implementation. But some survive. The danger is not so much in the conflict between problem finding and problem solving or implementing. The danger lies in removing the conflict by eliminating problem finding, or in letting any of the parties dominate. Then rigidity may set in, for the person or the organization or the society.

In summary

Managing can be thought of as a four-phase process of (a) problem finding, (b) problem solving, (c) implementing and (d) monitoring. But the first three need not and often should not occur in that order.

Problem finding is about identifying purpose, about creating interesting problems. It is seen as an active, leadership aspect of managing, but a phase that often calls for divergent and introspective thinking.

Problem solving is what most of us have learned a lot about in school. Analytic methods are our most powerful tools here, but even in this realm, managing often requires intuitive as well as analytic thinking.

Implementation is about the action part of the process—getting it done. Type-A implementation, emphasizing authority and control, derives from the rational view that implementation follows decision making, as it often must in large human organizations and in technical, nonhuman systems. Type-B implementation, using emotional, persuasive tools, has grown out of smaller, face-to-face human situations.

It is based in beliefs about human nature more than in beliefs about reason.

The monitoring phase provides the problem worker with feedback that permits continuous modification of all other phases.

Many conflicts arise at the points of juncture among the phases, but these conflicts are often themselves productive.

25 The volatile organization Everything triggers everything else

In the preceding chapter we looked at managing as a form of problem working, as a continuous juggling and interrelating of problem finding, problem solving, implementation, and monitoring. In this chapter, we go to the setting within which the manager does his managing—the organization. The key point we shall try to make is this one: Organizations are not the static structures depicted in organization charts, nor are they just collections of people, nor smoothly oiled man-machine systems. Organizations are all of the above, and then some. They are constantly changing networks of tasks, structures, information systems, and human beings, that are both simple and complicated, orderly and disorderly, placid and volatile. A large part of managing consists of trying to change those Rube Goldberg organizations so they will function better.

A diamond model of the organization

Consider the following hypothetical case.

> You are a manager. You think you have identified a typically ill-defined problem: One of your large field units, Division X, has turned in much poorer results than their forecasts had predicted. It doesn't seem to be performing its assigned tasks up to standard.
>
> So you decide to call in the local office of one of the reputable older consulting firms—Company S, the largest in town. They contract to take on the problem and send some people out to the unit to collect information.
>
> When they finally come in with a report, you scan it and then turn to the recommendations. They recommend the following: (1) Job descriptions need to be rewritten with greater precision (to get rid of squabbles about overlapping responsibilities). (2) The functional form of organization they now have at Division X ought to be converted to a product form. (3) In fact, Division X has grown

so large that it ought to be partially decentralized itself, with a lot more authority given to proposed new product managers. (4) And you may have to move a few people out, too. There is too much fat in the organization. (5) And so on.

Since you are a manager with an experimental turn of mind and a pocket full of money, you decide not to act on consultant S's report yet. You decide, instead, to knock on the door of another consulting firm, Company T, to get a second independent opinion.

You had gotten to know the first firm. You had found that the people in it were highly regarded and experienced in business organization. You now note, with some discomfort, that Company T looks different, though it also has impressive credentials. Company T is active in the Operations Research Society and the Institute of Management Sciences. Its business experience is not as extensive as that of firm S, but it has done a lot of recent military work, and its senior people all have Ph.D.'s. It seems to be made up of a group of whiz kids. But they have cut their hair and they sound reasonable, so you hire them to look into the same problems at Division X.

They send their people out to the unit, and they, too, come up with a report. But their conclusions are different from those reached by firm S. Instead of recommending modifications in the structure of the organization, they recommend modifications in the informational and control methods being used, modifications, that is, in the technology of managing. They want to program the inventory-control procedures being used in that division and to automate many of the purchasing operations. They want to modify the information flows, so that decisions can be made faster and at different points in the organization. And instead of talking about job descriptions and organization charts, their pockets are full of computers and software. You will have to hire some hotshot MBAs if you want to carry out their recommendations, because neither you nor any of your top people can fully understand what they are talking about.

But because (in this tale) you are really an experimental manager, and because your pockets are really full of gold, and because you don't satisfy easily, you decide you want a third opinion, so you call in the only other consulting firm in town, Company P. Its members have Ph.D.s too. Their offices aren't very elaborate. Their affiliations are different, too. They are members of the American Psychological Association, and/or members of the consultant network of the National Training Laboratories. They are clinical or social psychologists. And they view the world from the human side. They don't carry computers in their back pockets, or write job descriptions, or draw organization charts. Their favorite tools are the group discussion, the face-to-face meeting, and the open-ended interview.

So you ask them to take a look at Division X. And they, too, come up with a report. But, again, their report is different. It argues that the solution to Division X's problems lies in changing the attitudes of the people in that unit, in "unlocking the human potential" of Division X. Morale is low, they say. Apathy is high. People are constricted and anxious, afraid to speak up or take risks. What X needs is more openness, more participation, more involvement, more creativity.

So firm P's recommendation is that you approach the problem from a people perspective. They want you to set up an organizational development program in which you take groups of your people out to a country club for a week at a time to talk things over, to open up valid communication among themselves, to express what they really feel, and to develop much more mutual trust and confidence. Then they suggest you institute a team-building program within the organization.

Probably you could go on experimenting, but the board members are giving you strange looks by now, and the people in Division X are really up in the air. So you stop there and take a look at what you've gotten. Which of the three firms' recommendations should you follows? Which should you reject? Why?

Since you are the manager in this story, we'll leave it to you to answer those questions!

As of right now we have a situation that looks like this:

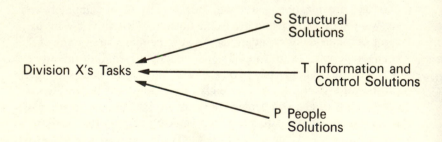

Group S wants to improve the performance of Division X's tasks by working on structure, by changing the organization chart and the loci of authority and responsibility. Firm T wants to solve the same problems informationally by improving the analytic quality of decisions and applying new techniques for controlling and processing information.

And firm P wants to solve the same problems by working on people and their interpersonal relationships.

But there is one more important point that needs to be made here before you decide which of these to use. They aren't mutually exclusive. The point is that the diagram above is incomplete. Because no one of these sets of recommendations, if implemented, will affect the tasks of Division X without involving each of the other points in that diagram. Structure and control and people are highly interconnected in organizations. If we go with firm S, and if we decentralize Division X, or if we change the organization chart, those changes will not only affect the task, they will change (perhaps adversely) people's attitudes and interpersonal relations. We will have to draw new arrows like these:

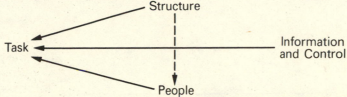

And if we play with that organization structure, we will also affect information and control requirements. The kinds of techniques that are now appropriate in a highly decentralized scheme—the accounting techniques for example—may have to be very different from those appropriate for highly centralized organizations. So add another arrow:

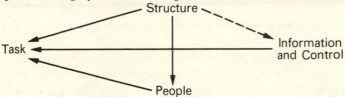

And similarly, if we hire the information-technology-oriented consulting firm, T and go on to introduce the computer and new information flows, then we can darn well expect effects not only on the way the job gets done, but also on structure and on people. If we centralize information in locations where we couldn't centralize before, we will find decisions being made and responsibilities being taken in places different from where they were being made and taken before. And while we may be talking about *de*centralization, that new information system may be pushing us toward centralization. We may also find that the kinds and numbers of people we need in our new, technically sophisticated organization may be quite different from what we needed before. Moreover, some things that were done by judgment and experience before will now be tightly programmed, and that will certainly affect the attitudes and feelings of the old-timers.

Finally, if we move in on the people side, hiring the people-oriented firm P, we will encourage our people to be more open and more honest in their communication, to take more responsibility, and to interact more with one another. But let's not for a moment think we can do those things without exerting great pressure on our existing organizational structure. The authority system will have to change, and old ideas about formal channels of communication will go out the window. And we will exert pressure on the information and control systems, too. Once they've developed a new outlook, people may want new tools or the abolition of old ones that may have been managerially useful but psychologically frustrating.

And so we keep adding more arrows until our diagram looks like this:

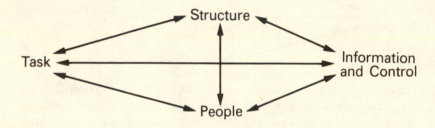

In this one, everything affects everything else! Although we started out to worry only about the relationship between structure and task, or information systems and task, or people and task, we end up worrying about the effects changes in any one of those areas will have on *all* the others. Some of those second-order changes may be very helpful, but some may be quite dangerous. And the manager has to somehow diagnose the second- and third-order effects of starting changes in any one of these entry points.

For organizations do not stand still. If we inject something into one part of the system, bells begin to ring and lights begin to flash all over the system, often in places we hadn't counted on and at times we hadn't expected.

This model we have just drawn is still incomplete because it is a picture of an organization in an empty world. Certainly if there is anything American organizations have learned in the last couple of decades, it is that the worlds they inhabit are anything but empty. The organization is very much shaped by its social life, by the pressures exerted on it by government, by consumers, by ethnic groups, and by hosts of other organizations. The modern organization is a city dweller.

It lives in a pressing, crowded world. And it presses back. So let's enclose our model in a world:

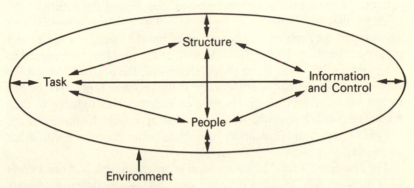

Managing the organization

All this is not to say that the complexity of the organization is so great that the manager can never predict what will happen when he tries to change one of these variables. It is only to say that an organization is complex enough to make any simple structural or informational or human model inadequate. We have made a lot of progress in understanding organizations in the last few decades. We now know a good deal more about ways of acting on structure or people or information technology; and we know somewhat more about how these elements are wired to one another. There is real progress in the organizational world. The three different solutions proposed by three different types of consulting firms in our example should not be taken as a sign that things have gone to pot. On the contrary, the different approaches are an indication of how much we have learned about organizations, and how much we know about ways to change them.

The three consultants in our tale may each be sold on his own product. Each may be overly enthusiastic about all that can be done by changing structure or information systems or people. Each may be partially and understandably blind to the perspectives of the others. But the manager need not be blind. He has lots more to work from than he did in the days when we so naively believed that the simple line drawing on the organization chart actually did capture the essence of his vital, volatile organization.

The next important question for the manager is this one: Are there any sensible rules about where I might start to bring about positive changes in my organization's performance? When shall I work on structure, when on information, when on people?

Here is a weak, but perhaps sensible, rule of thumb:

To decide whether he should devote his attention first to the structural consultant or the informational consultant or the humanistic consultant, the manager in our story should look first at the nature of the problem that he thinks he is trying to solve. For the moment, let's assume that the problem has been found, that the manager's values and purposes are clear. Then he should look at the problem with regard to *programmability*. That is, he should determine the degree to which the problem can be defined operationally. If the problem is of a type he has solved before, if he feels he knows a satisfactory way to solve it, then the best approach is probably a structural approach. If, however, the problem is novel and ill-defined, he may do better consulting with other people first.

The reasoning is this: If the problem is programmable—if one knows what steps to take to solve it—then one can usually define a sensible structure to carry out those steps. But if the problem is unusual, if it has no clear precedents, then his best tool is the human head—his own and his advisors'. In those unprogrammable problems, it doesn't make much sense to try to set up an orderly structure first, because no rational basis exists for choosing a structure.

Suppose, for example, the problem is to set up a new shoe factory in a new market in Texas. That's a fairly programmable problem. People who have worked in shoe manufacturing know a lot about how to go about solving that problem. They have enough experience and training in shoe manufacturing so that they can specify the steps involved in setting up a factory to produce X thousand pairs of shoes per month. They can make pretty good judgments about the equipment they will need and how that equipment ought to be aligned and how much space is required and what the steps from raw leather to finished shoes ought to be, and even how many people will be needed. That factory problem is a moderately programmable problem. It is not programmable down to the fifth decimal place, but an experienced person knows how to go about solving that problem. For that kind of problem, structural starting points seem to make good sense.

Now what's an unprogrammable problem? Consider this one: Suppose you are President Kennedy. You are awakened early one morning to look at some photographs of what the CIA says are nearly completed Russian missile sites in Cuba. What are operational steps that you can call upon to solve that problem? Where will you find the tools you need to establish an orderly program of activities to deal with that task? The answer, of course, is nowhere. We don't have programs for dealing with missile crises. Not only that, the president isn't even sure there is a crisis. He had dealt with the CIA a few months earlier at the

Bay of Pigs, and they had screwed him up rather badly. Now that same CIA insists those are pictures of missile sites, though the president thinks they look like tennis courts! So how do you approach such a problem? It doesn't make much sense to start by designing a structure, does it? But it might make good sense to begin by calling some intelligent heads together, giving them plenty of room and staff support, and setting them to work on possible approaches to the problem. The missile crisis is an unprogrammed problem. The best first tool we now have for dealing with such problems is the unfettered human mind.

If structure is a good place to start for programmed tasks, and people are a good place to start for unprogrammed tasks, what's the role of that third variable, information and control, in all this? One answer is that information and control technology is the handmaiden of structure. The primary function of I and C, one can argue, is to program what has hitherto been unprogrammable. Information and control systems help us to specify and operationalize things which had formerly been done judgmentally, by the seat of the pants. What was unprogrammable yesterday becomes programmable today, and what we had to solve judgmentally last week can be tackled in a more systematic way this week.

So our rule of thumb now reads: If the task is programmable, go structure first. If the task is unprogrammable, go people first.

But that is still only a partial rule. We must also worry about the secondary effects after we have chosen either the structure or the people route. For if we structure that programmable task too tightly, we're going to hear loud squeals from the people side of the system. And if we stay people-oriented on programmable tasks, our competitor may take it all. No rule of thumb can guarantee to make it easy for us.

The reader will note that as we conclude this chapter, we again come close to some of the issues raised in the preceding chapter. An unprogrammable task, for instance, represents a situation in which people don't know what they're doing. And that's close to the notion of problem finding—a very human process. And a programmable task describes a situation in which we do know what we're doing. And that's very close to our definition of problem solving. It's worth pointing out, too, that in large organizations, it's usually at higher levels that people don't know what they are doing! In contrast, the worker on the shop floor typically knows a lot about what he's doing. And that, of course, is precisely because we have been able to program what we call "low-level" jobs; they're considered "low-level" because it's fairly easy to teach lots of people how to do them. But we know very little about programming scientists or presidents, which may be why we worry so much more about finding "high-quality" researchers and presidents.

When we don't know how to tell people what they're supposed to do, we'd better be sure we get good people.

Here is another, even weaker, rule of thumb: As organizations grow larger, structural change becomes more useful (when we're trying to change large parts of that large organization). Large systems need formal structures for coordination and control, because face-to-face communication becomes too costly. In very small organizations face-to-face communication can do much of the job that structure must try to do for the large organization.

In summary

Organizations can be thought of as lively sets of interrelated systems designed to perform complicated tasks. We can try to manipulate at least three dimensions of those systems in order to improve task performance. We can manipulate the organization structure—the formal communication and authority work-flow systems. We can manipulate the informational and control technology. And we can manipulate the people systems—by changing people or attitudes or relationships.

But we must never for a moment forget that when we tamper with any one of these three variables, structure or information systems or people, we are likely to cause significant effects on the others, as well as on the task.

And we must never forget one other less controllable variable, the environment made up of other organizations and institutions, in which our organization is embedded.

In general, structural change seems an appropriate starting place to improve performance in programmable tasks, and the people side more appropriate on unprogrammable tasks. Structural change is also often the best available first step when trying to change very large units. Information and control systems can be thought of in part as "task converters," moving tasks from less programmed to more programmed states. They, therefore, are positively connected to structure.

26

Structure, people, and information technology Some key ideas and where they come from

In this last chapter we talked about several entry points into the organizational system: the structural, information, and people entry points. Useful theory and technique have developed around each of these points, aimed at providing the manager with handles for managing his organization. It is important to remember that these theories and techniques have not always been with us. They are human inventions. They have appeared on the organizational scene mostly over the last twenty years. They have entered organizations over fairly clear routes, and sometimes they have bumped into each other on the way.

In this chapter, we look back over those years to try to map out some of the key ideas and how they got started. Such an historical look can be useful, for without it, the mass of conflicting notions about managing can seem a disconnected hodgepodge of unrelated positions. But there is some order in it all, if we look at the picture historically, with ideas evolving to fit their times.

A few caveats are in order here:

First, even though this chapter describes things long past, our historical sketch is not meant just to offer curious folklore; nor is it history for history's sake. What started then is still with us now. The brick and mortar of much of our contemporary managerial thinking was laid down in those early years. Those same beliefs and practices can still be found on the factory floors of Pittsburgh and Detroit, and deeply embedded in the heads of directors and presidents in all sorts of organizations.

Second, most of the ideas behind the several managerial belief systems we shall consider have been around for much more than seventy years. Some of them have been around for centuries. But those ideas don't seem to take off and change the managerial world until someone invents some cheap and easily transferable techniques. It is techniques that turn those often dormant ideas into instruments of major change.

291

Third, the new in managing does *not* seem to drive out the old. What happens is that the new shunts the old over into a somewhat different niche, then the two coexist. When a new managerial invention comes along, it is added to the old. That "layering" effect tends, of course, to make things more and more complicated. The history of managing is a little bit like the history of medical practice. Most of the same diseases that were around in 1900 are around now. But practicing medicine must have been much simpler because the medical tool kit was much more limited. Rapid technological advance means that to be a good doctor, the modern doctor has to know a lot more than the old Doc did. Managing, too, is a more complicated business than it was in 1900 for the same simple reason: we know a lot more about it.

Let's go on now to look at three key inventions:

Scientific management: Its key ideas

One important set of ideas came into managerial thinking in America back around 1910. It was primarily concerned with structure and technology—the definition, measurement, and planning of the work process. Among the key figures in that "scientific management" movement was Frederick W. Taylor, a name most readers probably remember from their college textbooks. He was by no means the only significant contributor, but his thinking and his methods seem to have had the greatest impact on organizations.

Taylor was an engineer in the best sense of the word. He seemed also to have been a scientist, a questioning man, a fact-hunter.

If ever a movie is made about Taylor, the climactic scene will take place in the yards of the Bethlehem Steel Works shortly after the turn of the century. It will involve two main characters: Taylor himself, and an immigrant laborer named Schmidt. In the scenario, Schmidt is seen going about his work of moving pigs of iron, carrying them from position A to position B. Taylor, ever curious, ever imaginative, is watching Schmidt and conceiving a set of ideas that the world will later call *scientific management*.

As he observes Schmidt, he makes something like the following observations to himself: Schmidt is really doing two kinds of things: (1) He is using his arms and legs to move objects, but (2) he is also making decisions. The decisions are small ones but real ones nevertheless. Schmidt is deciding how to pile the pigs, whether to bend from the knee or the hip, and so on.

Taylor asks himself, "Is Schmidt doing this job in the best way that it can be done?" And he answers, "No."

Now he sets out to determine what the best way is. He searches for methods by which to measure work, and by which to compare alternative ways of doing the work. He argues that such search for the better way is a scientific job, a job that can be better done by people like himself than by people like Schmidt. So back to the laboratory he goes and there he devises the techniques of time-and-motion analysis, which he applies to Schmidt's job. From these, he and his colleagues go on to design an optimal plan for Schmidt's job. The plan specifies the nature of Schmidt's movements, the time that should be allocated to each distinct action.

Now Taylor returns to Schmidt with a message: "Let's stop doing it the way you are now doing it, and do it the way we have laid it out for you. Pick it up with your right hand, instead of your left; bend from the knee instead of from the waist, etc., etc., etc." He points out to Schmidt that what he (Taylor) has done is in Schmidt's and society's best interests for three reasons: First, more pig iron will be handled by the new methods, and that is certainly good for society. Second, Schmidt will end the day less fatigued than he was before, for Taylor will have taught him how to use his body intelligently. And third, Taylor, as an outsider, will urge the company to pay out to Schmidt some portion of the increase in profits accruing from this new method of work. For all these reasons it behooves Schmidt to carry out the work in the way that Taylor recommends. And it behooves the firm and society to adopt Taylor's methods, and to apply to many other kinds of jobs.

What Taylor is searching for is the best way to design and do work. He develops a technology for finding best ways, and in company with the industrial psychology of the time and the sophisticated managerial thinking about organizational structure, there emerges a whole conception of scientific management. In its ideal form it would yield a perfect fit between worker and work, so that he could do his work in the way best adapted to himself and most closely adjusted to the interests of the firm. The flow of work from position to position would be scientifically determined, the limits of activity of each worker would be scientifically measured, and so on. From Taylor's rib was born the whole concept of industrial engineering and the "efficiency man." And coming as it did at a time when production and manufacturing processes were proliferating and modernizing, it was consistent with what was happening in the world around it. No wonder it caught on. So that within a very few years hardly a manufacturing firm in America was without "efficiency men" and the paraphernalia of scientific management—the paraphernalia of job description, work standards, individual incentive schemes, organization charts, work-flow diagrams, and all of their entourage.

Scientific management did indeed seem to pay off. Along with the parallel work of many other innovators like Taylor, management became more formalized, jobs more specified, and mass-production technology, America's pride, came increasingly into being. The ideas that surrounded Taylorism became part of the standard vocabulary of almost every manager in the nation. The notion that work processes should be spelled out, that tasks should be measured and programmed, that responsibilities should be "commensurate" with authority—all these were ideas that generated either out of Taylorism or from other parallel sources that were quite consonant with Taylorism.

The cost of scientific management

But the modern reader in reviewing these last few paragraphs has probably already made a mental note of one nagging difficulty. It was made challengingly manifest by Taylor himself, with comments that were guaranteed to generate trouble even in 1911. He wrote, for example:

> Now one of the very first requirements for a man who is fit to handle pig iron . . . is that he shall be so stupid and so phlegmatic that he more nearly resembles . . . the ox than any other type . . . he must consequently be trained by a man more intelligent than himself. (F. W. Taylor, *Scientific Management* [New York: Harper, 1911], p. 59.)

The problem, of course, was the human problem. For what Taylor had done was to separate the planning, thinking, imagining parts of Schmidt from the moving, doing, acting out parts. He argued partially on the grounds that the Schmidts were a dull group—a rather dull argument. But he also argued it on the same grounds so often used today. In effect, he was saying that specialized and highly trained industrial engineers, equipped with modern tools, could do a better job of specifying how the work ought to be done than the people doing it.

But the human problem is there, and it was to haunt Taylor and the industrial engineers for a good many years to come. Even in 1911 social reformers took up the cudgel against Taylorism, arguing that Taylor was demeaning and degrading man. For what distinguished man from the ox any more than man's capacity to think and judge and make decisions? And if Taylor was removing those aspects from a worker's job, he was indeed dehumanizing the person. There followed a congressional inquiry into Taylor's activities, and there was much social uproar at the time. But the easily observable and obvious gains that Tayloristic methods generated seemed to overwhelm the social critics who could offer ideas and arguments, but no alternative techniques for getting work done better.

The unhappy industrial engineer

So the methods proliferated and expanded. And with that expansion came the second wave of attack; this time not from the social reformers who were interested in protecting Schmidt's welfare, but from the Schmidts themselves. And this time it came in a form that was more difficult to handle. It came in the form of slow-downs, sabotage, pegged production. It came in the form of socially organized resistance. And it led to the unhappy industrial engineer—"the efficiency man"—distrusted, often hated, by the people in the plant. When he showed up, work slowed down. When he set high standards, people professed they didn't know how to meet them. When he asked for suggestions, people hid the jigs they had rigged up to do the work faster.

In parallel, some of the unforeseen costs of other classical structural ideas began to show up. For along with Taylorism, other notions had emerged—about span of control and authority equaling responsibility, and the logical design of organizations.

While at lower levels human resistance seemed to be the major cost of Taylorism, the costs at higher levels were the costs of tight authoritarian structure. They came in the form of inextricably overlapping areas of authority, and overlapping responsibilities that resisted all efforts at separation, and in the form of "depersonalization" of relationships consequent to formalization and restriction of communication. These costs seemed to become greater and more noticeable as the decades passed, largely because the numbers and kinds of people in middle-management levels were growing so rapidly. White collars became more numerous, the complexities of staff relationships increased, the varieties of specialists grew; and the problem of coordinating their activities became much more difficult than it had been before.

The emergence of participative management

To fill this great breach up stepped the people-people. Under the influence of Taylorism organizations had indeed grown and prospered, but the human costs were becoming increasingly apparent. Human "resistance" became a major problem.

Let's now write a second script for a second movie to dramatize a second large phase in American managerial thinking—the people phase. To do so, we must turn to another setting and another time. This time we go to the Hawthorne Works of the Western Electric Company, in Cicero, Illinois. It is the late 1920s. The major characters are a group of Western Electric managers and researchers from the Harvard Business School on the one hand, and a group of workers from Western

Electric on the other. The researchers are present to study several problems, among them some that are strongly Tayloristic in their implications. They are there, among other things, to study the effects of lighting on the productivity of hourly workers performing fine assembly tasks. They go about their business by selecting a group of workers, placing them in a special workroom and maintaining productivity records, under various conditions of light, over an extended period. In our movie there is shot after shot of production charts, showing a sure enough climb in productivity with increasing foot-candles of light.

But with dramatic license, we now sneak a hero into the scene, some unknown (and imaginary) junior assistant. In the interests of science and truth, he argues that these findings will not be truly scientific unless a control is instituted. So he quietly begins to reduce the foot-candles of light (without saying anything to anyone). And now productivity should decline, but it does not. As the lighting goes down, the productivity continues to go up; and that, of course, is the moment of truth. For now the increases in productivity which had appeared to be caused by the lighting turn out to be independent of the lighting. It doesn't seem to matter whether the lights are bright or dim. These people continue to produce at an increasing rate.

And it is at this point that a new search begins. Now the findings must be accounted for. If it is not the lighting, what is it? And the search leads inexorably to the point that Taylor and his colleagues had been unable to handle. It leads to the social and psychological sides of people. It turns out that the increased productivity was caused less by lighting, than by attention. These workers were now in a small separate room. The environment was less formal. And a lot of other social and psychological factors were now operating that were much more difficult to measure and grasp than lighting. But ephemeral and intangible or not, they seemed to be closely and causally related to production.

Incidentally, it is worth pointing out that Taylor and his colleagues were not unaware of such human needs. They simply had no very good tools for dealing with them. But the Western Electric research stimulated a large new search for means and techniques for understanding and harnessing the social and psychological variables in the workplace.

From the late 1920s to the present, the people point of view has grown and prospered. The initial idea was simply that people would get things done better in organizations if they were willingly and enthusiastically involved in their jobs.

Thereupon we started to search for ways of getting such involvement. And gradually, through a series of steps and missteps, two key ideas emerged: First, that one powerful weapon for getting involvement and enthusiasm was the group—almost as a substitute for authority. People would be loyal to one another in groups, they would feel committed to groups that they had worked with. The second key idea was the idea of participation—essentially the idea that "people support what they help to create."

The war against Taylorism

Together these two led easily to the idea that workers ought to be involved in planning and decision making. But this new idea doesn't blend with Taylorism. In fact it's 180° away from Tayloristic solutions to the same problem. Taylor had argued that planning and decision-making should be taken away from Schmidts and given to specialized planners and decision makers. Now along comes the new people-oriented group, recommending that Schmidt's head be put back on his shoulders. It is no wonder then that clashes and small wars began to break out between these two conceptions.

At first the new participative people proceeded with considerable caution. They accepted existing organizational structures and worked within them. At Western Electric for example, they developed a program of counseling that lasted for a good many years. This early program was added outside of the regular organizational structure. Counselors could listen to employees; workers could spout their concerns and worries and complaints. But the counselors were to stay outside of the operational scheme of things. They were not to feed back information to top management. They were not, themselves, to induce any organizational changes. They listened. And when people, having thus expectorated their concerns, felt a little better, they were sent back into the same setting that had been there before. So the relief was likely to be temporary. And the treatments had to be continued as new problems built up.

On the other hand, relatively speaking, this kind of an external arrangement did not disturb the organization very much. It worked only on people without reference to structure. But radical and revolutionary as it was at the time, in retrospect it seems a weak and compromising solution. More daring experiments were yet to come.

These new experiments, usually spoken of now as experiments in "overcoming resistance to change," used some of the same ideas, and some different ones too. They used group methods especially, since they conceived of resistance to change as a function of (1) individual frustration and (2) strong group-generated forces. If one can therefore provide opportunities for need satisfaction and if one can also corner the group forces and direct them toward the desired behavior, then the best of all possible worlds will result.

Hence we began to get experiments that took the following typical and challenging (to Taylorism) form:

An hourly job that had been very carefully industrially engineered is the target. A group of workers is producing product X. The workers have been classified into three jobs: Job A, feeders, feed raw materials into a machine that turns out finished products. Job B, inspectors, sit along both sides of a continuing belt visually inspecting the finished products. Job C, packers, pack the finished product into boxes on pallets which are then taken away for shipment. The job has been studied and engineered in the best Tayloristic tradition. The speed of each machine has been set at an "optimal" level. The belt moves at a rate determined by the engineers and controlled by the foreman. The workers have even been selected by industrial psychologists so that the ones with high visual acuity are inspecting and the ones with high finger dexterity are packing, and so on.

And now onto this scene move the social scientists. They move into the home domain of the industrial engineer, to show him that he is all wet. They force a direct confrontation. They argue that by throwing the old industrial engineering standards out, replacing them with their new and better techniques—mainly the technique of the group meeting—they can get more productivity, less turnover, and more willing work than the engineers had ever achieved.

Now they sharpen up their major tool: the group meeting. They sit down with the people to "talk things over." They listen to the workers' gripes, to the things that they don't like about the way the work is done in their own jobs. Then they get down to some group decisions. One may be that they decide they want to swap off jobs, to overcome monotony. The inspectors will pack every once in a while, and the packers will feed the machines. They also decide that they, rather than the supervisor, should control the rheostat which sets the speed of the belt. The group argues that sometimes they like to work faster than the belt is going, and sometimes they like to work much slower. And so on. The group is thus now making a whole series of decisions usually made by management; decisions about the speed of the line, the jobs they will do, and when they will do them, much as Schmidt did before Taylor reached him. But these employees are acting in a group setting, following a group discussion. The outcome is a wiggly, uneven productivity curve, but with averages a good deal higher than under the previous engineered design, and with lowered turnover and higher morale as free riders.

Where has participative management found its home?

In the 1950s several such demonstrations occurred, showing that this much more human, much more participative approach could clearly increase productivity among hourly workers. Yet this approach has not swept American industry nearly as rapidly as Taylorism had swept it in the decades earlier. The preceding statement is a judgment, of course. Perhaps more employees are controlling more rheostats than this author is aware of. But in general it seems fair to say that the industrial engineer is by no means a gone goose. And work standards, job specifications, lines controlled by rheostats controlled by foremen, all of these are still a very large factor in American industry despite this apparently contrary evidence. In this viewer's opinion, these small wars between scientific managers and participative managers were not clearly won by the participative managers—not at the hourly level—certainly not by the 1960s.

One of the reasons may be that top managers felt anxious and uncomfortable about the apparent loss of control implied by these participative changes. Workers controlling rheostats might not be willing to give them up at some future date. There were fears, too, about the coordination problems that might be generated by lots of small groups operating more or less autonomously. Some things in the environment, like the development of national labor unions and legal controls over wages and hours required uniformity throughout the firm, and uniformity would be harder to achieve (or at least it so appeared), under participative management plans.

Whatever the reasons, it is probably fair to say that participative management began an orderly withdrawal, moving upstairs, where it would produce its greatest impact at the managerial rather than at the hourly levels where it had gotten its start. It was in middle and higher management that one found ever-increasing concern with participative notions during the sixties. Words like *communication* and *participation* have indeed become buzz words in managerial circles. The idea that staff people should interact and talk things over is now a commonplace. The idea that management people should lunch together and not worry too much about whether or not they return exactly at one o'clock is accepted practice. The idea of group discussions and conferences and meetings, despite their frustrations, has become a commonplace, too. The ideas of human-relations training and management development programs and lowering of decision points and encouraging team spirit had all shown up much more within management than they had at hourly levels in the sixties. Not by any means because its originators wished it so, participative management has entered American industry through the white-collar gate.

One of the results has been, in this observer's opinion, the development of a rather sharp and impenetrable line between hourly workers and managers. That wall has been created by many things in addition to the split between scientific and participative management. But it is now generally true in American management that one does not move easily from an apprenticeship in the machine shop to the presidency of a large company, even if one is bright. Movement to the top is easier if one starts out above the hourly worker line, as a sales or supervisory trainee. Hourly workers tend to stay hourly workers; in part, because they are trained differently, organized differently, controlled differently than managers and supervisors tend to be.

By the beginning of the seventies, however, the whole hourly worker question was being reopened, as a consequence largely of environmental pressures. Job enrichment programs were starting and there was even talk about alternatives to the assembly line, like those we discussed in chapter 23. It is as though the costs of Taylorism were becoming larger, relative to their payoff, because the expectations and attitudes of both the worker pool and society at large were changing in a direction that tended to reject the Tayloristic life.

The brave new world of information technology and management science

But our series of organizational movies is not yet complete. Let's back up a bit to a third one. Again we must change dates and costumes—to the 1950s and the gray flannel suit. And we change cast to a great extent. Our heroes now are mathematicians, computer folks, and such. While Taylor and his crew were armed with stop watches, and the participative people carried group meeting techniques in their back pockets, this new population rides on stage astride a glamorous new computer. They carry tools that did not exist for Taylor or the participative people, tools for measuring and analyzing, not what people do with their arms and legs, but what people do with their heads.

Like many movies, this one is an updated repeat of an old plot—the Taylor-Schmidt theme—but in modern dress. In lieu of Taylor, operations researchers and simulators are our stars, on one hand, and the middle manager stands in for Schmidt on the other. While Schmidt presumably achieved some fulfillment by being able to make minor decisions about how to handle pig iron, our new middle manager finds his fulfillment in making large and complicated judgmental decisions about how to estimate inventory or design products or allocate funds among a variety of alternatives.

And the computer people, sitting outside and observing these executives, can say in effect what Taylor must have said of Schmidt. Here are people who are doing things primitively, by the seat of their pants, by "know-how," and by "judgment," and by "experience." Surely there must be a better, a more scientific, a more systematic, a more logical way.

And with the help of new tools, they now search for that way and very often find it. They call it management science instead of scientific management. They find that they can solve complex multivariate problems that until now could be solved only by the good common sense and sound judgment of an experienced executive. They also find that they can often make complex decisions faster than they could be made before, by getting information into key spots more quickly and more fully than before. The climax of this movie, then, is not the tragic race between John Henry and the steam drill, but rather the race between the media executive in the ad agency and the computer.

This third wave makes its impact felt at several levels of the organization. Its effect on the Taylorized hourly worker is partially to eliminate the routine and monotonous from the human realm altogether, turning it over to the machine. Its effect on some participative middle managers may be to program them. This may be tantamount to doing what Taylor did to Schmidt. But looked at another way it simply means that we have once again found new and hopefully cheaper and easier ways of doing work. Human beings seem always to search for ways to program the hitherto unprogrammable. Management science shares with the earlier scientific management this push to understand, to order, to analyze the unanalyzed.

Managerial history and the problem-working process

The reader has probably already noticed a rough match between Taylorism and the structural point of view described in the last chapter; and between management science and the information and control entry point into the organization; and, of course, the reader has also noted that participative management maps nicely on what we described as the people approach in the preceding chapter. In chapter 24 we talked about the problem-working process, about problem finding, problem solving, and implementation, and it seems worth a paragraph or two just to connect this historical chapter with the ideas outlined back there.

Notice that scientific management and management science have something in common. They are both highly analytic approaches to the world. Both are ways of decomposing complex problems into more elemental forms and then recomposing them in a systematic and orderly way. Taylor could use his stopwatch to do that with several kinds of physical and routine work. Information technology tries to do it with more complex informational work. But they are cousins. They share a basic analytic methodology and a set of basic analytic values. They are, one might say, both concerned primarily with the problem-solving part of the problem-working process.

It is understandable, too, that both scientific managers and management scientists have generally tended to approach the implementation part of problem working in Type-A style. The Taylorist, having worked out a program for Schmidt, then explains to him (and, if necessary, orders him) to carry out that program. The management scientist, having worked out an optimal solution to an inventory-control problem, then wants the inventory people to use it. He may explain it; he may try to sell it; but if he has any trouble with implementation, he will probably take it upstairs to the company president and ask him to order people to do it. Scientific managers and management scientists tend to go the A route because in their analytic approach, problem solving usually precedes and is quite separate from implementation.

 Notice that participative managers are likely to be very much more concerned with Type-B implementation. That is, the high-quality solution itself is not their foremost concern. It is the useable solution, the one people will become committed to, that they worry about. Hence the emphasis on meetings, on small groups, on commitment to any solution that is satisfactory. But the reader will also notice that participative management is also somewhat concerned with issues of problem finding. There is a kind of faith in participative management circles that humans are highly imaginative critters. So if we can somehow provide them with the right conditions, the creativity will grow and flower.

But problem finding is still a peripheral rather than a central concern of participative management. None of these three perspectives on management, not Taylorism, nor participation, nor management science, has really centered its attention on the problem-finding process. Each of them pretty much starts with a problem. Indeed, as our conception of managing has become more influenced by inputs like participative management and management science, we probably tend to pay *less* attention to the still unprogrammed, uncomprehended, but perhaps critical front end of the managing game. The part of managing that is still virginal as far as most academics and consultants are concerned is the problem-finding part.

But even if problem finding has been ignored, significant advances have been made in the other areas. Since the turn of the century, important overlapping waves of progress have taken place.

And indeed, they can be called progress. Taylor offered analysis to an area which had not been analyzable. The ideas of participative management represent real progress both as mechanisms for improving productivity and for improving the personal satisfaction of people at work. The information technologist, a third wave, has added new kinds of analytic methods that impinge on areas never before subjected to analysis.

It is understandable that each of the three should feel it has the world by the tail, and that the best of all possible organizations will result from the complete application of his methods. But it is understandable too that in complex systems like modern organizations, none of these methods can be applied without affecting the others.

Nor can any of them be applied without generating some costs not initially foreseen by their inventors. Taylorism generated resistance and sabotage. Participation generated new problems of control, power, and coordination. Information technology has generated new social problems as well as those old ones of resistance and sabotage. And perhaps all three of them drew our attention away from problem finding.

If this historical rundown of overlapping waves of ideas seems only to complicate life for the manager, it should. For the manager of this and coming generations will have to cope with problems of interrelating and estimating the relative impacts of all three of these kinds of approaches and any new ones that may yet arise. He has to decide where in the organization they can best be applied, and if applied, what kinds of costs he can expect to show up elsewhere in his company.

In summary

Taylorism separated planning from doing, created the methods specialist and generated unforeseen problems of human resistance. It has found its more lasting application (at least in its original form) at hourly levels.

Participative management recombined planning and doing, but in groups. Though demonstrably applicable to hourly workers, it has thus far had its greatest impact on managerial levels; thus inadvertently contributing to an enlarged barrier to movement from worker to manager.

Information technology has reseparated planning from doing in think-type jobs. It affects all levels, and comes into at least partial conflict with participative ideas as an alternative method for managing both managers and hourly jobs.

These three are not discrete and irreconcilable. One need not choose one or another. Each is a step forward in organizational problem solving or implementation, if not in contributing to the fulfillment of the organization's members. And common sense tells us that these three do not represent the end of it. There will be fourth, fifth, and sixth major inventions out ahead.

One area begging for attention, and largely ignored by all these, is the area of problem finding.

27 Organizational goals and objectives Problem finding in action

This chapter is about something we don't know much about, organizational tasks and goals, where they come from and how they're managed.

It may seem silly to write about such obvious issues as organizational objectives. There's no great mystery about what any particular organization is trying to accomplish. That company makes and sells calculators and this one sells insurance. Companies make and sell some products or services; they try to do it at a profit; they try to grow and prosper. So what's the fuss? The fuss comes, in part, from the fact that some companies make lots of profit and grow fast and provide better goods and services than others. Why? And some of them start out cutting timber and end up running hotels, and others keep on cutting timber. Some become multinational; some stay domestic. Some create new products and others keep grinding out the old ones. How come?

Many of these differences can clearly be ascribed to differences in problem-solving skills or to differences in implementing skills or to differences in the availability of capital or to luck or to a whole collection of other things. But some of the important differences can be ascribed to differences in "imagination" or "leadership" or "strategy"; and those we would call problem finding.

All this suggests that some big differences among organizations begin at the front end, with the kinds of goals they choose to go after. So let's look, in this chapter, at how organizations seem to choose their goals and establish their purposes. Where do goals come from? Who sets them? Let's consider, too, why some goals seem to come alive and gain the commitment of the whole organization, while others simply "flop." And finally, let's talk a little bit about a related problem that sounds trivial but isn't. How can an organization know when its goals have been reached?

305

How do organizations find their problems?

Consider this curious question: How do organizations (or you, for that matter) find their problems? One answer is that they don't have to find problems anymore than you have to find the water when you're swimming. The problems are just there—all around you. The company has always made light bulbs, and its "problem" is to continue to make them cheaply, efficiently, and profitably. People in my family have always been farmers. When I grow up, I will be a farmer. It's just "natural."

And sometimes there is another answer, just a little bit different from the first one. If you ask any manager where he finds his problems, his reaction is apt to be laughter. He doesn't have to find problems; they find him. His desk is loaded with them every morning.

It's true, of course, that much of the world seems to work that way, with problems finding us rather than us finding problems. And it is probably also true, as some researchers have pointed out, that a special version of Gresham's law prevails, that people respond to the problems that find them before they respond to the problems they find for themselves. If there are specific problems with specific deadlines sitting on my desk, those are the ones I work on, not the unprogrammed things I might work on if there were no immediate fires to put out.

But this is precisely where a major organizational difficulty arises. Because programmed, specified deadlined problems seem to grow like weeds in organizations, and to demand our immediate attention, and because most of us respond to those problems first, organizations may become more *reactive* than *proactive*. They are buffeted by the waves instead of making on-course headway through the waves.

Then how do organizations get beyond this "local" condition of responding always to the immediate, pressing problems their environments toss at them? How do they, instead, act upon those environments to change them? And how do they get beyond the state of continuing to do what they have always done? For doing what you have always done is indeed dangerous in a volatile world of shifting demands and expectations.

Organizations use several methods to try to get out of those reactive boxes. Here are some of them:

1. One analytic way is to improve the organization's sensors. If we can get early warning about what's happening out there, we will have some time to plan, to make changes well in advance of the crisis. So let's develop our eyes and ears to sense market change, social change, economic change that might affect our business; and let's try to respond by adjusting our direction, our services, our policies accordingly. That's

not a foolish idea, and any organization without good external sensors is likely to get into trouble. In fact, in recent years many companies have gotten into trouble precisely because they did not sense what was going on out there.

But notice that sensing the environment is a peculiar sort of psychological game. Different people watching the same environment see different things. Some may see small shifts and treat them as large. Some may be observing large shifts but prefer to shut their eyes to them. So even the reality we perceive is to a great extent constructed out of our motives and our preexisting purposes. We must be sure that our sensors can sense even what we don't like to sense.

2. Another way organizations problem-find (and thereby avoid some distortion) is through maverick members of their own staffs. In some organizations one finds a few oddball persons who, by training or education or personality, insist on breaking Gresham's law. They work on the unprogrammed, the new, the novel, the unstructured, though their desks become piled higher and higher with day-to-day problems. Such people often find themselves in trouble in the organization both because they don't do enough "work" and because they tend to be irritants who raise disturbing questions. But organizations profit from their presence because they keep tossing in new and different perspectives.

3. Another way to problem-find is to loosen up the whole organization; cutting down the number of structured and programmed tasks. Job-enlargement programs fit into that category. So do many of the other participative activities designed to increase creativity among the organization's members. They can be thought of as ways of encouraging people actively to look for problems rather than to wait for them.

4. Still another way is to develop specialized search programs. Basic research is one. It is a searching mechanism, although what it is searching for is not entirely known. But precisely because its task is to search for the unknown, top managements are apt to feel uncomfortable about it. How does one control such unprogrammed activities? And how much of the resources of the organization should reasonably be poured into a well that seems bottomless? On the other hand, if we overcontrol basic research we destroy it. For then research would not be searching for new problems, but solving problems fed into it. How much does an organization need, somewhere in its structure, some open-ended, groping, searching bodies that don't know quite where they are going or quite what they'll find? Surely they will need more such scanning in more volatile environments.

It is here, too, that we get back to the old problem of the costs of pro-

gramming other more mundane jobs in our organization even when we
know how to program them. While we worry about the basic research
group spending its time doing useless things, we need to worry, too,
about a routine production group spending all its time doing only highly
programmed relevant things that are useful but unchanging, for the
nascent creative idea may be completely blocked in that controlled
setting. What we are talking about here, the reader will notice, is the
same difficult interface we talked about earlier, the one between divergent problem finding and convergent problem solving.

5. And then there's leadership. But here we are concerned not
with the implementing side of leadership; not with the power and
influence side; not with the capacity to get people to rally to your flag;
not even with the problem-solving side of leadership; not with the
brilliant analytic mind that goes right to the core of the problem; but
rather with the problem-*finding* side of leadership, the side with the
big dream and the high purpose. Certainly one way that organizations
find problems is through their leaders' visions. People in organizations
accept, to a very great extent, as their problems, those problems that
their leaders define.

We said earlier in this book, and it's worth repeating here, that one
sad and frequently occurring phenomenon in large organizations is
that juniors complain that their seniors fail to set clear goals; and
seniors, conversely, charge that their juniors aren't coming up with
creative goals for the seniors to approve. Each group blames the
other for failing to pick up the goal-setting ball. In the last analysis,
however, a large part of that ball carrying had better be done by the
people on top.

How do announced problems become
real problems? Implementing goals

One source of frustration for juniors in organizations is to develop a
brilliant new idea only to find that nobody will listen to it. A similar
source of frustration (and about as frequent) for organizational leaders, is to propose a great idea only to find that their people don't pick
it up and make it happen. That limitation in their power is a discovery
soon made by most people new to leadership. Even the king cannot
make some things happen.

So even leaders who have (1) great ideas, and (2) great power, soon
encounter that important implementation problem. How do they get
those ideas accepted and used by other relevant members of the
organization? Sometimes that part of the problem-working process
seems to be no problem at all. For example, when President Kennedy
defined the presence of Russian missiles in Cuba as a major crisis,

Americans accepted it as a major crisis and responded quickly and with commitment. But when the same Mr. Kennedy proclaimed the conquest of space as a major goal for American society, nothing much happened. Why, when some C.E.O.s announce a target for next year, does everyone in the company internalize that goal and go to work on it with zeal and resolution, while other C.E.O.s proclaiming similar goals get nothing but blank looks, resistance, and excuses?

A large part of the answer to that one lies in the relations between organizational leaders and organizational followers. The leader needs good internal sense organs. Part of his problem-finding process must be to take the needs of his people into account. He has to find problems that have real meaning to everybody in his organization.

Meaning, of course, can be "managed." So leaders have to worry about their internal PR, about setting up a problem carefully so that by the time it is officially made public, all the props and support systems that make it real will be in place. That's an implementation problem. President's aides announce major speeches well in advance of the speeches themselves. Rumors are carefully circulated. Allies and congressional leaders are briefed. Rewards for cooperation are defined. These are Type-A, perhaps Machiavellian, implementation steps. But if the problem does not make itself sufficiently real, the leader has to manage the process of making it real.

But he cannot always make problems real to his people, even with the best help in the world at his side. The reader will remember from the chapter on group pressure that if the distance between the leader's definition of a problem and followers' definition is very great, even the leader won't be able to make his view take hold. If the leader wants Z and his followers like A, then the leader has a lot of managing ahead of him before he can proclaim Z and expect it to be treated seriously.

The major point, then, is that for a leader to work a problem through, he needs not only to find the right one but to make it acceptable and valuable to other relevant members of his organization. And that is usually a complicated, incremental process.

How do organizations know when they have reached a goal? The monitoring process

This seems a beguilingly easy issue in organizational problem working. But people who have been around organizations know that it is not. Finding out how well it worked is especially difficult for those interesting unprogrammed problems in which no one knows quite what all the alternatives might be; and in which the delays between actions and effects are long ones. When delays between cause and effect are long, it is hard to isolate cause. Some primitive societies, for example, don't seem to make any logical connection between intercourse and child-birth nine months later. Too many other things happen over nine months that can account for the appearance of the infant. Too many other things often happen in our primitive organizational decision making, too. It's apt to be a long time, for example, between the intro-duction of an idea and the marketing of a product that it generated. Sometimes we can't remember the original idea. Sometimes the product flops—but is it because the market changed? Or because the idea was no good? These kinds of questions often make it truly difficult to determine whether or not a decision was a reasonable decision.

Besides, we live in a satisficing world. So all we are apt to know, if we know anything, is whether or not the decision we chose got us generally in the direction we wanted to go. We seldom know in organi-zations whether an alternative decision would have worked better than the one we chose.

Third, we have a kind of cognitive balance problem again. Once we have committed ourselves to an organizational decision, once we have built a plant or decided to manufacture widgets, there are lots of psy-chological forces to keep us from rejecting that decision. The failure of a decision has to be very dramatic indeed for it to be accepted as such. And even then, organizations have a strong propensity to develop silver linings for their failures.

But the thing that is clear is that feedback about the effects of be-havior is just as necessary for organizational learning as it is for indi-vidual learning. Getting quick and accurate feedback on organizational problems, however, is probably even harder than it is for individuals. Not only are the problems likely to be bigger and more complex, and the results apt to be delayed, but there are also problems of blocks and biases in internal communication. How quickly and accurately shall we report negative outcomes of something we have been responsible for? Do we dare tell the boss that his plan has flopped? Won't he feel that we just haven't done a very good job of implementing it?

Technology seems to be helping a good deal in speeding up the feedback process both within and without the organization. Telephones are faster than letters. Quick samplings of sales, statistically controlled, may tell us whether or not the style change is having the impact we want. Simulation devices allow us to pretest and get certain kinds of feedback before we have committed ourselves to a decision.

But technology has helped only a little to specify what we need to know about the world out there. Some of what an organization needs has been obvious for a long time—like consumer reaction to product changes. But other sources of useful intelligence about the environ-ment are harder to specify. What does the company need to know about the community in which it lives? About race relations? Drug abuse? Crime? The activities of college students? It's easy and safe to say that the company needs to know more than it ever did before. But exactly *what* and *how* are more difficult and not yet fully answered questions.

Yet we are probably making progress by turning our modern information technology toward the problem, by trying to model the important parameters of the environment so that the manager can better assess the likely effects of environmental changes on the organization, and the likely effects of changes by his organization on the environment. The techniques are progressing rapidly; the more human question of inputs—of what parts of the environment we really need to look at—is a little harder to handle.

Feedback mechanisms within the organization are perhaps more important than ever, too. Although most managers are ready and willing to grab new tools that will help them assess their impact on the market, they are less enthusiastic about new devices for sensing the internal problems of their organization. And it is on the internal side that one of the major people problems of organizations exists.

Still another source of bias in developing accurate and speedy feedback in organizations is the tendency of most of us to keep our pockets full of many different yardsticks. If our profits decline, can't we take solace in the fact that our share of the market went up? This tendency to select only the good yardsticks is one large part of the human balancing act. It is also a source of distortion in large organizations.

In the same vein, one of the key problems in getting accurate and quick feedback in organizations is the organization's own history. Suppose we have found a great problem. It has worked by all of our yardsticks. The effect of our success is often to cause us to lower our guard. We check less carefully, pay less attention to small cues, especially internal cues, when we are riding high on a previous series of successes. On the other hand, if organizations have met miserable failures, even greater distortions in feedback are likely to occur. For now the atmosphere is apt to be hostile and recriminative, and in that environment truth is hard to come by.

Once again, diversity of opinion looks useful. Organizations need those deviant small boys who claim the emperor is naked.

Single goals and multiple goals in organizations

For a long time economists liked to treat organizations as though they had single goals. Businessmen have often echoed this notion too, although they probably don't really believe it. The goal of the business, one often hears, is to maximize profits. But if one pushes that idea, one is likely to notice one important thing: Many people and groups within the firm in fact place *maximized* profit quite far down the list. They like to *improve* their profit positions. They feel good if they have done better than they did last year or if they have hit some target they set out to hit. And more important, there are many people and groups in organizations who place the whole profit issue fairly low on the list of operational goals. They will talk about improving quality, or getting a larger budget next year, or getting management to accept an organizational change.

This is only to say that in most organizations there is not one goal but a diversity of goals. Different individuals, different units, different groups are striving for different kinds of things. We solve a large part of this problem of different goals in the same firm by setting up formal roles and duties and expecting people to operate within them. We say to an employee, "When you come to work for us this is the job we want you to do." And most of us accept that role and spend a good part of our lives trying to achieve the goal associated with that role. But that isn't the only goal we strive for. We also try to enhance the role itself. Sometimes, even in trying to fulfill that role, we run into clear conflict with our own personal goals. That is the subject of the next chapter. But even if we operate within our roles, even if we do what we ought to be trying to do, even if our own personal motives are kept out of it, the goals of different parts of the organization are apt to be diverse and sometimes in conflict.

One important fact is that the meaningful, operational goals that people really work at tend to be local goals. Soldiers don't generally really fight for their country so much as they fight for their local units and their buddies. The district manager, although he is a good company man, may see himself as working mostly for his district.

No matter how much the planners try, they are not in most organizations able to set up a system of roles in such a way that all goals are consonant with all others. So that even if people do their jobs, conflicts of interest will arise. The organization, in fact, is not an orderly hierarchy of subgroups, each of which is striving toward some subgoal such that, together, they will maximize the company's total goals. That just isn't the way it works. The way it really works is much more like a political system. Group A wants a larger share of the budget. So does group B. There are active conflicts and competition to get their shares. Group C has to mediate between the two contestants, and it must worry about the negative effects on one if it finds for the other.

In summary

Managers don't have much trouble finding problems to work on. The world is full of them. But some managers do a better job than others of creating good problems instead of just fire fighting the ones that come along.

Several steps appear to help the active problem-finding process. Good sensors of what's going on in the world are important; so are diverse people inside the organization, people who look at the world in unusual ways; so are specialized search activities, like basic research programs.

Another critical problem-finding mechanism is organizational leadership. To a great extent, the problems they select are the problems that others accept.

But even in that transfer is difficult. Wise leaders do not assume that their people will automatically commit themselves to problems the leader has selected. They work at gaining such acceptance.

The other end of the problem-finding issue is monitoring, knowing when the problem has been worked through. In organizations, learning about results is harder than it looks. Feedback is often slow, distortion creeps in. Both information technology, and our old friend diversity of opinion, can help establish accurate feedback.

But goals set at the top are not the only goals to think about. The organization is a political system with subgroups that work for their own as well as the organization's goals. So a large chunk of the managing process must focus on bringing the local purposes of the various parts of the organization into some degree of alignment.

28   Managing people
        Work and satisfaction

Almost all of this book has been about managing people. So why a special chapter now? The answer is this: Managing people in large organizations often means managing many people you have never met, whom you may never even see. Yet you may set "policy" for them. It's that aggregate, "policy-level" kind of managing that we want to examine in this chapter. And that's often quite different from the face-to-face managing we talked about in earlier sections. In this chapter we consider company "philosophies" and "policies"; questions of how organizations should be designed to get good, committed work from lots of different kinds of people spread throughout many different locations. This chapter must therefore necessarily deal both with value questions and with questions of method.

Work, play, and people

There's a basic value question that needs to be considered forthwith.

Some people in industry feel that the impact of organizations on people's well-being is unimportant unless well-being influences productivity. Often, for example, industrial managers committed to a *structural* view hold that the eight hours a day people spend in their organizations are not hours designed for need satisfaction to begin with. They are *working* hours. Americans distinguish work from play precisely because work is not intended to provide contemporaneous need satisfaction. When one goes to work he should therefore feel that he is sacrificing his eight working hours in order to earn the wherewithal to obtain satisfactions *off* the job.

This clean-cut separation of work from play, and the value that underlies it, encounters two difficulties. First, it carries with it the unrealistic assumption, talked about in part 2, that people can actually make such a separation on some neat, rational basis. But people cannot shed their personalities at eight o'clock, nor their personal, non-organizational goals and interests. Even if they sign a frustration-in-exchange-for-pay contract, they are not likely to be able to fulfill their commitment. "Illogically" (but with the internal logic described in part 1) they go on using up organizational time trying to avoid personal frustration and to find positive satisfactions on the job.

Second, even if a manager could get his people to accept their jobs as necessary periods of frustration, he probably could not, if chapter 4 is right, get them to stop responding to frustration with aggression. Feelings of aggression are also outside the control of the contract.

Somehow, then, organizations have to deal with that work-satisfaction issue, instead of trying to finesse it. Somehow organizations have to deal with the fact that the whole person, not just his arms or legs, comes to work every day. Let's therefore take several characteristics of organizations and look at how they are likely to affect whole people's work and whole people's satisfaction.

Pyramids and people: The role of competition in work and satisfaction

Large industrial organizations are shaped more or less like pyramids. At least they become narrow at higher levels. Coupled, intentionally, with this narrowing design is a more-or-less-conscious effort by people at higher levels to encourage people at lower levels to climb. This effort need not be great to be successful because early training and education have already encouraged climbing behavior. Industrial organizations simply continue the process by offering greater rewards at higher levels, rewards that are perceptually real for most of us. They also help the process along by selectively screening out those with less intensive climbing desires.

These two factors, narrowing toward the top and desire to reach the top, combine to create *competition* for advancement. Such competition is likely to be less intense when the whole pyramid is rapidly growing and more intense as the growth rate decelerates. For when the whole pie is getting bigger, everyone can move with it. When the pie's growth ceases, but the diners' appetites do not, competition for a piece of it is likely to be more intense. Fortunately, however, the world is bigger than the company; so even when an organization has stopped growing, its members may continue to climb by leaving the organization —a characteristic and accepted phenomenon in some industries but one fought by management in others.

Still another escape, in static or slow-growth periods, can be found through personnel selection. It is possible to find competent people who do not like to climb or whose levels of aspiration will tolerate a more moderate rate of climb. Some American unions have found a need to remake or replace some of their people at the point at which the battle to organize gave way to the problem of consolidating the union and establishing more "gentlemanly" relations with management. The old-time battler, useful and effective in winning the war of organization, became a difficult problem when war gave way to diplomacy.

It should not be necessary to add, after the section on influence, that "remaking" people is not always a hopeless process. Experienced industrial counselors will probably agree that helping people to lower their levels of aspiration is one of their most common tasks. Counselors must deal with the young person who did not become superintendent after one year and the older one who did not become president—but whose best friend did. People can, in a great many instances, successfully learn to accept something short of supremacy.

If individual competition results from the combination of the pyramid and egoistic climbing needs, how does such competition affect the productive implementation of organizational tasks? It does not seem safe simply to generalize the advantages of interorganizational competition and apply them to interpersonal competition. A football team may compete successfully with other teams, but it does not follow that it will compete best if its members are in competition with one another.

Interpersonal competition also hits another complication that interorganizational competition manages to avoid: the problem of personal conflict between egoistic and social needs discussed in chapter 5. While parents and education have encouraged us to compete, our dependency has also encouraged our social needs. Climbing at the expense of others is unchristian and unsportsmanlike. So required interpersonal competition may disturb people and evoke feelings of guilt, feelings that are not usually present in competition between firms or other large organizations. Again, though, if the criterion is the total productivity of the organization, internal conflicts are relevant only if they hurt productivity.

Still another complication deriving from interpersonal competition is that people at higher levels in companies are the umpires and judges. In competition between organizations no such complication exists. The impersonal "market" is the judge of success. But within organizations the climbing game is played differently. The climber is largely dependent on the personal evaluation made of him by people at higher levels.

This personal element in the climbing process is much like what dependent children encounter. How "good" the job of mowing the lawn is depends largely on parents' reactions. It is a good job if they say so and a bad one if they say so. The youngster may learn that "good" depends as much on parental moods or on his ability to ingratiate as it does on the neatness of the lawn.

Considering all these complications, under what general conditions

can increasing interpersonal competition be expected to increase organizational productivity? At least three conditions come to mind: If
the jobs of the competitors are *independent,* not interdependent; if
objective, not subjective, *standards* for advancement can be established;
and if *success* for one *can be separated from failure* for others; then
interpersonal competition should result in a net increase in productivity.

Suppose, for example, that a sales manager decides to select an
assistant from among ten salesmen. The salesmen know that one of
them will get the job, but they do not know which one. Competition for
the assistant's job would probably increase total productivity if:

1. The salesmen operated in independent, non-overlapping territories.

2. The manager could devise and communicate an objective standard for selection. For example, he might select the person with the
greatest sales increase in the next six months over his past three-year
sales average. An objective standard is not easy to achieve. It requires
a method for equating territories; it must avoid the pitfall of encouraging salespeople to overload some customers and ignore others for the
short-term prize, and so on. And it must mean what it says: the subjective judgment of the manager must not count.

3. The salespeople see the objective standards as reasonable and
fair; the salespeople prefer the assistant's job to the satisfactions derived from being out in the territory; and they do not feel that they
are hurting one another in the process of striving for the promotion.

Such conditions are difficult to meet, and to the extent that they
are not met, the productive advantages of interpersonal competition
would be decreased.

In general, these conditions are probably easier to approximate at
lower than at higher levels. Jobs are often more independent of one
another at lower levels; measures of performance are easier, too. But
even at those levels, questions of job separation and individual incentives create difficult, perhaps impossible, problems. At higher levels,
where interdependent decision making plays a larger role, a design
for ideal competitive conditions is even less likely to be successful.

For at higher levels, as we suggested in the last chapter, jobs are
unique rather than standardized. They change, too; new problems show
up. The right decisions, even after they have been made, are often hard
to judge objectively. And probabilities play a larger part, so that a series
of successful decisions, or of unsuccessful ones, may occur by chance.
All these things force managers to evaluate high-level subordinates
more personally, more subjectively.

Further, the same characteristics of pyramids and people create
difficulties for superiors as well as for subordinates. One of the rewards
for the superior's own successful climb is the right to rule the roost, the

right to the attention and respect of subordinates. That reward must be partly given up when the manager is asked to set up impersonal, objective standards for his subordinates.

Managerial resistance to setting up objective standards, even where they are possible, is understandable. The best employee objectively may not be the best team member (for we want cooperation, too) or the easiest to work with. A successful pattern of people in a group, even if each is not perfect, may be more productive than a group of "perfect" but poorly related individuals.

Even where competition is an effective stimulus, the reward of promotion up the administrative ladder may not be a reward for some useful people. Research people and other professionals often fall into this group. The goals of many of them lie in their professions, not in the administrative hierarchy. But the traditional organizational pyramid builds on the assumption that higher levels in the organization are more important levels, more deserving of higher income and higher status. It becomes awkward for the pyramidal organization, therefore, to have a person at a lower level regularly contributing more than people several levels above him in the structure.

This picture of the costs of interpersonal competition can be easily overdrawn if one does not take into account the many other purposes the pyramid serves. It is a shape that simplifies many problems of communication and control. It is, on the face of it, a logical structure for handling the many levels of decision making that must go on in an organization. So, despite all the difficulties that are consequent to the competition created by the pyramid, there is not sufficient reason for abandoning it, especially since no good substitute is available. A more likely outcome will be a differentiating and separating of different parts of the pyramid, with the parts in less close contact with one another.

But if the emphasis on competition often causes trouble, the simultaneous emphasis on cooperation causes more. For like inconsistent parents, managers talk out of both sides of their mouths. While they want "aggressive," "competitive" young people, they also want people who "get along," who can "play on the team." The worst part of these clichés is the conflict they produce for the young person who wants to get ahead. Shall he or she be competitive or cooperative? Does the manager himself know what he wants, or ought he to spend some time, like our good influencer, reexamining his own motives and objectives?

Authority, dependency, and satisfaction

A second characteristic of industrial organizations is the hierarchical, unequal distribution of power among the members. Roughly, power follows the pyramid: higher levels have more of it; lower levels, less. An earlier chapter pointed out that this distribution is brought about primarily through the delegation of authority. Through authority (in addition to personal power) given people at higher levels, power is generally distributed through the organization so that more stays at the top than sifts to the bottom.

The other side of this coin is the psychological one. This distribution of power through authority means that people lower in the organization probably feel more dependent on higher levels than the other way around. So the hierarchical system of authority, in serving other organizational purposes, also causes feelings of dependency.

One important outgrowth of dependency, we have said, is ambivalence: the tendency simultaneously to like and dislike being dependent. That most of us like dependency is apparent when we lose it —when the lonely, independent assignment (like the presidency of the company) ultimately comes our way. That most of us also dislike dependency is shown by our efforts to attain the presidency.

Dependency, by splitting people down the middle, can affect organizational behavior in important ways. It can cause tensions in relationships between subordinate and superior, limiting freedom to communicate and increasing concern about the meanings of the superior's behavior. The signs of these difficulties show up everywhere in industry. At the office party the boss drops in and the atmosphere changes; some people drift away; others talk a little louder or a little faster. Idiosyncracies in the behavior of peers are passed over quickly, but the boss's oddities become legendary; his moods become prime subjects for gossip; his occasional offhand comments are scrutinized microscopically for their hidden but significant implications.

These behaviors are clues to the subordinate's perspective on the same problem higher management usually defines in terms of performance evaluation. Both perspectives recognize the extent to which life in an industrial organization is life in a medium of dependency, of continuous evaluation—a partial replication of childhood when every act was judged to be good or bad by adults. Such a medium necessarily must draw some of the subordinate's attention away from job functions so that he can focus it on methods of improving his position with superiors. To a greater or lesser degree, any assigned job becomes, in his medium, two jobs: One job is to carry out the assignment, to get the job done; the other (but not always secondary) job is to please the superior. Maybe the two tasks can be melded into one, or maybe the second one can be minimized (some alternatives are considered in the next chapter), but basically dependency causes concern over being judged in any task undertaken within the industrial setting.

Note that what we are talking about is partially an outcome of Type-A implementational thinking. If we make decisions at the top, then we must evaluate and control the performance of the people who carry out our decisions. But because those are real people down there, some unintended consequences emerge. Those people try to make their evaluations look good, regardless of actual task performance. So both game playing and the emotional consequences of dependency become free riders to be reckoned with. The organization is then driven toward more careful evaluation to separate the games from the truth. The devices used can become quite elaborate. But the more elaborate the performance-evaluation methods, the more elaborate the counterpoint of games and probably of distrust. So reams have been written about techniques of performance appraisal, yet almost no organization is satisfied with its performance-evaluation procedures. They are sources of constant complaint and require constant reinforcement by Type-A methods even to get superiors to use them regularly, because superiors—middle managers in the organization—find themselves caught up in the uncomfortable games, too.

Another factor bears on this dependency question. Partly to protect their relationships with their own superiors and partly on rational grounds, superiors tend to demand that subordinates objectively justify their actions, in advance of the actions themselves. This requirement may force people's dependency underground, so they act more and more independently, though they really would like a shoulder to weep on. The results of chronically unexpressable feelings of dependency can be serious, sometimes physically harmful, for the individual.

The same conditions can be organizationally harmful, too. Most executives are probably familiar with the problem of reporting back to top management some unhappy discovery about the adverse effects of one of top management's pet ideas. Often it is personally dangerous to communicate such information, despite behests by superiors to report the facts "objectively." Even the good subordinate may end up with a watered down, selective report of what he observed, though he cloaks it in the paraphernalia of facts and figures. And if the findings reflect on the subordinate himself, rather than the superior, objectivity becomes even more unlikely.

One result of this "evaluation fear" may be the loss of a most useful organizational tool—the sensitive, intuitive judgment of experienced people. Pressure on the superior to evaluate and on the subordinate to get a positive evaluation can team up to destroy unverbalizable judgment in favor of rational, objective justification.

For instance, the fact seems to be that we do not know very much about how advertising works. But to be businesslike, advertising people often have to act as if they do. There would be nothing inherently dangerous in such playacting if the actors knew they were acting and if they knew they were really using their uncommunicable knowledge and experience. Instead, they often behave as though they could write down and communicate all the relevant facts. The result, for the present, is that many business decisions have more the appearance of rationality than the actuality.

But there may be some hope in this realm. It may be that we can, as managers, learn better to understand and use the "gut feelings" of our own people as a valuable tool for managing. In recent years we have perhaps underestimated people's capacity to use nonanalytic, non-verbal styles of thinking. We have tended to ignore rather than exploit "intuition" and "judgment." But recently, over problems ranging from the assessment of individuals to the financial assessment of organizations, we have begun to revalue the human "feel" for things.

Perhaps, however, the statements just made need some modification. Experienced managers have always used those intuitive tools. When we speak about *beginning* to use them, what we really mean is that social scientists are rediscovering the wheel once again!

The jigsaw puzzle of individual responsibility

A third related characteristic of most organizations is that they live by the principle of individual responsibility. This is the belief that a task can be subdivided into person-sized pieces, each piece independent of every other and each piece just the right size for an individual. Some doubt exists about whether such an atomistic breakdown is even possible in complex modern organizations, and some doubt also exists about whether organizational charts which purport to demonstrate such a breakdown are reality or mirage.

The idea of individual responsibility probably grows out of the fact that industrial organizations are built from the top down, with a continuing need for control from the top. But as the size and complexity of organizations grow, control from the top becomes more difficult—at least the complete, unequivocal control that includes exclusive ownership of all significant decision-making rights.

With growth, management must ask: Now that we are so big that we must allow lower levels to make some decisions, how can we do so without giving up our independent sovereignty? The idea of responsibility to correspond with authority seemed like a good move. Top levels give subordinates some of their decision-making prerogatives, but they hold on to control over the relationship itself. Delegation of authority and responsibility are not irrevocable. They do not include a tenure clause. Thus, the dependency of the subordinate on the superior can remain almost intact. Moreover, by delegating specific, carefully defined areas of responsibility to individuals in individual-sized pieces, control from the top can be maximized. With one individual responsible for each separable phase of activity, difficulties can be spotted quickly and correctives can be applied to a manageable unit—an individual.

This is practical reasoning. In a structure controlled from the top, it makes sense to subdivide the total job into parts, to hold one individual responsible for each part, and at the same time to maintain control over means to the individual's key need satisfactions.

But these same ideas have some problems. The principle of individual responsibility assumes that all decisions can be made by individuals. It assumes also that the whole of an enterprise equals the sum of its separable areas of individual responsibility. These two assumptions lead the traditional concept of responsibility into difficulty in large modern organizations.

One difficulty arises when the assumption that the whole equals the sum of its individual-sized parts meets the factor of technical specialization. At that point the individual-sized parts stop being entirely independent of one another and become interdependent. The subparts and the sub-subparts begin inextricably to intertwine, and so, too, do individual areas of responsibility.

Consider, for example, an organization that is subdivided primarily along functional lines. It is made up of three major functions: procurement, manufacturing, and selling. Vice-presidents are in charge of these functions. Over time the company's products begin to grow in numbers, so additional people are assigned responsibility for supervising particular classes of products—"product managers." Still all products derive from the same raw materials; many are manufactured on the same production lines; and all are sold by the same sales force. Who is now responsible for the manufacture of product X—the manufacturing people or the product managers? Who is responsible for deciding how much raw material to procure for product X, especially if procurement of raw material for X automatically requires procurement of raw material for Y and Z? If the product supervisor is held responsible for the overall success of his product, but not for procurement, isn't he in the position of having responsibility without equal authority? Moreover, if the manufacturing vice-president is responsible for manufacturing, then what is the product manager's relation to him?

Overlapping circles of responsibility seem to show up more and more as organizations increase in size and complexity. Individual jobs become more and more dependent on other, previously unrelated jobs. Staff and service activities come into being, and defining their authority and responsibility becomes a nightmare.

Within the general medium of continual personal evaluation, subordinates must come more and more to demand wider and wider realms of authority in order to fulfill their responsibility. Private little kingdoms thus begin to emerge. Department heads get protective about their prerogatives and about other people moving in on their territory.

These complications are to be expected if a person knows he is being watched and judged continually and also knows that his job is defined in such a way that he cannot hope to do it adequately through his own efforts. He is dependent on his superiors for promotion and advancement and dependent on his peers for help in getting his job done; but he is evaluated by his superiors as though he were not dependent on either. So the plant superintendent is in continual conflict with the industrial-relations manager, because the superintendent's performance is partly dependent on his relations with his union. The industrial-relations manager, on the other hand, to do his job adequately, cannot permit plant-to-plant variations in labor contracts, even though a particular plant could profit from a special contract. The product manager is in continual conflict with the general sales manager because his products are not getting the sales attention he thinks they deserve. But the sales manager feels that he cannot do an adequate job unless he controls the way his salespeople subdivide their time and effort among products.

What are some ways out of these problems? One partial solution may be to allocate responsibilities more to groups, less to individuals; in effect, to delegate the delegation of individual responsibilities to the group. That's what we described in chapter 23 in the discussion of experiments with group-based factories.

Another current set of experiments centers around the "matrix" organization which we consider a bit elsewhere. The basic idea is to give up the notion of one person, one boss, in favor of multiple but systematically shared responsibilities.

Size

Still another set of human problems derives from the large numbers of people whose activities must be coordinated in modern industrial organizations. Large groups are harder to systematize and control than small groups. Large groups can, in fact, be different in kind as well as degree from small ones. We pointed out earlier that some communication nets, for example, are unique to small groups. They are not applicable to a ten-man group, let alone to a hundred men. For a group of five people, ten channels of communication are possible; but when the number of people increases to ten, forty-five channels open up, and when the number is one hundred, 4,950 communication channels are possible.

The point is that big groups are different from small ones. As organizations grow, some of the principles by which they are organized no longer apply. One writer has drawn some analogies from biology. He points out that Jack the Giant Killer's giant is sixty feet tall and well proportioned. He is ten times as tall as Jack, ten times as broad, ten times as thick through. His volume and mass are a thousand times those of Jack. But being built like Jack, his leg bones are probably ten times as wide and ten times as thick, or a hundred times as big as Jack's in cross-section. So now the giant has to carry a thousand times Jack's weight on supports only a hundred times as big. He probably cannot stand up. Simple proportionate increases in the size of each point do not necessarily make the system grow successfully. The same writer goes on to suggest that as industrial organizations grow, ideas such as span of control, the suggestion box, etc., which may have been useful at one point in an organization's size, lose their usefulness and require complete redesign.

Size, then, goes on to generate many varieties of individual human problems. Increased size increases every person's distance from people who influence his organizational fate. Although immediate superiors have a lot to do with determining where he goes, decisions beyond the immediate superior or even beyond the immediate superior's set limits on the speed and direction of his movement. Direct communication with those distant decision makers is almost impossible. The subordinate's anonymity increases, and so does his uncertainty about what will become of him. Each employee knows that he is being evaluated and also that he can have little effect on the information his evaluators use or on their interpretation of that information. So size adds to the tensions already instigated by the atmosphere of evaluation.

Size also separates people at the same level from one another. Because free and open communication among all persons becomes more complicated with growth, any one at any level becomes more isolated from others involved in other activities at the same level. So people's opportunities for a "general" business education, for varieties of experience, are fewer. Opportunities for an overview of the whole operation become more difficult. A modern production supervisor, for example, can easily live his life in a present-day organization and never meet a person who sells the product he is manufacturing. When related people and their related activities are mutually unknown, their perceptions of one another may become dangerously distorted.

Size, by increasing the complexity of communication, increases the probability of misinformation as well as the probability of decreased total information flow. As the number of people between a decision maker and his source of information increases, the probability of error and mistiming increases—a phenomenon that is most important because of its multiplying effects on attitudes as well as on the quality of business decisions. People, an earlier chapter showed, get frustrated and angry at one another when they have difficulty in sending or receiving information. Field people come to feel that the home office is made up of dunderheads, and the home office reciprocates the feelings. Managers recognizing these difficulties may try to compensate by forcing more information through the channels. They may require more periodic reports, set up forms, and themselves make it a point to disperse more information to more people. But though this counteraction may alleviate the problem, it may create additional difficulties—an oversupply of material that the recipient finds difficult to evaluate or even read. As long as the structure itself makes for long and difficult communication lines, changes in the structure itself would seem to be the only cure.

Changing organizations by changing people

If the problems just cited are some of the major people problems that cause a drag on both organizational work and human satisfaction, what's to be done about them?

In the early days, as we have pointed out, one answer was to use punishment and threat. Next, individual incentives were tried. Then we tried to keep people in line by manipulative means—by "making them think it's their idea." In all those cases we were looking at people after setting up a structure, which meant that structure took first place. The problem was to get people to work within it.

Since then another different kind of idea has moved in over a wide front. It is the idea that structure, in large part, ought to follow people. This is the idea behind the third consulting firm in chapter 25. If we can first develop a solid, loyal, hardworking group, with valid communication within it, then appropriate structure will follow.

O.D.: Organizational development

Over the last twenty years a significant effort at a people-first approach has been made in the United States and abroad. It is a Type-B approach and characteristically has emerged from psychological work with individuals and small groups. It involves a large number of different methods for trying to change the relationships among people in an organization, and the whole batch has generally come to be referred to in the United States as O.D., or organizational development.

The essence of O.D. is the building up of large organizations through building effective small groups. In turn, effectiveness in small groups is believed by O.D. people to emerge mostly from a high level of mutual trust among group members. It should come as no surprise, therefore, that much O.D. work aims at feelings. Its aim is to open emotional as well as task-related communication in order to develop mutually trusting, solid teams. The small team becomes the key functional unit and "team building" becomes one central activity of O.D. practitioners. These are work-based, task-oriented teams, and their purpose is to develop feelings of group responsibility and to enlarge individual jobs by making every individual in the team a planner as well as a doer.

A second major element of organizational development follows from the team-building emphasis. It is work on intergroup (or perhaps more properly interteam) conflict and cooperation. For as strongly motivated, task-oriented teams develop, the next problem becomes the relationships among teams in order to build up toward the integrated activities of the larger organization. And, of course, as team members emotionally identify with their own teams, they are likely to perceive other teams as outsiders or even as enemies. Much attention has therefore been paid to developing methods for resolving conflicts and for generating cooperation among the many teams.

O.D. practitioners use methods similar to those used for team building when they work on interteam building activities. That is, they deal with intergroup relations at a feelings level, too. O.D. methods therefore include intergroup confrontation meetings and intergroup discussions of their perceptions of one another. These serve as precursors to work on task, as efforts to develop integrated task activities among many groups. It is probably also fair to say that such methods *de*emphasize formal evaluation of individuals and focus evaluations around the performance of total teams, leaving the evaluation and "reeducation" of individuals to the teams themselves.

In recent years, particularly, O.D. people have moved upward from an emphasis on the small work group toward the design of total organizations. During this movement, the problem of *power* has reemerged as a major issue. The underlying ideology of O.D. has had a strong flavor of "power equalization" rather than "power differentiation." But as it moves toward larger units, O.D. must confront power problems just as Type-A approaches must confront human feelings and emotions as these approaches move downward through the organization.

In summary

Some characteristics of present-day industrial organizations necessarily affect people. Some of these effects are bad, either because they damage people or because they interfere with the problem-solving activities of organizations, or both. Perhaps none of the bad effects is so bad that it outweighs the advantages of control and economic integration that the same characteristics also provide.

The characteristics discussed are the pyramidal shape of organizations, with its tendency to increase interpersonal competitiveness; the hierarchical distribution of authority, with its tendency to increase dependency and "evaluation fear"; the idea of individual responsibility, with its assumption that a large and complicated task can be cut down into non-overlapping, individual-sized pieces; and the sheer size of modern organizations, with consequent difficulties of communication.

In general, each of these characteristics carries a potential for intensifying conflict and frustration in individuals and for increasing psychological pressures on the manager.

On the practical side, a variety of devices has emerged for trying to deal with human problems of organizations. Many of them are essentially Type-B approaches. One set operates under the umbrella label of organizational development. It seeks to develop psychologically strong small groups in organizations and then to build relationships among such groups, working from the bottom upward.

29

Organizational structure
Managing the situation
to manage the people

We've already talked a lot about organizational structure, but always in the context of other problems. In this chapter, even at the risk of redundancy, we want to focus on structure as a tool for managing people.

Structure is an important tool for managing for several different reasons: First, the manager himself has to live in the structural house that he builds. His structure frees or constrains him as well as his people. Second, structure is one of the major handles the manager can turn to change his organization's performance. Third, the structures people work in really do influence the way they behave. By changing structure, we can change behavior.

We are prisoners of structure

Let's take the last one first: how structure affects behavior. Much of this book has been about trying to change people's behavior directly, but a lot of it has also been about changing behavior by changing situations. Organizational structure is a large chunk of the total environment of people in organizations. And those structures really are important in limiting and shaping their behavior.

Strong evidence from a great many studies in a great many settings indicates that we are all, as it were, prisoners of structure. And in managing, structures are often much easier to change than people. We know, for instance, that the mistreatment of prisoners by guards can no longer be explained by calling the guards "sadists." Nor can the personality characteristics of hospital attendants explain cruel treatment of patients; nor can we explain the murderous behavior of Nazi underlings by pointing to weaknesses in their characters or to a special "German mentality." We know that we will get about the same behaviors from people of different backgrounds and different economic classes if we lock them into the same institutional structures. And we don't have to limit ourselves to institutions like concentration camps, prisons, and mental hospitals. The same effects can be found in armies, universities, and businesses. The institutional structure captures all of us to some degree. Notions about authority, specifications of "duties," of "responsibilities"—all these role requirements will sharply, though often unconsciously, influence our behavior. Some people do rebel against structures and some resist. But cutting across a wide spectrum of human differences, common situations generate commonalities in human behavior. And the old organization chart, though we kid about it, still defines a lot of the situation.

The notion that organizational structures are controllers of behavior is not at all a new insight. We have been changing structures in order to change behavior for a long, long time. Certainly if we were to ask managers what they would change in order to change an organization, the most frequent response would still be, "Change the structure." Change the specifications of who shall report to whom, the number of levels in the hierarchy, job titles, who shall answer directly to the president. These are all structural changes. We centralize structures or we decentralize them. We tighten job definitions or we loosen them. We redefine areas of responsibility. We redraw the chart. And by doing those things, we generate changes in behavior.

The process is not too complicated. Think back to the earlier sections of this book. People, we said, are creatures who seek satisfaction of their needs. Clearly, organizational structures tell us what kinds of behaviors are likely to produce need-satisfying rewards and what behaviors will produce punishments. We also said people are great balancers. A new organizational situation requires members to re-balance themselves. We said behavior affects attitudes, and vice versa. Organizational situations require certain definite behaviors—like arriving at the office at 9 A.M. Appropriate attitudes tend to follow. We said groups press individuals to conform to local standards. Organizations are full of structurally designed groups that press conformity. And so on. Organizational structures are for those reasons, and more, great behavior-modifying devices.

Managing structure

What are the ways the managers can do something about structure? And what are the likely effects of particular structural changes?

It may be a useful oversimplification to talk about two broad approaches to changing organizational structure. One is toward increasing hierarchy and formalism. The other is toward loosening the organization into a wider, more open network form.

The hierarchical approach seeks organizational effectiveness and productivity through impersonal order and system. It reflects an

analytic way of thinking from task backwards to organizational requirements. It seeks to specify communication lines, to squeeze out
slack, to pinpoint responsibility, to eliminate duplication of effort, to
monitor itself closely. In dealing with people, its major concern is with
constraining behavior into the narrow channels required to get work
done efficiently. Its logic is primarily the logic of subassemblies. We
must get A to do his bit and B and C to do their bits, and we must
design those bits so they can then be put together by D; and we must
make sure that A, B, C, and D do their bits on schedule and deliver
them to the right place. Then effective work will get done.

As organizations grow, the numbers of persons and activities which
must be so controlled and integrated also grows. But on paper, at least,
the advantages of the hierarchical approach also increase. For now we
can do things in large, economical batches and we can use our equipment fully, and clearly we need order and integration even more than
when we were small.

Notice (once again) that this tightening approach says very little
about the nature of man. Indeed, traditionally it has been plagued
with people trouble. People don't do what they're supposed to. So, in
general, it tends toward Type-A implementation; further tightening of
controls and narrowing of jobs, searching constantly for organizational
designs which will free it from the dysfunctional vagaries of human
nature.

The contrasting, loose-networks approach treats structure as a
second-order problem. It's a people-first approach. It starts with the
notion that human beings are naturally motivated, that they want to
be productive. It therefore views structure as the servant of motivation.
So the proponents of these people-oriented structures are generally
also proponents of decentralization, of matrix organizations, of job-
enrichment schemes and of group, more than individual, responsibilities. The emphases are on motivating, on creativity, on "developing"
people, on challenge, on generating ownership attitudes. They want
flexible, often only temporary, ad hoc structures to provide a home for
growth-motivated people. They argue that such flexible structures in
the long run will yield more productive outcomes.

Both groups are structuralists, nevertheless, in that both agree that
structure will influence behavior. One wants specific behaviors; the
other wants people to use their heads cooperatively in more wide-
open ways. In fact, most organizations (as we have said earlier)
do some of both, tightening at lower levels, and loosening at higher
levels, with structures based on task more than on any other single
variable.

What kind of structure would you prefer to live in?

Given these two extremes, which kind of organizational structure would you rather live in? Are you sure? Most people, at least in the United States, seem to prefer the second.

But if you like the tight one because it is clear-cut and orderly, remember that it is also probably relatively inflexible; so if you have a unique problem or a unique idea, you may have a very hard time getting the organization to let you do what you want to. You may be treated fairly, but impersonally.

And if you like the loose one, think twice too. You'll get very little feedback about how you're doing, perhaps very little credit for your individual contribution. There'll be lots of slop in the system, with important things happening before anyone bothers to tell you about them. And probably lots of long meetings.

And which would you like to manage? In the tight one you can give commands, but nothing may happen. You may be overwhelmed with decisions that lower-level people don't dare make by themselves. People may bow to you, but they may not level with you.

In the loose one, your subordinates may not pay much attention to you, except to complain when they can't get their way. You'll be trying to manage an oriental bazaar. Everybody will be negotiating for his own piece of the action.

The point, once again, is that you've got to pay the bills, whichever one you choose.

But few organizations are really as extreme as the models we've just caricatured. A loose organization has to compromise by being tight in some places in order to hold itself together. And a tight organization still has to be loose enough to cover crises and coordination problems and just to keep its people. If they weren't doing those balancing acts, they'd probably be on the road to self-destruction. But the two general styles do show up in different organizations.

Differentiation and integration

It's not just the personal preference of leaders that determines the kind of structures organizations develop. In fact, leaders often feel that their structures have a life of their own that makes them very hard to change—like the U.S. Government.

Structures are also shaped by tasks, by technology, by their social and economic environments. We shouldn't expect, should we, that the structures of an army, an ad agency, a hospital, and a railroad should all look alike? And they don't.

What seems to happen over the long run is that organizations shape themselves to match the demands made upon them by the worlds they live in. They *differentiate* in order to cope with differential pressures out there. If they make many products and sell in many markets, they develop highly differentiated structures at those interfaces. But as they put out separate tentacles to deal with different parts of the world, they must also make sure that they themselves don't break up. So they have to make *integrating* moves to counterbalance the differentiation. They have to tie pieces together with control systems and all sorts of coordinating devices.

These pressures to differentiate on the one hand, and to integrate on the other, keep managers jumping to manage the structure— especially if the environment they operate in is a rapidly changing one. Again we are oversimplifying, but it's probably fair to say that in relatively stable, unchanging environments, organizational structures— in the past—have tended toward hierarchy, toward tight integration. In volatile worlds of changing politics, technology, or markets, the general direction of organizational structures tends toward differentia- tion—toward loosening up to be able to cope with all that complexity. But counterexamples are not hard to find.

Hierarchical structure and authority

Ever since the early classical theorists, authority has been an over- weaning issue in managerial thinking about structure. Ever since the early classical theorists, Western designers of organizations have laid a heavy emphasis on the importance of factors like command, disci- pline, and authority in organizational design. Many of the early structuralists, indeed, drew their ideas from military organizations, so that this quasi-military flavor still shows through in many large American organizations.

Recently the emphasis on authority has noticeably declined. Unions, with their strong countervailing power, have helped make arbitrary use of authority unworkable. Professionalization and the dramatic rise of the technologist have also challenged the usefulness of authority as a managerial tool. As we have brought in employees who identify themselves more as professionals in some specialized fields and less as "locals," organizational authority has become a less effective tool. The human-relations movement also contributed to the decline of con- cern about who has authority over whom in organizations. It demon- strated that control can often be maintained with much less authority than we used to think.

But let us not confuse the decline in authority with a decline in organizational hierarchy in general. The hierarchy of roles in organizations serves purposes of coordination and integration that are becoming increasingly vital to organizational life. What is declining is not the hierarchy, but the tool called authority, essentially defined as the notion that some people must unquestionably obey others. That tool is probably considerably less important than it used to be, though it is still there. And it is, of course, just one dimension of hierarchical design.

The great early emphasis of structural people on authority led some of us for a while toward rejecting the whole structural approach. We tended, as we so often do, to want to throw out the baby with the bath water. Recently, however, we have begun to come back to structural questions from very different angles. We have come back to structure largely because we have been forced to—because it has become so patently obvious that structure is an aspect of organization (1) that we can manipulate, and (2) that has direct effects on problem working. If we decentralize, things happen—maybe not everything that we wanted to have happen—but things happen. If we change the definitions of roles of members of our organization, things happen. If we change communication lines by removing telephones, or separating people, or making some people inaccessible to others, things happen.

All of those kinds of changes are relatively easy for managers to carry out. So structural dimensions become doubly important—important because they constrain and thereby influence behavior, and important because they are readily manipulable. Yet there is an important limiting factor in the structural approaches. The structure of an organization makes some things possible, but it does not guarantee that they will happen. When we open up communication, as in the circle network, the structure will permit people to do things they could not do in the star. It does not guarantee that they will do them.

A new structural emphasis: The rising place of communication and role structure

In contrast to authority, American organizations have lately shown much more interest in problems of communication and coordination, and much more concern about redefining appropriate work flows. We have gotten more interested in who can talk to whom in organizations because as organizations have grown larger the losses from communication failures have become increasingly apparent. This emphasis on communication has also contributed to the decline of authority. Authoritarian organizations constrain and specify who can communicate with whom, and therefore tend to reduce the amount of communication. More recent structural approaches have tried to open up communications and have thereby come into conflict with notions of authority. Certainly both the communication-network experiments and the intergroup-conflict studies described earlier have demonstrated that the communication structure of an organization can influence the output and attitudes of its members, even with authority held out of the picture.

Something else is beginning to push students of management to take a second look at structural problems. And that is new knowledge and new ideas about structure. There has been a good deal of work, for example, in exploring the problems of roles in organizations, and conflicts between roles. We have begun to get some handles on more sophisticated ways of specifying roles than the old job description. And we have begun to understand the conditions under which particular roles, even conflicting ones, can be important and useful. Thus, for example, the idea of the "linking pin" role has been proposed. They are the liaison and the "broker" roles between groups in organizations. The linking-pin notion does not try to describe a job so that it will in no way overlap any other job—as the old job descriptions tried to do—but rather to recognize the interdependency of many jobs with others, and to include these overlaps.

We also know some things about the relationship between work flows and the people part of the organization. We are beginning to realize that if work steps are contiguous with one another in certain ways, the people who perform those steps are apt to establish relationships with one another and form groupings that they would not otherwise form. Earlier studies on housing developments have demonstrated the same point. The location of the garbage cans in an apartment building has a good deal to do with the kinds of friendships and relationships that develop within it.

We can also define *structure* broadly to include the whole culture of an organization, as well as its organization chart. When we take such a wide-angle view, the importance of structure for the modern organization becomes obvious. For now we are talking about the organization's overall style, its values and norms, its expectations about how its people will behave toward one another and toward the world out there, and its people's expectations about how the organization will behave toward them. Clearly such overall company "cultures" implicitly influence the behaviors of employees.

Organizational design: Some current notions

Most of these works, from communication research to the work on role conflict to the work on the relationship between work flows and interpersonal factors, are surface-scratching operations that are only beginning to reopen an old but terribly important issue—the issue of the design of organizational structures.

From another side new technology is reopening the same issue, for with computers and new analytic methods we have to make room (even in old-fashioned organizational structures) for new kinds of equipment, new kinds of people, new kinds of relationships. These two developments, rather than killing off the idea of organizational structure, are putting it back in the spotlight, making us ask ourselves again, "What is the ideal structural design for organization X?"

One answer to that question now seems clear. There is no ideal structure. Appropriate design is contingent upon task, environment, people, and the state of technology. It is also contingent on the imagination of its designers. Organizational design, like architectural design or product design, is a human creation. So we should not expect a fixed answer. We should expect new designs to be forever evolving. At the moment, perhaps because the environments of organizations have become more active and changing, the current ideal is a contingent design. Its targets are adaptability and self-modification rather than some optimal fixed form.

Perhaps we can go a bit further than that. Currently, for unprogrammed tasks, structures with less restricted communication and a looser authority hierarchy are favored generally. But check your environment's traditions and standards before you move that way. And check the history and expectations of your people before you radically alter the structure they have always worked in. And check your current technology, lest you discover that you could, with modern tools, program the previously unprogrammable task.

For more programmable tasks—that is, when we know pretty much how to do something—it now seems reasonable to move toward somewhat tighter (but not too tight), well-defined structures. But again, check the other conditions before you move that way. Check the culture into which you are inserting such an organization. Check the expectations of your people. Check the availability and cost of the support technologies that might help you tighten the system without losing the people.

There is another aspect of contingent structural design, too. Organizations aren't made of just one kind of stuff. They don't do just one kind of job. Increasingly it makes sense to think of large organizations as differentiated components of many smaller organizations, each performing its own set of tasks, in its own world, and structured accordingly. The large organization is thus a set of interconnected structures, rather than *a* structure. And more and more, as we suggested earlier, designers must worry about the integration problem, about sewing these structures together into an integral functioning whole. The problem is not so much setting up the factory or the research department; it is relating the factory to the research department with a minimum of destructive conflict and a maximum of mutual contribution.

In summary

The structures we live and work in change our behaviors, perhaps more than most of us realize. But structures are relatively manageable. Managers can tighten or loosen them, centralize or decentralize them. Both tightening and loosening have clear advantages in specific situations, but they also engender costs, for both manager and managed.

Though structures can be considerably modified by the efforts of managers, much of their form seems to evolve from the tasks, the technologies, and the environments in which those organizations exist. The more differentiated its world, the more differentiated the organization tends to become. More differentiation, however, requires some balance through integration. This "contingent" view is rising in importance in contemporary organizational design, while the older emphasis on authority as the key variable is declining.

Newer efforts at organizational design emphasize both the contingent view and the concept of the organization as a collection of differentiated smaller organizations.

30 Organizations and their environments From back then to out there

Organizations, like persons, are shaped by their times, and shape their times, too. If we look back over the last few decades, it seems quite easy to see how our business organizations have reflected our societies, and if we look ahead a decade or two, perhaps we can make some reasonable guesses about the relationships in the future. That's what we shall try to do in this chapter: to look, mostly from the manager's perspective, at the way organizations relate to society. And we shall do it by first reviewing much of what we have said earlier in this book, but with a broad base and a panoramic perspective. Then we'll go forward. Let's get a running start on the future by first backing up into the past.

Organization for productivity

Consider the American environment around 1900, an environment ripe for organizations designed for one great purpose: productivity. It was a relatively spare world we lived in then—sparse of people and of other organizations. Government was supportive. Vigorous entrepreneurs were heroes. The market begged for material goods. Our immigrant labor force was big and badly educated, but it was dedicated to finding a better world for its children. It was a period of personal immobility, too: people didn't usually move from one city to another. The family was big and important, in the European tradition. And it was a colonialistic period: the notion of the white man's burden, of an ignorant and somewhat irrational laboring class, was widespread, and with it the notion that the planning and thinking had to be done by the superior people, even over the objections of the ignorant childlike worker—for his own good.

Into this ripe setting—and no wonder—marched the organizational structuralists and technocrats, the classical organization theorists touting the gods of order and control, and the pragmatic technicians

337

like F. W. Taylor and Henry Ford. Taylor and his contemporaries, we said earlier, provided the techniques to back up classical organization theory, classical Type-A implementation techniques which separated planning from doing, so that large populations of noncraftsmen could be organized to produce large quantities of highly crafted products. Taylor moved the craft from the individual to the organization, and he got what he was after: productivity.

Now shift forward a few decades into the thirties and forties. In the United States, unions become strong, partially as a reaction to Tayloristic rigidities. Mr. Roosevelt's New Deal, with its new social orientation, moves in. At the same time, technology has begun to explode, and the explosion is magnified tremendously by World War II. Colonialism slows down. In the States, immigration slows to a trickle. Our people become much more mobile with improved communications and transportation. The early image of the glorious, heroic entrepreneur gives way to the caricature of the ruthless robber baron. He is watched more closely now and reacted to more strongly by a society that is somewhat more sensitive to the negative effects of unfettered profit seeking.

Under such conditions, what shape shall business organizations take? Or shall they, like turtles, develop shells that help keep them impervious to societal change?

As is so often the case, several, not necessarily consistent, things happen. Some firms change, but their first changes are ameliorative. They find Band-Aids to cover the minor wounds inflicted by the changing world. They become concerned about morale and human relations. They begin to worry about how to keep people happy while doing miserable jobs. They devise new incentive plans and suggestion systems. But they don't abandon the basic old Tayloristic structure. That is both productive and sacrosanct, and besides, they're getting locked into it by their investment in physical plants consistent with Taylorism. They continue to design the organization holes first and only then to search for the human pegs to fit them. The participative management movement begins to take shape in this period, and attacks Taylorism on Taylor's own playing field. These new social science types championing participative management try to show that participation and industrial democracy are better routes to the old nirvana of productivity than hard-nosed Taylorism itself. But in so doing they actually help to patch up Taylorism, to make it more endurable, more human, because *productivity* continues as the primary organizational goal and participation is touted only as a means to greater productivity. If we can make employees think it's their idea, the old argument runs, they will produce.

Organization for marketing and product innovation

But the emphasis on productivity began to show signs of cracking in those years, perhaps because of its own past success. Once we had produced a large number of refrigerators, the issue began to shift from producing more to marketing them better or to developing new products. Everybody could produce. Who could market? Who could innovate? These emerging questions led to a new emphasis, not on the management of production workers, but on the management of management itself. In this newly emerging executive world of marketers and technicians, the old Taylorism was just about useless. Time clocks in the research department just didn't make sense, nor did stopwatches in the president's office.

A different kind of managerial organization was needed. And gradually we backed into it. We began to worry about improving communication, about coordination, about setting up a climate for creativity. But we began to worry about these issues chiefly within the ranks of management itself, leaving the production worker pretty much in the hands of old Mr. Taylor.

Notice, however, that the new organization form that emerged was a more complex form than its predecessor. The new one was, in effect, divided into two layers—not only two classes of people but also two structures within which the two classes were expected to work. Type-B participative organizational structures began to be used widely, but almost exclusively within management—working toward the goals of growth and innovation—while well-structured Taylorism remained the rule for the organization of clerical and blue-collar production workers.

Within management, the theory of participation became almost an analog to the theory of the husbandry of plants. Neither social scientists nor anyone else really understood much about the *nature* of innovation and complex problem solving, but everybody needed them. The agronomists didn't understand how plants grew either, but they did the next best thing. They asked, "What are the conditions under which greatest growth occurs?" And the answers were that plants needed sunlight and moisture and appropriate soil chemistry. Under those conditions, but still mysteriously, plants grew. Participative theory and behavioral theory occupied about the same position with management. We didn't understand the processes, but we knew a lot about the conditions under which they flowered. We learned that autocracy tended to kill those attributes. So we marched in with human-relations training and brainstorming programs and O.D. and attitude surveys and a whole variety of paraphernalia intended to release managerial effectiveness within the diverse ranks of management. *Innovation* became a new organizational goal.

But as we all know, the new doesn't replace the old, it's just added on. So the goal of innovation was superimposed upon the old goal of productivity. Developing managerial potential became a major new means added to the old. The old industrial relations department stayed; but a new management development department was added on.

Then the informational organization

But once again our world insisted on changing. Enter the real technological explosion of the mid-fifties. Enter the computer and information technology and management science. Now for the first time we could seriously reexamine the catalyst theories of participative management. Now we could ask, "What is the true nature of problem solving? Of creativity? Of innovation?" Part of the answer was clear: Since by now we had an excellent theory of information processing, perhaps we could even build artificial problem-solving devices to substitute for, or at least to supplement, human abilities.

Perhaps it was not accidental that this whole new analytic-informational package came to be called "management science," for it was very much the same as Taylor's old scientific management, but it rode a computer instead of a stopwatch. It was Taylor's scientific management in that it separated the planning of decisions from the decision making itself, just as Taylor had separated the planning of physical work from doing it.

Now what kind of organizational changes could be expected to accompany this brand new capacity to program the hitherto unprogrammable, this new ability to replace at least some classes of human judgments with systematic procedures?

One major change was the emergence of a new quality of dynamism in the organizational world, a new quick feedback cycle that permitted the organization to know the effects of what it had just done and therefore to become a much more self-modifying system. (In the past we hadn't always been sure of the effects of what we had done, of what had caused what.) Hence also a new temporary quality in organizational life. This temporariness was mirrored in the nature of the information technology itself, which even now continues to grow at an exponential rate. And it was reflected in the attitudes of the new population of professionals who rode upon this technology, a highly mobile group, with the typical attitudes of professionals everywhere: high professional loyalty, low organizational loyalty.

Another and opposing change was the extension of humanistic, participative management even further upward into the still unprogrammed, open-ended areas at the top of the organizational hierarchy, while simultaneously tightening up controls over other parts of the organization, particularly sectors of lower middle management. As a result the organization became even more differentiated, with even more different parts operating within different organizational forms, forms that ranged from open, loosely controlled structures to the most minutely controlled structures imaginable. For the people behind management science, for the whiz kids, the planners, and for top management itself, the new technology made for a less programmed world, more ambiguous, more challenging, more judgmental, more open-ended. As for the guy on the line, he continued to be told what to do, how to do it, and which finger to do it with.

By the sixties, the old Tayloristic organization, steered by its traditional tasks and its traditional structure, found itself either supplanted or dominated by this new form, steered by its new technology and by its highly trained professional planners. Viewed as a whole, the organization became not one structure but many structures, not an undifferentiated mass but a highly differentiated set of subsystems capable not of a single task but of a wide range of tasks, from routine to creative. And the new challenge was the one we mentioned in chapter 29, the articulation of the parts with one another, more than the operation of any particular part.

In the new technological world, the old meaning of the word *productivity* began to fade away. It referred less and less to getting ten more engines to roll off the line. It began to take on a "systems" connotation. Productivity meant making the whole system work. Business schools gradually dropped their courses in "Production" in favor of courses called "Operations Management" and "Systems Analysis," aimed at putting the whole thing together, at articulating the several parts.

It was with this problem, articulation, that the new organization of the sixties began to struggle. The new central issues were not just production, or even just imaginative marketing, but rather problems like these: How do we get the subparts of this system to coordinate with one another so we can solve that huge problem out there? How do we reduce conflict and competition among these parts? How do we deal with our new prima donnas who are forever at each other's throats?

The sociopolitical organization

Another way of saying all this is to say that the newly added organizational problems became increasingly like political problems of whole societies, because the new large organizations had become like a society, a complex set of interacting power groups with different backgrounds, different objectives, different mores, different beliefs.

Now what about the seventies and eighties? What's happening to the organizational environment? And how are organizations likely to respond?

This author's clouded crystal ball shows some big things happening out there, and several of those things are the unforeseen harvest of the organizational past we have just been discussing. For not only do social changes cause changes in organizations, but the organizations in a society cause social changes.

Values, we all know, are changing, and so are attitudes toward industry. A few years ago if a company had wanted to build a new plant in my town, it would have been welcomed as a supplier of new jobs and a contributor to the local economy. Not quite so now, at least not for a significant portion of the population. A new plant now means new jobs all right, but new jobs mean new people, new people means overcrowding, overcrowding means less open space and more destruction of the physical environment.

Perhaps such apparent value changes, especially among the young, are transient. But if the reader will return his thoughts to part 1, he will remember that attitudes once formed are not readily reversed.

Another real change we are undergoing is an organizational population explosion. The population of organizations, in the United States at least, is climbing at a much more rapid rate than the population of people.

For almost any given organization this growth has already meant an environment very different from what it was. The organization, whether it likes it or not, finds itself an urban apartment-dweller rather than the occupant of an isolated cabin. No longer can it wander at will across virgin terrain firing its shotgun at anything that moves. What moves may be another organization. The neighbors claim our organization is too noisy; the government claims it is unlawful; the competitors complain that it is unfair; youth claims that it is immoral; the local society for the protection of the green hills claims that it befouls the atmosphere; and the world union people claim that its activity is an insult to our Canadian neighbors. The empty world is gone. Privacy—organizational privacy—is gone. And the exploitive, devil-may-care, roughhouse, produce-it-and-peddle-it organization of the early days is going, too. Organizations are caught in a large, permanent traffic jam.

Moreover, the people inside organizations are members of the outside society. So their values are changing. Pressures for change are thus building from within. Employees are seeking a new, but not yet well-defined, quality of life. And so are managers.

Couple these changes with the continuing expansion of those that lay just behind them: The continuing growth of technology, the still shrinking world, the even higher levels of education, the high degree of professionalism, and the massive size and complexity of new organizational tasks. Let's wrap that bundle up and ask how organizations will reshape themselves in the decades ahead.

Part of the answer looks reasonably clear. Upon the Taylorized blue-collar organization of the early 1900s, we superimposed the participative white-collar organization of the forties and early fifties; and then upon that we began to superimpose the information-processing organization of the late fifties and sixties. My guess is that the new superimposition, the new layer, is the sociopolitical organization of the seventies and eighties. The problems of the short term future will lie not so much within the organization as between it and society. We shall have to look much more to the social and family life of organization. We shall begin to know organizations by the company they keep. The future will be social, political, interorganizational.

Way back at the beginning, before Taylor, in the virgin world, organizations were nomadic. They were wandering, entrepreneurial bands of people. They were companies in the original sense of that word: companies of human beings. With Taylorism and Henry Ford, that nomadic form gave way to a more static life-style. Organizations became like tough, independent farmers, staking their claims, carving out their plots of land, and exploiting their soil—routinely, but also autonomously. Then the knowledge explosion provided a kind of rebirth of nomadism. Organizations no longer had to be anchored to their traditional tasks and to their traditional structures. The new, highly flexible technology and the new, high-powered technologists could provide a different sort of anchor. The organization could become mobile again, searching for tasks unlike anything it had undertaken before. It could become nomadic again not in a geographic sense, but creatively, searching for new applications for its new resources, including its pensive, and perpetually hungry technology.

But these nomadic organizations will be nomads in a crowded and interdependent world. Now the environment is more differentiated, more populous. It provides more opportunities, but it also makes for harder going. In the new environment, the traditional free-moving, autonomous business organization will surely have to give way. So will the tough-thinking, rapid-fire, decision-making, crisis-eating company president. So too will the kindly morale builder. The appropriate new company president begins to look much more like (heaven help us!) a politician who must juggle both the conflicting forces rising from within the organization, and those pressing in from outside groups.

He or she will need wit and sensitivity as well as analytic skills. And he or she will need what the black brothers call "soul."

Such an image of a company president may seem almost 180 degrees from the current beliefs of many managers. Many of them felt, for example, that current business types, tough and decisive, should have been running universities in the early seventies. Then student disturbances would have ceased forthwith. But the converse may be the more likely future: not that business types will run universities like businesses, but that university type will run businesses like universities.

For the university may present an interesting parallel to the business organization of the future. Internally it is made up of many diverse groups over whom the administration can exert little direct authority. The faculty is a collection of prima donnas who may have some departmental loyalty, but mostly are loyal only to their professions. The students are a kind of transient body, vocally self-interested, but neither clearly consumers nor employees, neither well organized nor rational. And then there are the board of trustees and the community groups and all other factions of society who feel it appropriate to exert pressure on the university—factions ranging from local industry, which wants more engineers and business students; to women's groups, who want more women on the faculty; to the black community, which wants black studies and more black students; to the alumni, who want a better football team.

In that kind of setting the university president does not sit at a command post, punching out action decisions and ordering people about. On the contrary, he arbitrates, he confronts, he debates, he negotiates. And out of the negotiation process he tries to build not only viability and innovativeness, but adaptiveness.

Enter, too, the "litigious" world, where everybody sues everybody else; in which the lawyers must be consulted before we hire Mary Smith away from our competitor, or before we fire Joe Blow.

Company presidents in the next couple of decades will have to be political, legal, and diplomatic jugglers, inside the organization and outside.

All this projects an organizational world which is very different and yet in many ways very much the same. It is not, we must repeat, a question of the new replacing the old, but of the new added on to the old. Certain tasks, for example, and certain kinds of industries are likely to remain highly routinized. The changes they will be experiencing are perhaps of only two kinds: they will be automating, and they will be involved in a new blue-collar participative revolution because economics and sociology will force them to make the life of the production worker a more challenging one.

At the middle levels of line management, which had been going slowly participative in the fifties, the two quite polar trends should continue and remain somewhat in conflict. In partial opposition to the participative trend is an accelerating trend toward greater programming and control, emerging from management science. We are already seeing some of the oddities generated by those counterforces; for example, greater centralized control over greater decentralization.

But upward and outward in the organization, among the planners, the staff people, and top management itself, there perhaps we should expect a desperate race for the better utilization of human resources. It is with our staff people and our higher levels of executives, with our technologists and professionals and researchers that we shall continue to search for the conditions that catalyze creativity and give us future direction.

Certainly one place we shall search is outside the traditionally constrained realms of rationality and logic. We shall do much more work on problem finding. We shall probably come to value and even to utilize effectively "right hemisphere" kinds of divergent thinking that we have characteristically ascribed to artists and women rather than to managers. Indeed, for reasons that have very little to do with organizational wishes and a lot to do with the wishes of women we shall bring more women into the organization. Despite ourselves, we shall thus have added an important new diversity and some much-needed new skills in finding problems and working them through.

If, finally, we take the total situation we are facing—the shrinking world, the explosion of knowledge, the organizational population explosion, our massive social and economic tasks, emerging new value systems—at least one thing seems clear: Rigid old authoritarian mechanisms will slowly fall to lower and lower positions, for they were designed for an orderly, slowly changing, almost static world. Organizational ambiguity, uncertainty, and irregularity have already become the normal state. We shall have to build new tools and new organizational structures to deal with that sort of continuously exploding world. Another thing is also certain: management will never be simple again.

In summary

Since this is our last chapter, we have taken the liberty of painting with a very broad brush. Our thesis is interactional—that organizations respond to their times, and the times to their organizations. Grossly we seem to have moved from productivity-oriented organizations to marketing-oriented organizations to informational organizations, and perhaps we are now moving to sociopolitical organizations. Each stage is reflective of the pressures of the times, some of which are reactive to earlier pressures by organizations on the times.

But these stages have been more additive than serial, building one upon the other rather than succeeding one another. The outcome is therefore greater diversity and pluralism among organizations, and greater complexity within.

Questions

Part 1

Chapter 1

1. If people behave to satisfy needs, why will some people starve to death before they give away a secret? Are they satisfying needs?
2. We said in this chapter that "people are alike" in their efforts to satisfy needs. Do you think that Eskimos are like us in their efforts? How about the inmates of mental hospitals? Do they all abide by the same rules? Or do the rules apply only to "normal" people?
3. If all our behavior is "caused" because things in the world stimulate our needs, how can people be held responsible for anything they do? Aren't they just pawns, pushed about by the environment? So why punish the murderer? Why not punish the world that "caused" his murdering behavior?
4. What is a "habit"? Is it behavior that is an execution to the rule that "people behave to satisfy needs"? What needs can the "habit" of biting one's nails satisfy?
5. Is there any such thing as a really free choice? If behavior is caused, isn't the choice always predetermined by the cause?
6. Think of whatever it is you want most. Suppose you got it. Would you then sit on your tail, fat and happy? Do "satisfied" people really stop searching and trying? Do we have to keep people dissatisfied to keep them working?

Chapter 2

1. Most of us would like our children to be independent and ambitious but not hostile or suspicious of the world. How can we get the former qualities without the latter?
2. Suppose I gave you a newborn infant and the following assignment: "Train this child so that at age five he is badly spoiled." What

behavior might I mean by "spoiled" behavior? How would you carry out the assignment?

3. Now consider the exactly opposite treatment. Are you sure that it would not spoil the child equally well?

4. Suppose I gave you a new employee and the same assignment. How would you spoil him?

5. Look back fifteen or twenty years. Do you think your personality has changed as much as your body? Or would your mother still recognize your personality even if she couldn't recognize your face or voice? Just how have you changed? New needs? New ways of satisfying needs?

6. We often say that children are dependent on their parents. Are parents independent of their children? Are managers less dependent on employees than vice versa?

7. We keep on comparing parents with bosses. Is the comparison fair? How is a boss different from a parent? How is a good boss different from a good parent?

8. Which levels of needs in the hierarchy operate for you? In the classroom? On the job?

Chapter 3

1. If it is true that each of us sees the world through the rose-colored glasses of his own needs, is it ever possible for people to be objective? How about scientists? Are they objective? What if we get the perceptions of several people instead of one? Does the pooling of perceptions make for greater objectivity?

2. Suppose you were an advertiser of automobiles. Suppose you know some people want power more than safety and some want safety and are a little afraid of power. Do you think you could advertise both without scaring off all your customers?

3. Suppose you hold an opinion about something. You find that your boss and all your peers hold the opposite opinion. You don't know why they do, just that they do. Do you think your opinion would be changed? Do you think anybody else's would? Why?

4. We sometimes say that businessmen perceive the whole world in terms of their business. If there's a flood they only think about how it will help or hurt their business, and so on. If that is true, do you think businessmen's perceptions should be "broadened" so that they would perceive the world as public-spirited citizens instead of just as businessmen? Why or why not?

5. Do you and your spouse see children, politics, and friends the same way? Do you perceive some things differently? Is it necessary that

two people see the world from the same angle in order to get along together? If not, why not?

6. Do you have an "act"? Does it work?

7. Consider the first born in your family. Is he or she more affiliative or more responsive to social pressures than the others? Why? Or why not?

Chapter 4

1. Suppose you wanted to raise your child to act like the "third person," to treat most adverse experience as a deprivation instead of as a frustration. What kind of experiences would you want to put him through?

2. If you set high standards for junior executives, some of them will experience failure. Does that mean you should not set high standards?

3. Subordinates often frustrate their supervisors by acting stupidly or by making mistakes. A competent supervisor, when frustrated, will want to blow off his aggression at the subordinate. Should he? What does it teach the subordinate? If he doesn't blow off, what should he do with his feelings?

4. Suppose you have an ambitious subordinate. He's pretty good but not so good as somebody else. You appoint the somebody else to a new job. How do you tell the ambitious subordinate that he didn't make it?

5. Suppose you have an employee who you feel sure will never go much further than he is now. But he wants to. Would you tell him he isn't going to get far in your organization? Would you tell him to keep trying? What would you do?

Chapter 5

1. If I put two quarters on a table and tell you you may have one, will you be in conflict over the choice? What if you know one of the quarters is burning hot, but you don't know which one? Conflict? What's the difference between the two cases?

2. Is it "right" for parents to try to build conscience into their children? Wouldn't we be mentally healthier if we didn't feel guilty over things? What would life be like in a conscience-less society?

3. Does repression serve any purpose? Suppose we didn't deny to ourselves the existence of some of our own needs. Could we get along any better in the real world?

4. Is it possible for people to recognize their own needs and still ignore them? Can someone who knows he's jealous of another person get

along with him? Could he get along better if he were not conscious of being jealous?

5. Many people get anxious or even freeze up altogether when they have to make a speech or presentation. Why do you think that happens? What kinds of people would it not happen to? How do people learn to feel scared of an audience? Or is it "just natural"?

6. Suppose one of your children (whom you love) suddenly married a strong advocate of a political position you hate. How would you feel at first? A couple of years later? What would you do?

Chapter 6

1. We use dollar bills frequently. Do you know how many times the figure "1" appears on one? Can you draw a good facsimile? If you can't, why can't you? Haven't you had a lot of "experience" with dollars? You've also had a lot of experience with the alphabet. Can you say it backward as fast as you can say it forward? Why not?

2. Do you think machines can be designed to replace middle managers? Or is there some quality about human problem solving that will always make it superior to machine problem solving?

3. Do people learn better and better under more and more pressure? Do you? Do people learn better when there is no pressure?

4. Suppose your company were trying to decide how much to invest in research. Is there a single best answer to that question? What steps would you go through to find a satisfactory answer?

5. Suppose I give you a crossword puzzle to do and you do it. Does that teach you anything about doing other crossword puzzles faster? Does it teach you anything about wanting to do other crossword puzzles faster? Suppose I put a very tight deadline on the first one. Would that help you do later ones better than a loose deadline on the first one?

6. In question 5, suppose I paid you by the puzzle done. Would that help?

Chapter 7

1. Categorize yourself. Are you, in your own opinion, an iconic-intuitive type? Or a symbolic-analytic type? Have you always been? Will you always be? How do you know? Can you cite examples?

2. Do you think think there is any relationship between cognitive style and "radicalism" or "conservatism"? How and why? Or why not?

3. Are we an enactively and iconically "mute" society? Have we become symbolically skilled at the expense of those other modes of understanding?

4. If intuitive-iconic types ran the world, what sort of world would it be?

5. Consider some person(s) with whom you find it hard to communicate. Is cognitive style a factor in the problem? If so, can you translate your communication into his style?

Chapter 8

1. When critics of the "establishment" attack it as hypocritical, they seem to mean that it holds to logically inconsistent attitudes and values. For example, it is against pot but for bourbon. It is against violence but for capital punishment. Do such "inconsistencies" serve any social purpose at all?

2. Following up on question 1 above, are there any political organizations, right or left, that are perfectly consistent in their positions?

3. If logical argument is such a poor means for bringing about attitudinal change, why do we put so much emphasis, in schools and in the political process, on debate and argument?

4. What about the ethics of attitude change, especially by nonrational, affective means? Should advertisers use sex or masculinity or fear of social isolation in their approaches? If they shouldn't, should political or social groups who want to effect change? Should you, if you want to get someone close to you to stop smoking?

5. Do you think it's true that "you believe what you do" and that "you do what you believe"? Is one of those "truths" truer than the other?

6. Consider the following common view, among older people: "Once these crazy kids get out of school and have to make a living, they'll settle down and vote Republican, too." Is the statement psychologically sound? How about this one from the other side? "Don't let them seduce you into the Establishment. Once you're in, you'll be brainwashed." Also true?

Chapter 9

1. After reading this chapter, how would you handle the job of selecting a new research director?

2. Suppose a test salesman came to your door. Suppose he claimed he could evaluate your executives, showing you their strengths and weaknesses. How would you decide whether or not to buy?

3. Do you think top management should pick people for promotion who can get along with top management? Or should their ability to get along with present management be irrelevant? Or neither of the above?

4. Suppose your company were using tests to decide promotions. Do you think you should know your own results? Should you know

other people's results? Do you think the use of tests for this purpose would make you like your company better? Would it make you work harder?

5. What about the ethics of assessment centers? Should executives (or anybody else) be required to go through several days of personal evaluation? And should the findings then be made available to the executives' superiors in the hierarchy? To all of them? All of the findings? Should subordinates also be informed of their boss's purported strengths and weaknesses?

6. Do you think *you* are, as they say, "in touch with your feelings"? How do you know? Can you separate your feelings about another person from the "facts" about him?

Part 2
Chapter 10

1. How would you decide whether communication in your organization is "good" or "bad"? What would you look at? How could you test it?

2. Is it possible for people to respect a superior even if they know he makes many mistakes? Does a superior need the respect of his subordinates to function?

3. In general, is two-way communication easier between peers than between superior and subordinate? Why or why not?

4. How is the communication between man and woman before they are married different from after they are married? When is it more valid? Why?

5. Why are receivers often frustrated by one-way communication? Why do they get emotional about it, even in a game situation like the experiment described here? Why don't they just feel deprived and treat it lightly? What needs are involved?

6. What about communication between blacks and whites in the United States these days? Do the same rules apply as between any two peers? What are the special problems involved in trying to achieve interracial communication?

Chapter 11

1. Sometimes a superior will say: "Go down to the Oshkosh plant and bring their quality control into line, but don't upset people down there." Is it possible to change organizations without upsetting people?

2. When you feel anxious or uncertain about your ability to do a job, can you admit it to your boss? To your spouse? Would it help if you could? Why or why not?

3. Have you ever begun to like someone you disliked at first? Why did it happen? Did you ever dislike him more as you got to know him better? Why?

4. The supermarket, people say, has depersonalized the old personal relationship between housewife and grocer. Is that, in your opinion, bad or good? Hasn't the large company depersonalized relationships among its members? Is that bad or good?

5. In some companies the threat of firing is kept ever present. In others everybody knows that nobody ever gets fired. What are the pros and cons from the management point of view?

Chapter 12

1. Sometimes we say that children want someone to exert authority over them, to require them to do certain things. They cannot decide everything for themselves. Does the same hold true for people in industry? Should a superior use his authority if his subordinates seem to want him to? Would you then say he was using his authority "restrictively" or "rewardingly"?

2. Sometimes a supervisor has to use his authority to enforce a rule he himself does not believe in. Should he claim he believes it? Should he pass the buck by telling his people that he is only doing what top management is forcing him to do?

3. Should top management use its authority to make middle management act as though it believed in all company policies? Or should it allow middle people to tell their subordinates they disagree with a policy?

4. Sometimes bosses worry about using their authority, even when they feel they should. They don't like to fire someone or bawl people out. Why do they feel this way? Is it only because they don't like to hurt other people?

5. Even if we don't want to use our authority to restrict people, don't we have to? Aren't people restricted just by their awareness of our authority? Can we abdicate our authority?

6. Are you obedient to authority because it is authority? Or don't you pay any attention to the position of the person asking you to do something? Or are you responsive only to the message itself? Are you sure of your answers?

7. Should you be obedient to people in authority? Always? Never? What would society be like if no one paid attention to rank?

Chapter 13

1. Do teachers traditionally use coercive power in dealing with students? Can you cite examples from your own educational life? If so, were other means of influence available to the teacher?

2. Is anyone ever really powerless in a relationship with another person? A prisoner? A slave? A student? A worker?

3. This chapter argued that American business organizations are quite civilized. Do you agree or disagree? Why? Are universities more "civilized"? Is the medical profession? The military? Government agencies? The church?

4. Are you a coercer of others? Do you control anybody's behavior by exploiting fear? By using reductive techniques? Do any organizations to which you belong employ such techniques?

5. How does one draw the line between ethically "legitimate" and "illegitimate" pressures? Is it legitimate for me to demand that my employees work actively for the Republican party? That they cut their hair? Is it legitimate for me to "let it be known" that employees who work for the Democratic party are looked upon with favor? Ditto for long hair?

Chapter 14

1. Consider the notion of "making them think it's their idea." Does it work? Is it right? What needs in A might be operating if he chooses to approach B this way?

2. In selling situations, under what conditions need a salesman's motives be kept to himself? How about non-selling situations?

3. Do you know anyone who tries to use his relationship with you as a means of influencing you? How do you respond?

4. Is "participation" ever "manipulative"? When?

5. How can you determine whether or not a person is "sincere" in his opinions? Are you ever insincere? When?

6. Do you ever use "vicarious" means to get what you want? Do men or women do that more often? Are you sure?

Chapter 15

1. Is it possible for a subordinate to influence his superiors? How would you go about convincing your boss that your idea is better than his? Would you have to go over his head to higher authority? Any other alternatives?

2. Suppose you were starting on a new job as office manager of a small plant. On your very first day the manager says: "I know it takes time to change a department, but I want you to do something right away about the people in your group. They've been coming in at all hours of the morning. The old office manager was very lax about it. Do something about it fast, because it's hurting morale in other departments." What would you do? Suppose the people you were dealing with were all old-timers and you were young and new.

3. Suppose you are a market-research executive reporting to the president. The sales manager thinks market research is nonsense, but to finance any studies you have to get sales department funds. How would you attack the problem?

4. Suppose a friend asks you for advice on a personal problem. You think you have just the right advice to offer. Would you give it? Do you think it would be accepted? Why or why not? What is "advice" anyway?

5. A good department head under you comes to you very upset because he can't get his people to accept a methods change, even though other departments are succeeding. How would you handle him? Would you try to make him feel better? How would you help him?

6. Are you a good user of other people's counsel and advice? Should you be?

Chapter 16

1. I once had a job in which the incentive rate was based on the productivity of a three-man work group. The foreman used to put one new or unskilled man with two experienced ones and then change the group every few days, arguing that it kept the bonus down and and motivated the two good men to train the third. What do you think of his arguments?

2. If you got a big raise in pay, would you work harder? If you were promised a big bonus for completing a particular assignment successfully, would you work harder at it?

3. In some multiple incentive plans, employee committees have a right to full information about sales planning and progress. They also have a right to criticize the sales department and to suggest changes. If you were the sales manager, what would you think of such a policy?

Part 3
Chapter 17

1. "It's obvious that in a crisis decisions have to be made by the one person in charge." Do you agree? Why or why not?

2. When we say, "That was a really good decision!" what do we mean by "good"? Do we always mean the best answer? Or the decision we liked best? Or the decision our people suggested?

3. If you let your three children decide for themselves how to use one bicycle among themselves, have you abdicated parental authority?

What if the decision is about the one family car? Or how late they can stay out on Saturday night?

4. Consider the last group meeting you attended. Did it make decent decisions? Why or why not?

5. Is it true that you are more likely to support what you have helped to create than what other people have helped to create? Can you find examples from your own life?

Chapter 18

1. Suppose you resolved to say exactly what you felt from this moment on. Do you think you could actually do it, even if you wanted to? How do you think the people around you would react to it? Would you make friends or lose them?

2. Have you ever felt one thing in a group meeting and said another? Why? Did this covering up help the group solve its problem? Would it have helped more or less if you had said what you felt?

3. Do most people in a work group or a classroom make the same judgments as you do about other members? Do they all think the way you do about the people who you think talk too much? How do you know whether your opinion is shared? If it is, what ought to happen? If it isn't, how ought you to behave?

4. If you were chairman of a committee and thought people were covering up their real feelings and taking the safe course, just yessing, what would you do about it? How would you do it?

5. Should the senior person on a committee serve as chairperson? The junior person? Is seniority irrelevant?

Chapter 19

1. Sometimes we feel that particular people are "bad" committee members. Just what is a bad member? How does one decide that a person has talked too much? Or not enough? Is it "bad" for a committee that one of its members is grumpy or disagreeable?

2. Suppose one member of your committee insists on putting his feet upon the table, or swearing, or doing something else others don't do. Should he be stopped? Why or why not?

3. Should a group chairperson not express his own opinions for fear that group members will disagree with him? What if he has useful opinions? Does "permissiveness" exclude the leader?

4. Suppose a supervisor operates his department "democratically." At a meeting his people decide to do something he thinks is wrong. Should he shut up and go along? Should he veto?

5. Suppose the supervisor agrees with his people but knows that his boss would disapprove. Should he shut up? Should he say that he knows the people upstairs would disapprove? Should he veto without explanation?

6. Even if you wanted to, could you use different leadership styles on different occasions? If you can be tough, can you also, on other occasions, really behave in a way that your members will see as permissive? Or vice versa?

7. Are there people in the world who are leaders no matter where they are or what the situation? Do you˙ know any? How did they get that way? And what have they got that makes them that way?

8. In what kind of tasks would you want deviant thinking in your group? When wouldn't you want it?

9. Do you know any "chronic deviants"? Why do they behave that way? Has their tendency to deviate affected their influence in the organization? Which ways?

Chapter 20

1. When a group has won a competition, we said, its internal morale and solidity go way up. Then how come when some African nations for example, win their independence, they get into internal conflict among themselves?

2. Is conflict among groups in a business organization ever useful? When?

3. In competitions like the ones we described, it is usually the lowest-level executives in a group who fight hardest for their team and against the enemy. Can you explain why that happens?

4. If an "enemy" group is supposed to cause our group to become more cohesive, what about Vietnam? Did Vietnam increase American cohesiveness? Why not?

5. Design a program whereby two groups could produce two independent products and then select one of them, with minimum conflict and maximum final acceptance of the one selected.

6. "Groups may get into squabbles about small issues, but when the chips are down—if the survival of both groups is at stake—people manage to work things out." Do you agree? Do you think British unions and managements will work things out to keep the British economy from going down?

7. Many of us tend to pooh-pooh compromises as ways out of conflict situations, denigrating them as violations of "principles" and "integrity." Do you think your organization could survive without compromise?

Chapter 21

1. Does your boss (or do you) say that his "door is always open"? Is it? Would it be a good idea if it were? Should the president of a company with ten thousand employees try to make himself accessible to any one of them who wants to see him?
2. What is the actual pattern of communication in your department? Does everyone communicate freely with everyone else? Would freer communication help? How would you go about encouraging it?
3. Suppose you are the personnel manager of a small company. The president says: "Our communication is lousy around here. People always claim they didn't get the word. I don't hear about problems till after someone has fouled them up. You're the personnel manager. Do something about it!" What would you do?
4. How would you go about cutting down the disorderliness and wastefulness of a two-way, equalitarian communication net without destroying its advantages?

Chapter 22

1. Do you think it's possible for a university to teach people to be managers? Or is "experience" in nonmanagerial jobs necessary?
2. Does personal counseling have any proper place in management development? Or should one's personal life be his own business? Should we involve the spouse? What is a person's own business and not the company's? Where should the lines be drawn?
3. Do you think a manager trained in the airplane industry could move to the ladies underwear industry and still be successful? Is "managership" distinct from any *particular* company?
4. How about the transfer from managing a small company to managing a large one? Is that possible? Why or why not? How about the other way, from large industry to small?
5. Can you teach an old manager new tricks? How?
6. If you were running a business school, how would you prepare a student for management in the 1990s?

Chapter 23

1. Suppose we design some work around a group of eight people, to increase commitment and challenge. After two years, all eight people have learned to do all the jobs in the group. Is there any challenge left? Should we expect second-stage trouble at that point?
2. Do you like working in groups? Does everybody?

3. Is it true that attitudes toward work have changed significantly? Are yours very different from those of your parents? Which way?

4. Suppose people don't want to participate. Should we make them? Or "educate" them to like it? Or leave them alone?

5. Imagine a factory to make shoes in 1990. How do you expect it to be set up? How would you *like* it to be set up?

Part 4
Chapter 24

1. Consider your own formal education. Is it true that most of it was relevant more to problem solving than to either implementing or problem finding?

2. Consider your last effort to implement something. Why did you do it? Did you find the problem, or did someone else? Would you have implemented it if someone hadn't told you to?

3. What about your career? Did you make it? (or will you make it?) Or did it just happen to you? (or will it just happen to you?)

4. How does someone decide what he "really" wants?

5. Are you a type-A or a type-B implementer?

6. Under what conditions might it be possible to use type-B implementation if you were the commanding general of an infantry division? How about if you were the manager of a dog food plant? How about it if you were a first grade teacher?

7. Under what conditions do you get your best ideas? When you're alone? In a group? Do you think you understand why?

Chapter 25

1. If I invented an inexpensive automatic typewriter that could take dictation and convert it to type, would it affect the *structure* of an American business firm? Would it affect *people*? How?

2. Suppose I invented a fast, cheap, and easily accessible psychoanalysis, guaranteed to change any of us from neurotics into stable, secure, psychologically healthy types. Would organizational structures change? Would the tools of organizations change?

3. *Should* people be treated alike in organizations, no matter what their jobs or status? Why or why not?

4. *Are* people treated alike in the organizations you know? If not, what factors determine how they are treated?

5. "At any level in an organization we find people who are organizational superiors to other people who are organizational subordinates. This superior-subordinate relationship is basically the same whether it be between foreman and worker or between president and VP." Do you agree or disagree? Why?

Chapter 26

1. Has your work ever been programmed by someone else? What was the outcome?
2. Is Taylorism dead?
3. Do you treat your family "Tayloristically"? "Participatively"? How did your parents treat you?
4. From your observations, is the wall between middle and top management bigger or smaller than it was ten years ago? Guess about its size ten years hence.
5. Do you think you are better equipped to plan and schedule the housework of your spouse (or parent, or somebody else) than he is? Why? Do you think you could get him to accept your plans? If he won't accept them, are the plans therefore worthless?

Chapter 27

1. Consider any organization you belong to: By what means did it really reach the most recent major decision it made?
2. What made you decide to read this book?
3. Again consider some organization you belong to: Does it have any machinery for resolving internal conflicts? What machinery? How did it develop?
4. Does your organization know when it has solved a large problem? How?
5. How can any organization become "more sensitive" to its environment?
6. Suppose your boss asked you to design the "right" organization for five years from now. How would you go about doing it?

Chapter 28

1. What are you trying to teach your children about cooperation and competition? Why?
2. Is "cooperation" the same as "conformity"? Can people be independent and individualistic and yet cooperative? Or does one negate the other?
3. A friend of mine is an executive in a small plant owned by his family. He says that everybody tries to know everything, everybody is the boss, everybody countermands everybody else's orders. Though he admits they all say what they think and the business is profitable, he wishes it were "better organized" so that each executive would stay in his own area of responsibility. Do you think "better organization" is called for? If so, what would it consist of?

4. Do you think your specific job could be so defined that it would be really independent of other jobs?

5. Would more valid communication help or hurt your organization? Why?

Chapter 29

1. Have you ever been a "prisoner" of structure? Or are you a free agent?

2. If a person two levels below you came to you directly with a work problem, how would you react?

3. If a man one level below you went directly to your boss with a work problem, how would you react?

4. Is there too much communication in your organization, or too little? How much is too much? How much is too little?

5. Can two people be given joint responsibility for a job?

6. Are all segments of any large organizations structured in the same way? Should they be? If not, what are the costs of having a system in which different parts of the whole operate by different rules?

Chapter 30

1. Will the new attitudes and values of the young change future organizations? Or will the young be brainwashed before they achieve enough power in the organization to change it?

2. Lots of people want business organizations to behave with more "social responsibility." What is the social responsibility of the local car dealer?

3. If you felt your organization was out of touch with society, how would you get it in touch? Would you set up a department of social sensitivity? Why or why not?

4. If the organizational world does become stickier and more crowded, won't organizations be less free? And won't that make entrepreneurial activity more difficult? And won't that in turn limit individual freedom?

5. "Organizations will continue to move the world. If you want to change the world, change organizations." Do you agree?

6. One last question: Can life in a large organization be fulfilling, rewarding, etc., for you? Can life outside an organization be fulfilling, rewarding, etc.?

Notes and
suggested readings

Some references that I list are nontechnical, some quite technical. I have starred (*) the ones that should require no special background, though they are not necessarily lazy reading. Although some of the others are difficult, I have included them for readers interested enough in a special problem to want to track it down.

I also beg the indulgence of those scholars and practitioners whose ideas and results are mentioned without appropriate references to the source.

Part 1. People one at a time

The material in chapters 1 through 5 is based on many sources. The design and some of the specific examples came primarily from Douglas McGregor and Irving Knickerbocker. They had laid out this kind of material for an introductory course in psychology for engineering students at the Massachusetts Institute of Technology, and I taught it there for a couple of years a long time ago.

Chapters 1 and 2

For a comprehensive view of growth motivation, see:

*Maslow, A. H. *Motivation and Personality*. New York: Harper and Row, 1970.

*Maslow, A. H. *The Farther Reaches of Human Nature*. New York: Viking, 1973.

For a general review of motivation, see:

Weiner, B. *Theories of Motivation*. Chicago: Markham, 1972.

Another useful book that covers the territory in these two chapters, and a good deal more is:

Hall C. S. et al. *Theories of Personality*. New York: Wiley, 1970.

For the relationship of motivation to work, try:

*Ford, R. N. *Motivation through the Work Itself*. New York: American Management Association, 1969.

*Herzberg, F. *Work and the Nature of Man*. Cleveland: World, 1968.
*Steers, R. M., and Porter, L. W. *Motivation and Work Behavior*. New York: McGraw Hill, 1975.

In chapter 2 there is a brief consideration of executive personality. For more, see:

Campbell, J. P. et al. *Managerial Performance, Behavior, and Effectiveness*. New York: McGraw-Hill, 1970.
*Levinson, H. *The Exceptional Executive*. Cambridge, Mass.: Harvard University Press, 1968.
*Maccoby, M. *The Gamesman*. New York: Simon and Schuster, 1976.
*McGregor, D. *The Professional Manager*. Edited by C. McGregor and W. G. Bennis. New York: McGraw-Hill, 1967.

For comparative work on managerial motives among executives from several nations, see:

*Haire, M., Ghiselli, E., and Porter, L. *Managerial Thinking: An International Study*. New York: Wiley, 1966.

And for the work on achievement motivation, see:

*McClelland, D. C. *The Achieving Society*. Princeton, N. J.: Van Nostrand, 1961.

And more recently,

*McClelland, D. C. *Power: The Inner Experience*. New York: Halsted, 1976.

On the intrinsic-extrinsic issues, see:

Deci, E. *Intrinsic Motivation*. New York: Plenum, 1975.

For a review on women and the fear of success (the original work was done by Matina Horner), see:

*Tresemer, D. "Fear of Success: Popular but Unproven." *Psychology Today* 7 (1974): 10, 82–85.

And for vicarious achievement, see:

Lipman-Blumen, J. and Leavitt, H. J. "Vicarious and Direct Achievement Patterns in Adulthood." *The Counseling Psychologist,* vol. 6, no. 1, Spring 1976.

Chapter 3

The reader may be interested in other perceptual illusions. Any introductory psychology text is likely to have half a dozen. The figure in this chapter is from a German psychology laboratory and was drawn before 1900. For some really impressive perceptual illusions, people willing to do a little carpentry will find the following useful:

Ittleson, W. H. *The Ames Demonstrations in Perception*. Princeton, N. J.: Princeton University Press, 1952.

For a fascinating consideration of the human "act," see:

*Goffman, E. *The Presentation of Self in Everyday Life*. Garden City, N. Y.: Doubleday, 1959.

For work on interpersonal perception, try:

*Hastorf, A. H. et al. *Person Perception*. Reading, Mass.: Addison-Wesley, 1970.

Some of the implications of differential perception have evolved in recent years into what is now called "attribution theory." See:

Harvey, J. H., Ickes, W. J., and Kidd, R. F., eds. *New Directions in Attribution Research*. Hillsdale, N. J.: Lawrence Earlbaum, 1976.

Chapters 4 and 5

The reader may be interested in this classic:

*Lorenz, K. *On Aggression*. New York: Harcourt, Brace and World, 1966.

The original source on cognitive dissonance theory is:

Festinger, L. *A Theory of Cognitive Dissonance*. Evanston, Ill.: Row, Peterson, 1957.

For the end-of-the-world study see:

*Festinger, L. Riecken, H. W.; and Schachter, S. *When Prophecy Fails*. Minneapolis: University of Minnesota Press, 1956.

For elaboration of some of the issues in these two chapters see any good text on personality like:

Hall, C. S. *Theories of Personality*. New York: Wiley, 1970.

Lazarus, R. S. *Personality*. Englewood Cliffs, N. J.: Prentice-Hall, 1971.

And for more on the relation between personality and management (in AT&T) try:

*Bray, D. W., Campbell, R. J., and Grant, D. L. *Formative Years in Business*. New York: Wiley, 1974.

Chapter 6

The reader will get a good picture of current learning theory from:

Hilgard, E. R., and Bower, G. *Theories of Learning*. New York.: Appleton-Century-Crofts, 1967.

Some other important books on thinking and problem solving are these:

Bruner, J. S.; Goodnow, J. J.; and Austin, G. A. *A Study of Thinking*. New York: Wiley, 1956.

Miller, G. A.; Galanter, E.; and Pribram, K. H. *Plans and the Structure of Behavior*. New York: Holt, Rinehart and Winston, 1960.

And on behavior modification, see:

Bandura, A. *Principles of Behavior Modification*. New York: Holt, Rinehart and Winston, 1969.

For the work on higher-order problem solving as studied by machine simulation:

Reitman, W. *Cognition and Thought*. New York: Wiley, 1965.

Newell, A., and Simon, H. A. *Human Problem Solving*. Englewood Cliffs, N. J.: Prentice Hall, 1972.

*Simon, H. A. *The New Science of Management Decision*. Englewood Cliffs, N. J.: Prentice Hall, 1977.

It is also from Professor Simon that I borrowed the analogy of the needle in the haystack.

Chapter 7

For cognitive development in the child, see:

Bruner, J. S. et al. *Studies in Cognitive Growth*. New York: Wiley, 1966.

*Bruner, J. S. *On Knowing: Essays for the Left Hand*. Atkinson, 1965.

For a somewhat different view of human consciousness, and creativity, see:

*Ornstein, R. *The Psychology of Consciousness*. San Francisco, Calif.: Freeman, 1972.

For cognitive style differences among British school boys see:

*Hudson, L. *Contrary Imaginations,* London: Methuen Press, 1967.

And for some of the problems involved in communication between people with different styles, see:

Huysmans, J. *The Implementation of Operations Research*. New York: Wiley-Interscience, 1970.

*McKenny, J. L., and Keen, P., G. W. "How Managers' Minds Work" *Harvard Business Review,* May-June 1974.

A broader social view of some of the same problems appears in:

*Snow, C.P. *Two Cultures and a Second Look*. Cambridge: Cambridge University Press, 1969.

And for a good summary of what we know about the problem of creativity in organization, see:

*Steiner, G. A., ed. *The Creative Organization*. Chicago: University of Chicago Press, 1965.

Chapter 8

There is much good work on attitudes and attitude change. Two of the best and most readable are:

*Bem, D. J. *Beliefs, Attitudes and Human Affairs*. Belmont, Calif.: Brooks-Cole, 1970.

*Zimbardo, P. G., and Ebbeson, E. B. *Influencing Attitudes and Changing Behavior*. Reading, Mass.: Addison-Wesley, 1969.

On organizational culture, see:

Ouchi, W. and Jaeger, A. "Type Z Organizations: A Better Match for a Mobile Society." Research paper no. 314 (revised February 1977). Graduate School of Business, Stanford University, Stanford, California.

Chapter 9

I have purposely avoided citing the source of the excerpt from a test report.

For a good contemporary analysis of personality assessment, see:

Mischel, W. *Personality and Assessment*. New York: Wiley, 1968.

For nondirective interviewing, see:

Rogers, C., and Dymond, R. F., eds. *Psychotherapy and Personality Change*. Chicago: University of Chicago Press, 1957.

Korchin, S. *Modern Clinical Psychology*. Basic Books, 1976.

For a good review of experience with assessment centers in industry, read:

*Byham, W. C. "Assessment Centers for Spotting Future Managers." *Harvard Business Review,* July–August 1970.

Part 2. People two at a time

Good background for this whole part may be found in these two commentaries on American culture:

*Reich, C. A. *The Greening of America*. New York: Random House, 1970.

*Riesman, David et al. *The Lonely Crowd*. New York: Yale University Press, 1950.

For more microanalytic examinations of interpersonal behavior, try:

*Bennis, W. G. et al. *Interpersonal Dynamics*. Homewood, Ill.: Dorsey, 1968.

*Hall, E. T. *The Hidden Dimension*. Garden City, N. Y.: Anchor-Doubleday, 1969.

Chapter 10

More details on the feedback experiments described can be found in:

Leavitt, H. J., and Mueller, R. A. H. "Some Effects of Feedback on Communication." *Human Relations* 4 (1951): 401–10. Reprinted in A. Paul Hare, Edgar F. Borgatta, and Robert F. Bales, eds., *Small Groups* (New York: Knopf, 1955).

Chapter 11

For a thorough background on these approaches, see:

*Bennis, W. G.; Benne, K. D.; and Chin, R. *The Planning of Change*. New York: Holt, Rinehart and Winston, 1976.
also
*Lippit, R., Watson, J. and Westley, B. *The Dynamics of Planned Change*. New York: Harcourt, Brace, 1958.

Chapter 12

Our definition of authority is more psychological than many. Traditional organization theorists define it variously:

Brown, Alvin. *Organization of Industry*. New York: Prentice-Hall, 1947. Here it is called "the aspect of responsibility which represents its power of performance."

*Peterson, E., and Plowman, E. C. *Business Organization and Management*. Homewood, Ill.: Richard D. Irwin, 1946. Here it is called "the power to make and issue executive decisions."

For a more realistic definition and analysis see:

Simon, H. A. *Administrative Behavior*. New York: Free Press, 1976. The original work on obedience may be found in:

*Milgram, S. *Obedience to Authority*. New York: Harper and Row, 1974.

Chapter 13

On "protest absorption" see:

Leeds, R. "The Absorption of Protest." In *New Perspectives in Organizational Research,* edited by W. W. Cooper et al. New York: Wiley, 1964.

Much of the best literature on power comes from political science. See:

*Gamson, W. A. *Power and Discontent*. Homewood, Ill. Dorsey Press, 1968.

*Schelling, T. C. *The Strategy of Conflict*. Cambridge: Harvard University Press, 1960.

*Sorenson, T. C. *Decision Making in the White House*. New York: Columbia University Press, 1964.

See also:

*Zaleznik, A. "Power and Politics in Organizational Life." *Harvard Business Review,* May–June 1970.

or try:

*Mao Tse-tung. *On Guerrilla Warfare*. New York: Praeger, 1961.

and on brainwashing, see

*Schein, E. *Coercive Persuasion*. New York: Norton, 1961.

Chapter 14

Take a look sometime at good old:

*Carnegie, D. *How to Win Friends and Influence People*. New York: Pocket Books, 1958.

See also:

*Martin, N. H., and Sims, J. H. "Power Tactics." In *Industrial Man*, edited by W. L. Warner and N. H. Martin. New York: Harper, 1959. Also reprinted in H. J. Leavitt and L. Pondy, *Readings in Managerial Psychology* (Chicago: University of Chicago Press, 1964).

*Zimbardo, P. G., and Ebbeson, E. B. *Influencing Attitudes and Changing Behavior*. Reading, Mass.: Addison-Wesley, 1969.

Chapter 15

*Argyris, C. *Interpersonal Competence and Organizational Effectiveness*. Homewood, Ill.: Dorsey, 1962.

*Bennis, W. G.; Benne, K. D.; and Chin, R. *The Planning of Change*. New York: Holt, Rinehart and Winston, 1976.

Material on AA is available from many sources. One is:

Alcoholics Anonymous. New York: Works Publishing Co., 1939.

See also:

*Carl Roger's most recent book *On Personal Power*. New York: Delacorte, 1977.

Chapter 16

The "hygiene" theory is from:

*Herzberg, F. *Work and the Nature of Man*. Cleveland: World, 1968.

For work on satisfaction and its measurement, see:

Smith, P. C. et al. *The Measurement of Satisfaction in Work and Retirement: A Strategy for the Study of Attitudes*. Chicago: Rand McNally, 1969.

For insights into the psychology and sociology of incentives, see:

Lawler, E. E. *Pay and Organization Effectiveness: A Psychological View*. New York: McGraw-Hill, 1971.

The overpayment experiments were conducted at General Electric Company. See:

Adams, J. S., and Rosenbaum, W. B. "The Relationship of Worker Productivity to Cognitive Dissonance about Wage Inequities." *Journal of Applied Psychology* 46 (1962): 161–64.

On performance appraisal see:

Whisler, T. L., and Harper, S. F. *Performance Appraisal: Research and Practice*. New York: Holt, Rinehart and Winston, 1962.

Kellogg, M. S. *What to do about Performance Appraisal*. New York. Amacon, 1975.

See also:

Lawler, E. E. and Rhode, J. G. *Information and Control in Organizations*. Pacific Palisades, Calif.: Goodyear, 1976.

Part 3. People in threes to twenties

For general background on group behavior, see:

*Shepard, C. *Small Groups*. San Francisco: Chandler, 1964.

Cartwright, D., and Zander, A., eds. *Group Dynamics*. 3d ed. New York: Harper and Row, 1968.

Chapter 17

See any of the books mentioned above, plus:

Collins, B. E. and Guetzkow, H. *A Social Psychology of Group Processes for Decision Making*. New York: Wiley, 1964.

And for a fascinating small group analysis of some major U.S. decisions, see:

*Janis, I. L. *Victims of Groupthink*. Boston: Houghton-Mifflin, 1972.

Chapter 18

Hare, A. P. *Small Group Process*. Chicago: Free Press, 1969.

For a more managerially oriented view try:

*Schein, E. H. *Process Consultation*. Reading, Mass.: Addison Wesley, 1969.

On T-groups and sensitivity training, try:

Bradford, L. et al. *T-Group Theory and Laboratory Method*. New York: Wiley, 1964.

For an extension of T-group ideas in organizational development, see:

*Beckhard, R. *Organizational Development: Strategies and Models*. Reading, Mass.: Addison-Wesley, 1967.

Chapter 19

*Kiesler, C. A., and Kiesler, S. B. *Conformity*. Reading, Mass.: Addison-Wesley, 1969.

see also:

*Janis, I. L. *Victims of Groupthink*. Boston: Houghton-Mifflin, 1972.

For a "contingency" theory of leadership, try:

*Fiedler, F. *A Theory of Leadership Effectiveness*. New York: McGraw-Hill, 1967.

On the "contingency" idea, I have drawn heavily from a useful model of group leadership by:

*Vroom, V. H. and Yetton, P. W. *Leadership and Decision Making.* Pittsburgh: University of Pittsburgh Press, 1973.

Chapter 20

The long example illustrating group conflict is taken from a letter written by John W. May, a Hartford, Connecticut, executive, to the *Saturday Review* and paraphrased in the issue of 1 June 1962.

The innovative work here has been done in large part by:

Sherif, M., ed. *Intergroup Relations and Leadership.* New York: Wiley, 1962.

Much work was also done by R. R. Blake and J. Mouton, one report of which appears in the Sherif book.

Much additional work has been done on conflict in the last few years. On methods for managing conflict, see:

*Filley, A. F. *Interpersonal Conflict Resolution.* Glenview, Ill.: Scott Foresman, 1975.

*Walton, R. E. *Interpersonal Peacemaking: Corporations and Third Party Consultation.* Reading, Mass.: Addison Wesley, 1969.

Chapter 21

The networks research was stimulated and led by Alex Bavelas. For more, see the summary:

Glanzer, M., and Glaser, R. "Techniques for the Study of Team Structure and Behavior." *Psychological Bulletin* 58 (January 1961): 1. See also:

Collins, B., and Guetzkow, H. *Social Psychology of Group Processes for Decision Making.* New York: Wiley, 1964.

Chapter 22

Most of the interesting work in this area has come out of the human-relations movement, so I refer the reader to the works of Argyris, Blake, Likert, McGregor, and the National Training Laboratories, all noted elsewhere in these suggested readings.

Try these for a rundown on recent goings on:

House, R. J., ed. *Management Development.* Ann Arbor: University of Michigan, 1967.

Taylor, B. and Lippitt, G. L. *Management Development and Training Handbook.* London and New York: McGraw-Hill, 1975.

In addition, some important efforts are being made to develop cognitive training tools, such as business games. See, for example:

*Cohen, K. J.; Dill, W. R.; Kuehn, A. A.; and Winters, D. R. *The

Carnegie Tech Management Game. Homewood, Ill.: Irwin, 1964.
For a novel and impressive approach, see:
*Revans, R. W. *Developing Effective Managers: A New Approach to Management Education.* New York: Praeger, 1970.

Chapter 23

For the Scandinavian experience:
*Swedish Employers Confederation. *Job Reform in Sweden,* 1974.
See also:
*Hackman, J. R. and Suttle, J. L., eds. *Improving Life at Work.* Santa Monica, Calif.: Goodyear, 1977.
For recent data on job satisfaction, see:
*Katzell, R. A. et al. *Work, Productivity and Job Satisfaction.* New York: The Psychological Corporation, 1975.
Cummings, T. G. and Srivastva, S. *Management of work: A sociotechnical systems approach.* Kent, Ohio: Kent State University Press, 1977.
See also for recent information on the Scanlon Plan:
*Frost, C. R. et. al. "The Scanlon plan at the Dana Corporation." In *Breakthrough in Union Management Cooperation,* edited by J. A. Loftus and B. Walfish. Scarsdale, N. Y.: Work in America Institute, 1977.
And to feel what it's like to work, read:
*Terkel, S. *Working.* New York: Avon, 1975.

Part 4. People in hundreds and thousands

Some classic general works in this area include:
*Barnard, C. *The Functions of the Executive.* Cambridge, Mass.: Harvard University Press, 1938.
*Drucker, Peter. *The Practice of Management.* New York: Harper, 1954.
*McGregor, D. *The Human Side of Enterprise.* New York: McGraw-Hill, 1960.
March, J. G., and Simon, H. A. *Organizations.* New York: Wiley, 1958.

Chapter 24

For an interesting view of what managers actually do, see:
*Mintzberg, H. *The Nature of Managerial Work.* New York: Harper and Row, 1973.
And for a different, but not that different view, see the study of American college presidents by

Cohen, M. D. and March, J. G. *Leadership and Ambiguity*. New York: McGraw-Hill, 1974.

And for a moderate elaboration of this chapter try:

Leavitt, H. J. "Beyond the Analytic Manager." *California Management Review,* vol. 17, no. 3 (Spring 1975) and no. 4 (Summer 1975).

Leavitt, H. J. "Problem Finding, Problem Solving and Solution Implementing: Creativity in the Context of Working Problems Through." *UCLA Educator,* vol. 18, no. 2 (Spring 1976).

Much of the work on implementation is in the political science literature. For example, a study of the implementation of a federal program in Oakland:

Wildavsky, A. B. and Pressman, J. L. *Implementation*. Berkeley, Calif.: University of California Press, 1973.

But see also:

Mumford, E. and Pettigrew, A. *Implementing Strategic Decisions*. London: Longman, 1975.

Chapter 25

The work by March and Simon (see above) is a good place to look for a picture of the organization as a dynamic system. So are:

Cyert, R. M., and March, J. G. *A Behavioral Theory of the Firm*. Englewood Cliffs, N. J.: Prentice-Hall, 1963.

Emery, F. E. *Systems Thinking*. London: Penguin, 1970.

*Lawrence P., and Lorsch, J. *Organization and Environment*. Homewood, Ill.: Irwin, 1969.

Perrow, C. *Organizational Analysis*. Belmont, Calif.: Wadsworth, 1970.

*Weick, K. *The Social Psychology of Organizing*. Reading, Mass.: Addison-Wesley, 1969.

Chapter 26

For a good historical view, see:

*Kempner, T. T. and Wills, G. *Management Thinkers*. Baltimore, Md.: Penguin, 1970.

For good summaries of alternative positions, try:

*Lawrence, P., and Lorsch, J. *Organization and Environment*. Homewood, Ill.: Irwin, 1969.

And a couple of classics:

*Taylor, F. W. *Scientific Management*. New York: Harper, 1911.

Roethlisberger, F. J., and Dickson, W. J. *Management and the Worker*. Cambridge, Mass.: Harvard University Press, 1939.

Chapter 27

Alexis, M., and Wilson, C. *Organizational Decision Making*. Englewood Cliffs, N. J.: Prentice-Hall, 1967.

March, J. G., and Simon, H. A. *Organizations*. New York: Wiley, 1958.

For more on the relationship between task and structure, try:

Woodward, J. *Industrial Organizations: Theory and Practice*. Oxford: Oxford University Press, 1965.

Perrow, C. *Organizational Analysis*. Belmont, Calif.: Wadsworth, 1970.

*Mintzberg's *Nature of Managerial Work* (New York: Harper and Row, 1973) will be useful here, too.

Chapter 28

Addison-Wesley has published a set of little paperbacks about organizational development. See especially in that series:

*Beckhard, R. *Organization Development: Strategies and Models*. Reading, Mass.: Addison-Wesley, 1969.

For strong statements of the participative position, see:

*Likert, R. *The Human Organization*. New York: McGraw-Hill, 1967.

*Marrow, A. *Management by Participation*. New York: Harper and Row, 1967.

Chapter 29

A coverage of actual structures of many large companies is provided in:

*Holden, P. E. et al. *Top Management*. New York: McGraw-Hill, 1968.

A fascinating analysis of hierarchical structure in general is:

Simon, H. A. "The Architecture of Complexity." In *The Shape of Automation for Men and Management,* edited by H. A. Simon. New York: Harper and Row, 1965.

See also:

Weick, K. *The Social Psychology of Organizing*. Reading, Mass.: Addison-Wesley, 1969.

*Galbraith, J. R. *Organizational Design*. Reading, Mass.: Addison-Wesley, 1977.

*Lawler, E. E. and Rhode, J. G. *Information and Control in Organizations*. Pacific Palisades, Calif.: Goodyear, 1976.

*Whisler, T. L. *Information Technology and Organizational Change*. Belmont, Calif.: Wadsworth, 1970.

Chapter 30

See again:

*Lawrence, P., and Lorsch, J. *Organization and Environment*. Homewood, Ill.: Irwin, 1969.

Thompson, J. D. *Organizations in Action*. New York: McGraw-Hill, 1967.

See also several British works:

Burns, T., and Stalker, G. M. *The Management of Innovation*. London: Tavistock, 1961.

Rice, A. K. *The Enterprise and Its Environment*. London: Tavistock, 1963.

Woodward, J. *Industrial Organizations: Theory and Practice*. Oxford: Oxford University Press, 1965.

And consider again the references to Chapter 23, as well as:

Leavitt, H. J., Dill. W., and Eyring, H. E. *The Organizational World*. New York: Harcourt, Brace, Jovanovich, 1973.

Index

375